MARKETING HOSPITALITY

MARKETING HOSPITALITY

Third Edition

CATHY H. C. HSU
TOM POWERS

John Wiley & Sons, Inc.

Library of Congress Cataloging-in-Publication Data

Hsu, Cathy H. C.
  Marketing hospitality / by Cathy H. C. Hsu and Tom Powers.—3rd ed.
     p. cm.
  ISBN 0-471-34885-6 (cloth : alk. paper)
  1. Hospitality industry—Marketing.   I. Powers, Thomas F.   II. Title.

  TX911.3.M3 H78   2001
  647.94'068'8—dc21
                                                                    00-043381

Printed in the United States of America

 9 8 7 6 5 4

Contents in Brief

Contents

3 The Macro and Micro Environments of Hospitality Marketing

Market Segmentation and Target Marketing 65

 Marketing Information and Research 93

6 Marketing Strategy 123

7 The Marketing Plan 149

The Hospitality Product   169

Place in Hospitality Marketing: Distribution 201

10 **Place in Hospitality Marketing: Location** 225

11 The Price of Hospitality   245

12 Marketing Communication: Advertising   267

13 Marketing Communication: Sales Promotion, Public Relations/Publicity, and Personal Selling

14 Marketing at the Unit Level 317

Preface

This book was written primarily for students in hospitality management programs. Most of these students will work in the industry; many of them already do. Because of the way hospitality businesses are structured, the overwhelming majority of graduates will spend their careers on the operations side of the business. The focus of this text, however, is marketing—not really an activity separate from operations but an *integral part* of it, especially at the unit level. Therefore, we combine attention to the theories and knowledge of marketing with a strong emphasis on applications in hospitality operations.

Certainly, the body of theory and knowledge is important to students. However, being able to put practical experience together with a sound grasp of theory is even more important. After (or even before) graduation, most students will work for a multiunit company, either a chain or a franchise organization. This larger context requires a comprehension of the strategies and planning of the business so that managers can implement such strategies with proper knowledge and an understanding of their purpose. The design of this book strives to help students develop the necessary knowledge through a logical presentation and explanation of concepts and theories and to provide students with real-life examples to help them bridge the gap between theory and practice.

The more immediate concern of graduates and working students is the challenge of day-to-day unit operations, where most people spend several years before moving on to corporate responsibilities. Because of the importance of achieving success at the unit level, this text places significant emphasis on trade sources, such as industry conferences, and the collective wisdom of practitioners garnered from their years of practical experience. The framework for these practical applications, naturally, is provided by the academic knowledge of marketing.

This book was also written for professors who teach hospitality marketing. This text, designed for a one-quarter or one-semester course, can be used in either one of the two types of marketing classes. Most hospitality curricula include two courses in marketing. The first is a principles of marketing course. *Marketing Hospitality* provides the basic foundations of marketing theory necessary for the introductory course when it is taught by hospitality faculty. In many programs, however, the introductory course is taught by business faculty. Hospitality faculty then teach a second course, often called Hospitality Marketing Management or Advanced Hospitality Marketing. This text is suitable for this second course taught by instructors who wish to emphasize the *applications of marketing.*

A valid concern of instructors is the usefulness and effectiveness of a textbook. Before working on this third edition, a survey of hospitality marketing instructors was conducted to identify desired topics, appropriate approaches, and preferred "add-ons" of a hospitality marketing textbook. Hospitality students' learning styles have also been researched (by the lead author Cathy H. C. Hsu) over the past 10 years. The findings indicate that hospitality students learn best through hands-on experiences and practical application of ideas. Preferences of both instructors and students were taken into consideration and incorporated into the design of this book. It is only appropriate for authors of a marketing textbook to understand end users' needs and wants because of the very nature of the subject matter—a subject that focuses on how to satisfy consumers.

Both of us have used the first and second editions of this text in the classroom for several years and have been pleased with students' reactions. Students (even anonymously) have indicated that they liked the book and found it easy to read. Other instructors who have used the book report similar results. Instructors also like the industry examples and discussion, the detailed and current information, and the overview of the industry. We have worked hard to maintain the strengths of the book. Significant emphasis has been placed on industry examples in the main body of the text. In addition, case studies are used to develop students' awareness of contemporary issues and practices related to the subject matter of the various chapters. Examples are drawn primarily from foodservice and lodging operations. When practices are different in the two sectors, topics are analyzed separately. Additional illustrations are derived from travel and tourism businesses such as airlines, casinos, and tour operators.

To reflect instructors' preferences and changes in service marketing practices, virtually all chapters have been rewritten and reorganized. Students are provided with an overall picture of the marketing activities in hospitality organizations in Chapter 1. Chapter 2, "Hospitality Services," was added to offer a systematic review of the differences between products and services. Students are introduced to the differences early so that they will have a more focused perspective when evaluating the internal and external environmental factors as reviewed in Chapter 3. The discussions of consumer behavior and marketing research in Chapters 3 to 5 have been expanded to include a more detailed examination of the underlying principles.

Chapter 6, on marketing strategy, has also been redesigned to focus on the increasingly important issue of strategic planning. Students are then taken through a step-by-step process of developing a marketing plan in Chapter 7. The discussion of marketing mix elements has been updated to reflect current industry practices. The yield management concept is explained in more detail, and the actual calculation of pricing has been minimized, based on the suggestions of a number of instructors. The emphasis in the second edition on branding, distribution, and unit-level marketing is retained in this edition. A list of Internet resources is provided at the end of each chapter, allowing instructors and students to visit the Web sites of the various companies and associations mentioned in the chapters.

An *Instructor's Manual* (ISBN 0-471-35737-5) with test questions accompanies this textbook. The *Instructor's Manual* includes course syllabi, objectives, lecture outlines, key words and concepts with definitions, Internet exercises, answers to the Discussion Questions in the textbook, and Classroom Discussion Exercises. In addition, there are several Field Research Projects. The Test Bank and PowerPoint slides are available to qualified adopters at www.wiley.com/college.

Cathy H. C. Hsu
Tom Powers
March 2001

Acknowledgments

This edition of the *Marketing Hospitality* could not have been completed without the assistance of many individuals. First of all, I would like to thank Tom Powers for giving me the opportunity to work on the revision as coauthor. I can only imagine how much thought and love he invested in the first and second editions. I am honored to be chosen to continue to carry the torch of such a legend in hospitality education. Tom has provided tremendous guidance, not only with regard to content but also in the area of writing perspectives and strategies, throughout the revision process. He has given me the freedom to change and be creative, and yet kept me focused and on the right track. I learned tremendously from Tom and am in his debt.

I would also like to thank the Department of Hotel, Restaurant, and Institution Management and Dietetics (HRIMD) at Kansas State University (K-State) for its financial support in terms of facilities, supplies, and research assistants. The encouragement of Dr. Judy Miller, head of the HRIMD, is sincerely appreciated. The productive environment she has created made the completion of this project possible, and the congeniality of my colleagues at K-State made it an enjoyable one.

Dr. Li-Chun Lin, University of Tennessee, assisted with the survey of hospitality marketing instructors to identify topics included in their courses, the sequence of content areas covered, and supporting materials desired by instructors. The survey results were used in planning this revision. My research assistant, Dr. Jeong-Ja Choi, who was a doctoral candidate at K-State during the revision process, deserves special recognition. She spent countless hours conducting research and checking references. A special thanks to Ms. Lisa DeNicola, who was an undergraduate student at K-State, for her persistence and hard work in obtaining photographs and permissions of all copyrighted materials.

Finally, I would like to thank my family for their encouragement. I am extremely grateful for the understanding and moral support of my husband, Dr. Thomas S. C. Sun, the persistence and work ethic that I learned from my dad, and the optimistic personality that I inherited from my mom. I am thankful and blessed.

Cathy H. C. Hsu

A number of colleagues across North America have generously given their time to review portions of this book. We appreciate the invaluable comments provided by Terence McDonough of Erie Community College and other anonymous reviewers. Their objective evaluation of the content identified areas for improvement.

JoAnna Turtletaub, Senior Editor at John Wiley & Sons, encouraged us to undertake this revision and has provided valuable advice. We would also like to thank all the editorial and production staff who have worked on this edition for their professionalism and dedication.

We appreciate the cooperation and support of all companies and individuals who provided us with their advertisements and photographs and granted us permission to use them in this edition. These print materials are an integral part of the book.

We are in debt to many colleagues and friends who have given us ideas, reviewed portions of the book, and provided invaluable comments. Their assistance and friendship are treasured.

Cathy H. C. Hsu and Tom Powers

MARKETING HOSPITALITY

1

Marketing—
Everybody's Job

When you have finished reading this chapter, you should be able to:

- Discuss three basic approaches to the market.
- Describe marketing as a way of thinking.
- Explain tensions between marketing and operations.
- Discuss four common bases for organizing the headquarters marketing unit.

If one of the employees in the manufacturing plant that produces your T-shirt is unhappy on the day your shirt is made, it is unlikely that you will even know about it, nor is it likely to affect the quality of your T-shirt. However, you probably have had the experience of dining in a restaurant where your server was unhappy—and *what* a difference that can make in your dining experience.

The product in hospitality is the experience of the guests. This experience has both a **goods** component (e.g., food) and an interactive component, which we call **service.** In practice, hospitality employees become part of the product (experience). In one way or another, *every* employee is part of the guests' experience, because the typical hospitality organization is highly personal and interactive. One unhappy server in a restaurant can ruin the guests' whole dining experience.

To simplify, we can divide customers into two types: first-time guests and repeat guests. New guests often decide to try an operation as a result of advertising and promotion, but they can also make the decision based on word-of-mouth—that is, because of other people's experience. Repeat patronage, on the other hand, comes almost entirely as a result of satisfactory prior experiences. To provide those satisfactory experiences and to secure repeat customers takes the effort of every member in the hospitality organization. In hospitality operations, everyone is a **part-time marketer** (Gummesson 1998), because every member is essential to the success of a marketing program in some way. Therefore, it is essential for anyone planning a hospitality career to understand this important subject called *marketing.*

This chapter considers what the marketing concept is and how it can be distinguished from other points of view. The function of marketing and how a marketing department fits into the overall corporate management structure are also discussed.

Three Approaches to the Market

Some people argue that the key to attracting and keeping customers is the product. As the saying goes in the movie *Field of Dreams,* "If you build it, they will come." Another common view is that selling is the way to gain customers. Its proponents typically say, "Nothing happens until somebody sells something." In fact, there is considerable merit to both of these views, but they see only part of the picture. We consider each briefly and then turn to a third way of approaching the market—the marketing perspective.

A Product Orientation

In the years just after World War II, hotel occupancy was at an all-time high. Flushed with success, hotel owners saw the new roadside motels as a passing fad because *they knew* what a good hotel was—the type of hotels that they offered, not the roadside motels. However, 10 years later many of those same hotels were facing declining occupancies and revenues. The roadside motels provided convenience and lower rates and were stealing customers from the traditional "established" hotels. The hotel operators thought that the products that *they* designed were the most important success factor.

Some restaurateurs have suffered from a similar orientation. They defined what a restaurant was in terms of their own tastes and preferences—what *they* liked in a good restaurant. For them, the product defined by tradition was sacred. In today's marketplace, operations of this type are disappearing and being replaced by those that are in tune with changing consumer demands. The fact is that consumer needs, tastes, and preferences are rapidly changing, and it is the *consumers* who define what will and will not succeed. Operators who have a **product orientation,** however, have a point in that good products and efficient operations are essential to an effective marketing program. For that reason, we devote considerable attention to such products and services in later chapters. Remember, however, that the right products alone are not enough for success.

A Sales Orientation

It is quite common in hospitality organizations to find people who think of selling as the entire extent of marketing. This point of view is typified by the idea that the key to business success is to "get out there and sell." The assumption is that if you sell hard enough, the guests will buy. Therefore, the focus of a **sales orientation** is still the product, or what an operation has to offer. Operators who think marketing is just advertising and selling fall into this category; so do operators who look only at the promotional side of their businesses.

Selling is a very important business activity; however, the real danger of the sales orientation is that any success due to selling may create an illusion that "sell, sell, sell" is the way to prosper. When an operation offers products and services that fit the needs and preferences of its guests, selling can contribute greatly to the success of that operation. However, when guests' tastes change or the operation fails to satisfy the guests for any reason, the sales orientation is doomed to failure. Remember, satisfying the guest is the key to repeat sales and a vital part of marketing.

A Marketing Orientation

To adopt a **marketing orientation,** the reasoning process about what we offer begins with consumers' needs and wants. We must discover the customers' needs, wants, and preferences and provide products and services that meet their needs and wants and match their preferences. It is what customers think and feel, not what operators know or can sell, that defines the business. A leading hospitality marketing researcher put it this way:

> *The sole difference between competitive restaurant volumes is simply the better definition of guests' needs. There may be many today who are foolish enough to believe that consumers continue to come to your restaurants just because of your offering . . . but they don't!*

Marketing begins with customers' needs and wants. (Photo courtesy of Peter Menzel/Stock Boston.)

Rather, they come to satisfy their own needs, which happen, at the moment, to be satisfied by your products and services. (Rice 1983)

The three approaches to the market are summarized in Table 1.1.

Marketing

As noted earlier, a marketing orientation is really a way of thinking, a philosophy. That philosophy is translated into action by various marketing activities. The American Marketing Association defines marketing as:

The process of planning and executing the conception, pricing, promotion, and distribution of ideas, goods, and services to create exchanges that satisfy individual and organizational goals. (Bennett 1995)

The marketing process, as indicated earlier, begins with customers. Specifically, the process starts with a particular group of customers, often called the **target market.** It is the needs of this market that define the products and services that can be suc-

TABLE 1.1 Three Approaches to the Market			
Approach	Stresses Importance of	Advantages	Weaknesses or Problems
Product	Our product Our know-how	We know how to do this	Offering something customers may not want
Sales	What we have to sell Our commitment	We can decide to make this effort	May not result in sales if customers are not satisfied
Marketing	Customers' needs and wants Customers' points of view Customers' values	Recognizing new needs may stimulate demands We stress both product and selling efforts Offerings change with the consumers	More difficult to implement than product or sales approach Requiring careful analysis of problems and plans Requiring more than operating know-how

cessfully developed and brought to the market. In manufacturing, marketing is generally carried out by a separate unit of the company. Although there are marketing departments in hospitality firms, everyone in the organization is involved in marketing because good performance by everyone is needed to secure repeat sales. The activities that constitute marketing are often referred to as the **marketing mix,** a term underlining the fact that marketing involves several related activities.

The Marketing Mix

The problem with the product and sales orientations of marketing discussed earlier is not that they are wrong, but that they are only partly right. Marketing actually involves a variety of activities, not just producing and selling products. These activities are commonly summarized as the **Four Ps:** product, price, place, and promotion. A marketer mixes these elements into a solution that will satisfy consumers in the face of competition. The marketing mix must take into account the following:

- Providing *products (goods and services)* that consumers need or want
- Offering products in a *place* that is convenient to the guests
- Setting a *price* that will generate a profit while providing value to the guests and taking into account the prices of competing goods and services
- Informing prospective guests of the offering by *promotion,* including advertising, personal selling, and other forms of marketing communication

Marketing as a Social Force

One very broad definition of marketing describes it as "the creation of satisfied customers." Marketing involves discovering consumer needs and satisfying those needs. An example will make the underlying idea clearer.

Some years ago, the mortgage on the Mayflower Hotel in Plymouth, Michigan, was about to be foreclosed and the hotel was ready to go out of business. Anyone with common sense, people said, could see that the building would eventually be demolished to make way for something more useful. Fortunately for Plymouth, and many thousands of future guests, a young man two years out of college with some *uncommon* sense saw that run-down old hotel as an opportunity. Ralph Lorenz managed to persuade the hotel's board of directors to let him take over the operation and try to revive it—against all the best and wisest advice.

The hotel was in a terrible physical condition. Years of unprofitable operation had left it in sad disrepair. However, it was in an area of large manufacturing plants, and Ralph saw a need at those plants that his hotel could serve. Every plant had a bowling league, so he approached company personnel managers, union officials, and bowling league officers with this proposition: "Bring your busloads of bowlers to my hotel for their bowling banquets and I'll give them the biggest T-bone steak they ever saw for one dollar over my cost." Ralph was able to offer that incentive because he and one waiter, with the help of a couple of high school students, could serve that very simple meal. As for the meal preparation, he needed only minimum kitchen help. He, the cook, and the dishwasher cleaned up when the events were over—and the hotel cleaned up financially because the bowlers came, hundreds of them, almost every night for months.

Gradually, Ralph was able to reinvest the profits of the bowling banquets to repair the hotel coffee shop and dining room. The Mayflower Coffee Shop became a local gathering spot, and, in time, the hotel's reputation for friendly, prompt service attracted people from Detroit and beyond. As one successful year followed another, the revenues from the food operation were used to refurbish the hotel's guest rooms.

Ralph and his hotel became a focal point in Plymouth. As nearby Detroit grew, many bedroom communities exploded in population but became characterless. Although today's Plymouth is unquestionably a suburb of Detroit, it remains a distinctive place—in large part because the Mayflower Hotel has kept the small-town community spirit alive.

An important point in this success story is that Ralph recognized the needs of the market. In the short run, he saw a need for low-cost, but big-portion, meals and used the space in an old, run-down hotel to fill that need. In the longer run, he recognized the need for a local gathering spot and invested the profits from bowling banquets to refurbish his hotel so that it could become a town center. In the very long run, he recognized the need for a facility not only to meet the demands for food and lodging but also to provide a focus for the community. Members of the community rewarded his efforts with repeat patronage. Another important point of the story is that Ralph did not do it alone. His friendly, efficient crew of "part-time marketers" was a big part of the success because it was they who provided the service.

This story embodies the central realities of marketing. Ralph saw a need, and by meeting that need in a new way, he created value for the customers and for the community. The hospitality industry puts all of us in the role of host or hostess; therefore, our natural concern is the pleasant experience of our guests. Consequently, the guest-centered reasoning that underlies marketing fits perfectly with the very nature of hospitality services.

Marketing is equally appropriate for institutional operators, both for-profit and not-for-profit organizations, such as those engaged in health care, school foodservice, and college dining. Some hospitals offer gourmet meals, specialized room service, and a whole array of homelike amenities. Special services are tailored to patient needs. For example, some hospitals offer romantic candlelight dinners for new parents and specialized services designed for senior citizens. Some also provide concierge service on certain floors, with meals served by professional servers. In nonpatient foodservice, a hospital's bakery that serves the public can become a profit center. Because of the inconsistent funding levels from year to year, school foodservice has also increased emphasis on marketing to maintain or raise schoolchildren's participation rates, the percentage of students eating meals at school, in order to acquire the necessary dollars to support its staff.

In college dining, the emphasis on marketing has been so prevalent and successful

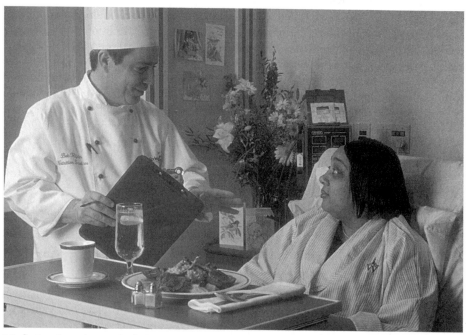

Marketing is an increasingly important management tool in health care. This hospital improves its competitive position by having the chef visit patients in the hospital room and find out their preferences. (Photo courtesy of Sodexho Marriott Services, Inc.)

that sales have actually increased in spite of declining enrollments. Certainly, the increasing presence of national brand names, such as Taco Bell and McDonald's, on college campuses is evidence that contract companies and institutional operators are responding to what their customers want.

Some may insist that marketing must be connected to profits, which is fine as long as a broad definition of profit is used. Nonprofit operations, such as foodservice in some institutions, have the goal of breaking even, which means that they set out to achieve neither a loss nor a profit. In other words, they have a "zero profit" goal. Subsidized operations, such as school foodservice, set out to achieve a loss on sales, which is covered by a subsidy. In this case, they have a "negative profit" objective. Both non-profit and subsidized operations must achieve a level of sales that gives them enough revenue to keep their personnel employed and to maintain their services. Marketing can help them reach the desired level of sales.

Marketing and Society

Marketing is an important part of the way of life in a free society. In a free society, within the limits of the law, people choose for themselves what they want to be and want to do. The mechanisms of a free society maximize people's opportunity for choice. And this is exactly what marketing does, because marketing is based on the autonomy of individual consumers.

Business organizations have come to realize that they have responsibilities to society and to the environment, in addition to their traditional objectives of making a profit. Consumers today are more aware of and concerned about social and environmental issues. Therefore, to satisfy consumers' demands, businesses must demonstrate similar awareness and concerns. Marketing and public relations campaigns are typically the vehicles used to deliver the message that they care. For example, many casinos donate part of their revenue to programs for the treatment of pathological gambling; "green hotels" use biodegradable cleaning supplies and provide certain services only when guests request them; and many restaurants and hotels publicize the fact that they have an effective recycling program. Case Study 1.1 illustrates one corporation's effort to conserve the environment.

CASE STUDY 1.1

McDonald's and the Environment

More than two decades ago, McDonald's began to find ways to conserve energy in its restaurants. In 1996, the company opened four energy-efficient restaurants that featured innovative technologies for cost and energy savings. As a member of the U.S. Environmental Protection Agency's voluntary "Green Lights" program, McDonald's has ensured that all of its newly constructed restaurants have energy-efficient lamps and fixtures for interior lighting. All existing company-owned units have also been converted to energy-efficient inside lighting. These changes significantly reduce pollution and save energy.

McDonald's has also reduced packaging by more than 20 million pounds since 1990. By trimming the size of its napkins and straws, the company has decreased the amount of materials used to produce these products by 2 million pounds annually. As for recycling, McDonald's has identified more than 200 items in its restaurants that can be made from recycled materials. Recycled products used include bags, cartons, and Happy Meal boxes; tables and chairs; booster seats; serving trays; Playland surfaces; and building materials.

McDonald's commitment is guided by the following principles:

- Effectively manage solid waste by reducing, reusing, and recycling.
- Conserve and protect natural resources.
- Encourage environmental values and practices.
- Ensure accountability procedures for suppliers.

McDonald's has worked closely with communities around the world in educating consumers on important environmental issues. Several programs have been developed for implementation, and brochures are available for distribution.

Source: "McDonald's Environmental Affairs," *McDonald's and the Environment.* (Oak Brook, IL: Author, 1996).

Marketing cannot solve all our problems, but it is a rational approach to the offering of choices. Marketing has played an increasingly important role in contemporary society and the free market economy. When an effective marketing program is in place, it creates a win-win situation for the marketers and the consumers.

Organizing and Managing the Marketing Function

As discussed earlier, marketing responsibilities in hospitality businesses are distributed throughout the organizations. This section reviews the division of marketing responsibilities between marketing and operations staff, some of the possible conflicts between marketing and operations, and how these can be resolved. The basis for organizing the marketing unit is also discussed.

Like many other service businesses, the hospitality industry follows the manufacturing and packaged goods industries in organizational structure (see Figure 1.1). Typically, in most manufacturing companies the marketing department handles and is responsible for most of the marketing function. However, because of the interactive nature of hospitality services, only part of the total marketing function, such as advertising and sales promotion, can be managed by a traditional marketing department.

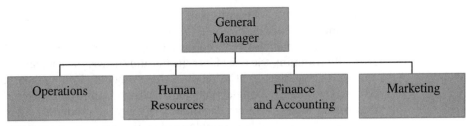

FIGURE 1.1 A traditional organizational structure.

In a hospitality organization, the employee—including his or her attitudes and behaviors—is a part of the experience the customers purchase. The physical products, such as food and guest rooms, are important, but an unpleasant interaction with an employee can ruin a guest's experience.

The marketing department can conduct promotional activities to secure trial purchases by new customers and remind existing customers to return. However, advertising an operation that is poorly run can actually decrease sales when customers are driven away by unhappy experiences. To obtain repeat sales and develop cross-sales opportunities, successful interactions between guests and service employees are a must. Those interactions are most likely to be beyond the control of the marketing managers and the marketing department. In fact, operations managers are responsible for the employees' interactions with guests. Because the success of a marketing program depends on the efforts of operations personnel to secure repeat patronage, it is important that the commitment to marketing start at the very top of the organization—with "the boss" to whom both the operations and marketing departments report. Only top management can develop the necessary organizational structures and procedures to create a collaborative working environment for managers and staff in the various departments.

The Marketing Department in Multiunit Companies

Marketing as an organizational unit in hospitality businesses has gained increasing recognition and status in recent years. Most chain organizations have a marketing executive at the vice president level. The marketing department usually has responsibilities for advertising, public relations, and design of promotional programs and supporting media, as well as for market research.

The increasing use of market research extends marketing executives' interests into what has traditionally been operation's domain. One objective of research may be to investigate customer satisfaction, which can include questions about products offered, services received, prices charged, quality of experience, and convenience of location. Research results can be used by heads of marketing and operations and other senior managers for strategic planning, product development, and other important functions. As noted earlier, operations now has responsibility for service activities that have traditionally been part of the marketing function. Marketing is now involved in activities that have historically been the domain of operations. The potential for "turf" disputes is obvious.

Conflicts Between Marketing and Operations Departments

Three management functions are actively involved in creating and delivering services: marketing, operations, and human resources (see Figure 1.2) (Lovelock 1999). Because of the almost simultaneous production and consumption of products and services in the hospitality industry, the three departments have to work closely together to ensure satisfaction in customers' experiences. The close interaction between the three departments and the broadening of the marketing domain necessarily lead to the crossing of organizational lines and, thus, potential for **organizational conflict,** especially between the marketing and operations departments. Marketers see their responsibilities as including development of new product concepts, distribution and pricing strategies, and communication programs, as well as monitoring the activities of competitors. However, when marketers seek to become involved in product design and service delivery, operations managers may resent their efforts as an intrusion into the operations domain (Lovelock 1992).

There are three major areas of conflict between marketing and operations personnel. First, there is friction between operations' goal of *cost control* and marketing's interest in *maximizing revenue* through new products and services. "Because of the ways in which they are evaluated, operations managers tend to be concerned with improving efficiency and keeping down costs, whereas marketers look for opportunities to increase sales"(Lovelock 1992).

Second, the two departments have different *time horizons.* Marketing executives may be more oriented to customer concerns and eager to create an early competitive advantage, or they may be aware of competitive activities and feel a sense of urgency to respond to the competition. They may also be more conscious of the promises made

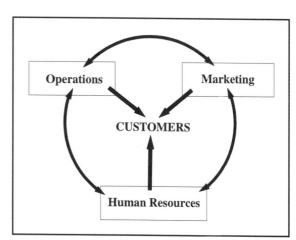

FIGURE 1.2 Management functions and customer service.
Source: Adapted from C. H. Lovelock and L. Wright, *Principles of Service Marketing and Management* (Upper Saddle River, NJ: Prentice-Hall, 1999), p. 20.

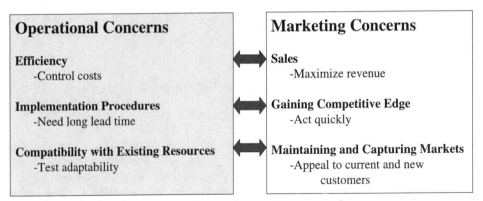

FIGURE 1.3   Conflicts between operations and marketing personnel.

in the company's advertising and promotion and thus concerned with prompt adjustments in operating priorities to fulfill those promises. Operations executives, however, are more aware of the thousands of little problems of daily operation. With greater understanding of the difficulties of implementing change and achieving quality, operations people are likely to seek more lead time for detailed planning, staff training, and system testing to refine new operating procedures.

The third area of conflict relates to *compatibility*. How well does a new product fit into the operation? The marketers may see the attractiveness of the new product to existing and prospective customers; however, if the product is incompatible with existing production facilities, expertise, and employee skills, the idea is unrealistic. There is, however, a difference between recognition of a bad fit and *resistance to change*. Operations managers deal with numerous problems every day—posed by employees, guests, equipment, weather, competitors, and other factors. Once they develop a "system" to solve these daily problems, they have a vested interest in the status quo and are reluctant to introduce new products and services, especially when the ideas are not their own. Both incompatibility and resistance to change cause delay in implementing new ideas. However, their causes are different and require different solutions.

These three areas of tension—revenue versus cost orientation, different time horizons, and perceived fit of new products—become more important as marketing grows in significance in hospitality organizations. Figure 1.3 illustrates these contrasting points of view.

Resolving Conflicts

The different and sometimes conflicted perspectives of marketing and operations personnel pose a challenge for managers in both functional areas. The distinction between marketing as a central office function and operations as unit-level function has to be minimized. Some large firms are moving marketing staff and significant marketing decision-making power to the regional and unit levels to establish a clearer linkage between operations and marketing. The danger, however, is that unit-level managers may have a purely operational perspective. Therefore, another necessary step is for operations managers to obtain the proper training to gain a broader view of the organization's functions, including marketing. This requires training *not just* in marketing as a separate subject, but in marketing as a part of an interdisciplinary approach to management.

Similarly, marketing people must be trained so that they are aware of the operating realities. This means, at a minimum, a significant cross-training effort for marketing personnel that involves working assignments for a substantial period of time in operations or, better yet, the promotion of operations people with specialized training in marketing into marketing positions.

Closer involvement of operations and marketing in joint committees and task forces, as well as increased informal working contact between operations and marketing, will help each side see and understand the problems of the other. Until marketing understands operations and operations sees marketing as a part of its necessary competencies, the conflict between the two points of view will continue to present costly problems.

Internal Marketing

Internal marketing means applying the philosophy and practices of marketing to the people who serve the external customer so that (1) the best possible people can be employed and retained and (2) they will do the best possible work (Taylor and Cosenza 1997). Internal marketing involves identifying the company's internal customers, its employees, and realizing there is a need to take a marketing approach to securing their support in fulfilling the company's mission. Organizations can use a number of marketing tools, similar to those used in external marketing, to motivate employees. This is especially important when employees are in contact with customers and are thus part of the product. Only when we have happy employees will we have happy customers. Therefore, management must package jobs and their rewards in a way that fits the needs of its customers—employees in this case. Internal marketing is discussed in more detail in the next chapter.

Organizing the Marketing Unit

The basis for organizing the marketing unit varies according to the needs of the particular companies. The four most common approaches to departmentalize the marketing component are functional, geographic, market, and product. In the **functional** approach, the marketing unit is organized around basic marketing activities such as advertising, sales, and market research. Therefore, under the marketing manager, there may be an advertising manager, a sales manager, and a market research manager. This is a common organizational structure in smaller companies.

With the increasing emphasis on localized marketing as competitive conditions

(Broken lines indicate functional staff supervision.)
FIGURE 1.4   Marketing department: Geographic organization

change from market to market, more organizations have established regional marketing departments based on the **geographic** distribution of their operations. Area marketing directors, as shown in Figure 1.4, usually report to the directors of operations for their respective regions. A senior marketing executive at the corporate level supervises the area marketing staff by advising and reviewing marketing plans, activities, and results. The corporate office also provides the general marketing plan within which local plans are prepared.

At the hotel property level, marketing activities are usually organized by **market** (i.e., customer group). For example, one sales manager may handle the convention and tour market, while another handles the corporate accounts. Under the director of marketing, there may be a group sales manager, a key account sales manager, a banquet sales manager, and a tour sales manager. Contract foodservice companies are also often organized by customer group. Business and industry, colleges and universities, schools, and health care facilities are the largest customer groups.

The **product** approach is not commonly used to organize a marketing unit, probably because it is unusual to market different menu items separately. However, corporations with multiple brands or concepts may have separate marketing teams to take care of the different products. For example, in a certain company, the pizza and Mexican restaurant divisions may each have their own marketing teams even though they are owned by the same company. Or a corporation may have a marketing unit for its hotel division and another unit for its restaurant division.

Often, a combination of organizational approaches is used. Some restaurant companies have their headquarters marketing group organized functionally, but they also use regional marketing managers. Contract foodservice companies often have geographically designated sales territories but divide the work within a territory by market.

Summary

What the customers purchase in hospitality businesses is an experience. Employees' attitudes and behaviors are a part of the experience or product. Therefore, all employees are part-time marketers. The marketing concept begins with the customers and their needs and wants and delivers products that meet those needs and wants. Marketing consists of a mix of activities that includes product, price, place, and promotion, the four Ps of marketing. Marketing is a pervasive force in our society and is used by both for-profit and nonprofit organizations.

The conflicting viewpoints of marketing and operations are contrasted in Figure 1.3. Operations tends to be concerned with costs and stability, whereas marketing is consumer and competitor conscious and focuses on sales. The basis for organizing the marketing unit, as discussed in this chapter, varies according to the needs of the particular companies.

Key Words and Concepts

Goods	Marketing orientation	Internal marketing
Service	Target market	Functional
Part-time marketer	Marketing mix	Geographic
Product orientation	Four Ps	Market
Sales orientation	Organizational conflict	Product

Resources on the Internet

American Hotel & Motel Association. *http://www.ahma.com*

American Marketing Association. *http://www.ama.org*

Hospitality Sales & Marketing Association International. *http://www.hsmai.org*

McDonald's Corporation. *http://www.mcdonalds.com*

National Restaurant Association. *http://www.restaurant.org/*

Sales and Marketing Management. *http://www.salesandmarketing.com/smmnew/*

Discussion Questions

1. Why is marketing everyone's job?
2. What are the three approaches to the market? Why is the marketing approach superior?
3. What are the elements of the marketing mix?
4. What are the major conflicts between the operations and marketing departments? Why do these conflicts exist?
5. How is the marketing unit usually organized in a firm?

References

Bennett, P. D. ed. (1995). *Dictionary of marketing terms*. Chicago: American Marketing Association.

Gummesson, E. (1998). Implementation requires a relationship marketing paradigm. *Journal of the Academy of Marketing Science, 26*(3), 242–249.

Lovelock, C. H. (1992). The search for synergy: What marketers need to know about service operations. In C. H. Lovelock, ed. *Managing services: Marketing, operations, and human resources* 2d ed., pp. 392–405. Englewood Cliffs, NJ: Prentice-Hall.

Lovelock, C. H., and L. Wright. (1999). *Principles of Service Marketing and Management*. Upper Saddle River, NJ: Prentice-Hall.

Rice, G. D. (1983). Target marketing: The art of segmentation. *Proceedings, Chain Operators Exchange*, 5–6. Chicago: International Foodservice Manufacturers Association.

Taylor, S. L. and R. M. Cosenza. (1997). Internal marketing can reduce employee turnover. *Supervision, 58*(12), 3–5.

Hospitality Services

(Photo courtesy of Corbis Images.)

When you have finished reading this chapter, you should be able to:

- Describe the characteristics of hospitality services.
- Explain the relationship between the marketing and operations functions.
- Assess service quality and identify the gaps in service quality.
- Identify the important aspects of service quality control.
- Apply queuing theory in managing demand.
- Explain the importance and components of internal marketing.

One of the real dangers hospitality companies face is that their product will become a commodity. After all, how much *real* difference is there between the physical aspects of different brands of hotels or between menus of various restaurants? If they are all pretty much the same, the danger is that they will be treated like other commodities, in which the general quality grade (e.g., US Choice beef, US #1 Fancy vegetables) and the price are the only buyer considerations. In this circumstance, profit margins are thin and the opportunity for differentiation is minimal.

In hospitality, the great opportunity for differentiation is **service.** The point at which a guest interacts with a hospitality operation (i.e., its people, facilities, and systems) is called a "moment of truth" (Normann 1984)—a time when the guest matches his or her experience with the promise of performance made by the operation. This chapter further explains why everyone working in the hospitality industry is an active participant in his or her company's marketing mission, given that operations and marketing are so closely tied together.

The quality of service is vital to a company's operational and financial success. The following sections consider what services are, what service quality is, and how quality is controlled in a service operation. Psychological considerations in waiting line management are discussed, inasmuch as waiting lines are common occurrences in many hospitality operations. Internal marketing is also reviewed, because the management of service operations depends on selling employees on their work and developing a service culture.

Hospitality Service Characteristics

With the increase in automation in hospitality businesses, it is important to note that service is rendered not only by *people* but also by electronic and mechanical *devices* and complex *systems* maintained by hospitality companies. For example, in-room television checkout, minibars, and reservation systems all provide service with minimal human involvement. Therefore, the following definition of service encompasses all kinds of service encounters:

> *A service is an activity or series of activities of more or less intangible nature that normally, but not necessarily, take[s] place in interactions between the customer and service employees and/or physical resources or goods and/or systems of the service provider, which are provided as solutions to customer problems.* (Grönroos 1990)

From a guest's point of view, the service is an *experience.* It is the sum of everything that happens to him or her in connection with a transaction or series of transactions. Services, including hospitality services, differ from goods in several aspects (Lovelock 1996).

Intangibility

When a manufactured product is purchased, the consumer receives something tangible. When a car or a computer is purchased, the customer acquires that product for his or her own use. Although the manufacturer may provide safety warnings and maintenance directions for a product, how the consumer uses it is essentially his or her own choice. However, the essence of a service transaction is that what is purchased includes both tangible goods and intangible services. In addition to the tangible food and beverages, foodservice and lodging operations also provide an intangible service, convenience, hospitality, social contact, atmosphere, relaxation, and, perhaps, entertainment. A meal in a restaurant may be delicious, but if the room in which it is served is unattractive and dirty, the *experience* is likely to be a failure for many guests. If a guest is provided with a lovely room but only after a long argument about the rate or reservation, the guest's stay is ruined from the beginning.

When a customer purchases a computer, he or she is not only buying the CPU or the keyboard, but also the *benefits* of speed and convenience. Thus, there is an intangible component in any transaction. However, when you purchase a product, it is a physical thing that you can take with you. A service, on the other hand, is generally consumed at the time of purchase. It is not a thing that can be possessed. It is experienced. The product, then, is in large part the performance of the service organization. Because of their **intangibility,** it is much harder for guests to test or evaluate services than tangible goods. They have no direct means of knowing how good the services are before purchase.

People as Part of the Product

When a service is provided in a hospitality operation, guests tend to be there in person. Therefore, a service usually involves people on *both* sides of the transaction. At dinner, there is the wait staff and the guest. In a hotel, the front office staff and the guest interact. With automation, some personal service is replaced by equipment, such as in-room checkout via TV. Services of this type only make those personal contacts between service staff and guests more important. Hence, employees *and* guests are literally part of the product.

Because there are people involved, services are *less standardized* than products. Two different service personnel can do a good, but somewhat different, job in rooming a guest. Even the same server can provide variations in services, depending on the server–guest interaction. Highly standardized behavior is often not possible and frequently not desirable. Service personnel are usually more effective if they are able to be themselves. Managing a service transaction often involves accepting varying results, depending on the circumstances. Because **people are part of the product,** the service industry also encounters very different challenges in regard to quality control. Once a manufacturing process is standardized, it is likely that most products produced will meet the quality standards. However, quality control in services is different because of the human element. Hospitality operations can standardize service proce-

Two servers performing the same tasks does not guarantee that customers will receive the same level of service. Careful specification of procedures and selection of employees can go a long way toward reducing problems in customer service. (Photo courtesy of Catherine Ursillo/ Photo Researchers.)

dures, yet each guest is different and each person providing the service is different as well. A guest rarely receives exactly the same service when visiting the same hospitality operation at different times. This does not mean that quality control is impossible, but it is subject to variation.

The way service is delivered has changed dramatically in the past few decades. The hospitality service industry moved from serving mainly a "class market," dealing mostly with a relatively small upper-income group, to serving a "mass market." Self-service, which is popular in the mass market, involves the guests not only as the recipients of service, but also as active players. Therefore, the guests' own behaviors have an effect on their satisfaction with the service provided. For example, how well a guest can use the automatic check-out equipment in the guest room, how well a guest can serve him- or herself in a cafeteria, or how well a guest can pour a cup of coffee in a hotel lobby has a significant impact on that guest's overall experience in the hospitality operation.

In hospitality services where interaction among individuals is intensive, guests not only come in contact with service personnel but also have contact with other guests. A noisy neighbor in a hotel or a loud party at the next table in a restaurant may ruin a guest's experience—one that the hospitality operation staff has tried so hard to perfect. Therefore, service staff, guests themselves, and other guests are all part of the product.

Demand Patterns

Hospitality operations tend to encounter peaks and valleys in demand. Restaurants are hectic at mealtime, but business is usually slow between meals. Resorts have on-seasons and off-seasons. Business-oriented hotels experience midweek surges in demand, but are often not as busy on the weekend. Because of the variability in **demand patterns,** service marketing and operations management are often concerned with "managing demand." This involves thinking through the needs of the guests and the organizations, and managing the marketing mix to meet the different challenges that occur during different demand periods. For example, marketing personnel may conclude that higher prices and advertising focusing on the need for reservations are the best approach to manage peak periods, whereas special discounts and heavy promotion are required to increase occupancy during off-seasons. The two extremes in this simplified example illustrate how to manage demand by adjusting elements of the marketing mix to meet changing market conditions.

Perishability

In manufacturing, products not sold today keep their value in inventory and can be sold later. However, an intangible service has to deal with the issue of **perishability.** An unsold airline seat or an unoccupied guest room cannot be sold after the flight has departed or the night has passed. Similarly, when a guest leaves a restaurant because the waiting line is too long, the revenue from that particular meal is lost forever. Because services are produced and consumed at the same time, they are highly perishable and there is no way to build an inventory. The inability to store excess production in inventory makes capacity utilization critical to the management and marketing of services.

Channels of Distribution

The **channel of distribution** of packaged goods includes brokers, wholesalers, retailers, and other intermediaries. The hospitality industry has different kinds of channels of distribution. For example, travel agents and tour wholesalers sell rooms for many hotels. However, these arrangements are rapidly changing because of the enhancement of the global network of reservation systems (discussed in Chapter 9). The global distribution system (GDS) is increasing the reach of individual properties and the types and number of intermediaries. These developments provide a challenge to lodging marketers. Similarly, home delivery of foodservice is now provided by independent contractors. In a sense, take-out and delivery services make the customer's home an extension of the foodservice operations.

Franchise systems are another form of distribution. Instead of distributing goods, franchise systems distribute a *format for doing business.* These systems determine the kinds of experiences individual franchise units provide for their guests. Therefore, franchise systems distribute the ultimate in intangibles—ideas.

The distinctive characteristics of hospitality services are summarized in Figure 2.1.

INTANGIBILITY
   -Product is experienced.
   -Product includes both goods and services.
   -Guests are purchasing the performance.
   -It is harder to evaluate quality of services than products.

PEOPLE AS PART OF THE PRODUCT
   -Employees are part of the product.
   -Services are less standardized than products.
   -Quality control is more challenging for services than for products.
   -Guests are directly involved in all service transactions.

DEMANDS PATTERNS
   -Demand levels have peaks and valleys.
   -Marketing mix is used to manage demand.

PERISHABILITY
   -Unused capacity is wasted.
   -There is no way to build an inventory.
   -Capacity management is crucial.

CHANNELS OF DISTRIBUTION
   -Channels of distribution increase in importance.
   -Franchising is a form of distribution.

FIGURE 2.1   Distinctive characteristics of hospitality services.

Hospitality Service Marketing System

As discussed earlier, from a guest's perspective, the product purchased is an experience. However, from the organization's point of view, the "service product" is a deliberately orchestrated *event*. The best way to think of the service product is as a continuum, with all intangible interaction on one end and pure physical goods on the other. Service products vary from an extreme of almost all tangible goods, such as a sandwich from a vending machine, to almost entirely intangible service interactions, such as making a flight reservation through a travel agent. There are very few products that are purely goods or services (Shostack 1977).

Three Overlapping Service Systems

As mentioned earlier, the service product is a complex phenomenon made up of everything that happens to guests. Figure 2.2 provides an overview of the complex hospitality service marketing system. The hospitality service, from guests' perspectives, comprises three **overlapping service systems** (Lovelock 1996). Only a small portion of

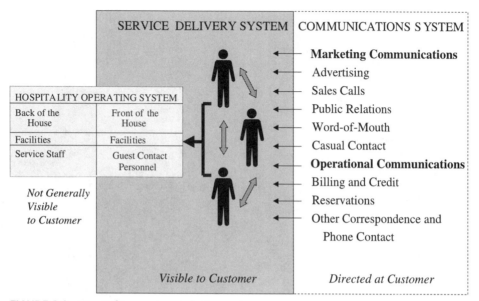

FIGURE 2.2   Hospitality service marketing system.
Source: Adapted from C. H. Lovelock, *Services Marketing,* 3d ed. (Upper Saddle River, NJ: Prentice-Hall, 1996), 55.

these systems is under the direct control of marketing; most are under the supervision of operations.

The **service delivery system** is concerned with where, when, and how the service product is delivered to guests. It includes front-of-the-house facilities, such as dining rooms, lobbies, front desks, and guest rooms, and front-of-the-house personnel who are (or should be) trained for guest contact. As shown in Figure 2.2 and mentioned earlier, other guests are also part of the service delivery system, because guests affect each other's experience of the operation. For example, a group of noisy conventioneers or bus tour members bursting into the lobby of an upscale hotel may change the perception of the regular guests of the hotel as to the type of operation they are staying in—and the value of their stay. The fact that guests are part of the product has serious implications in selecting appropriate target markets.

The **hospitality operating system** is where the work gets done for the guests. Part of the operating system is physically located in the service delivery system visible to the guests. The front of the house is deliberately designed, physically and organizationally, to achieve an appropriate impression while providing important functional services. The back of the house provides the utilitarian production activities essential to the delivery of service, such as housekeeping, food production, and engineering.

The intent is that the back of the house is kept out of sight of the guests, but the operating reality is that guests do step into service corridors, interact with housekeepers, or wander into the kitchen (by mistake or as part of exploring the operation).

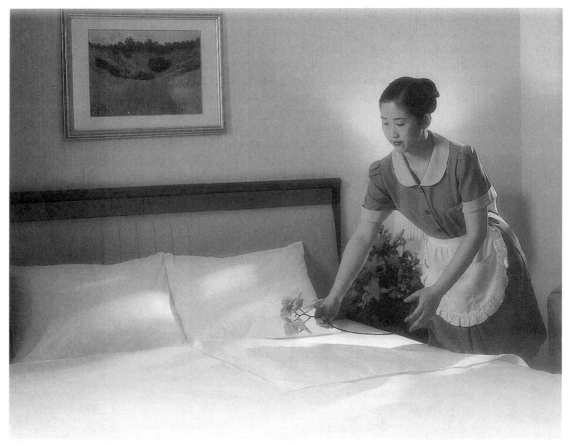

An occasional contact with back-of-the-house personnel may alter the guest's view of the operation—for better or worse. (Photo courtesy of Evergreen International Hotels.)

"Back stage" has a special authenticity for guests. They know that the front of the house is "on stage" and that the impression there is a carefully created one. For this reason, experiencing the back of the house is sometimes perceived by guests as finding out what things are "really like" in an operation. Therefore, cleanliness and order in the back of the house and friendly, courteous staff are important to a successful operation. They can have an impact on guests' perception of the entire facility.

The **communications system** includes planned marketing communications, such as advertising, promotion, and public relations, and operational communications, such as billing statements and reservation confirmation. The efforts of a courteous front office agent can easily be destroyed by rude communication with the accounting department, inept reservations staff, or even by an unanswered letter.

Service Quality

Quality, experts agree, "is whatever the customer says it is, and the quality of a particular product or service is whatever the customer perceives it to be" (Buzzell and Gale 1987). As you can see, the emphasis is on the customer and on perceived quality. There are objective measures of service that can be expressed in numerical terms, such as service time, errors in food orders, and length of waiting time. These are proxies (indirect measures) that are useful in tracking service quality. However, the product is, ultimately, the customers' experience, and their *subjective* evaluation of that experience is the final determinant of quality.

Quality Dimensions: Technical and Interpersonal

Quality can be conceptualized broadly along two critical dimensions. The first is the **technical dimension:** Did things go right? Was the hot food hot? The reservation in order? The room cleaned? The second is the more difficult **interpersonal dimension.** Was the server friendly? Did service staff go the extra mile to be helpful? Did the guests feel welcome? The technical dimension represents *what* the customer receives; the interpersonal dimension stands for *how* the customer receives the service.

Technical quality issues are relatively objective and measurable. Technical quality, however, is generally the minimum expectation of guests. "Even when an excellent solution is achieved, the firm may be unsuccessful if the excellence in technical quality is counteracted or nullified by badly managed and handled buyer-seller interactions" (Grönroos 1990). Yet interpersonal success without technical competence is also unsatisfactory. For example, excellent service at the front office cannot make up for the missed wake-up call. Therefore, both technical and interpersonal dimensions of the service quality are critical to the success of a hospitality operation.

Measuring Service Quality

Results of research on service quality and customer satisfaction have indicated that consumers use five criteria to assess service quality (Berry, Zeithma, and Parasuraman 1992):

Tangibles	The appearance of physical facilities, equipment, personnel, and communication materials
Reliability	The ability to perform the promised service dependably and accurately
Responsiveness	The willingness to help customers and to provide prompt service
Assurance	The knowledge and courtesy of employees and their ability to convey trust and confidence
Empathy	The provision of caring, individualized attention to customers

Of the five criteria, only "tangibles" is strictly technical. "Reliability" can reflect both technical and interpersonal dimensions. The others clearly relate to interpersonal aspects of the service encounter. Therefore, one can never overstate the importance of people in service operations.

Service Quality Gaps

Researchers have also studied the causes of service failures. Five specific **service quality gaps** between what actually happened and what should have happened were identified:

Misunderstanding	What management understands customers want is different from what customers really want.
Communication	Management has a correct understanding of customer preferences, but these are not translated properly into service quality specifications.
Performance	Adequate service standards are set but not properly carried out by the organization and its employees.
Overpromising	Marketing communications promise more than the firm can deliver.
Expectations	The service experience is, for whatever reason, inconsistent with the customer's expectation.

Addressing the factors associated with service failure in the preceding list, the following guidelines have been developed for service quality enhancement and customer satisfaction:

1. It is absolutely essential to understand *what value is* to the guests.
2. *Understanding alone is not enough.* Management must translate its knowledge into policies and procedures and communicate its understanding to the rest of the organization.
3. It is also not enough simply for everyone to agree on service standards. *Performance is critical.* The performance that we provide has to meet the service standards. This is what the guests will experience.
4. An organization must *deliver* what it promises and avoid overpromising in its promotion.
5. The expectation established by all forms of communication, including word of mouth, must be met by the operation.

Service Quality Control and the Zero-Defect Goal

In the manufacturing industry, the goal of quality control is to reduce defects to a minimum. A strong product quality control program not only reduces defects but also ensures that defective products are removed from inventory for modification or elimination. In hospitality services, however, there are no rejects, just unhappy customers. Because a "defect" is an event that happens to a guest, there is no way to do a recall. Under these circumstances, the argument for a **zero-defect standard** is compelling, but may be unrealistic:

> *The fact is that in services, no matter how rigorous the procedures and employee training or how advanced the technology, zero defects is an unattainable goal. Unlike manufacturers that can adjust inputs and machinery until products are uniformly perfect, service companies cannot escape variation. Factors like the weather and the customers themselves are beyond a company's control.* (Labovitz and Chang 1987)

Setting a zero-defect target, although an unattainable goal in any absolute sense, *does* help an organization focus on minimizing service problems. Moreover, although guests can be demanding, most of them are not unreasonable. The standards an operation must reach are based on guest expectations. Delay or even a moment's inattention in a luxury operation is an annoyance, to say the least, and a potentially serious defect in operating quality. However, waiting lines are a part of life at a theme park. No one expects Ritz quality at a quick-service restaurant.

Even though most guests have reasonable expectations, service failures are a serious problem because they reduce the likelihood of repeat patronage and good word of mouth. Therefore, programmatic efforts to reduce quality defects are essential to the success of a hospitality operation. Case Study 2.1 summarizes one company's quality management program.

CASE STUDY 2.1

Quality at the Ritz

The Ritz-Carlton is the first and only hospitality firm to win the Malcolm Baldridge National Quality Award, which recognizes exceptional achievement in the practice of total quality management principles, given by the U.S. Department of Commerce in 1992. In 1999 it won the award a second time and is thus the first and only service company to win the award two times. There is only one other American company, Xerox, that has earned the distinction more than once.

The Ritz-Carlton's total quality management (TQM) program begins with an absolute commitment by senior management to the development and implementation of TQM. This not only includes a policy promise, but involves a pledge of approximately one fourth of the senior executives' time. Following from this top management commitment is an engagement by unit-level managers and the employees with whom they work.

"Great food, great product, great service, and great costs are not enough," said President and COO Schulze of The Ritz-Carlton Hotel Company, L.L.C. "We have to find a way to be even better. Real quality means zero defects and 100 percent customer retention." The essence of this philosophy has been refined into a set of core values collectively called "The Gold Standards." New employees receive a two-day orientation that emphasizes the corporation's service culture. The concepts are reinforced in daily departmental "lineups" attended by all employees. And The Ritz-Carlton is an industry leader in providing 120 hours of training per employee per year.

The Ritz-Carlton's motto is "We are Ladies and Gentlemen Serving Ladies and Gentlemen." It is the responsibility of each employee to create an environment of team-

Three Steps of Service	"We Are Ladies and Gentlemen Serving Ladies and Gentlemen"	THE RITZ-CARLTON® HOTEL COMPANY, L.L.C. Credo	The Employee Promise
1 A warm and sincere greeting. Use the guest name, if and when possible. **2** Anticipation and compliance with guest needs. **3** Fond farewell. Give them a warm good-bye and use their name, if and when possible.		The Ritz-Carlton Hotel is a place where the genuine care and comfort of our guests is our highest mission. We pledge to provide the finest personal service and facilities for our guests who will always enjoy a warm, relaxed, yet refined ambience. The Ritz-Carlton experience enlivens the senses, instills well-being, and fulfills even the unexpressed wishes and needs of our guests.	*At The Ritz-Carlton, our Ladies and Gentlemen are the most important resource in our service commitment to our guests.* *By applying the principles of trust, honesty, respect, integrity and commitment, we nurture and maximize talent to the benefit of each individual and the company.* *The Ritz-Carlton fosters a work environment where diversity is valued, quality of life is enhanced, and individual aspirations are fulfilled, and The Ritz-Carlton mystique is strengthened.*

work and lateral service so that the needs of the guests, and of each other employee, are met. All employees are also empowered to satisfy customer demands. When a guest has a problem or needs something special, employees are expected to break away from their regular duties to address and resolve the issue.

The Gold Standards, as embodied in the Credo Card, are printed on a pocket-size laminated card. Every employee carries this in his or her pocket, a constant reminder that guest satisfaction is the highest mission.

Source: The Ritz-Carlton Company. (2001). *Ritz-Carlton homepage* [On-line]. Available: http://www.ritzcarlton.com/

The Cost of Quality

The significant reduction of service defects appears to be an expensive project. Yet, there are good reasons to believe that improving quality will actually *reduce* costs. Costs of quality can be divided into the good, the bad, and the ugly (Labovitz and Chang 1987). The **good costs** are the costs involved in problem prevention, such as good hiring practices, quality-oriented training and supervision, and compensation related to quality performance. These costs represent a long-term investment rather than a short-term, temporary fix. The **bad costs** are the costs of inspection and correction, including supervisory personnel's time, increased food and beverage costs due to replacement, decreased operational efficiency due to time spent on corrective actions, and additional training and employee turnover costs. Even though it is good to identify and correct problems before guests complain, this is only a short-term solution. Inspection and correction activities must be repeated again and again if the root of the problem is not resolved.

The **ugly costs** are the costs of service defects. The failure of preventive activities and inspection and correction actions will allow substandard performance to be delivered, which results in unsatisfied guests. When guests complain, at least the operation gets a second chance to correct its mistakes and try to compensate the guests for their inconvenience. It is possible to turn an unsatisfied guest into a happy guest before his or her departure. Actually, this is the least expensive form of ugly costs. If a guest leaves the property unsatisfied with the problem unresolved, there are three very expensive ugly costs of service defects: lost customers, efforts to attract new customers, and bad word of mouth. The cost of lost business can be viewed this way:

> At Club Med, one lost customer costs the company at least $2,400: a loyal guest visits the resorts an average of four times after the initial visit and spends roughly $1,000 each time. The contribution margin is 60 percent. So when a Club Med customer doesn't return, the company loses 60 percent of $4,000, or $2,400. It also has to replace the customer through expensive marketing efforts. (Labovitz and Chang 1987)

The cost of gaining a new customer is estimated at about six times the cost required to retain an existing one (LeBoeuf 1987). Finally, there is the negative word of mouth.

People are much more likely to complain to their friends and peers than to the service provider. One study suggests that a typical dissatisfied customer will tell 8 to 10 people about a bad experience, and 1 in 5 will tell 20 (LeBoeuf 1987). Because the recommendations of others play a key role in consumers' decisions about which hospitality operations to patronize, the impact of "disrecommendations" is certainly a significant cost, though one that never shows up clearly on a company's financial statements.

Given the costs attributed to service errors and the savings that can be realized by avoiding such errors, we can say that "quality is free" (Crosby 1979). Another way to look at the various costs of quality is summarized by the "1-10-100 Rule" (Labovitz and Chang 1987). Basically, every $1 spent in prevention (good) costs will save a company $10 in inspection and correction (bad) costs and $100 in customer complaint (ugly) costs.

Enlisting the Customer in Quality Control

Management should actively seek opinions from customers in the development and implementation of a quality control program. Customers should be encouraged to be involved in such programs so that their needs can be better served. Very often, customers get involved only when there is a problem or something to complain about. Even then, management should see complaints as valuable sources of information to identify problem areas. However, a more proactive approach should be taken to prevent problems from happening. Service guarantees and other programs to obtain customer feedback can have a positive impact on both service standards and customer retention.

Guarantees. Striving for perfection helps focus the quality control effort; however, we have seen the objective difficulties in actually achieving a zero-defects goal. Yet this does not mean that customer satisfaction cannot be guaranteed. Because of the intangible nature of service, a **guarantee program** can enhance customers' confidence and reduce their risks in making purchase decisions. Even though zero defects is an almost unattainable goal, the commitment to error-free service can help force a company to provide the best service possible. In addition, there are several benefits that can derive from a guarantee program:

- It makes the company ascertain its customers' definition of good service (reduces the misunderstanding gap).
- It sets clear performance standards (reduces the communication gap).
- It generates reliable data through customer compensation when performance is poor. Such data can be used for system redesign or training program development.
- It forces a company to examine its service-delivery system for possible weak points in the corporation or in the individual units in order to reduce the guarantee program cost.
- It builds customer loyalty, sales, and market share.

- The financial commitment from management makes a strong statement about its emphasis on customer satisfaction.

The Promus Hotel Corporation, the franchisor and operator of Hampton Inns, Homewood Suites, and Embassy Suites, pioneered the 100 percent satisfaction guarantee to guests. In each of its hotels, guests are promised high-quality accommodations, friendly and efficient service, and clean and comfortable surroundings. The company's promise, "If you're not completely satisfied, we'll give you your night's stay for free," has enhanced the company's reputation with the target markets it serves. A good service guarantee should have the following characteristics (Hart 1988):

- *Unconditional.* The objective is to satisfy the customers, not to argue with them about what circumstances are covered. When a guarantee has many conditions, it loses its power.

Hampton Inn celebrated its 10th anniversary of the 100 percent satisfaction guarantee. (Photo courtesy of Hampton Inn.)

- *Easy to understand.* The guarantee should be written in simple, concise language that pinpoints the promise. Customers then know exactly what they can expect, and employees know exactly what is expected of them. For example, use the "10-minute lunch" guarantee, rather than the "quick-lunch" guarantee, to communicate the speed of lunch service.
- *Meaningful.* A guarantee should cover the aspects of a service transaction that are important to the customers and should provide a significant payout if the promise is not kept. Do not guarantee something the customers already expect, such as a clean room.
- *Easy to invoke.* A customer who is already dissatisfied should not have to jump through hoops to report a problem. Similarly, customers should not be made to feel guilty about invoking the guarantee. Companies should encourage unhappy customers to speak up.
- *Easy to collect.* Customers should not have to work hard to collect compensations. The procedure should be easy and quick—on the spot, if possible.

Once a guarantee program is installed, we must make sure that we play the game fairly. An antagonized customer who feels that the guarantee has not been honored in his or her case is a customer who is not likely to come back but is likely to become a source of negative word of mouth. Therefore, offering a guarantee carries with it an obvious need to mean it and fulfill the promise. From time to time there may be a few guests who cheat and try to receive the payout without just cause. However, the costs of these cases are minimal as compared with the benefits generated by a strong guarantee program.

Customer Feedback. Customer complaints can also be solicited through the use of toll-free telephone numbers and Internet Web sites, which encourage people to report problems by making it easy to do so. Asking customers, face-to-face, is a more direct way to obtain feedback. When a front office employee or a server queries customers about their experience, specific questions should be asked to encourage honest answers. The usual question, "How is everything?" is not the most effective in generating a specific response. Most customers reply to general questions with a single word, "Fine." Questions should be addressed to a specific aspect of the service, such as, "Was your steak done to your liking?" Finally, questionnaires administered on a regular basis to samples of guests and comment cards placed in prominent locations are additional means of obtaining valuable customer-retention and service quality information.

The reaction to a complaint should be prompt and involve solving the problem when possible, even if the company is not at fault. After the guest's departure, it is a good idea to follow up with the customer through a phone call or letter. This immediate personal attention is appreciated by the guest, and the staff dealing with the complaint has an opportunity to work with the guest to determine what additional actions will be needed. It is important to realize that an organization's ability to respond can be greatly enhanced if it empowers its employees to solve a guest's problem on the spot (Labovitz and Chang 1987).

Managing Demand Through Queuing

As mentioned earlier, because of its perishability, we cannot build up our service inventory. When the demand exceeds supply, or the number of arrivals at a facility exceeds the capacity of the system to accommodate them, waiting lines, or "queues," occur. Psychological studies reveal that people often think they have waited longer for a service than they actually have. Overestimates can be as high as sevenfold (Lovelock 1996). Therefore, operations must manage the experience of waiting in line to minimize the perceived time lag for the guests. None of the **queuing** management techniques makes a line move faster, but they do make the time pass more quickly and pleasantly. David Maister (1985) has formulated eight principles about managing demand through queuing. They are summarized in Figure 2.3.

When customers are given something to do or are entertained while waiting, the wait appears to be shorter. Restaurants can pass out menus to guests waiting to be seated. Some restaurants put their menus on the wall so that people can read them. While customers read or "study" the menu, they may discover items of which they were not aware. Therefore, not only does the restaurant make the wait more pleasant, it also takes advantage of the wait time to do some creative marketing. In some instances, ski resorts train staff to provide entertainment for guests when lines get too long at ski lifts. At Disney theme parks, waiting line areas are decorated so as to give people something to look at, and they are often visited by "cast members." Some restaurants have a gift shop beside the waiting area so that guests can browse the merchandise. Hotels often place mirrors next to the elevators to allow guests to check their appearance and help them pass the time.

- Unoccupied waits feel longer than occupied waits.
- Preprocess waits feel longer than in-process waits.
- Anxiety makes waits seem longer.
- Uncertain waits seem longer than known, finite waits.
- Unexplained waits seem longer than explained waits.
- Unfair waits seem longer than equitable waits.
- The more valuable the service, the longer people will wait.
- Solo waits feel longer than group waits.

FIGURE 2.3 Principles of waiting.
Source: Adapted from D. H. Maister, "The Psychology of Waiting Lines," in J. A. Czepiel, M. R. Solomon, and C. F. Surprenant, eds., *The Service Encounter* (Lexington, MA: Lexington Books/ D.C. Health, 1985), 115–122.

A preprocess wait—that is, waiting to start—is less acceptable to guests than other periods of waiting. This is another reason for operators to give guests a menu to study while waiting for a table—to encourage a sense that the process *has* started. Postprocess waits, such as waiting for a bill or waiting to check out, are also annoying. Express check-out is designed to eliminate the postprocess wait. Servers should be trained to minimize guests' postprocess waits.

Anxiety can make a wait seem longer. When guests have time constraints, anxiety leads them to overestimate the waiting time. Servers may be able to identify guests with time pressures and try to alleviate their concerns and reduce their anxiety. Children are especially not good at waiting for food. As children get fidgety, adults in the same party are likely to become frustrated, and this mood may also affect other guests' dining experience. Therefore, it is a good idea to keep children occupied so as to reduce anxiety for everyone.

People also wait more patiently when they know approximately how long they will be waiting and why they are waiting. Disney theme parks have done a good job of informing visitors by placing a sign indicating the estimated wait time. Most diners, seeing a line of people waiting for tables, are interested in finding out how long the wait will be. Restaurants should provide an honest estimate of the wait time.

Unfair waits, real or perceived, are likely to upset guests. Foodservice and lodging operations should have flexibility in accommodating guests with different needs so that the "first come, first served" rule is followed. Part of the responsibility of marketing is to create value for the hospitality service. The more valuable the service is, the longer people are willing to wait. Waiting can also be more tolerable when people feel that they are part of a group, perhaps through interaction with others.

Taking reservations in advance is one way to minimize wait time by matching supply with demand. When a room reservation request at one property cannot be met, a reservation at a nearby property can be offered. Similarly, when a dinner reservation at 8:00 P.M. cannot be accommodated, a table at 8:30 P.M. may be offered. Managing waiting lines and taking reservations are ways to manage demand in an industry in which supply cannot be inventoried.

Internal Marketing

As shown in Figure 2.4, the hospitality marketing cycle begins with promotional activities that stimulate interest in the company's offering. A potential guest may inquire about the service offering and pricing. If the inquiry is handled properly, a favorable purchase decision is likely. Therefore, the success of the initial contact with the operation is critical in turning a potential guest into an actual guest. When the guest arrives, a positive first impression will help retain his or her current patronage. On the other hand, a negative first interaction may discourage the guest from staying

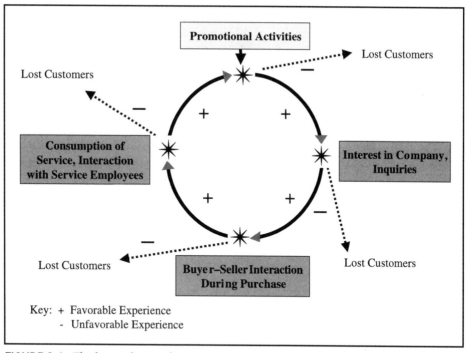

FIGURE 2.4 The hospitality marketing cycle: marketing and operations.
Source: Adapted from C. Grönroos, *Service Management and Marketing: Managing the Moments of Truth in Service Competition* (Lexington, MA: Lexington Books, 1990), 130.

and completing the current purchase. While a guest is consuming the service, successful encounters enhance the experience and build repeat business. Unpleasant experiences can spoil the current purchase and reduce repeat visits. Therefore, at each stage of the cycle, customers are gained or lost on the basis of their evaluation of the experience. Customers' assessments are based on the performance and attitudes of *all* employees, including both marketing and operations personnel.

Given the importance of people to an operation's success, it is not surprising to learn that service orientation sessions that include all personnel have been carefully developed. They are often called **internal marketing** programs. Internal marketing is a philosophy for managing personnel and a systematic way of developing and enhancing a **service culture.** The focus is on how to develop customer-conscious employees. Because the skills, customer orientation, and service mindedness of employees are critical to customers' perceptions of an operation and to their future patronage, internal marketing is considered a prerequisite for successful external marketing performance (Grönroos 1990). The overall objectives of internal marketing are to (1) attract and retain good employees and (2) ensure that the employees are motivated for customer-oriented and service-minded performance and therefore successfully fulfill their duties as "part-time marketers."

Employee Recruitment and Retention

One of the authors of this book (Tom Powers) interviewed operations executives at Disney World and asked how they train their employees to be so friendly. The surprising answer was, "We don't." The executives indicated that they took care of friendliness by aggressively screening people who applied to be "cast members," as Disney calls its employees. According to Southwest Airlines CEO Kelleher, "If you don't have a good attitude, we don't want you no matter how skilled you are. We can change skill levels through training. We can't change attitudes" (Teasley and Robinson 1998). In an effort to match employee personalities to those of its customers, Southwest even invites its most frequent flyers to interview and participate in the screening of potential new employees. Similarly, a Marriott official observed, "We can train people to do any task, but to get people with a friendly attitude, it starts with recruitment and hiring" (Grönroos 1990). Careful employee selection, therefore, is critical to successful service-oriented operations.

At Four Seasons, a key employment criterion is whether the candidate is a person with whom current employees will like to work. Several interviews, including a meeting with a senior executive, are conducted before a final decision is made. This approach is effective not only in assessing the applicant but also in communicating to the candidate the importance of the job and a sense of the company's values.

In many service organizations, the high-customer-contact jobs are also entry-level

Internal communication programs of all kinds are an important part of efforts to motivate operations employees. (Photo courtesy of Sodexho Marriott Services, Inc.)

positions, such as counter workers in quick-service restaurants and bell staff in hotels. The organization places its success in the hands of the newest and least-trained employees (Tansik 1988). Therefore, the orientation and training of all employees is extremely important to success in providing quality service. In addition to the necessary technical skills, it is important for all employees to develop an understanding of the entire organization and how it functions in a market-driven culture. An orientation to the company's philosophy, culture, and priorities, such as the two-day classroom program provided at the Ritz-Carlton, should help new employees adapt to the operation's environment and be successful at carrying out the company's objectives. Continued employee training and development activities are also important to refresh and enhance employees' technical, communication, and personal skills, as well as to reemphasize the importance of quality service. A well-trained and service-oriented employee is the most critical resource to the success of an organization. Service guarantees will actually be disastrous if internal marketing is not properly implemented and not all employees are prepared and motivated to act in a service-oriented manner.

A Service Culture

A **corporate culture** can be sensed as an internal climate within an organization. More formally, corporate culture may be defined as "the pattern of shared beliefs and values that give the members of an institution meaning, and provide them with the rules for behavior in their organization" (Davis 1984). A corporate culture is a powerful communication tool for "nurturing a service culture that will shape employee behavior more effectively than rules and regulations can" (Davidow and Uttal 1989).

A service culture provides the rewards and encouragement necessary to motivate employees to go out of their way to perform superior service. A service culture exists when there is an appreciation for good service and when giving good service to internal and external customers is considered a natural way of life and one of the most important measurements in the organization. Internal marketing can be a powerful tool in developing a service culture. For example, internal marketing activities can enable employees to understand and accept an organization's business objectives and strategies and to develop service-oriented communications and interaction skills. Internal marketing activities can also be designed to develop a service-oriented management and leadership style, which is a fundamental requirement in any service culture.

Once management is committed to service quality, employees can quickly sense the commitment and orientation and tend to be more dedicated to service quality. Management in a service culture usually takes care of its internal customers—employees—first, which leads to higher job satisfaction. Happy employees are likely to stay with their current employer and have a higher level of performance, which means satisfied customers. With satisfied customers who visit repeatedly and develop brand loyalty, the profitability of the operation is bound to increase. This favorable process usually continues in a circular pattern, as better profitability provides the means to maintain and further improve service-oriented attitudes among the personnel. Figure 2.5 shows the linking of service and profitability (Reich 1997).

FIGURE 2.5 The service–profit chain.
Source: Adapted from A. Z. Reich, *Marketing Management for the Hospitality Industry: A Strategic Approach* (New York: John Wiley & Sons, 1997), 107.

Summary

Hospitality services differ from manufactured goods in a number of characteristics: intangibility, people as part of the product, demand patterns, perishability, and channels of distribution. The service product's complexity can be described by three overlapping systems—the service delivery system, the hospitality operating system, and the communications system—in a service operation. Service quality can be achieved only when employees have both the technical and interpersonal skills required. The five criteria used by consumers to assess service quality are tangibles, reliability, responsiveness, assurance, and empathy. The five common service quality gaps are related to misunderstanding, lack of proper communication, inadequate performance, overpromising, and lack of consistency between expectations and experiences.

The zero-defect goal is ambitious, yet it helps an organization to aim high in providing service quality. Ensuring quality service reduces the bad and ugly costs, which are usually much higher than a good (prevention) cost. Customers should be encouraged to provide feedback by the offering of guarantees and other information-collecting mechanisms.

Because there is no inventory in supply, managing demand is critical. The handling of sometimes unavoidable waiting lines is an important part of demand management. Moreover, internal marketing programs should be implemented to attract and retain good employees and to cultivate a service culture, which are essential elements in service quality and long-term profitability.

Key Words and Concepts

Intangibility	Interpersonal dimension	Expectations
People are part of the product	Tangibles	Zero-defect standard
Demand patterns	Reliability	Good costs
Perishability	Responsiveness	Bad costs
Channel of distribution	Assurance	Ugly costs
Overlapping service systems	Empathy	Guarantee program
Service delivery system	Service quality gaps	Queuing
Hospitality operating system	Misunderstanding	Internal marketing
Communications system	Communication	Service culture
Quality	Performance	Corporate culture
Technical dimension	Overpromising	

Resources on the Internet

Club Med. *http://www.clubmed.com*
Hampton Inn. *http://www.hampton-inn.com/*
Malcolm Baldrige National Quality Award.
   http://www.quality.nist.gov

The Ritz-Carlton. *http://www.ritzcarlton.com*
Southwest Airlines. *http://www.southwest.com/*
The Walt Disney Company. *http://disney.go.com/*

Discussion Questions

1. What are the characteristics of service? What impact do they have on operations?
2. How can service quality be measured?
3. What common gaps occur in service? How can they be avoided?
4. What are the limitations of a zero-defect goal? What are its uses?
5. Is quality free? Why?
6. What are the uses of a guarantee program? What makes a guarantee program successful?
7. What are the implications of managing demand through queuing in service operations?
8. What is internal marketing?
9. What kind of corporate culture is appropriate to a service organization?

References

Berry, L. L., V. A. Zeithaml, and A. Parasuraman. (1992). Five imperatives for improving service quality. In C. H. Lovelock, ed. *Managing services: Marketing, operations, and human resources.* 2d ed., pp. 224–235. Englewood Cliffs, NJ: Prentice-Hall.

Buzzell, R. D., and B. T. Gale. (1987). *The PIMS principles: Linking strategy to performance.* New York: The Free Press.

Crosby, P. (1979). *Quality is free.* New York: McGraw-Hill.

Davidow, W. H., and B. Uttal. (1989). *Total customer service: The ultimate weapon.* New York: Harper & Row.

Davis, S. M. (1984). *Managing corporate culture.* Cambridge, MA: Ballinger.

Grönroos, C. (1990). *Service management and marketing.* Lexington, MA: Lexington Books.

Hart, C. W. L. (1988). The power of unconditional service guarantees. *Harvard Business Review, 66*(4), 54–62.

Labovitz, G. H., and Y. S. Chang. (1987). *Quality costs: The good, the bad and the ugly.* Boston: Organizational Dynamics.

LeBoeuf, M. (1987). *How to win customers and keep them for life.* New York: G. P. Putnam's Sons.

Lovelock, C. H. (1996). *Services marketing.* 3d ed. Upper Saddle River, NJ: Prentice-Hall.

Maister, D. H. (1985). The psychology of waiting lines. In J. A. Czepiel, M. R. Solomon, and C. F. Surprenant, eds. *The service encounter.* pp. 113–123. Lexington, MA: Lexington Books/D.C. Health.

Normann, R. (1984). *Service management: Strategy and leadership in service businesses.* New York: John Wiley & Sons.

Reich, A. Z. (1997). *Marketing management for the hospitality industry: A strategic approach.* New York: John Wiley & Sons.

Shostack, G. L. (1977). Breaking free from product marketing. *Journal of Marketing, 41*(2), 73–80.

Tansik, D. A. (1988, November). *Balance in service systems design.* Research report presented at the Seinsheimer Symposium on Business. New Orleans: Tulane University, Freeman School of Business.

Teasley, R. W., and R. Robinson. (1998). Southwest Airlines. In R. C. Lewis, ed. *Cases in hospitality strategy and policy.* pp. 15–42. New York: John Wiley & Sons.

The Macro and Micro Environments of Hospitality Marketing

When you have finished reading this chapter, you should be able to:

- Identify elements of the macro environment and their implications.
- Analyze elements of the micro environment and their implications.
- Discuss major demographic trends and their implications.
- Describe factors influencing buyer characteristics.
- Explain the buying process as problem solving.
- Illustrate the perception-forming process.
- Understand the risks associated with purchase decisions.

```
┌─────────────────────────────────────────────┐
│  Macro Environment                           │
│         -Economy                             │
│         -Society and culture                 │
│         -Politics                            │
│         -Technology                          │
│         -Ecology                             │
│   ┌─────────────────────────────────────┐    │
│   │  Micro Environment                  │    │
│   │     -Competitors                    │    │
│   │     -Customers                      │    │
│   │                                     │    │
│   │   ┌─────────────────────────────┐   │    │
│   │   │  Hospitality Marketing      │   │    │
│   │   └─────────────────────────────┘   │    │
│   └─────────────────────────────────────┘    │
└─────────────────────────────────────────────┘
```

FIGURE 3.1 Environmental influences on hospitality marketing.

Hospitality marketing takes place in a complex environment. On one hand, there are forces, such as the economy and social change, in the remote **macro environment** that affect the way operations conduct business. On the other hand, there are competitors and consumers in the immediate **micro environment** who interact with businesses and influence their marketing and operations. The environments of marketing are summarized graphically in Figure 3.1. Elements of the macro and micro environments are discussed throughout this chapter.

The Macro Environment

Economy

Consumers' spending on hospitality services is discretionary spending. The share of household budgets spent on food away from home declined slightly during the recession of the early 1990s (Putnam and Allshouse 1999). "When people have to cut back on expenses, eating out and entertainment outside the home are the first things to go" (American Demographics 1995). Company travel budgets are also among the first to be cut in a recession. Therefore, hospitality industry sales reflect general business conditions and respond to trends in the economy. Hospitality firms, especially in the lodging segment, rely on mortgages to fund new construction. Thus, high interest rates can discourage the development of new properties and additions to existing facilities. Low interest rates and easy availability of money, however, can result in building booms—and then in oversupply, which makes a marketer's challenge even tougher. Other economic factors that must be considered include GNP (gross national product) growth, disposable and discretionary income, the inflation rate, consumer confidence and willingness to spend, the unemployment rate, the availability of credit, and currency exchange rates.

Different segments of the industry are affected differently by the various economic factors. For example, when income growth is flat, the impact on quick-service and fine dining restaurants, or on budget and luxury hotels, is not the same. Whereas high-end hotels and fine dining restaurants may see recession as a threat, economy hotels and quick-service restaurants (QSRs) may see it as an opportunity. During a recession, the **squeeze effect** (every level of the market tries to "squeeze" its prices to increase market potential) is likely to occur. For example, as shown in Figure 3.2, fine dining restaurants try to be a little more informal and provide a wider range of menu prices so as to solicit some of the theme restaurant customers and thus broaden the market. Theme restaurants may use special pricing to entice the upper end of the family-style restaurant market. Family restaurants, in turn, reduce their prices or promote special deals to attract those who usually go to QSRs. Finally, QSRs develop "value meals" to retain their current customers and encourage frequent repeat visits. The same effects can be seen in the lodging segment during a recession.

Society and Culture

As social and cultural values, beliefs, and opinions change, opportunities are created for new products, services, and concepts. As people become more concerned about secondhand smoke, more restaurants, even in states where a complete smoking ban is not required, have become completely smoke-free. Hotels also provide nonsmoking

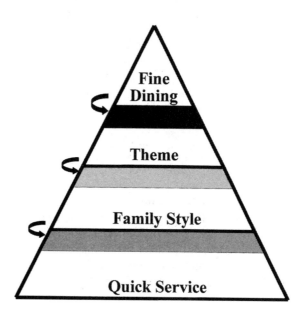

FIGURE 3.2   The squeeze effect.

rooms or floors in response to the contemporary climate of the social environment. Another major social and cultural trend is the desire for fitness and health, which has triggered a whole array of new products and services, such as spa resorts, fitness facilities in hotels, and healthful menu items. QSRs have switched from using animal fat to vegetable oil as a frying medium for french fries and other fried menu items. Many restaurants are also flexible in providing substitutions for menu components. Case Study 3.1 describes a hotel's effort to serve low-fat, low-cholesterol food.

CASE STUDY 3.1

"Cuisine Naturelle" for the Health Conscious

Hyatt hotels' development of a new line of low-fat, low-cholesterol menu items, called Cuisine Naturelle, is explained by the company's vice president of food and beverage, Philip Kendall: "What we're doing is putting the choice back into healthy eating and giving diners more options for eating well-balanced, good-tasting food. . . . This menu proves to diners that they can eat beef, pork and pasta with cream sauce and still have dessert, if the meal is prepared properly."

Cuisine Naturelle was created in response to Hyatt's research indicating that travelers are interested in eating low-fat, healthful meals but demand a variety of choices when doing so. A 1989 National Restaurant Association report showed that 55 percent of diners rate nutrition as their top concern but choose food based on taste. Therefore, each Cuisine Naturelle selection is marinated or prepared with less than one teaspoon of oil, and only natural, additive-free, organically grown fruits and vegetables, fresh herbs, and special cuts of meat are used.

Test marketing in 10 hotels revealed that the Cuisine Naturelle menu, which accounted for only 10 percent of the menu, was responsible for 30 to 35 percent of total sales. Nutritional information is provided for all items on the menu. The menu is available in full-service restaurants and coffee shops, as well as through catering and room service, in all 104 Hyatt hotels in the United States, Canada, and the Caribbean. To implement the new menu, all Hyatt kitchens have been restocked and redesigned to accommodate the new way of cooking.

Source: Hyatt Corporation. (2000). *Explore Hyatt: Cuisine Naturelle* (On-line) Web site: http://www.hyatt.com/athyatt/services/naturel.html

Today's consumers are experienced diners and travelers. They demand quality and value. They know what they can and should receive for their money. Therefore, creating value and striving for quality service are top priorities for most hospitality operations. Food safety and responsible alcohol service have also received the attention of consumers. Operators and marketers may see these trends as opportunities to develop a competitive advantage over other organizations. With the increased awareness of cultural diversity, the demand for ethnic specialty restaurants has grown tremendously. In addition to the staples of Mexican, Italian, and Chinese restaurants, Thai, Spanish, South African, Vietnamese, and many other types of ethnic restaurants have also gained popularity.

Demographic changes have a significant impact on social and cultural values and trends, as well as on consumer preferences in products and services. Demographics are objectively measurable characteristics in the population, such as age, income, and family structure. Some of the major **demographic trends** are discussed in the following paragraphs.

Age. This section discusses a number of the principal age-based consumer segments in today's market. The characteristics of various age groups are summarized in Table 3.1. The senior (55+) market will become increasingly important as people live longer and healthier. This is a significant market not only because of the large number of senior citizens but also because of the amounts of their discretionary income and leisure time. Although their incomes may not be as high as those of younger families in peak earning years, many seniors have significant spending power because of their

TABLE 3.1 Characteristics of Generations

	Seniors	Boomers	Gen X	Gen Y
Born	1945 or earlier	1946–1964	1965–1978	1979–1994
Age in year 2001	56 and older	37–55	23–36	7–22
Population	56 million	72 million	17 million	60 million
Family	Mom, dad, grandma, grandpa	Mom, dad	Mom or dad	Mom or dad or grandma
Caucasian	85%	75%	69%	66%
Defining idea	Duty	Individuality	Diversity	Anything goes
Style	Team player	Self-absorbed	Entrepreneur	Every person for him- or herself
Work is . . .	Obligation	Exciting adventure	Difficult challenge	Unknown
Education is . . .	Dream	Birthright	Way to get ahead	Cultural experience
Money management	Save	Spend	Hedge	Spend
Technologies	Typewriter Rotary phone	IBM Touch-tone phone	Macintosh Cell phone	Netscape Motorola flex-pager
"In" crowd	Nightclubs	Rock clubs	Rave clubs	Swing clubs
Water	Tonic water	Perrier	Evian	Caffeinated
Designers	Christian Dior	Calvin Klein	Donna Karan	Tommy Hilfiger

Source: Adapted from Greg Flack, "Food Service Trends Beyond 2000," Shuggart Lecture Series. Manhattan, KS, April 21, 1999.

Seniors account for a large percentage of pleasure travel. Identifying and catering to their tastes is of growing importance. (Photo courtesy of Carnival Cruise Lines.)

accumulated wealth and reduced financial obligations, such as child rearing costs and mortgage payments. The greatest change in the size of the senior market, however, lies ahead when the baby boomers reach the senior stage of their lives.

The aging of the baby boom generation (people born between 1946 and 1964) has tremendous implications for the hospitality industry. Marketers are likely to pay attention to this group because of its size and its disproportionate purchasing power. **Baby boomers,** in general, are well educated and upwardly mobile; therefore their purchasing power is likely to grow as they enter middle age—a prime income-earning stage of their lives. This is the group partially responsible for the growth of the all-suite hotels and the increasing popularity of upscale casual restaurants.

Generation X-ers, born between 1965 and 1978, are in their young adulthood years. This generation differs from previous generations of young adults in many important respects, including their behavior as consumers. They are well traveled and consume more fast food (Ritchie 1995a). They grew up surrounded by commercial messages, are skeptical of hype, and do not like overstatement. If we wish Generation X-ers to visit our operations, the offerings must be perceived as useful. They are not likely to purchase for reasons of status or to make a statement, but to fulfill a genuine need (Ritchie 1995b).

Generation Y-ers, born between 1979 and 1994, are the new age group, also known as the millennial generation. Most of them are still in school and living with their parents. Some, however, have become independent consumers. This generation includes 60 million youngsters, more than three times the size of Generation X—the largest group to hit the American scene since the 72 million baby boomers. This is also known as the Internet generation, which means greater differences between individuals because the Internet drives diversity. Because of their young age and limited consuming experience, many of the characteristics of these individuals as consumers are still unknown. However, they do respond favorably to humor, irony, and the unvarnished truth (Newborne 1999). This is the generation to watch in the next few decades.

Working Women. As more women work outside their homes, families have more income and less time for food preparation and long vacations. This means more dinners away from home, more carry-outs from restaurants and grocery store food counters, and more mini-vacations. More women in business also means more women business travelers. In fact, women are expected to constitute half of all business travelers in 2002, as compared with only 1 percent in 1970 (Khan 1999). Significant implications for hotel room amenities and services include extra security, makeup mirrors in the bathrooms, and skirt hangers in the closet, to name a few. Case Study 3.2 is an example of the Wyndham Hotel's effort to capture the women travelers market. The large number of working women has also affected corporations' media and communication strategies.

CASE STUDY 3.2

Women on Their Way by Wyndham

Wyndham Hotels & Resorts has developed an ongoing program to better serve the needs of the growing number of women business travelers. The Women Business Travelers Advisory Board was created to advise the company on the development and evaluation of new products and programs. For example, the advisory board suggested the upgrading of bathroom toiletries. As a result, the hotels switched to the *Bath & Body Works* brand shampoo, conditioner, and body lotion. Women also consistently indicated a preference for a sophisticated, yet informal, setting for conversation. The company responded by creating a "signature" library, now a design feature in Wyndham Garden Hotels.

Wyndham hotels offer other elements that have particular appeal to women, such as open, well-lit lobbies and hallways; interior corridor access to all guest rooms; real hook hangers, including skirt hangers; healthful cuisine; exercise facilities; hair dryers; in-room iron and ironing board; and shower massage.

A special Web site has also been developed for women travelers, which contains information and travel tips for women by women. Topics include health and fitness, packing, safety, technology, time management, and staying sane. Another feature of the Web site is a women's forum where women business travelers can post messages to discuss particular issues or provide tips and encouragement to each other. The Web site also provides links to other women travelers and related sites.

Source: Wyndham IP Corporation. (2001). *Women on their way* (On-line). Web site: http://www.womenbusinesstravelers.com

Family Composition. Later marriages and delay in having children, as well as families choosing to remain childless, have had a significant impact on the hospitality industry. DINKs (Dual Income No Kids) are the wealthy couples with more leisure time. They are restaurants' more frequent customers (a night out on the town), and they can afford to travel more (a weekend out of town) and use more expensive accommodations. Later marriages and a high divorce rate also mean more single-person and single-parent households and more women as household heads. Individuals in such households have different consuming needs and preferences, as compared with traditional household members. Single-parent families, especially those headed by women, tend to have lower incomes. Although they are not as good customers for hospitality in general, they do patronize QSRs.

Politics

Federal, state, and local government actions affect hospitality operations and marketing. For example, a limit on the amount that can be deducted for business meals and business entertainment has hurt many upscale restaurants. The restaurant industry continues to experience pressure from the federal government, and from some state governments as well, to improve nutritional labeling for menus. Local zoning laws have a direct impact on the location of businesses, and city ordinances affect the types of signs a business can display. Court rulings can also change the types of products offered. For example, after one QSR was successfully sued for the high temperature of its coffee, many other QSRs lowered their coffee temperature and removed hot chocolate from their menus.

One of the major activities of both state and national trade associations, such as the National Restaurant Association and the American Hotel and Motel Association, involves government affairs. Both associations are recognized for the effectiveness of their lobbying activities. At the state and local levels, destination marketing agencies, such as state tourism offices and convention and visitors bureaus, play an important role in building sales for the hospitality industry in their regions.

Technology

The greatest impacts of technology on hospitality operations are in the area of communications and the amount and quality of information available. Computerized point-of-sales (POS) systems have revolutionized the analysis of restaurant operating results. Unit managers know profit results on an hourly basis. And this information is available immediately to area managers and headquarters staff. Other technological applications include property management systems, food production and storage, facility safety and security, energy control, marketing and information systems, customer ordering and payment systems, and the use of peripheral equipment.

For example, computers are used to keep track of a guest's history on spending, frequency of visits, and product preferences. Hotels offer automatic check-in and check-out. QSR customers can place their orders on a touch-screen computer terminal. Many QSRs have also installed an order confirmation system, with a screen displaying items ordered, at the drive-thru to reduce order-taking errors. Some restaurants take orders via fax machine for pickups. Other restaurants provide beepers to waiting guests so that they can walk around the block to pass the time. Many operations also use the Internet for promotion, distribution (making reservations), and public relations activities. Hotels, resorts, casinos, and cruise lines have taken advantage of "smart card" technology to make it easier for guests to spend money and to monitor guest activities.

Furthermore, the computer and communications technologies have created a whole new world of entertainment, which can be a major competitor of hospitality

This computer system illustrates the use of wireless technology in a casino operation. (Graphic courtesy of Ameranth Technology Systems, Inc., www.Ameranth.com)

operations. Consumers have a choice of going out for entertainment or of staying home and and being entertained. "Virtual vacation" is already available on the Internet.

Ecology

Ecology refers to the relationships between human beings and other living things and the air, soil, and water that support them (Pearce and Robinson 1997). Businesses have an obligation to protect the natural resources available so that they can operate in an optimal environment as long as possible. Consumers have also shown interest in environmental protection and have demanded that businesses behave in an ecologically friendly manner. Therefore, the implementation of environmental policies can become a point of competitive advantage.

The Business Council for Sustainable Development has used the term *eco-efficiency* to describe corporations that produce more useful products and services and at the same time reduce resource consumption and pollution (Pearce and Robinson 1997). One of the most important steps a company can take in achieving a competitive position with regard to an eco-efficient strategy is to fully capitalize on technological developments as a way of gaining efficiency. For example, energy-saving equipment is available and computers can be used to cut down on paperwork. Current technologies allow the guest room temperature be controlled at the front office so that when the rooms are not occupied, the climate system can be turned to the energy-saving mode.

Many hospitality organizations have implemented environment-friendly programs. For example, many restaurants serve water only on request, and hotels ask guests to keep towels on the rack if they will be used again so that they will not be washed unnecessarily. Some restaurants, such as Long John Silver's, use recyclable and biodegradable packaging materials (Long John Silver's 2001). Case Study 1.1 (in Chapter 1) describes McDonald's efforts in protecting the environment.

The Micro Environment

The most important factors in the micro environment are a firm's competitive position and the composition of its customers. An operation has more influence on its micro environment than on the macro environment. Therefore, operators and marketers can be more proactive in dealing with competitors and customers than with politics and technology.

Competitors

One variable used to define an industry's structure is its concentration or fragmentation. A **concentrated industry** is one in which sales are dominated by only a few companies. A **fragmented industry** is one in which no company has a significant market share (Pearce and Robinson 1997). Within the hospitality market, only the QSR segment has reached the stability of a concentrated industry. McDonald's is clearly the market leader; however, there are challenges from existing players, such as Taco Bell and Burger King. It is reasonable to say that McDonald's has a strong lead, but not strong enough to eliminate competition.

The casual restaurant segment is more fragmented and competitive. Operators are witnessing "changes in market dominance as new concepts and faster-growing chains nip away at veteran players who, in many cases, are slowing up their core brands' unit growth in order to develop new chain concepts" (Prewitt 1999).

The lodging segment of the industry appears to be dominated by very large chains because of the few franchisors' brand names used by literally thousands of properties. However, lodging consists of franchised properties with many owners. Property owners change their brand names at surprisingly high frequency. Therefore, the current industry structure is not one of market dominance, but one of fragmentation and extreme competitiveness (Powers 1992).

In recent years most of the growth in the hospitality industry has occurred in chain and national brand operations. Hospitality leaders, such as McDonald's and Marriott, have maintained or increased their market shares. The percentage of independently owned, nonfranchised operations has declined. It is estimated that 27 percent of restaurants fail within the first year. The marketplace for independent operations is much more competitive than it was just a few years ago.

The high degree of competition in both the hotel and the restaurant segments affects pricing strategies and all other elements of the marketing mix. The relatively fragmented nature of the industry means that the environment will remain highly competitive and unpredictable.

Customers

The goal of marketing is to influence **consumer behavior.** To do this, marketers must understand how and why customers behave the way they do. We first examine the characteristics of buyers, then discuss their buying process.

Characteristics of Buyers. Three categories of buyer characteristics have significant influences on individuals' purchasing behaviors. **Societal influences** include the impacts of families, culture/subculture, socioeconomic status, and reference groups. **Personal situations** comprise an individual's age, life cycle stage, and psychographic characteristics. A buyer's perception, attitudes, and personality are the relevant **psychological influences.**

Societal Influences. Families are important to hospitality marketers for two reasons. First of all, children learn how to be consumers from their parents. Therefore, understanding and educating parents as consumers may yield long-term returns on the investment. Second, family decisions are especially important to hospitality operations because, in many cases, our customers are families and decisions about entertainment, vacations, and dining out are more likely to be joint family decisions. Joint family decisions, by definition, involve more than one person's input, and each member may have a particular opinion or source of information. Moreover, each individual may play a different role in the decision-making process. Therefore, an understanding of the dynamics of family decision making, the role each member plays, and the members' sources of information can help marketers better attract the family market.

Research has shown that children are likely to influence decisions for purchases consumed by the whole family, such as food items, vacation plans, entertainment, and restaurant choices. It is also argued that commercial messages received by both children and parents can help children get their requests. Therefore, both McDonald's and Disney, for example, have advertisements designed for children and for adults.

A **culture** is a distinctive way of living shared by a group of people. It is socially shared, it is learned, and it is gradually changing. Cultural values are learned through socialization as individuals grow up. In the United States, each decade, such as the 1960s, 1970s, and 1980s, seems to have its own cultural theme. For example, because of the focus on family values in the 1990s, Las Vegas and many other tourist destinations have positioned themselves as "family destinations."

In a given society, certain segments of the population may be represented as **subcultures** because of their distinct values and customs. Subcultures can be identified based on a number of factors, such as age, geographic region, and ethnic background. People in different age categories, such as Generation X, baby boomers, and seniors, have different consuming behaviors. Geographic regions can also be used to define subcultures because of the differences in tastes, values, and behaviors. On the global level, such regions may include Europe, North America, and Asia. Within the United States, Southern, New England, and Midwestern are some of the distinct regions. An example of regional differences is that iced tea served in the southern United States is usually presweetened, whereas in the Midwest it is not. Southerners are also more inclined to eat biscuits than the rest of the country, and hominy grits are hardly ever offered outside the South.

The most important subcultural groups in the United States are defined by ethnic origin. The two largest minority subcultures are the African American and the Hispanic. Hispanics are well on their way to becoming the largest ethnic minority in the United States. This population growth is fueled by the immigration of young adults (Pearce and Robinson 1997). Studies have identified differences between subcultures in media usage preferences and purchasing behaviors, as well as in perceptions and attitudes.

Socioeconomic status refers to the position of an individual or family on a social scale based on criteria that are valuable to the society. In the North American society, occupation, education, and income are used to define the prestige or power of an individual and to assign him or her to a particular social class. There are no absolute lines between classes, and social class is measured by a combination of factors. For example, a college professor who has a Ph.D. degree and earns $45,000 a year may enjoy a higher social status than a factory foreman who has a high school diploma and makes $60,000 annually. Social classes are important to marketers because consumers in the same class usually display similar patterns in what they buy, where they live, how they shop, and what they read.

Most Hispanic people understand English, but advertising in Spanish nevertheless has a strong appeal for them. (Photo courtesy of Pizza Hut.)

A **reference group** is a group that serves as a reference point for individuals in the formation of their beliefs, attitudes, and behaviors. Reference groups are important to marketers because they are consumers' sources of information and influence. *Primary reference groups* include family and close friends. These are the individuals consumers relate to on a regular, face-to-face basis. *Secondary reference groups* comprise fellow church and professional association members. Contact with these individuals is not as close or frequent as with primary reference group members. Neighbors, fraternal members, and classmates can constitute either a primary or a secondary reference group, depending on how close consumers are to these people and how much contact they have with them.

A third type of reference group is the *aspiration group*—the group to which consumers would like to belong. An "anticipatory" aspiration group is a group you anticipate joining at some future time. For example, you may anticipate that you will be one of the highly successful business persons or CEO of a hotel corporation. A "symbolic" aspiration group is a group that you would like to belong to, although you know that you are not likely to become a member. For example, you do not think you will be a successful professional football player or a movie star, even though you would very much like to be one. The "Want to be like Mike" slogan used by the Gatorade advertisement is a classic example of using a member of the symbolic aspiration group to influence consumers' purchase behavior.

Travelers in different stages of their life cycle have different needs and preferences when selecting a lodging property. (Photo courtesy of Holiday Inn.)

Personal Situations. A consumer's interests are also affected by a number of factors that are specific to the individual but may be shared with many others. These factors offer solid grounds for grouping consumers into various market segments. As consumers age, their interests and needs, and abilities to satisfy their needs, change. Therefore, different marketing strategies are required to attract people of different age groups. **Life cycle stages** tend to parallel changes in age; however, different individuals experience life differently, especially during the stages of young adulthood and middle age. With today's freedom of choice and alternative lifestyles, it is impossible to determine an all-inclusive set of characteristics for each life cycle stage. However, Table 3.2 summarizes the principal life cycle stages and some suggested consumer characteristics related to each stage.

To reiterate the importance of the baby boomer generation, this group accounts for nearly one-third of the North American population and is moving into middle age, a period when incomes rise and different consuming needs develop. These are prime hospitality customers. In fact, baby boomers account for slightly more than half of all restaurant visits. Constituting another key age group and life cycle stage are the seniors, people aged 65 and older. Even with various levels of health problems, most seniors under age 75 remain active, are relatively prosperous, and have lots of leisure time. This makes them a prime target for hospitality services. Studies have shown that seniors travel more, travel greater distances, stay away from home longer, and are more mobile (Miller 1996). In addition, seniors are one of the most prosperous age groups in the U.S. population. As Anthony Marshall (1997) has accurately pointed out, the "the silver market is lined with gold."

Patterns of activities, interests, and opinions **(AIO)** are the primary measurements of individuals' **psychographic,** or lifestyle, characteristics. Among the common psychographic categories are the health conscious, price conscious, and environmental protectors. The task of hospitality marketing is to recognize and fill the needs generated by people's ways of life. For example, the recent proliferation of spa resorts is a reaction to the needs of stressful professionals who are willing and able to pay for the pampering of their bodies and souls. Mini-vacation packages are developed for dual-career families, often combining a short vacation with a business trip for one of the partners. The short vacation and the couple's generally time-pressed way of life and relatively high income mean that the quality of the experience is often more important than the cost. Off-season special deals are often designed for individuals who are both price conscious and flexible as to travel schedules—many of whom are senior citizens.

Psychological Influences. A number of psychological factors influence consumers' behaviors and are important considerations for hospitality marketers. Psychology is a complex study; therefore we confine our attention to just three consumer characteristics: perception, attitudes, and personality.

The saying that marketing is not a battle of products, it is a battle of perceptions sums up the importance of consumer **perception.** The success we have in creating quality perceptions and in marketing services largely depends on the way our customers perceive our services. Perceptions are also important to marketers because they tell us how consumers see the world. Perceptions are subjective ways of interpreting

TABLE 3.2 The Life Cycle and Hospitality

Life Cycle Stage	Age	Hospitality Industry Consumer Characteristics
Childhood		
Early	5 or under	Need toys and child portions. May require baby-sitter in hotels.
Late	6–12	Important influence on choice of place to eat out. Resort hotels provide recreation programs for pre-teens.
Teenagers		
Younger	13–15	Becoming independent consumers but most commonly without significant independent income. Major influence on dining out. Recreation facilities in hotels used independently.
Older	16–19	Independent consumers, often employed part-time. High need for social activity.
Young Adulthood		
Young singles	20–24	In labor force and/or postsecondary education full-time. Adequate income for small-scale use of hospitality services, such as for dating. Travel with family or on very low budget.
Young married	25–34	Predominantly two-income families, but family formation expenditures and investments often reduce funds available for travel. Like lively, informal dining places. High interest in travel.
Middle Age		
Young middle age	35–49	Income rises considerably, but children at home or in college require significant continuing support. Highest propensity to eat out, travel.
Advanced middle age	50–64	Income at peak, though sometimes reduced at early retirement. Very high propensity to travel. Eat out less often than young middle-age groups.
Senior Citizens		
Young old	65–74	Fixed but adequate income. Retirement means an affluent leisure class. Generally healthy and vigorous. Intent to enjoy life. Regular, but less frequent, restaurant customers. Some special diet considerations.
Old	75–84	More health problems; often widow or widower living alone. Prone to depression. May require nursing home care. Special diet considerations more prevalent.
Very old	85 and over	Most rapidly growing population segment in North America. One of 5 live in nursing homes; 7 of 10 are women. Frail elderly, but also some alert and very prosperous elderly. Often require special diets and assistance.

and assigning meaning to stimuli. They are subjective because each person evaluates messages in a different way.

Figure 3.3 illustrates the perception-forming process. To begin, the individual has to be *exposed* to the message. Consumers are exposed to thousands of commercial messages each day. Just by looking around the room where you are situated, you can get a sense of how many commercial messages you encounter daily. For example, do you see a beverage container with a logo on it? What about a pen with a logo? A T-shirt with a brand name printed on it? Are there any other products showing either a brand name or another advertisement? Simply because you are exposed to these messages does not mean that you pay attention to all of them. Consumers pay *selective attention*, based on their needs, preferences, past experiences, and attitudes. For example, suppose two people are driving into a busy shopping area. Both of them are surrounded by literally hundreds of stimuli: traffic lights, other vehicles, pedestrians, road signs, shops, and billboards, to name a few. One person is driving a car that is about to run out of gas, and the other is an hour overdue for lunch. It is likely that one of them will notice the gas station signs and that the other will pay attention to restaurant signs.

Even when you do pay attention, it does not mean that you can *comprehend* the message the way the sender would like you to. For example, suppose you and a friend are watching television together and a new commercial is shown. The two of you may come up with different explanations of the message being sent, yet perhaps neither of you has received the message as intended by the sponsor.

Finally, how many of the messages you are exposed to, pay attention to, and understand can you remember? This is the *selective retention* stage of the perception-forming process. If the driver who is looking for a restaurant is highly cost conscious,

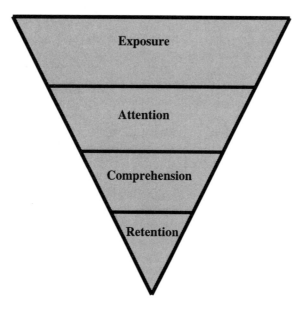

FIGURE 3.3 Perception-forming process.

he will remember the QSR signs and quickly forget about the upscale restaurants. That is, the driver will hold on to those stimuli (restaurant signs) that most closely fit with his interests and needs. Perception forming is a very selective process and is important to all areas of marketing because it tells us how consumers see the world. To survive the highly competitive process of attracting customers, marketers must develop clear, attention-getting messages that fit the needs of consumers.

Attitude is a consumer's overall liking or preference for an object, which may be a product, a service, or an operation. Attitudes are learned, because we develop attitudes based on past experiences. Once attitudes are developed, they are enduring and difficult to change. Identifying consumer attitudes toward an operation or a product is important because an individual's attitudes can directly influence his or her behavioral intention (e.g., intent to visit or purchase), which is a predictor of the actual behavior (e.g., actual visit or purchase) (Ajzen 1991). Therefore, when a consumer has a positive attitude toward a restaurant, this individual is likely to think about visiting the restaurant and to actually dine in the restaurant.

Personality consists of a pattern of characteristics and habits that makes each individual unique. A useful way to think of personality is in terms of a person's self-concept (Mehta 1999). People have an *ideal self-concept* and an *actual self-concept.* The ideal represents what you would like to be, even though it is sometimes unrealistic. The actual represents an honest assessment of who you are. People tend to buy products and services to enhance their self-concept, so that they can be one step closer to the ideal image, or to reflect their actual self-concept. Therefore, marketing can encourage the consumer to "be the person you know you should be" by offering opportunities to achieve higher social status, greater relaxation, or another ideal state. Marketing can also try to match products and services to people's self-concept. For example, a luxury hotel may appeal to people who "think" of themselves as successful and well-to-do, as well as to those who really are. A resort may appeal to individuals who perceive themselves as young, active, and fun loving, and to those who actually are. Although people's personalities do affect their buying behavior, the complexity of the human personality is such that it should be used only to provide general guidelines, rather than to construct a viable market segment.

The Buying Process. Before consumers reach the actual purchase stage, they go through the steps of a problem-solving process. Consumers may appear impulsive and sometimes irrational, but they are not unreasonable—they make a purchase for a reason, which is to solve a problem. Therefore, the consumers' **buying process** can be thought of as the problem-solving process illustrated in Figure 3.4.

Problem Awareness. Consumers do not begin a decision process until they perceive a difference between what they have and what they must have (a need) or what they have and what they would like to have (a want). The difference must be great enough to create a "problem" for the consumer to take action. Therefore, part of the mission of marketers is to help consumers develop an awareness of their problems. Marketers may also heighten consumers' sense of urgency with their problems and inform them that the marketers' operation represents a solution to such problems.

FIGURE 3.4 Consumer problem-solving process.

For example, a country inn near a metropolitan area may use consumers' increasing concerns about the noise and pressure of big city living, and the need to get away from it all, as a marketing opportunity. Marketing communications can highlight the hectic daily schedule as a problem that seriously erodes the quality of urban life. A relaxed dinner or weekend retreat at the tranquil country inn can be offered as the solution.

Information Search. Once consumers are aware of a problem, they look for solutions. In other words, they search for information. Several factors must be considered to fully understand this stage of the problem-solving process: the importance of the decision, the amount of prior experience, the perceived risk, and sources of information.

The *importance of the decision* to be made dictates the amount of time and effort to invest in that decision. The decision to pick a QSR for lunch between classes is not nearly as important as the selection of a nice restaurant for a first date. Thus, the extent of the information search for the quick lunch decision is very limited and the decision is made in a moment, whereas the decision for the first date will take longer. The second determinant of the scope of the information search is *prior experience.* When people plan to go to a distant resort in an area they have never visited before, they will probably consult a travel agent or friends who have been there. Because of the intangible nature of hospitality services, uncertainty is high when no prior experience exists. As a result, the **perceived risk** of making the wrong decision is relatively high.

Risks associated with a purchase decision may be financial, social, or performance related. The degree of *financial risk* is a function of the cost of a product or service and whether it can be purchased with the consumer's discretionary income. For example, the consumer who has saved for four years to purchase a vacation package runs a much higher risk than those who can pay for the same package from their discretionary income.

Social risk involves the possibility that the guest will be embarrassed to be seen using a particular product or service or will be concerned about using the product or service the wrong way. For example, Motel 6 found that customers were hesitant to admit that they stayed at Motel 6 because they were afraid of being labeled as "cheapskates" or as persons who could not afford "decent" accommodations (Cunningham and Dev 1992). Another example is an individual who has an opportunity to attend a banquet at an exclusive club but is worried about the formality of table manners and is afraid that the club will be too snobbish for her taste.

Consumers evaluating a distant resort may have concerns about whether facilities and amenities will be acceptable (performance risk) and about how well they will fit in (social risk). (Photo courtesy of Corbis Images.)

Performance risk involves the possibility that something will not work. For example, there is the risk of encountering an unsanitary restaurant, an unsafe aircraft, un-healthful food, or unfriendly service. The higher the total perceived risks, the more involved the consumer is with the decision, which means that more information is needed to help make the best decision.

Because of the intangibility factor, customers tend to rely more on social sources of information, such as word of mouth, than on commercial sources of information, such as advertisements, when purchasing services. It has been confirmed by the National Restaurant Association's study (1998) that informal or interpersonal recommendations are substantially more important than information provided by the operations themselves. It is worth noting that word-of-mouth communication, unlike other media, cannot be bought. It can be earned only through superior operating performance. This demonstrates the close relationship between operating performance and marketing in securing repeat patronage discussed in Chapter 2.

Alternative Evaluation and Purchase Decision. One way to evaluate alternatives is to use a single criterion to screen all options. Options that do not meet this criterion are deleted from the list before other factors are even considered. If two restaurants are equal on the single most important criterion, such as price, then evaluation may proceed on the second most important variable, perhaps location.

Another way to evaluate alternatives is to develop a mental weighted average that includes several factors weighted according to their importance. Factors used to evaluate a vacation destination may include climate, distance from home, airfare, hotel room rate, and attractions. Consumers do not actually "compute" an average to reach a decision, but a similar kind of weighting process takes place in their minds. Each decision variable is intuitively weighted by its importance, the relative performance of each destination on each factor is assessed, and the total scores of all destinations are compared to select the best option.

Before a purchase decision is made, at any point during the course of action, consumers may completely stop the problem-solving process or go back one or more steps to repeat some of the activities. For example, a couple, planning the celebration of their 25th wedding anniversary, finding that none of the alternatives fits their schedule or budget, may decide to search for more alternatives. Or, they may even go back to the very first stage and question whether a celebration is necessary—whether they have a problem.

Postpurchase Evaluation. When a major purchase decision is made, consumers may still have a number of concerns that have been only partly resolved in the decision-making process. This set of concerns and the feeling of discomfort is referred to as **cognitive dissonance.** For example, once a decision has been made, we may ask ourselves, "Did we make the right decision?" Consumers usually find **postpurchase evaluation** more essential with services than with products because, without prior experience, services are more difficult to evaluate and distinguish from each other. As a result, consumers are less confident about their decisions. After the purchase, consumers will continue to search for information to support their decisions. From the marketer's perspective, this suggests the need to provide some reassurance in the immediate postpurchase period. Something as simple as a personalized reservation confirmation or a thank-you note may help to ease the consumers' minds and reinforce the feeling that they made the right choice.

Another part of the postpurchase evaluation is conducted after the services have been provided. Customers compare their expectation with the actual experience and classify the experience as either satisfactory or unsatisfactory. When there is an *overpromising gap,* as discussed in Chapter 2, unreasonable expectations are created and disappointment and dissatisfaction are bound to happen. However, if what was promised was delivered, customers are more likely to be satisfied and to offer positive word of mouth.

The problem-solving process can be a learning experience for both new and veteran consumers. Yet a consumer solving the same problem again and again is not likely to spend much time on the process and may not even go through the entire process step by step. Therefore, the process can be characterized as a continuum with two extremes. **Complex decision making,** at one end, means the consumer goes through every stage of the process at least once and makes a highly involved decision. At the

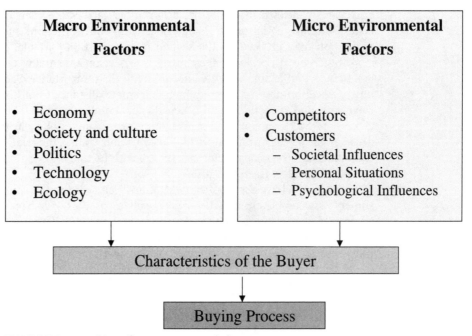

FIGURE 3.5   Variables affecting consumer behavior.

other end, a solution is selected on the basis of prior satisfactory experience without much thinking, which is called **habitual decision making.** Figure 3.5 graphically summarizes all the variables involved in consumer marketing discussed earlier.

Summary

Components of the macro and micro environments affect the way consumers behave and the way marketers conduct business. Macro environmental factors include economy, society and culture, politics, technology, and ecology. A micro environment is composed mostly of competitors and customers. Marketers need to understand the characteristics of buyers and their problem-solving processes to effectively attract and retain their visits. Consumers' characteristics are formed on the basis of societal influences, personal situations, and psychological influences. Societal influences come from family, culture and subculture, socioeconomic status, and reference group. Psychological influences include perception, attitudes, and personality. A buyer's problem-solving process encompasses the problem awareness, information search, alternative evaluation, purchase decision, and post-purchase evaluation stages. Risks associated with a purchase decision include financial, social, and performance-related risks.

Key Words and Concepts

Macro environment
Squeeze effect
Demographic trends
Baby boomers
Generation X-ers
Generation Y-ers
Ecology
Micro environment
Concentrated industry
Fragmented industry

Consumer behavior
Societal influences
Personal situations
Psychological influences
Culture
Subcultures
Socioeconomic status
Reference group
Life cycle stages
AIO

Psychographics
Perception
Attitude
Personality
Buying process
Perceived risk
Cognitive dissonance
Postpurchase evaluation
Complex decision making
Habitual decision making

Resources on the Internet

American Demographics.
   http://www.demographics.com/publications
Hyatt Hotels. *http://www.hyatt.com/*
Long John Silver's.
   http://www.ljsilvers.com/aboutfaq.htm

Nation's Restaurant News.
   http://www.nrn.com/resources/
Women on Their Way by Wyndham.
   http://www.womenbusinesstravelers.com/

Discussion Questions

1. What are the environments of hospitality discussed in this chapter? How do environmental elements affect marketing?
2. What are the characteristics of buyers, as identified in this chapter? What is the significance of each?
3. What are the different types of reference groups?
4. How can a buyer's perception influence his or her purchase behavior? How is a perception formed?
5. How can a person's personality affect his or her buying behavior?
6. What are the stages in the buying process?
7. What kinds of risks are associated with purchase decisions?

References

Ajzen, I. (1991). The theory of planned behavior. *Organizational Behavior and Human Decision Processes, 50*(2), 179–211.

American Demographics. (1995). The future of spending. *American Demographics, 14*(January), 13–19.

Cunningham, M. W., and C. S. Dev. (1992). Strategic marketing: A lodging "end run." *The Cornell Hotel Restaurant Administration Quarterly, 33*(4), 36–43.

Khan, S. (1999). Aiming to please women. *USA Today,* (June 10), B1–B2.

Long John Silver's. (2001). *FAQ* (on-line). Web site: http://www.ljsilvers.com/aboutfaq.htm

Marshall, A. (1997). Seniors have big travel budgets but need accommodation. *Hotel and Motel Management, 212*(6), 17.

Mehta, A. (1999). Using self-concept to assess advertising effectiveness. *Journal of Advertising Research, 39*(1), 81–89.

Miller, J. (1996). Golden opportunity. *Hotel and Motel Management, 211*(April 1), 45–46.

National Restaurant Association. (1998). *Tableservice restaurant trends–1998.* Washington, DC: Author.

Neuborne, E. (1999). Generation Y. *Business Week, 3616* (February 15), 81–84, 86, 88.

Pearce, J. A., II, and R. B. Robinson Jr. (1997). *Strategic management: Formulation, implementation, and control.* Boston: Irwin/McGraw-Hill.

Powers, T. F. (1992). The advent of the megachain: A case of the emperor's new clothes. *Hospitality Research Journal, 16*(1), 1–12.

Prewitt, M. (1999). *More top dinner houses nurture secondary brands to augment growth momentum* (on-line). Web site: http://www.nrn.com/resources/T100_dinner.html

Putnam, J. J., and J. E. Allshouse. (1999). *Food consumption, prices, and expenditures, 1970–97* (SB-965). Washington, DC: U.S. Department of Agriculture, Economic Research Service.

Ritchie, K. (1995a). *Marketing to Generation X.* New York: Lexington Books.

Ritchie, K. (1995b). Marketing to Generation X. *American Demographics* (on-line Serial) Web site: http://www.demographics.com/publications/ad/95_ad/9504_ad/9504af02.htm

4

Market Segmentation and Target Marketing

When you have finished reading this chapter, you should be able to:

- Define segmentation and target marketing.
- Explain the advantages of segmentation.
- Discuss the criteria for successful market segmentation.
- Describe the major types of hospitality market segments.
- Explain the importance of psychographic and geo-demographic segmentation.
- Discuss buying centers and their various roles.
- Identify the hospitality industry's principal organizational segments.

Segmenting and Targeting Markets

After World War II the market for hospitality services enjoyed a major growth period. Quick-service restaurants (QSRs) challenged the old "mom and pop" restaurants; motels challenged hotels. As more organizations entered this growing market, operators needed to gain an advantage over competitors. Gradually, a new consumer-based way of thinking about hospitality has become the rule. The question then arises, "Who are our customers?" Operations cannot be all things to all people. Which group, or groups, of customers can we serve best? The answer to this dilemma is **market segmentation,** a process of dividing the market into different groups of consumers who have common needs and wants. A **market segment** is a group of individuals with enough characteristics in common that they will react in a similar way to a marketing appeal.

There are four basic criteria for market segmentation. A good segment should be identifiable, measurable, of adequate size, and accessible. Holiday Inn's targeting of hearing-impaired persons offers a helpful illustration of these points.

1. *Identifiable.* Hearing-impaired persons include those who are totally and partially deaf and those who have limited hearing ability.
2. *Measurable.* Numerical measures should be available to indicate the size of the market segment. In this case, Holiday Inn learned that the number of people who were totally deaf was 2 million, with an additional 9 million with significant hearing impairment and an estimated 10 million more with some hearing impairment.
3. *Adequate size.* A market of as many as 21 million potential travelers was clearly significant. In fact, during the first year that services for hearing-impaired persons were offered, the company gained 40,000 to 50,000 room-nights from this segment.
4. *Accessible.* It must be both possible and economically feasible to reach the segment. There are numerous publications directed at hearing-impaired persons. On the other hand, people feeling like a weekend splurge sounds like a good market segment. But how would you find them? It may not be economically feasible to communicate with them.

Target Marketing

Among clearly defined segments, marketers must choose one or more segments that they can best serve, based on what each segment demands and what the operations can provide. Once the proper market segments have been identified, target marketing is the logical next step. The segments chosen become **target markets,** and the entire marketing program is designed for these targets.

In this chapter, most of the discussion focuses on segmentation. However, segmentation is undertaken for the purpose of **target marketing**—that is, shaping the marketing program and marketing mix to meet the needs of a specific segment or segments. From time to time, the discussion turns from segmentation to target marketing to make the connection clear.

Why Segment?

The rationale behind segmentation, mentioned earlier, is a good basic starting point. Segmentation gives us a way to understand a marketplace that is diverse and changing. We can, however, be more specific about the advantages of market segmentation:

1. Fundamentally, segmentation ties the operation and all its marketing activities to *consumers*—not to all consumers, of course, but to some recognizable group or groups of consumers who can be expected to respond in a similar way to a marketing appeal.
2. A segmented marketing strategy is aimed at specific consumer groups. As a result, operators and marketers have a clear *reference group* to use as a benchmark for making decisions.
3. Segmentation allows the selection of consumer groups that offer the best *profit potential* at various times. For example, a deluxe resort in a warm climate may target wealthy people and expense-account travelers during the busy season, and rate-sensitive travelers in the off-season.
4. The process of analyzing markets by segment may reveal an *unserved or underserved segment.* For example, people being relocated or those attending an extended training program have special needs that are not met by traditional hotels. They are less interested in on-premise foodservices, prefer more spacious rooms with adequate work space, and require more opportunities for after-work socializing. Extended-stay properties were developed to meet the needs of this segment.

Market segmentation not only helps us understand what people want in a product, it also gives a good idea of the price they are willing to pay and where they want to be served. In addition, segmentation offers an opportunity to make more effective use of promotional media by identifying those that can reach the target markets effectively.

Types of Segments

Market segments can be identified by their geographic, demographic, psychographic, benefit, and purchase behavior characteristics. We should note that there is no single best segmentation approach. Actually, most marketers use a combination of segmentation techniques. For example, a company may combine geographic characteristics with a consideration of demographics and lifestyle to derive a viable target market.

Geographic Segmentation

A key element in the marketing mix is place. Geographic considerations—where the operation is and where the customers are—are obviously important. However, marketers sometimes overlook them. There are a number of ways to look at **geographic segmentation,** and each of them has special applications in hospitality marketing.

Political. One approach to geographic segmentation follows political subdivisions: state, county, and city. For example, state-level associations and organizations have annual or even more frequent meetings that produce significant convention and room-night business. A restaurant may define the target market as the city of Ames, Iowa, and the communities within 20 miles of Ames. A hotel may periodically analyze car license plates in their own or competitors' parking lots to identify the **trade area**—a geographical area containing the customers of a particular firm or group of firms for specific goods or services (Bennett 1995).

Census. The U.S. Bureau of the Census divides the country into nine regions, as shown in Figure 4.1 The census also reports statistics by state. A **primary metropolitan statistical area (PMSA)** refers to a city, such as New York, that is part of a larger population group. PMSAs have a population of at least 1 million. PMSAs are then combined in a **consolidated metropolitan statistical area (CMSA).** Minneapolis and St. Paul, for example, are each a PMSA and are combined into the CMSA of Minneapolis-St. Paul. The next smaller unit is a **metropolitan statistical area (MSA).** MSAs are integrated economic units with a population of at least 50,000 and are not part of a larger population concentration. Cities such as Fargo, North Dakota, and Reno, Nevada, are MSAs.

Census figures are further broken down into tracts that cover areas ranging in population size from 2,500 to 8,000 people. An even smaller area, the block group,

① New England

② Middle Atlantic

③ South Atlantic

④ East North Central

⑤ East South Central

⑥ West North Central

⑦ West South Central

⑧ Mountain

⑨ Pacific

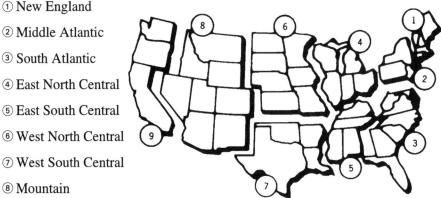

FIGURE 4.1   U.S. census regions.

contains an average of 350 families, the approximate size of a neighborhood. Block group data offer opportunities to target market specific neighborhoods and to assess precise data on a particular group at a manageable cost. The U.S. Bureau of the Census collects a great deal of detailed information on families and individuals in each area, and some market research firms offer even more specific information. Because the census is taken only once every 10 years, statistics become less useful as time passes and population increases or decreases within the census unit. However, the Bureau publishes *Population Estimates,* based on data collected from a sample of the population rather than a census. Commercial statistical sources also offer updates.

Postal Zones. Postal zones are identified by zip codes, which is another geographic segmentation variable readily available to marketers. The nine-digit zip codes can even identify people by city blocks and apartment buildings. Identifying customers by zip code is a quick and easy way to determine the neighborhoods providing the most customers for a restaurant and the cities generating the most guests for a hotel.

Media Coverage. Another geographic segment, used in planning television advertising, is the **area of dominant influence (ADI).** The ADI of a major metropolitan center includes any county that receives the city's television signals more than half the time. There are more than 200 ADIs in the United States that are measured and updated periodically. ADIs are used not only to plan television marketing, but sometimes also in developing a location strategy for restaurants during a chain's expansion. The intent is to locate new operations in the same or a few other ADIs so that media purchases can be concentrated in those particular ADIs. In addition, ADIs are commonly used by franchisors to set up local advertising cooperative units.

Demographic Segmentation

Whereas geographic segmentation looks at *where* the customers are, **demographic segmentation** looks at *who* the customers are. Some common demographic measures are age, gender, family size, family life cycle stage, income, education, and ethnic background.

Age. As noted in earlier chapters, one of the strongest driving forces in the North American economy has been the baby boom. The baby boom generation stimulated the growth of fast food in the 1950s and 1960s, when many families had several young children. As baby boomers became teenagers, they were themselves fast food customers. The movement of this generation into the more affluent middle age has been one reason for the growth of casual dining. As shown in Table 4.1, the average household foodservice spending increases as the age of the household head increases, up until the age of 54.

Even though many purchase behaviors are affected by how old the consumers are, *when* a person is born can also determine the individual's lifelong preferences. These lifelong impacts based on year of birth are referred to as the **cohort effects.** Cohort

TABLE 4.1　Weekly Expenditure for Food Away from Home by Age of Household Head	
Age	Amount Spent per Week
All units reporting	$36.94
Under 25	24.46
25–34	36.40
35–44	43.90
45–54	49.77
55–64	37.42
65–74	28.19
75 and over	16.60

Source: Data derived from *Consumer Expenditure Survey* (Washington, DC: Bureau of Labor Statistics, 1997).

effects relate to the particular perspectives of an age group (cohort) toward different products and services. Some cohorts commonly referred to are baby boomers and Generation X.

Gender. One of the ways in which women and men differ is in their eating preferences. Several years ago, Wendy's sought to increase the number of women customers by introducing one of the first QSR salad bars. Taco Bell, on the other hand, sought to increase its share of the male dining-out market by introducing the double beef burrito, a heartier menu choice designed to appeal to men's bigger appetites. In these two cases, women were a *target market* for Wendy's, and Taco Bell targeted men. Table 4.2 shows the differences between the sexes according to their food preferences (Lydecker 1994).

As for lodging preferences, women business travelers consider security, personal

TABLE 4.2　Differences Between the Sexes	
Men Are	Women Are
• More taste-driven in their food choices	• Highly concerned about nutrition
• More in sync with restaurant portions	• Likely to eat less
• Confirmed meat lovers	• Confirmed fruit lovers
• Comforted by familiar foods	• More adventurous in food choices
• More likely to crave entrées than desserts	• Snackers with a sweet tooth
• More frequent restaurant patrons	• Apt to eat out less often

Source: Lydecker, T. (August 1994). Men & Women: Two different markets sharing a table. *Restaurant USA*, pp. 26–30.

TABLE 4.3 Weekly Expenditures for Food Away from Home by Household Size

Size	Household Spending per Week	Per Capita Spending per Week
1 person	$23.56	$23.56
2 persons	40.37	20.19
3 persons	41.23	13.74
4 persons	45.42	11.36
5 or more persons	44.58	[a]

[a] A price figure for per capita spending is not available for this open-ended category, but it is less than $8.92.

Source: Data derived from *Consumer Expenditure Survey* (Washington, DC: Bureau of Labor Statistics, 1997).

services, and low prices to be relatively more important selection criteria. The availability of irons and ironing boards, room service, and bathrobes is also important. Men place greater emphasis on services and facilities than women do (McCleary, Weaver, and Li 1994).

Family Size. Table 4.3 shows the importance of singles *and* families to foodservice operations. Singles are the best individual customers, with the highest per capita spending per week. Even though per capita spending declines as the size of household increases, total household expenditure on foodservice continues to rise as the family size increases, up to four persons.

Income. There is a strong positive correlation between foodservice purchases and income. When incomes rise, people not only spend more in absolute dollars, but can also afford to spend a higher percentage of their food budget on food away from home (Table 4.4). Income segmentation, whether targeting the higher- or the lower-income groups, makes sense because the spending levels of various income groups suggest the patronage at different types of restaurants.

Ethnic Background. By the year 2005, about 28 percent of the U.S. population will be African American, Hispanic, or Asian, an increase from 22 percent as recently as 1990 (U.S. Bureau of the Census 2001). Asians and Hispanics are the fastest-growing population groups. Ethnic groups generally have distinctive tastes in food and, often, in ambience. They also respond differently to advertising appeals. Although 80 percent of Hispanic people are either fluent in or able to understand English, advertising in Spanish has a strong appeal. Different cultural values also make different types of appeals effective.

TABLE 4.4 Expenditures for Food Away from Home by Income Segment

Annual Household Income	Amount Spent per Week	Percentage of Weekly Food Budget
All Households reporting	$37.15	39.4%
Under $5,000	19.17	36.8
$5,000–9,999	14.38	28.8
10,000–14,999	16.37	28.3
15,000–19,999	21.71	30.0
20,000–29,999	27.08	34.3
30,000–39,999	35.12	37.4
40,000–49,999	42.46	40.7
50,000–69,000	51.23	42.8
70,000+	76.23	47.9

Source: Data derived from *Consumer Expenditure Survey* (Washington, DC: Bureau of Labor Statistics, 1997).

Demographic Segmentation: Effectiveness. Demographic data are readily available and are one of the least expensive forms of information. They are also often related to the way customers choose hospitality services. Case Study 4.1 illustrates several hospitality operations' efforts to target specific markets based on demographic characteristics. The use of several demographic variables together to define a market segment can further enhance their effectiveness. Obviously, not all 30-year-olds behave the same way. Some are rich; some are poor. Families headed by 50-year-olds vary in their behavior not only according to income, but also according to family structure. Families with children at home or in college usually have less disposable income than families without dependent children. Therefore, the statistics of any single demographic capture only one dimension.

CASE STUDY 4.1

Targeting Specific Markets Based on Demographic Characteristics

Because of increased competition, many hotels target specific markets based on their unique needs for physical products as well as for intangible services. Choice Hotels International has designed rooms in Econo Lodge and Rodeway Inn hotels with the special needs of mature travelers in mind. These "Senior Friendly Rooms" feature brighter lighting, levered door handles and faucets, in-room coffee makers, large-button telephones and TV remote controls, and large-digit alarm clocks. Sleep Inns, also franchised by Choice Hotels, offer an oversized walk-in shower and brighter lighting. Mike Cothran, Rodeway Inn brand management vice president, noted, "We know that Rodeway Inn hotels have special appeal for value-seeking guests, particularly senior citizens. That is why we have targeted our marketing to highlight that 25 percent of our rooms are designated Choice Room for seniors, with special amenities."

Also to target the growing number of senior citizens, the Olive Garden Italian restaurants offer the Menu on Cassette, which allows blind and visually impaired guests to hear what is on the menu. "People are losing their sight at an older age and are not learning to read advanced braille," noted Carol Adams, director at the Center for Independence Technology and Education in Orlando, Florida, who assisted with the development of the menu program. Most visually impaired people who become so at a later age have learned to cope through the assistance of family and friends, and from memory. The Menu on Cassette, used in all of the company's restaurants, provides an overview of the menu and price ranges. The Olive Garden does offer braille menus; however, they are more helpful to people who have learned braille, mainly those who were born blind or who lost their sight at an early age. In addition to the cassette tapes, The Olive Garden also introduced large-print menus.

Knights Inn targets professional truck drivers through a variety of activities, such as attending the Mid-America Trucking Show, maintaining a Trucker On-Line Resource Center, and offering the King of the Road Club. The Trucker On-Line Resource Center (http://www.knightsinn.com/ctg/cgi-bin/KnightsInn/trucker_resources/) provides links to truck stops, trucking companies, unions, weather and road conditions, mapping sites, insurance companies, Departments of Transportation, and many other useful sites. Knights Inn is committed to providing clean, comfortable rooms at great value prices. Knights Inn understands that one of the trucker's biggest expenses, after insurance, fuel, and truck payments, is lodging. The King of the Road Club offers free local calls, prepaid calling cards, a free coffee thermos fill up upon departure, and full tractor-trailer parking at most locations.

Knowing the significant size of Generation Y and that baby-boomer parents would appreciate some peace and quiet time alone during a family vacation, Hyatt Resorts developed Camp Hyatt. At Camp Hyatt, kids can enjoy many supervised activities that are special to each resort's location. They can learn all about plant life, animals, local culture, history, and geography, as well as snorkel, water slide, and explore the desert or rain forests. Camp Hyatt is available at most Hyatt Resorts in the continental United States, Hawaii, the Caribbean, and at participating destinations worldwide.

Sources: Choice Hotels International. (2001). *Home page* (on-line). Web site: http://www.hotelchoice.com; Olive Garden. (2001). *Our menu* (on-line). Web site: http://www.olivegarden.com/menu.html; Hyatt Corporation. (2001). *Hyatt's camp* (on-line). Web site: http://www.hyatt.com/hyatt_resorts/camp/index.html; Knights Franchise Systems, Inc. (2001). *Trucker resources* (on-line). Web site: http://www.knights inn.com/ctg/cgi-bin/KnightsInn/trucker_resources/AAAAQdACQAAA1NdAAM

Moreover, demographic characteristics do not take consumers' attitudes and values into consideration. A wealthy individual may be *able* to stay at an expensive hotel, but may choose to visit a more economical property on a family vacation. Middle-aged customers may choose to visit restaurants with a younger image because they *feel* young, or want to feel young. Nor do demographics alone provide enough information for marketers to select the appropriate advertising context or buying appeal.

Demographics are an important starting point for segmentation, but adding the life-style dimension gives greater depth to the picture.

Psychographic Segmentation

A resort may know the average age, family status, and number of children of its guests, but this does not necessarily indicate what their preferences are and, therefore, how the resort should program its activities. For example, are its customers adventurous or do they prefer a resort where they and their children can spend some quiet time together? Psychographics provide clues that are qualitative in nature. **Psychographic,** or lifestyle, **segmentation** relates to consumers' interests, attitudes, beliefs, values, and personalities. Psychographics is sometimes referred to as **AIO,** which stands for activities, interests, and opinions.

Activities include work-related and social activities, entertainment, sports, and vacation preferences. A consumer's *interests* may be centered on family or job, work or recreation, food or fashion, or any combination of these. *Opinions* can be measurements of products or of political, economic, or social issues of the day (Plummer 1974). Segments defined by AIO research provide insights into factors such as the consumer group's time or price consciousness, their venturesomeness or self-confidence. Do they like risk? Buy impulsively? Have an optimistic or a pessimistic view of life? Figure 4.2 gives examples of the AIO elements and contrasts AIO with demographics.

A syndicated lifestyle segmentation technique that has attracted attention in food-service is the *Values and Lifestyle (VALS)* system developed by SRI International. VALS 2, an updated version, uses two dimensions—self-orientation and resources—to identify eight segments of adult consumers who have different attitudes and exhibit distinctive behavior and decision-making patterns (SRI International 1997). Figure 4.3 illustrates the eight segments arranged by self-orientation and resources.

"Self-orientation" refers to the consumer's approach to buying. Individuals who are *principle-oriented* are more likely to purchase on the basis of beliefs, as opposed to feelings, desire for approval, or opinions of others. *Status-oriented* consumers look for

Activities	Interests	Opinions	Demographics
Work	Family	Themselves	Age
Hobbies	Home	Social issues	Education
Social events	Job	Politics	Income
Vacation	Community	Business	Occupation
Entertainment	Recreation	Economics	Family size
Clubs	Fashion	Education	Dwelling
Community	Food	Products	Geography
Shopping	Media	Future	City size
Sports	Achievements	Culture	Stage in cycle

FIGURE 4.2 AIO elements and demographic factors used in segmentation.
Source: Adapted from Joseph T. Plummer, "The Concept and Applications of Life-Style Segmentation," *Journal of Marketing* (January 1974): 34.

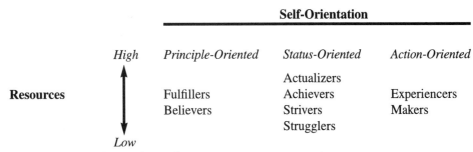

FIGURE 4.3   VALS 2 psychographics segments.
Source: Adapted from SRI International, 1997. *Values and Lifestyles: Psychographic Segmentation* [on-line]. Available: http://future.sri.com/VALS/VALS.seg.shtml

products and services that demonstrate these individuals' success to their peers. *Action-oriented* consumers are guided by a desire for social or physical activity, variety, and risk taking. "Resources" refers to the full range of psychological, physical, and material means, such as education, income, self-confidence, health, eagerness to buy things, intelligence, and energy level. If you are interested in taking the VALS survey and finding out what type of consumer you are, visit the SRI Web site at http://future.sri.com/vals/vals2desc.html.

Foodservice companies have used VALS in developing new restaurant concepts and menu offerings, as well as in site selection, design, and the development and execution of promotional campaigns. Psychographic segmentation is intended to give a personal dimension to the development of market segments and is often used in combination with demographic characteristics. Segments constructed in this way provide a more detailed description of consumers.

Benefit Segmentation

If the benefits provided by an operation are to capture consumers' real needs and wants, then **benefit segmentation** can be really powerful because it matches the product offerings to the consumers' preferences. In restaurants, some people seek convenience and speed, others focus on nutrition or flavor, and still others may look for atmosphere or variety. When selecting a vacation resort, some may ask for a peaceful and quiet place to relax, whereas others may see adventure and exciting activities as a way to reenergize. Once the reasons or the important attributes used in the selection of a restaurant or hotel are identified, operators can design products and services offering those benefits and communicate with the specific market segments, highlighting the benefits provided.

Behavior Segmentation

Behavior segmentation deals with the actions, or behaviors, of individual consumers. Three common factors used in segmenting by behavior are **user status, user frequency,** and **usage occasion.**

User Status. Consumers are divided into nonusers, first-time users, and repeat users. Marketers can separate first-time users from nonusers by campaigns encouraging a trial purchase. An increasingly common approach is to single out repeat users, or current customers, as a priority segment, because the cost to retain existing customers is much lower than to obtain new ones. Marketers can further segment current users into smaller groups based on user frequency.

User Frequency. Current users are divided into light, medium, and heavy users. Pizza delivery operations, for example, often target principally the heavy users, who account for as much as 80 percent of their business. Hotels and restaurants, like airlines, have come to recognize and target heavy users by offering them rewards and discounts for repeat patronage with their frequent traveler or diner programs. Casinos are known to aggressively encourage frequent repeat visits with "comps."

Usage Occasion. *When, how,* and *why* consumers use an operation are both distinctive and important factors. In restaurants, the meal occasion offers important insights into consumers' needs and preferences. Typical meal occasions are breakfast, lunch, and dinner. Snack occasions are midmorning, midafternoon, and late evening. McDonald's has used occasion expansion as a major business builder, first with breakfast as a meal occasion and later with chicken nuggets as a snack occasion. McDonald's success suggests the power of this form of segmentation.

Another time-based usage occasion segmentation is seen in seasonal variations in resorts and weekday–weekend differences in hotels. Weekend customers are more likely to be pleasure travelers, whereas weekday guests are most often business people. As for resorts and other vacation destinations, off-season guests are often price sensitive and seek bargain rates. In-season guests tend to be very demanding in service quality because they are paying top rates.

Segmentation according to *how* users use a restaurant, such as drive-in or takeout, is another example of usage segmentation. These two segments have different requirements in regard to packaging, service, and, sometimes, price. These distinctions are useful bases for planning an operation, as well as for marketing activities.

The "why" of a purchase also offers a means of segmentation related to the customers' buying purposes. Hotel guests are commonly divided into business, convention, and pleasure travelers. Each group has somewhat different facility requirements, rate sensitivities, and interests. Restaurant customers can be divided into similar segments, such as family dining, business meals, and romantic occasions. Customers dining for particular occasions often prefer a different atmosphere, price range, and menu offerings.

Combining Segmentation Approaches

Each of the segmentation approaches has its advantages and limitations. It is more effective, under most circumstances, to use a combination of segmentation approaches. For example, in addition to using demographics as a way to segment the market, psychographics and benefits sought can be used to further define the market

The service needs of the delivery market set it apart as a specific operational segment. (Photo courtesy of Domino's Pizza, Inc.)

segments. A segmentation matrix can be used to identify all possible markets with a combination of segmentation approaches. Geo-demographic segmentation is a specific example of combining the geographic, demographic, and psychographic characteristics of consumers.

Segmentation Matrix. The segmentation of markets can be fine-tuned by identifying segments within segments. The result is a **segmentation matrix** that allows us to focus on particular markets in planning the product, pricing, and promotion. The first step in building the matrix is to identify the market segments based on two segmentation approaches. For example, we may identify four segments based on family status and three segments based on psychographics. Then we display all the segment combinations on a four-by-three matrix. For example, Figure 4.4 shows the 36 possible market segments of a restaurant based on the "when" and "how" usage occasion segmentation techniques. Because consumer needs are often different on weekdays and weekends, they are considered as different market segments.

Primary resources should be allocated to those segments that can generate the most return. Therefore, segments with the greatest potential should be identified and listed in order of importance. Both the size of the opportunity and the operation's ability to competitively serve the market segment should be considered when ranking the segments.

This Ritz-Carlton ad uses demographic (age, income, and family life cycle), psychographic (interest in having a perfect wedding), and usage occasion as segmentation criteria. (Photo courtesy of The Ritz-Carlton Hotel Company, L.L.C.)

	Snack/meal Occasion	Breakfast	Midmorning	Lunch	Midafternoon	Dinner	Late evening		
Dine-in		1[a]	11	5	11	9	11	Weekday	Time of week
Carry-out		2	12	6	12		12	Weekday	Time of week
Delivery								Weekday	Time of week
Dine-in		3		7		10		Weekend	Time of week
Carry-out		4		8				Weekend	Time of week
Delivery								Weekend	Time of week

(Leftmost vertical label: Where food is consumed)

FIGURE 4.4   Segmentation matrix based on usage occasion.

[a] Rank order of importance

Geo-demographic Segmentation. Neighborhoods are usually made up of people with similar demographic and lifestyle characteristics. Using the block-group-level census data, neighborhoods, of approximately 350 households, are studied in detail. The boundaries of block groups are defined by actual city streets, so they are similar to real neighborhoods. Geo-demographic information is especially powerful because it provides objective, measurable demographic information in combination with a lifestyle picture of the people involved.

The process of building a **geo-demographic segmentation** system begins with an analysis of census data to identify key factors in order to cluster the population. The analysis includes demographic data, such as age, income, education, occupation, and home ownership, as well as consumer attitudes, product preferences, and media use (Francese 1994). Information from commercially available databases are combined with the census data to achieve the final segmentation system.

There are four neighborhood-based cluster systems commercially available. *ACORN* features 43 highly targeted neighborhood clusters, ranging from the "Top One Percent" to "Distressed Neighborhoods." Based on analyses of the country's 226,000 neighborhoods by 61 lifestyle characteristics, such as demographics and key determinants of consumer behavior, ACORN offers information on TV viewership, newspaper readership, type and frequency of restaurant patronage, and hobbies, among other factors (CACI Marketing Systems 2001). *ClusterPLUS 2000* incorporates demographic data with product usage, lifestyle interests, and media habits to define 60 neighborhood cluster designations. Each cluster can be further divided into 8 subclusters.

MicroVision 50 is a micro-geographic consumer targeting system that uses aggregated consumer demand data as well as census data to accurately classify every household in the United States within one of 50 unique market segments. These segments are defined with the use of more than 200 variables. Each segment consists of households that have similar life cycles and share common interests, purchasing patterns, financial behaviors, and products/services demands (New America Information Services Group 1998). For example, zip code 66503 (Manhattan, Kansas) comprises 56 percent "Movers and Shakers," 19 percent "Established Wealth," and 10 percent "Country Home Families" (National Decision Systems 2001). The MicroVision profile then gives businesses a look at consumers in each specific segment.

PRIZM, one of the oldest lifestyle cluster systems, defines every neighborhood in the United States in terms of demographically and behaviorally distinct clusters. PRIZM contains 62 segments in 15 social groups, ranging from the affluent executives of "Blue Blood Estates" to the remote rural families of "Blue Highways" (Claritas 2001). The 15 groups reflect their members' degree of urbanization—from rural to urban—and income. In addition to census data, PRIZM uses a network of more than 1,600 local sources of periodically updated demographic data. To measure the degree of urbanization, PRIZM divides the United States into 900,000 geographic cells. Figure 4.5 shows how the PRIZM clusters are put together—through data analysis, individuals with similar demographic, geographic, and behavioral characteristics are grouped into the same cluster.

Geo-demographic, or neighborhood, segmentation has two major uses that are particularly important to restaurants. Restaurant chains often rely on the population within a small radius for the bulk of their business. Therefore, geo-demographic information can help in location analysis and selection. It is also useful for direct mail. The block groups with lifestyles that fit those of the restaurant's target market can be

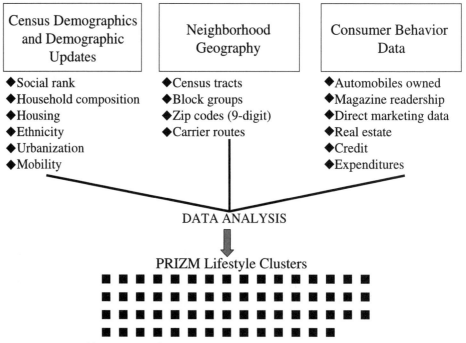

FIGURE 4.5 Building PRIZM Clusters.
Source: PRIZM Lifestyle Segmentation (New York: Claritas).

selected for mailing. In addition, geo-demographic segmentation is used as a basis for planning other forms of advertising. For example, newspaper advertising supplements can be inserted into zip-code-zoned editions of newspapers.

Segmenting Organizational Markets

There are many organizational customers in the hospitality industry. Hotels commonly sell to organizations, in addition to individual guests. Contract foodservice companies sell their services exclusively to client institutions, but also need to satisfy the individual guests. Chapter 13 looks at personal selling, which, in hospitality, is almost exclusively directed at organizational customers. In this chapter the focus is on understanding organizational customers and their behaviors.

Organizational Buying Behavior

Organizational customers are conventionally seen as "rational" purchasers who emphasize logical considerations, such as price and functionality. The typical view of these customers as being "task-oriented" is not wrong, but it is not entirely correct, either. People who make purchasing decisions for companies and institutions are humans and therefore can react emotionally, based on self-interest and ego. They must also deal with uncertainty and risk.

An organization's buying is usually the responsibility of more than one person. The group of people involved in the decision is referred to as the **buying center.** For example, when a university chooses a contract foodservice company, the buying center will likely involve the dean of student affairs, the vice president of finance, and perhaps the president, depending on the scope of the project. Other members of this buying center may include one or more representatives of the student body, faculty, and staff. In such a complex decision process, it is important to be aware of the many roles that buying center members may play: users, influencers, buyers, deciders, and gatekeepers (Webster and Wind 1972).

Users, in this instance, may include the students, faculty, and staff who are foodservice customers. The dean of students, along with students, faculty, and staff, are certainly the *influencers,* who help define needs and set selection criteria. The *buyer,* the person with formal authority to close the deal, is probably the vice president of finance. *Deciders* are those who have either formal or informal power to make the decision. In this case, the decider is the president by him- or herself or in concert with one or more other senior officials. *Gatekeepers,* the people who gather information for the decision process and control the information flow, can include the purchasing manager and the president's assistant. Table 4.5 offers another example illustrating the various roles in a buying center.

Organizational buying decisions are more complex than individual decisions. They are made by a group, which may or may not be formally appointed and whose mem-

Organizational buying decisions are made by a group of people known as the "buying center." (Photo © Michael Abramson—Woodfin Camp and Associates.)

bership may change as the buying process unfolds. The various members of the buying center may play one or more roles in the process. An analysis of how the buying center functions, who plays what role, can be crucial to the salesperson making the typical "big-ticket" sale that characterizes organizational purchases. It is important to note that all variables influencing individual purchase decisions also affect each of the buying center's members. Therefore, the better the sales representatives are acquainted with members of the buying center, the better the chance of success in influencing the final decision.

The logic of segmentation applies to organizational markets as well. Two areas of hospitality marketing, in which the target includes organizational customers and their buying centers, are discussed in the following sections.

Lodging's Organizational Customer Segments

Individual Business Travelers. A major part of the marketing effort to reach individual business travelers involves marketing to the organizational affiliates of those travelers. Local business traveler generators include companies that are headquartered

TABLE 4.5 Who Participates in the Organizational Buying Decision?	
Buying Decision Role	Participant
Gatekeeper	The manager's secretary raises the question of planning for the Christmas party at a staff meeting in late October. During the period the decision is under consideration, he will maintain and circulate files of proposals and related information.
Influencers	A committee is formed to choose a location and menu. Any person of high informal or formal status not on this committee is likely to be consulted by committee member(s).
Decider	The manager—based on budget, the committee's recommendations, and her own judgment—makes the final decision.
Buyer	As the company (buyer) will pick up the check, the manager must submit final plans for approval to the home office.
Users	Everybody has a good time!

in the local area or companies that have a significant number of people visiting them. Professional organizations, such as consulting firms, and businesses with people whose work takes them on the road are also significant sources of business.

An important question here is who the *buyer* is, as opposed to who the consumer is. If the secretaries are the ones making the reservations, they become a significant target of the marketing effort, even though they may never stay in the hotel themselves. The same is true of travel managers or meeting planners for a business or professional organization in a distant city. Individual business travelers are a vital segment for most hotels, but they are often booked through their organizational affiliations.

Business travelers can be further segmented in a number of ways, such as by travel budget size or frequency of visits. Hotels may segment organizations by size and number of room-nights generated, targeting those that provide a large volume of business by offering special rates and services. Case Study 4.2 shows how one hotel designs its products and services to meet the needs of business travelers.

CASE STUDY 4.2

The Club Hotel by DoubleTree

After interviewing business travelers from across the United States, DoubleTree Hotels found that these customers want a place that helps them with the ultimate purpose of their trips: getting their jobs done. From much analysis and the input of several leading companies that serve business people, OfficeMax, Au Bon Pain Bakery Café, and Steelcase furnishings, Club Hotel by DoubleTree created the Club Room—equal parts den, office, and café.

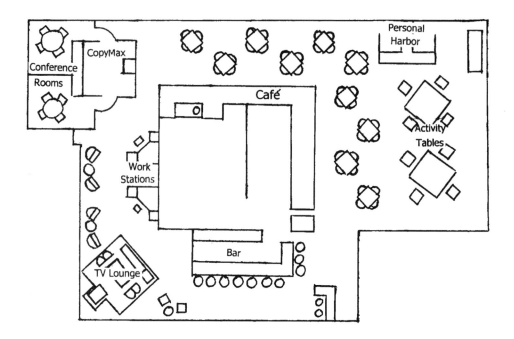

The Club Room has many features that address the needs of today's business travelers. The first is a private mini-office, called a Personal Harbor, for workers who need to get serious work done while on the road. The second is a table, called an Activity Table, that is wired for electrical equipment and a data port for those who want to be connected to the office or the Internet while having a drink and watching TV. The third is a mini-meeting room that seats up to six people for spontaneous conferences of small groups. All of these facilities, designed by Steelcase, are free of charge. The fourth is an Au Bon Pain Bakery Café—a food and beverage offering based on the concept of "not fast food, but good food fast." Moreover, a 24-hour self-service CopyMax business center provides a laser printer, fax, and copying machine, available through a credit card swipe.

Source: Club Hotels. (2001). *Club Hotel: The Club Room* (on-line). Web site: http://www.doubletreehotels.com/ClubHtls/club.html

Group Markets. Different group business segments have quite different needs and characteristics. Several such segments are identified in Table 4.6. Some possible ways for targeting those segments and their characteristics are also summarized in the table. **Corporate meetings** is a market made up of corporations that require accommodations to hold management meetings, sales meetings, training sessions, and seminars. This market can be further divided by size of meeting or dollar amount spent

Business travelers have distinctive needs and preferences. (Photo courtesy of Holiday Inn.)

TABLE 4.6 Targeting Lodging Organizational Market Segments	
Segment	Contact and Characteristics
Individual Business Travelers	Contacting local or distant referral source
	Special rates for high-use organizations
Group Markets	
Corporate meetings	
Large	Special facilities
Small	
Business and professional associations	
Large	Convention hotel facilities for large conventions and trade shows
Small	Small meeting rooms
Tours[a]	Special pricing to wholesalers
	Sales calls on tour packagers
Other Organizational Markets	
Airline crews	Contract price, quiet rooms
Government	Special rates
SMERF	Special rates

[a]Includes incentive houses.

per participant. Depending on size and budget, corporations have different needs and preferences in regard to their meeting facilities.

Business and professional associations hold meetings, conventions, and trade shows. This segment generates individual room-nights and meeting room business, but a distinctive characteristic is its requirement for convention and trade show space. Smaller organizations and state-level conventions may be served by typical full-service hotels. However, the large-convention market is a specialized segment that is served by convention hotels. Trade shows usually require specialized facilities developed specifically for their purposes by convention hotels and civic convention centers.

Another major organizational segment is **tour operators.** Travel wholesalers often purchase blocks of hotel rooms over a period of time, along with airline seats and other travel components, and then sell them as vacation packages to individual travelers. These rooms are usually purchased at a considerable discount and, for this reason, are often considered a low-profit-margin sale. However, because of the known quantity, relatively low marketing costs, and the fact that hotels do not have to worry about credit and collection, the cost of doing business is significantly reduced. Although there are individual end users involved, from a hotel sales perspective, travel wholesalers are organizational customers.

A more specialized type of travel wholesalers, **incentive houses,** arrange corporations' incentive travel packages, such as a week in San Juan, Las Vegas, or the Lake

Some hotels offer special convention rates during slow periods to increase demand.

of the Ozarks. *Incentive travel* packages are awards received by corporate employees who achieve superior performance or win sales contests.

Other Organizational Markets. In cities with a major airport, airline crews offer a significant volume of business. Rooms are usually sold on contract at a fixed rate for an extended period of time. Because of their irregular work schedules, airline crews have special needs. For example, they may occupy the rooms for only a relatively short period of time; therefore, quick check-in and check-out procedures are expected. They may also need to sleep while everyone else is at work or at play. Quiet rooms away from traffic and with heavy drapery to block out daylight are desirable. The discount offered in the airline contract makes this an unattractive segment when occupancy rates are high, but the guaranteed volume makes it attractive when business is slow.

Government agencies generally reimburse their employees at a fixed rate per day, called a *per diem*, making this a very rate-conscious segment. *Government rates* are often well below most other special rates, which makes this segment similar to the airline crew segment in terms of price. Many government agencies centralize their travel arrangements. The buyer may be a travel manager, much like the purchasing person in an airline company or other corporations that contract for rooms. Government employees, in this case, are the end users, or guests.

SMERF stands for social, military, education, religious, and fraternal organizations. Because the SMERF markets are extremely price sensitive, many organizations in these segments are accommodated in off-seasons at favorable rates. Their business is generally not sought after during peak or shoulder seasons (periods between high and low demand times that still generate sufficient revenues to cover operating expenses and/or generate a profit) unless they are willing to pay higher rates.

Contract Foodservice's Organizational Customer Segments

Contract foodservice companies should be concerned with two groups of customers. As in any other foodservice operations, the guests or end users must be served satisfactorily and cost-effectively. This is the consumer market. The other group of customers, the buyers or clients, is the organizational market. These are the decision makers in selecting a contract foodservice operation. Both groups are important, yet with distinctively different functions, preferences, and motives.

Table 4.7 shows the major segments and the bases on which they can be further subdivided. In addition to the criteria listed, two other approaches can be used to divide the market. First, the entire contract foodservice market can be divided into users and nonusers. Institutions that have never been served by a contract company are usually least receptive to the use of contract companies. The sales approach here must often overcome the reluctance of the client's buying center to give up control of an important element of its institution. For institutions that have worked with a contract company, the sale is generally a competitive one—that is, it involves competing with other contract foodservice providers.

Business and industry accounts have needs ranging from executive dining rooms like this one to cafeterias and even fast food.

Good relations with a client institution's buying center require a smooth working relationship with student customer.

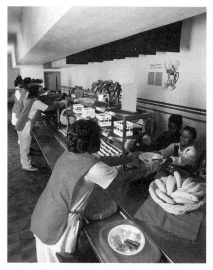

Most schools operate under tight federal guidelines.

Health care is characterized by a highly professionalized environment.

Organizational customers in institutional foodservice can be segmented by the particular needs of the client institution. (Photo courtesy of ARAMARK.)

Leisure services operate in specialized facilities, and very large crowds create a need for very high volume operations.

TABLE 4.7 Contract Foodservice Market Segmentation

Segment	Subsegmentation Base
Business and industry	Size of company Manufacturing vs. white collar
Colleges and universities	Size of institution Public or private Residential or commuter
Schools	Primary or secondary Public or private
Health care facilities	Acute care (hospitals) Extended care (nursing homes)
Other institutional segments	
Leisure services	Stadiums, arenas, parks
Correctional services	
Retailers	
Conference centers and hotels	
Senior living centers	

Another overall segmentation approach is based on the fee structure. Some contracts specify a flat fee, whereby the cost of the operation is assumed by the client institutions. Regardless of profit or loss, the contract companies are paid a fixed service fee. The clients, in this case, are typically very cost sensitive. Other types of contracts tie the service fee to the profit. The contract companies have full profit-and-loss responsibility. In this circumstance the clients are not as much concerned with costs, because the contractors have to control or absorb the excessive costs.

Business and Industry (B&I). B&I can be further segmented by size. The very large accounts, such as those with 3,000 to 5,000 employees, have different consumer characteristics than companies with 1,000 employees. Companies with fewer than 300 employees are usually served by vending operations. Another way to segment this market is to divide it between manufacturing plants and white-collar operations and other offices. Types of services desired and menu preferences often vary between manufacturing and office employees.

Colleges and Universities. This market can also be segmented by size. Generally, very large institutions operate their own foodservices and are therefore not likely to purchase contracts. Public and private institutions, as well as residential and commuter institutions, usually serve students of different backgrounds and needs. Therefore, as organizational customers, they all have different needs and preferences.

Schools. The public–private variable divides the school market. In a private school, the sale is usually made to a small buying center in the school, whereas in a public school the sale is usually to a large central administration at the school district level. Another way to divide the market is to distinguish between primary schools (kindergarten through eighth grade) and secondary schools (ninth through twelfth grades). The consumers in secondary schools are substantially different from those in primary schools, which gives the clients, or schools, a considerably different set of concerns.

Health Care Facilities. A primary distinction in this segment is between acute care facilities such as hospitals, and extended care facilities, such as nursing homes. In extended care facilities, the emphasis is on helping the residents enjoy life and providing foods that are good for both the body and the soul. In acute care settings, on the other hand, the pressure to move patients out of the hospitals as soon as possible translates into pressure on dietary departments to educate patients to any new diet requirements and help them to become accustomed to these requirements as quickly as possible.

Other Institutional Segments. Leisure services can be divided into sports and entertainment (stadiums and arenas), convention centers, and national and state parks. Correctional facilities are a fast-growing segment, and a number of specialized companies have sprung up to serve them. Another growth area for contract companies is retailing, with supermarkets seeking institutional foodservice companies to run their service-intensive foodservice operations. Contract companies also manage foodservice in training and conference centers and in some hotels.

Summary

In order to relate to millions of consumers, we need to segment markets into groups of individuals who have some common characteristics from a marketing perspective. Target marketing involves manipulating the elements of the marketing mix to appeal to a particular target market. The principal segment types, as discussed in this chapter, are geographic, demographic, psychographic, benefit, and behavior. Employing more than one segmentation approach at a time, such as a segmentation matrix combined with geo-demographic segmentation, is often useful.

Organization buyers usually account for the "big-ticket" sales. To be successful, marketers have to understand the buying center structure and be familiar with members of the center. Organizational marketing can also benefit from segmentation. Lodging's organizational markets include business travelers, corporate meetings, associations, tour groups, incentive travel, airline crews, government, and the catch-all group

SMERF. Contract foodservice companies are generally segmented into business and industry, colleges and universities, schools, health care facilities, and other institutional segments such as leisure services, correctional facilities, and retailing.

Key Words and Concepts

Market segmentation
Market segment
Target markets
Target marketing
Geographic segmentation
Trade area
Primary metropolitan statistical area (PMSA)
Consolidated metropolitan statistical area (CMSA)
Metropolitan statistical area (MSA)

Areas of dominant influence (ADI)
Demographic segmentation
Cohort effects
Psychographic segmentation
AIO
Benefit segmentation
Behavior segmentation
User status
User frequency
Usage occasion
Segmentation matrix

Geo-demographic segmentation
Organizational customers
Buying center
Corporate meetings
Business and professional associations
Tour operators
Incentive houses
SMERF
B&I

Resources on the Internet

CACI Marketing Systems.
   http://demographics.caci.com/Databases/ACORN.html
Choice Hotels International.
   http://www.hotelchoice.com
Claritas Inc. *http://www.claritas.com/*
Club Hotels. *http://www.clubhotels.com/*
Hyatt Hotels. *http://www.hyatt.com/*
Knights Inn. *http://www.knightsinn.com/*
National Association of Reunion Managers.
   http://www.reunions.com
National Decision Systems.
   http://laguna.natdecsys.com/lifequiz.html

New America Information Services Group.
   http://www.site-right.com/microvision.htm
Olive Garden Italian Restaurant.
   http://www.olivegarden.com/
Society for the Advancement of Travel for the Handicapped. *http://www.sath.org*
Society of Government Meeting Professionals.
   http://www.sgmp.org
SRI Consulting.
   http://future.sri.com/vals/vals2desc.html

Discussion Questions

1. What are the four basic criteria for segmentation?
2. Why is segmentation helpful to marketers?
3. What is target marketing? Provide an example, from your own community, of an operation that targets a particular market.
4. Based on what characteristics can a market be segmented? Provide an example of each segmentation approach, showing how characteristics can be used to shape a marketing program.
5. What does "psychographic" mean? Give two or three examples of psychographic segments.

6. How can customers' behaviors be used to segment a market?

7. What is geo-demographic segmentation?

8. How are consumer and organizational buying behaviors different?

9. What is a buying center? What are the major roles in a buying center?

10. What are the various organizational customer segments in the lodging industry? What are their specific needs?

11. What are the various organizational customer segments in the foodservice industry? What are their specific needs?

References

Bennett, P. D., ed. (1995). *Dictionary of marketing terms.* 2d ed. Chicago: American Marketing Association.

CACI Marketing Systems. (2001). *Databases: ACORN® lifestyles* (on-line). Website: http://demographics.caci.com/Databases/ACORN.html

Claritas. (2001). *Neighborhood segmentation—PRIZM* (on-line). Web site: http://www.claritas.com

Francese, P. (1994). What is cluster analysis for? *Marketing Tools* (April–May), 50.

Lydecker, T. (1994). Men & women: Two different markets sharing a table. *Restaurants USA, 14*(7), 26–30.

McCleary, K. W., P. Weaver, and L. Li. (1994). Gender-based differences in business travelers lodging preferences. *Cornell Hotel and Restaurant Administration Quarterly, 35*(1), 51–58.

National Decision Systems. (2001). *A zip code can make your company lots of money!* (on-line). Web site: http://laguna.natdecsys.com/lifequiz.html

New America Information Services Group. (1998). *MicroVision Profile Maps* (on-line). Web site: http://www.site-right.com/microvision.htm

Plummer, J. T. (1974). The concept and application of life style segmentation. *Journal of Marketing, 38*(1), 33–37.

SRI International. (1997). *The proven segmentation system* (on-line). Web site: http://future.sri.com/vals/vals2desc.html

U.S. Bureau of the Census. (2001). *National population estimates* (on-line). Web site: http://www.census.gov/population/www/estimates/uspop.html

Webster, F. E., Jr., and Y. Wind. (1972). *Organizational buying behavior.* Englewood Cliffs, NJ: Prentice-Hall.

Marketing Information and Research

When you have finished reading this chapter, you should be able to:

- Describe major sources of information used in making marketing decisions.
- Identify common hospitality research concerns.
- Provide examples of marketing research in action.
- Explain the marketing research process.
- Understand the research instrument design principles.
- Discuss the value of database marketing.

The previous two chapters considered some general approaches to analyzing consumers, including consumer behavior models and market segmentation approaches. This chapter analyzes consumers for the purpose of making specific marketing decisions.

As the level of competition in the hospitality industry continues to increase, total spending for marketing will continue to rise. These significant expenditures are not something that operators can afford to gamble with. As we move from the unit level to corporate headquarters, the expenditures rise to an astronomical level, with McDonald's alone spending $2 billion a year on marketing. To ensure that their marketing dollars have the maximum impact, marketers need solid, fact-based information to help them make the best marketing decisions.

Marketing Intelligence

Marketing intelligence includes not just market information, but the whole spectrum of external environment information needed to support key decisions about products, prices, and other management and marketing issues. Knowledge of the economy, labor market conditions, legislative and regulatory development, and pertinent events such as social changes and technological advancement is essential. All of this information is available from public sources, but keeping abreast of it, a process called **environmental scanning,** takes time and effort.

A variety of raw data flow into an organization. Some information comes from the routine operation of a hotel or restaurant. However, because of the importance of pertinent facts in making the best decisions, businesses also seek information from readily available public sources and customers and, sometimes, through the perfectly legal observation of a competitor's activities.

Internal Company Sources

Many of the routine operational reports generated in hotels and restaurants are useful sources of marketing information. For example, a hotel's property management system contains data on the percentage of double occupancy for each night of the week. After comparing this ratio to the industry or company average, the hotel manager may decide that low double occupancy is the reason that the property's average daily rate (ADR) is not as high as it should be. Efforts to promote more family or convention business may help increase double occupancy and, therefore, the ADR.

Reservation data are routinely used to make marketing, as well as operational, decisions. For example, data on the number of room requests that have been turned away may reveal an opportunity to construct a new property or an addition to the existing property. The Sheraton's decision to build a $750 million property in Las Vegas was based significantly on the Sheraton reservation system's record of 140,000 turned away room-nights each year (Macdonald 1994). Further analysis of reservation requests by room type should provide useful information on the types of rooms to build.

Point-of-sales (POS) systems have revolutionized the extent of information available in foodservice operations. Sales information can be provided in great detail, such as by item sold, restaurant unit, time of day, and region. Properly programmed and monitored POS systems can indicate the degree of success for special deals, evaluate the popularity of new products, and even track sales of individual servers. For example, at the end of a shift, the manager may determine how many bottles of wine were opened for a special offer, how many portions of a new menu item were ordered, and how many of each were sold by individual servers. The same types of information can be available by unit and region, or on a company-wide basis.

Mrs. Fields' Cookies has a comprehensive computer network that allows two-way communication between the various units and headquarters. Based on historical data, each unit manager receives a forecast for the day by product item. Headquarters also monitors the sales level of each store and updates its forecast by the hour. When sales are below expectations, the computer will suggest merchandising techniques, such as providing samples to storefront traffic, to pick up sales. A company's comptroller, the market research department at the corporate level, or the operation's manager or analyst at the unit level can periodically assemble information from various reports to identify trends or solve particular problems.

Modern point-of-sale cash register systems automatically provide reports that are—or can be—rich in marketing information. (Photo courtesy of Sodexho Marriott Services, Inc.)

Competitor Information

Management also needs information on the company's specific competitive environment. Competitor intelligence can be collected routinely by using a clipping service to monitor the local and trade press. Competitors' marketing activities should be observed and analyzed. Getting on competitors' mailing lists may be one way to collect information. Hotel sales staff commonly visit competitors to monitor their announcement boards to identify the group functions that are being held at these properties. Reports on this kind of information are of interest not only to a property's salespeople, but also to the national sales staff. Many companies require their executives to shop their foodservice competitors on a regular basis. Brief written reports of those visits, often including sample menus, can provide headquarters staff with an insight into competitive conditions in local markets.

An activity as simple as counting cars and examining license plates in a competitor's parking lot can yield valuable information, such as the trade area. Many hotels know the occupancy and ADR of the neighboring properties through the informal exchange of information, or gossip, among sales and front office staff. Actually, occupancy information is sometimes exchanged by hotels' front desks on an hourly basis to facilitate the placement of overflow customers.

Marketing Information Systems (MIS)

Marketing information systems should be organized in such a way to provide both marketing and operations personnel at all levels of the organization with the information they need to take appropriate competitive actions. Ideally, unit-level marketing information, such as competitive shopping reports, should be provided on a regular basis in summary form to higher levels in the organization. In addition, information gathered by headquarters that is relevant to regional and unit marketing and line managers should be summarized and distributed for their use.

The danger of an operations-dominated company in such a busy world is that there will be pockets of information that are not fully understood and utilized by various levels of management. Only those directly involved in data collection and analysis truly understand how to interpret and use the information. Another danger, with the help of sophisticated computers, is information overload. As marketing and operations managers are bombarded with data, they tend to get lost among all the items of information and numbers.

Marketing Research

Marketing research responds to specific needs for information with specially designed studies. Marketing research can use secondary data (information not gathered for the immediate study at hand but for some other purpose) and/or primary data (original data collected specifically for the purpose of the project at hand). If secondary data can answer the research questions under investigation, secondary research can often save the time and expense of conducting original research.

Secondary Research

"Secondary research is . . . finding the answers to questions other people have asked and applying them to your own problems" (Association of Independent Information Professionals 2001). There is a huge body of information readily available from government agencies, civic organizations, associations, and trade sources at little or no cost.

Government Agencies. The *Statistical Abstract of the United States,* published by the U.S. Bureau of the Census, is a compilation of statistical data on the economy, population, and social and political structure of the United States. It contains summary data and provides references to other more detailed sources of information. Data on banking activities are distributed in the *Federal Reserve Bulletin,* published by the U.S. Department of Commerce. These activities are sometimes used as an indicator of the level and direction of economic health in a community.

Current population reports, published by the U.S. Bureau of the Census, provide updated information on special topics on an annual basis. The Census Bureau also publishes periodic studies on a wide range of population-related subjects. The census of population is taken every 10 years. It provides information on population by geographic region, including a detailed breakdown of the demographics of each region. The census reports contain factors such as distribution of the population by gender, marital status, age, race and ethnicity, family size, and employment and income statistics. The census of housing, also conducted every 10 years, provides data on areas and types of buildings, as well as their size, condition, rentals, and average value. Other census reports, available every 5 years, survey retail and wholesale trade, service industries, manufacturers, mineral industries, transportation, agriculture, and state and local governments.

Data are also published by state agencies, providing information on tourism at the state level, which often is available from the state tourism promotion office. This office may also have information on travel patterns and spending behavior for a state's regions and large cities. Feeder areas, locations where most visitors come from, may also be identified.

Regional, county, and city planning agencies, as well as traffic engineering offices, are useful sources of information on traffic patterns. They can provide maps indicating traffic counts for major streets. These agencies are also good sources of information on planned changes in the roadway system, which is crucial in decisions on location selection.

Civic Bodies and Associations. The local Chamber of Commerce usually has a statistical profile and description of a community's economy, including information classified by types of activity (e.g., manufacturing vs. service). A list of large employers is usually available as well. The list describes each employer's location, nature of business, and number of employees. This information is helpful in developing an understanding of the economic life of a city and can assist in creating a prospect list. Most local Convention and Visitors Bureaus publish statistics on visitors to their communities and provide a forecast of future visitation and lists of conventions booked in the next few years.

Trade Sources. The trade press provides a great deal of information on competing companies and trade practices. *Restaurants & Institutions* publishes an annual study, *The Institutions 400,* which ranks the 400 largest hospitality firms and institutions and provides insightful information about growth and success in the foodservice industry. *Hotel* magazine each year publishes a similar study of worldwide hotel chains. The *Hotel and Travel Index* lists most hotels for major cities worldwide; the *American Hotel and Motel Red Book* also has a roster of hotel properties.

Accounting and consulting firms that have specialized practices in hospitality publish annual studies, providing information on city, regional, and national occupancies and operating statistics. Industry forecasts and analyses provided by Smith Travel Research sometimes serve as the basis for accounting companies' reports and publications. The National Restaurant Association's (NRA) research department publishes an annual profile of foodservice businesses in *Restaurants USA.* In addition, NRA issues restaurant operating results and a number of regional market research reports. State restaurant and lodging associations also publish reports or newsletters that cover local trends and issues. Conferences hosted by state or national trade associations are other sources of industry information.

Assessing Secondary Research. Secondary data have the advantage of being readily available. They are especially useful in the early stages of a market research effort when the problem is being defined and background information is being sought. However, secondary research almost never addresses the specific question that the researcher wants to answer. Because secondary data are collected for others' research purposes, the types or sources of data may not apply to the situation at hand. Furthermore, when using the results of secondary research, one must be aware of the potential bias of the researchers who conducted the study. For example, Chambers of Commerce or trade associations may explain the data to their own favor.

Another potential problem with secondary research is that there is so much information. Busy managers, especially those in small operations in which they have to take care of everything, may not have time to sort through all the materials. There are, however, professionals who will conduct information searches for a fee. Many of these professionals are members of the Association of Independent Information Professionals (Association of Independent Information Professionals 2001).

Syndicated Studies

There are numerous **syndicated studies** on market research that are commercially available. One of the most widely known is *Consumer Reports and Eating-Out Share Trends* (CREST). CREST provides reports on purchases of food prepared away from home, based on consumer diaries provided by a panel of 13,000 participating households. Summary information from CREST is published monthly in *Restaurants USA*. Many restaurant chains subscribe to CREST's special studies, which provide information on their market share and trends in their restaurant segment and geographic area. The geo-demographic lifestyle studies of neighborhoods, discussed in Chapter 4, are useful in conjunction with a restaurant trading area study to determine good geographic target markets for direct mail and other promotions.

Another major food industry consulting and research firm is Technomic, Inc., which publishes statistical updates on current industry trends and profiles on emerging concepts in *Technomic Foodservice Digest, ConcepTrac,* and *Future Food Trends* (Technomic Inc. 2001). For the hotel segment, Smith Travel Research provides data on current trends and includes periodic analyses of various market segments and observations on industry performance in *Lodging Outlook* (Smith Travel Research 2001).

Primary Research

Primary research is the most precise way of gathering information about a marketing problem. Primary research requires the development of specific research questions, a research design to answer those questions, and the collection and analysis of original data. The following sections discuss applications of primary research in the hospitality industry and examine the research process in detail.

Common Concerns in Hospitality Marketing Research

Some of the most common areas of concern in hospitality marketing research include customer identification, product research, customers' reactions to promotions, and tracking studies. Each of these is discussed briefly in the following sections.

Who Are Our Customers?

One way to identify a restaurant's **customer base** is by conducting a trading area study that deals with the question, "Who are the restaurant's customers?" in strictly geographic terms. Employees can be instructed to ask customers where they have just come from and where they live. An alternative to identifying the addresses of customers, who may not want to give them to a stranger, is to ask for the zip code. These data provide two kinds of valuable information. First, they help to provide a picture of the geographic draw of the restaurant. Second, they indicate the proportion of customers who come from work or home, by meal period. The "from home" and "from work" customers can be considered two different segments because of their differing preferences and needs.

When a sufficient number of responses have been received (e.g., 100 to 200), each geographic area can then be plotted on a street map with color coding to show the concentration of customer distribution. This not only tells operators who their customers are in terms of location, but also indicates any underreported markets that have potential to be significant sources of business. Those neglected areas should be targeted with marketing efforts to draw more customers.

Product Research: What Do Our Customers Want?

Under the general topic of **product research,** we can look at customer purchase behavior—what products and services they buy, whether they like the sample product provided, and what they think they would like in a proposed product. Customer purchase behavior or usage studies can provide a basis for market segmentation. This can be accomplished by surveying a sample of the population that includes the operation's customers to identify the heavy, medium, and light users and their demographic characteristics. A less precise approach to looking at consumer purchase behavior is to make an estimate based on the observation of an operation and its customers. In fact, we hear this kind of judgment being made frequently: "Most of my customers are . . ."

Hotels can study what customers would like to see in a hotel room before designing or renovating guest rooms. Customers are given a list of features a room may have and a price list that specifies a cost for each feature. The customers are then given play money and asked to "buy" the list of features they think represent the best value until they spend all their money. Based on the dollar amount attached to each feature, the relative importance of each from the customer's perspective can be identified. Important features can then be incorporated into room designs. A specific example of using market research in guest room design is presented in Case Study 5.1

CASE STUDY 5.1

"The Room That Works": Market Research in Hotel Room Design

Marriott International is a leader in the application of market research to lodging product design. The very successful Courtyard by Marriott guest room was designed on the basis of consumer research. Actually, the Courtyard by Marriott slogan is "The Hotel Designed by Business Travelers." Recently, Marriott formed an alliance with AT&T and Steelcase, a furniture manufacturer, to study the needs of contemporary business travelers. The study provides a good example of a market research process that begins very broadly and gradually becomes more specific until it reaches a conclusion.

The situation facing business travelers was summarized by Marriott's director of market research, Daniel Bretl:

There is an overwhelming need for people to get more done at all times. With globaliza-
tion and increased technology, people are traveling more than ever. With corporate
downsizing, they have to get more done.

This created a need for a room that would accommodate the special requirements of
busy business travelers.

The first step in the research process was a review of secondary research, including
existing research from Marriott and Steelcase as well as information from industry
sources. From the review of secondary information, Marriott added a number of questions regarding traveler needs to a tracking study it regularly conducted.

Using information collected to this point, a research agenda was identified, and a
series of focus groups was planned. Six focus groups were conducted in Atlanta, Chicago, and San Francisco. With the results from this qualitative research, three room
prototypes were developed and installed in Marriott hotels for the field test. Guests
who occupied the rooms were not informed of the experiment. The field test results
provided the basis for preparing two more room prototypes, which were constructed
and examined by business travelers. These travelers were asked to evaluate the two
room types in comparison with each other and with a standard Marriott room. The
room type most likely to generate incremental visits to Marriott hotels was identified.

"The Room That Works" incorporates features that the target market, business
travelers, sought. Specifically, the new room design includes the following:

- A large console table and a mobile writing desk (slightly lower than the desk and partially stored underneath it) so guests can move the table to the window and work from natural light if desired
- Two power outlets and a modem jack mounted in the console top
- A movable desk light
- A fully adjustable ergonomic chair
- A reach-anywhere phone

Continuing with its research focus, Marriott completed an extensive customer study at more than 40 hotels to determine the best high-speed in-room Internet solution. For its combination of user-friendly design, speed, and security, the STSN (Suite Technology Systems Network) has been selected to provide high-speed Internet access in Marriott hotel guest rooms, including Courtyard by Marriott rooms. Marriott will offer STSN at a minimum of 100 hotels by year end 1999 and at more than 500 properties by the end of 2000.

Sources: Personal interview (1996) with D. J. Bretl, previous Marriott Director of Market Research; Marriott International. (2001). *Marriott to offer high-speed Internet access in guest rooms, meeting rooms, and business centers* (on-line). Web site: http://www.marriott.com/news/0902STSN.asp; Marriott International. (2001). *Courtyard by Marriott* (on-line). Web site: http://www.courtyard.com/

A variety of product decisions are studied by market researchers. Taste panels sample actual products to determine whether they like or dislike a product and why. Sensory evaluations are conducted by many restaurant corporations before the introduction of new menu items. Taste panels are asked to rate the sample on characteristics such as color, taste, smell, texture, and appearance. Based on the panelists' evaluations, revisions in recipe or presentation are made to enhance quality and consumer appeal.

Copy Testing

To determine their likelihood of acceptance by consumers, advertising ideas are often tested early in the design stage before production expenses are incurred. This practice, called **copy testing,** is particularly common with television advertising because of the expensiveness of the production and media time. Other types of advertisement can also be evaluated by the methods described here.

Advertising can be evaluated through questionnaires administered in person (usually in shopping malls), by mail, or by telephone. However, experimental research, a basic approach to market research, is often used in copy testing. Two kinds of experiments are used: laboratory and field. A **laboratory experiment** is an investigation in which researchers create a situation with specific conditions so as to control some variables and manipulate others. A **field experiment** is a research study in a realistic situation in which one or more independent variables are manipulated by the re-

The "experts" in this respondent group were children who helped a hotel develop its children's menu. (Photo courtesy of Spencer Grant/Photo Researchers.)

searcher under as carefully controlled conditions as the situation allows (Bennett 1995).

In a laboratory experiment assessing a television commercial, an audience is recruited and shown programming selected by the researcher, including the commercial under investigation. All variables, including the viewing content, audience composition, and audience attention, are under the control of the researcher. All audience members provide feedback in the same way, as required by the researcher.

Copy testing using a field experiment may be conducted, for example, by showing a commercial to a selected number of homes on cable television or to all homes in a test city on cable or broadcast television. In a laboratory setting, the studio audience will certainly sit through the program. In the field setting, however, some viewers may not even turn the television on; others will use the commercial break to do other things or to "whiz" through the channels.

The laboratory setting provides tighter control, costs less, speeds data collection, and provides greater confidentiality of the research findings. However, because they know they are being observed, and wishing to please the researchers, people may react differently than they usually do. The field test offers less control of the situation, and for this reason, the results are more realistic. Moreover, because a larger sample group is exposed to the commercial in a field test, it may be possible to track actual purchase behavior and infer a cause-and-effect relationship.

In conducting copy testing, the following topics and questions can be addressed (Mortimer and Matthews 1998; Mehta 1999):

Persuasiveness	Will the audience buy or want to buy?
Communications	Does the audience hear the main point?
Recall	Does the message break through the clutter?
Self-involvement	Can the audience relate to the message?
Credibility	Does the audience believe it or not?
Clarity	Does the audience understand it or not?
Tastefulness	Does it offend the audience?
Stimulation	Is the message exciting or dull?

Tracking Studies

A **tracking study** follows consumers over a period of time, rather than perceiving them at a single point in time. A common method for conducting such a study is to perform a series of surveys based on a random sample of the market area. Results of the first study are used to establish a base for comparison in later studies. Subsequent studies track changes in consumer behaviors and attitudes.

Although the issues to be studied vary from operation to operation, the topics listed in Figure 5.1 provide a good example of the scope of these studies. Tracking studies are usually conducted to identify consumer changes to evaluate the effectiveness of introducing a new product, new marketing techniques, or service quality standards.

Customer profile studies can contrast the demographics of heavy and light users for a particular restaurant, compare these profiles among competing operations, and monitor the changes in customer composition over time. *Operation awareness* should be tracked to determine the effectiveness of marketing programs. There are three levels of awareness. The highest level is the "top of mind." For example, when a traveler is asked to name a hotel, the first hotel mentioned has the highest level of awareness. The second level is the "unaided recall," which includes all the hotels mentioned without prompting. The lowest level of awareness is "aided recall." The traveler cannot

Customer profile
Operation awareness
Trial purchase
Patronage frequency and occasions
Advertising awareness and recall
Customer attitude and operation's image
Preferred product/service characteristics
Customer preference by occasion

FIGURE 5.1   Possible topics of a tracking study.

Restaurant Attribute	Hotel Attribute
Quality of food	Clean room
Friendly service	Simple check-in
Value for money	Cleanliness of facility
Convenient location	Décor
Variety of menu	Nonsmoking rooms
Décor	Convenient location
Seating arrangement	Security
Atmosphere	Desk or worktable in room
Clean dining area	Free morning paper
Nonsmoking area	In-room safe
Neat employee appearance	Room service
Clean rest rooms	Pet allowance
Fast service	Personal care items
Ample parking space	Value for money
Portion size	Free breakfast
Clear menu description	Express check-out

FIGURE 5.2 Possible operation attributes to be included in an attitude tracking study.

recall the name of the hotel without prompting. An aided recall question is, for example, "Have you ever heard of the Little Apples Hotel?"

Trial purchase studies go a step further to determine the percentage and demographics of those who have tried the restaurant or hotel and each of the major competitors. *Patronage frequency and occasions* studies analyze how often customers usually visit the operation in a specified period of time, such as during the previous one month, and for what purpose. Results can be used to calculate market share by occasion and to identify the strength of each market segment. *Advertising awareness and recall* can also be tracked to measure the aided and unaided recall of advertising. Once the awareness level is established, respondents can be asked what ideas or topics were mentioned in the ads, to help establish what was perceived by the audience. The advertising medium that has the best recall record can then be identified.

Attitudes toward an operation and its *image* can be measured by asking respondents to rate the operation on a list of attributes, using a scale of 1 to 5 or 1 to 7. Respondents can be asked to rate the attributes from excellent to poor, or, based on comparison with competitors, from far superior to far inferior. A list of possible attributes is provided in Figure 5.2. Key *product and service features* can also be included in the list to see which features are positively related to the likelihood of customer trial or repeat business. *Customer preference by occasion* can be measured by asking respondents to identify the operation of choice under different circumstances. A sample form is provided in Figure 5.3.

Market research before and after an advertising or promotional campaign helps measure the impact of that campaign on factors such as awareness, attitude, trial, and frequency of visit. A series of studies, beginning with a baseline study before any

Which of the following four restaurants do you prefer most when dining for different occasions? Check one for each occasion.

	Restaurant			
	A	B	C	D
1. Eat lunch alone	____	____	____	____
2. Eat lunch with friends	____	____	____	____
3. Eat lunch with family	____	____	____	____
4. Eat evening meal alone	____	____	____	____
5. Eat evening meal with friends	____	____	____	____
6. Eat evening meal with family	____	____	____	____
7. Take a date out for the evening meal	____	____	____	____
8. Order food to go (take-out)	____	____	____	____
9. Order delivery to work	____	____	____	____
10. Order delivery to home	____	____	____	____

FIGURE 5.3   Customer preference by occasion.

special promotion has taken place, provides the insights needed to evaluate the company's ongoing marketing program. The results can also serve as the basis for preparing future marketing and advertising programs.

The Research Process

A funnel can be used to illustrate the **research process,** as shown in Figure 5.4. It begins with the broadest possible scope by developing an understanding and definition of the problem. In this stage, the research is preliminary. As the research progresses, it becomes more specific and pointed.

Problem Definition

The major emphasis in **preliminary research** is on gaining insights, uncovering ideas, and finding possible explanations—not on getting *the* answer (Churchill 1995). A preliminary investigation is used for some or all of these purposes:

1. To establish more specifically the nature of the problem so that it can be more fully researched
2. To establish priorities for future research
3. To improve understanding of the practical problems ahead in a proposed research project
4. To improve general understanding of a problem area or to clarify the concepts that are applied to it

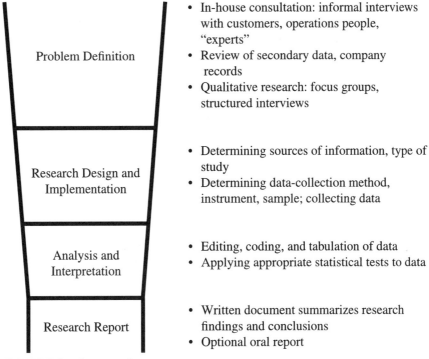

FIGURE 5.4   The research process.
Source: Kenneth G. Hardy, University of Western Ontario.

At the exploratory stage there may be a laundry list of possible problems. For example, when sales are off, marketing may suggest that the problem is poor food or service. Operations may point to superior marketing by competitors, perhaps using coupons or other promotional activities. Store managers may express concern that prices are too high. Top management may wonder whether general economic conditions are the root of the problem. Preliminary research attempts to reduce all these possibilities to a manageable list, which can then be studied through conventional, quantifiable research techniques.

The major tools of preliminary research are a literature search, an examination of in-house information, a key informant survey, and the use of qualitative research techniques such as depth interviews and focus groups. A **literature search** involves reviewing the trade, business, and professional press, as well as published statistical sources and syndicated studies. A search of the company's internal records, such as sales records, quality control reports, and customer comment files, may help narrow the problem.

A **key informant survey** involves interviewing people who are likely to have some insight into the problem. Key informants may include operating managers, sales staff (including servers and desk clerks), other operations employees, suppliers, and consultants. In some situations, analysis of selected cases may prove useful. For example, units with the best and worst operating results can be studied and compared.

Qualitative research techniques can be used to develop better understanding of the problem. **Depth interviews** begin by posing a general topic to the person being interviewed. The interviewer's task is to encourage the respondent to talk freely on the topic. Beyond the opening question, the interview is basically unstructured. The interviewer can ask questions to clarify points made by the respondent in order to develop an in-depth understanding of the respondent's perspective.

Focused group discussions, or **focus groups,** usually include 8 to 12 participants and a trained facilitator. The focus group is a little more directive than a depth interview, in that the facilitator uses a topic outline to guide discussion. The facilitator must balance openness and an accepting attitude with the need to keep the discussion on the subject and to cover all the topics specified. The facilitator should encourage interaction among group members to prevent a series of monologues; no one member should be allowed to dominate the group. Focus groups are often observed through one-way mirrors while they are being conducted. Some sessions are also audio- or videotaped. The record of the discussion and the impression of the observers and facilitator are analyzed.

A limitation of the qualitative research techniques is that respondents are not representative of the general population, and therefore results are not generalizable or projectable. For example, one group of researchers listened to a group of senior citizens discussing food choices and restaurant preferences in a focus group. The seniors spent quite some time discussing healthful menu items in a lively session, making the issue appear to be important. However, the second and third focus groups of seniors did not find that issue interesting or worth discussion. This variation is a good illustration of the fact that such groups are not representative.

Follow-up research is often needed to verify the preliminary findings generated by depth interviews and focus groups. These preliminary research findings are useful in developing a research agenda and often provide useful background for the development of research instruments, such as questionnaires.

Research Design and Implementation

Once the purpose of the research and the nature of the problem are defined, decisions must be made in regard to the type of research and data collection method, source of respondents, and data collection instrument.

Type of Research and Data Collection Method. Research can be conducted by experiment, observation, or survey. Examples of field and laboratory experiments were discussed earlier. Another example of field **experiment** is the use of various cities across the country as test markets by quick-service restaurants (QSRs). Before introducing a menu item nationwide, QSRs usually offer the item in selected markets to evaluate its performance. Sales of operations in the test markets are compared with those of same-size operations in similar markets to determine an item's popularity and success. Potential problems of such field experiments include external variables that cannot be controlled by researchers. For example, weather, special events, and competitors' marketing activities during the test period can influence the outcome of the experiment.

The **observation** method can be used to monitor customer behaviors and reactions to certain products, services, or marketing techniques. For example, a secret shopper can be hired to visit a hotel and observe the service quality and operation procedures from a customer perspective. Notes are taken during the observation for later analysis and discussion. Servers can also be asked to observe guest reactions when a new upselling technique is used. After a trial period, servers' notes from their observations can be summarized to determine the effectiveness of the upselling method.

The **survey** is the most popular research method in the hospitality industry because it is adaptable to a variety of situations and is relatively inexpensive. Data can be collected by different means, including face-to-face, telephone, and mail surveys. Conducting a survey in a shopping mall or on the street is an example of *face-to-face* data collection. Data on product or advertising awareness can be collected this way. Face-to-face data collection provides the opportunity for probing and clarification, and it allows personal observation of the respondents' reactions and body language. However, the training of interviewers and administration of interviews are costly, difficult, and time-consuming.

Telephone surveys are usually conducted in the evenings or on weekends. A satisfaction survey performed shortly after a customer's visit is commonly done via telephone. A telephone interview is less expensive than the face-to-face interview, but the opportunity to observe respondents is, for the most part, lost. The length of the questionnaire must also be limited to the time the interviewer can hold someone's attention on the phone. *Mail* surveys are frequently used in the hospitality industry because of their relatively low cost and the ability to distribute the questionnaire to a large number of people. However, the response rates of mail surveys are usually lower than those of face-to-face and telephone surveys, and they offer no chance for clarification or further questions and answers.

Source of Respondents. Operations usually do not have enough time or money to do census studies, in which everyone in a certain population is surveyed. A census may be done in a private club when the total number of members is relatively small or when a census is seen as politically correct to avoid offending any members who otherwise may not be consulted. Generally, a *sample* of the population is used for data collection. It is critically important to be sure that the sample is drawn from the correct population. For example, a large foodservice company was considering entry into the pizza business. Its researchers used a sample drawn from the general population; however the company's target market was frequent users, mostly 18- to 26-year-olds. The company was misled by the results of the study because the sample was drawn from a population different from the target market.

The use of **probability sampling,** whereby everyone in the population has an equal chance of being selected, is desirable because the sample drawn is more likely to be representative of the population. An example of probability sampling, called *systematic random sampling,* is to select every *n*th name in a hotel guest database. Asking a computer to randomly select 300 names from the guest database is another probability sampling method, *simple random sampling.* Hotel operators can also randomly select several dates and survey all guests registered on those days, using a method called *cluster sampling.*

If the use of probability sampling is not possible or financially feasible, **nonprobability sampling** may be used. *Convenience sampling,* drawn from readily available respondents, such as classmates or shoppers in a mall, is often used. To have a little control over the composition of respondents, *quota sampling* can be used. For example, 100 males and 100 females are surveyed, or 100 heavy users and 100 light users are interviewed. Because not all individuals in a population have an equal chance of being selected, researchers must be aware of the potential sampling bias. Depending on the importance of the decision to be made, this bias may be tolerable. Researchers are always faced with the question of whether the value of the information is equal to or greater than the cost of obtaining it.

Data Collection Instrument. Regardless of the data collection and sampling methods, a **research instrument,** or questionnaire, is needed. A good questionnaire is not easy to develop. Several issues, as shown in Figure 5.5, should be addressed by the researcher when designing a questionnaire. First, the questionnaire should be kept as short as possible. Therefore, only the *necessary* questions are asked. We also need to consider the *ability* and *willingness* of the respondents to answer the questions. Do they have the knowledge required to answer the questions correctly? Can they make the necessary judgments? Will they answer the questions honestly? Respondents may think that some questions are too personal or embarrassing to answer. To reduce their uneasiness, they can be asked to check one of a number of categories instead of filling in the blanks. For example, we can list income, age, and education level in categories.

The *format* of the questionnaire is the next decision. Should the questions be open-ended or closed-ended? Open-ended questions are similar to short-answer questions on a test, whereas closed-ended questions are like multiple-choice items. Face-to-face

What information is required?
Can respondents answer the questions?
Will respondents answer the questions?
What format should be used?
Which question comes first?
What should the questionnaire look like?
What words should be used?
Which scales should be used?
Should the organization's name be disguised?

FIGURE 5.5 Instrument design considerations.

data collection allows more use of open-ended questions, and mail surveys require the almost exclusive use of closed-ended questions. Open-ended questions can provide in-depth information that cannot be obtained by closed-ended questions. Open-ended questions are more difficult to analyze and summarize, but closed-ended questions are usually more difficult to design.

Once we have developed the questions, we need to decide their *sequence*. The interesting questions should always be listed first to catch respondents' attention and to encourage their continuation of the survey. More difficult and personal questions, such as those on demographics, should be located toward the end of the questionnaire. The *layout* of the questionnaire can also influence the response rate. Layout decisions include the font size, paper and print color, paper size and material, graphics, and design.

The *wording* and phrasing of the questionnaire determines the accuracy and quality of the responses received. *Common language*, not professional jargon or trade terminology, should always be used. Only words with one universally understood meaning should be used. For example, does the question "How often do you dine out for dinner?" refer to lunch or supper? People from different regions of the country or various parts of the world may have different explanations of the word "dinner." The question "How much are you willing to pay for a room in a luxury hotel?" is also vague. What do you mean by "luxury"?

Questions should also be phrased in *neutral terms* to avoid leading the respondents to reply one way or the other. Moreover, each question should contain only one inquiry to make sure that the results are meaningful. For example, the question "Do you prefer large restaurants or small, quiet restaurants?" actually tries to measure two things—the size of the restaurant and the quietness of the restaurant. A respondent may indicate a preference for a small, quiet restaurant, even though the size does not matter and quietness is what she likes. Precise *instruction* should always be given to ensure that respondents complete the questionnaire properly. For example, are they supposed to check, circle, or fill in the blanks? Are they supposed to select only one answer or all answers that apply?

A response *scale* must also be selected. The most commonly used is a 5- or 7-point rating scale. For example, 5 = extremely satisfied and 1 = extremely dissatisfied, or 5 = extremely important and 1 = not at all important. Alternately, respondents can be asked to rank order items on a list, or to check one or all appropriate items.

A final question must be considered: Will the research sponsor be openly identified or will it be *disguised?* Most researchers identify their organization and the purpose of the study. Sometimes, however, the purpose of the research may be disguised so as to avoid respondents' tendency to provide answers they think the researchers would like to hear.

Data collection requires the research manager to develop procedures, train research workers to follow them, and oversee the research to ensure that the data collection process does not bias the responses. Returned questionnaires must be checked to be sure that directions have been followed. When necessary, incorrectly obtained data are deleted so that they will not be included in the analysis.

TABLE 5.1 Percentages and Means of Survey Items

	Excellent 5	Good 4	Very Good 3	Fair 2	Poor 1	Don't Know	Mean
1. Quality of meeting rooms	24.8%	24.0%	21.7%	11.2%	18.3%	8.7%	3.26
2. Value for money of meeting room facilities	22.8	18.3	21.9	12.1	11.8	13.1	2.89
3. Quality of guest room accommodations	22.8	35.7	23.1	8.7	0.8	8.9	3.44

Data Analysis and Interpretation

Once the data collection process is accomplished, the completed responses are analyzed and results are summarized and interpreted. Simple tabulation gives the percentage of responses to each question. Table 5.1 shows the percentage and mean of each item related to hotel meeting room and guest room facilities. A cross-tabulation, in Table 5.2, shows responses divided between respondents who had used the hotel for conferences and those who had not. Comparisons are often made between genders and between education and income levels. More sophisticated statistical analyses can be performed to further study the relationships between variables.

In addition to analyzing the data, researchers must interpret the findings and assign meanings to the numbers. For example, the numbers in Table 5.2 show that more respondents who had not used the property indicated good meeting room and hotel facilities as an important factor in the choice of a hotel. This could mean that nonusers perceive the property as having less-than-desirable meeting room and hotel facilities.

TABLE 5.2 Cross-Tabulation of Survey Items

Most Important Factor in Choice of Hotel	Used Property for Meetings and Conferences					
	Yes		No		Total	
	Number	Percentage	Number	Percentage	Number	Percentage
Location of hotel	28	40.0	9	11.3	37	24.7
Contact person	0	0	3	3.8	3	2.0
Conference service	9	12.8	8	10.0	17	11.3
Meeting room facilities	10	14.3	24	30.0	34	22.7
Guest room accommodations	0	0	2	2.5	2	1.3
Hotel facilities	15	21.4	24	30.0	39	26.0
Other	8	11.4	10	12.5	18	12.0
Total	70	100	80	100	150	100

Preparation of the Research Report

In the final analysis, conclusions must be drawn from the information collected. At this point, judgment, experience, and common sense must come into play, because the meaning of statistical reports is usually not self-evident. Statistics can help them to reach conclusions, but researchers and managers have to make the final decisions. Possible actions based on data in Table 5.2 include (1) developing a marketing campaign toward nonusers to change their perceptions about the hotel and meeting room facilities, (2) conducting a comparative analysis to determine whether the hotel's facilities are really worse than those of competitors, and (3) launching another research study to collect more detailed information from nonusers to find out exactly why they had not used the property for meetings and conventions. Researchers usually include possible actions in the final report and may recommend priorities. However, managers have to make the decisions and select the most appropriate actions.

The research process is summarized graphically in Figure 5.6. Case Study 5.2, the story of a company turnaround based on market research, shows the importance of marketing research in hospitality operations.

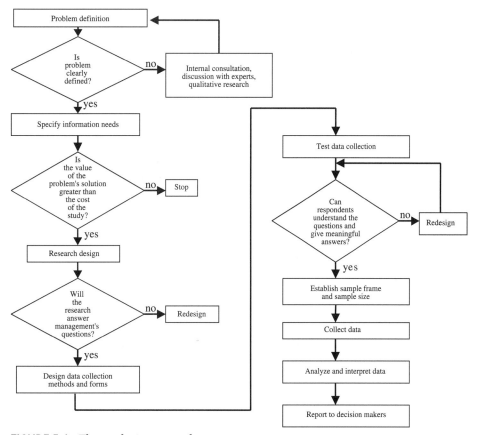

FIGURE 5.6 The marketing research process.
Source: Adapted from Burke Marketing Institute, Cincinnati, Ohio.

CASE STUDY 5.2

Marketing Research Lays Ground for Turnaround at Round Table Pizza

When Round Table Pizza undertook a self-assessment, it had approximately 150 stores, all concentrated in California. Marketing research revealed that Round Table was ranked the last in brand and advertising awareness among consumers. Round Table was, in effect, an undifferentiated and unmarketed brand. The research also revealed widespread consumer skepticism about pizza chain restaurants and the quality of their products, in a market where independents had more than 50 percent of the market share.

The company set out to position Round Table as the premier pizza restaurant. To achieve this goal, it determined through marketing research what consumers wanted and shaped its operation to meet those expectations. The promises in its advertising reflected the reality in its operations:

1. *Dough:* The crust dough is made *fresh* daily in the restaurants. Many pizza operators use already prepared, frozen dough to make their crusts—not Round Table. Its commercial stated, "We don't thaw pizza, we make it."
2. *Cheese:* Round Table's three-cheese blend is made from specially aged, *whole* milk mozzarella cheese. Aged cheddar and provolone cheeses complete the blend. The blend is applied to the pizza *fresh*, never frozen.
3. *Sauce:* "Prepared fresh in our stores with our own secret spice formula—not precanned at some distant packing plant."
4. *Meat toppings:* Round Table uses only the highest-quality meat—meat that contains no fillers, binders, or extenders.

Frozen, dehydrated, and precooked were not part of the Round Table concept.

In the first year following the new advertising, sales increased more than 30 percent. Over the next five years, Round Table experienced explosive growth, expanding to more than 400 restaurants. As shown in the following table, Round Table had moved to number one in market share in the Pacific states. Round Table focused on consumers, found out what they wanted, gave it to them, and told them what it was doing. It all began with determining what the consumers wanted. As of 2000, there were more than 500 Round Table restaurants in the western United States, Asia, and the Middle East.

Attitude and Usage—Unaided Measurements			
	Advertising Awareness		Best Quality
	Before Repositioning	After Repositioning	After Repositioning
Round Table	16%	45%	54%
Major Competition			
Chain A	47%	19%	14%
Chain B	23%	11%	8%
Chain C	30%	14%	6%
Chain D	—	11%	3%
All other chains	—	14%	10%

Sources: Maverick Solutions, Inc. (1995). *Round Table Pizza: History* (on-line). Web site: *http://www.waiter .com/roundtable/history.html;* Round Table. (2001). *Round Table—History* (on-line). Web site: http://www. roundtablepizza.com/press/rthistory.htm; S. Bergen, "Pizza . . . a Fresh Experience." *Proceedings, Chain Operators Exchange.* (Chicago: International Foodservice Manufacturers Association, 1985).

Consumer Information: Mining the Guest Database

The process of using a guest database for marketing purposes is referred to as **database marketing (DBM).** Specifically, DBM is:

an approach by which computer database technologies are harnessed to design, create, and manage customer data lists containing information about each customer's characteristics and history of interactions with the company. The lists are used as needed for locating, selecting, targeting, servicing, and establishing relationships with customers in order to enhance the long-term value of these customers to the company. The techniques used for managing lists include: 1. database manipulation methods such as select and join, 2. statistical methods for predicting each customer's likelihood of future purchases of specific items based on his/her history of past purchases, and 3. measures for computing the life-time value of a customer on an ongoing basis. (Bennett 1995)

Tracking Guest Transactions

The basic worth of DBM is that it is even more powerful than other means of segmentation, such as demographics or psychographics. As one expert put it,

In a hierarchy of value, what someone has done is much more insightful than who someone is. I can't really tell very much about whether you are likely to come to my restaurant and what

you are likely to eat from knowing your income or your age. But I can tell a lot if I have the detailed information on a few meals you've had. (Dunn 1994)

The process starts when an operation begins to keep track of who its customers are. A hotel, for example, will log each visit by a customer in its guest history file. Guest history files actually have long been a feature of luxury hotels. In the 1930s, the guest history file in Chicago's Palmer House, recorded on 3 × 5 cards by hand, filled a room the size of a modern midpriced hotel lobby. What is different now is the accessibility of the information and its storage devices—computer disks, tapes, and CDs. The information on who the customers are and what their preferences are can be used to build customer loyalty.

Tracking customer transactions is fairly straightforward for hotels, because they begin the transaction with registration. Restaurants, however, have found ways to accumulate information as well. One of the major sources of guest information is a frequency program.

Frequency Marketing

The term **frequency marketing** derives from the frequent-flyer program launched in 1981 by American Airlines (Colloquy 1998). American's computerized SABRE reservations database provided a simple and accurate way to track customer purchase behaviors and to manage the awards accounting. Fiercely competitive situations encouraged marketers to reconsider the potential for building sales through programs aimed at current customers rather than new customers.

The inducement for guests to sign up for a frequency program is that there is some reward for frequent patronage. Rewards can be divided into two categories, *hard* and *soft*. Hard rewards have actual monetary value, such as discounts, a free bottle of wine, a free meal, or a free night's stay. Soft rewards include such benefits as special reservation handling, personal recognition, and other perks. As soon as a diner signs up for a frequent-diner card, his or her name, address, and usually some demographic information are available to be logged into the restaurant's database. Table 5.3 lists some sample programs offered by restaurants (Colloquy 1997).

The real advantage of an effective frequency program is the customer information the sponsor accumulates through the program's ability to track customer patronage behaviors, creating the ability to customize the marketing effort to the high-value customers. The database can also identify those customers who are heavy spenders; which of those heavy spenders could spend even more; which light customers could become heavies; which are true loyalists versus those who are convenience shoppers; and which are most expensive to serve because they visit infrequently, pay the lowest prices, and consume the most service (Barlow 1999).

Database marketing is sometimes referred to as **relationship marketing,** because once an organization has a guest database, it can use that information to build and enhance relationships with its customers. Because the goal of these programs is to encourage more frequent patronage by current customers, such marketing is also called *loyalty marketing.*

In 1983, members of Marriott's frequent-guest program earned points for every night stayed and every dollar spent at participating properties. All the other major hotel chains have adopted the concept of inviting high-value guests to enroll in their frequent-guest programs. (Photograph courtesy of Colloquy/Frequency Marketing, Inc.)

Database marketing does not have to be aimed solely at a company's current customer base. It can also be expanded to a program of marketing to others who are similar to current customers. Using demographic and geo-demographic databases available from information suppliers, it is possible to locate potential customers who fit the current customer profile. These people are logical target markets for promotion. Therefore, the advantages of DBM include building the loyalty of existing customers, expanding market share through identification and acquisition of potential customers, providing a basis for revenue stream analysis, and reducing marketing costs over the long run by allowing a company to use its marketing budget more efficiently by targeting more precisely.

Using the DBM Program

In most businesses, 20 percent of the customers generate 80 percent of the business; thus, it is clearly in an operation's interest to know which of its customers are frequent visitors. It is also useful to know their average spending. With time, the DBM program may suggest segmenting the customers based not only on frequency but also on the dollar value of their patronage. Extra-valuable customers deserve special rewards and recognition. Some airlines, for example, make sure that exceptionally frequent travelers are never bumped from crowded flights and are given special consideration when lines are long or flights are cancelled.

TABLE 5.3 Frequent-Dining Programs

Sponsor/Program	Structure	Benefits	Data Collection	Communications	Notes
Burger King Kid's Club					
	• N/A	• Free kid's meal on birthday • Discounts with partner airlines, such as $99 round-trip on TWA • Kids' meals toys • Welcome package includes card, secret code name, personal door hanger, riddle cards, and stickers	• Name, address, and birthday • Membership list not for rent	• *Adventure* quarterly newsletter features puzzles, games, encourages interaction among members • Periodic mailings support in-store promotions such as Disney's *Hunchback of Notre Dame* or *Toy Story* toy giveaway ties • Toll-free number for member questions	• Launched 1990 to develop a "value-added" program that would be "interactive" with its members • Designed to build "long-term" relationships
California Café CafE Club					
	• 1 point/$1 • Accepts credit cards • Membership card must be present • Mail in statement to acquire Dining Certificate	• 100 bonus enrollment points • 250 points = $25 Dining Certificate, 500 points = $50 Dining Certificate • 50,000 points = 7 day, Seven Seas Radisson cruise for two, plus a variety of other travel packages, private tours, and dining at renowned wineries, spa retreats, etc.; can be "purchased" with points • CafE Club points can be credited only to the member making payment for dining events	• General demographics plus food preferences and other CafE Club locations visited	• Telephone number • Web page • CafE Club statement every 2 months (active members only) with total point accumulation • Quarterly newsletter features special events, exclusive offers, bonus earning opportunities, and current list of award opportunities • On-line newsletter	• Participating restaurants include California Cafes, CafE Del Rey, Napa Valley Grilles, and Alcatraz Brewing Company • Liquor control laws in some areas prohibit point credit for alcoholic purchases

T.G.I. Friday's Gold Points

Points	Rewards	Member Data Collected	Communication	Results
• 10 points/$1	• 500 bonus enrollment points • Double, triple and double-triple points offered on sales receipts • 1,250 points = free appetizer • 5,750 points = $15 certificate • 11,000 points = $30 certificate • 19,000 points = $50 certificate • 37,000 points = $100 certificate • 80,000 points = Radisson Weekend • 125,000 points = free U.S. airfare • 250,000 points = Radisson Seven Seas Cruise	• Name, address, phone, birth date, business zip, and average visit frequency • Visit locations, dates, times, purchase amounts • Gallup in-store surveys • "Capability" to determine what members eat	• Purchase receipts indicate point balances and ongoing bonus offers • Web site and toll-free number • Members-only 800 number	• As of February, 1997, 32 members have taken the cruise • "Several million" members, about 300,000 new members a week • About 50% of base is "active" • Average spending and total sales accounted for by members are "significantly higher" than those of non-members • Some program changes made since launching; i.e., the point system has increased

McDonald's McBreak Card

Points	Rewards	Member Data Collected	Communication	Results
• 1 point/$1 • Receipt indicates cumulative point total	• Rewards range from free cup of coffee or soda (10 points) to a deluxe sandwich (75 points)	• Name, address, birthday information, including names and birthdays of children	• Point status, reward, and marketing messages; incentives for returning a different time of day; coupons and reminder of points needed for next reward found on receipt at point of sale	• Launched 1997 in Dallas/Fort Worth test market • Hoped to have 500,000 members by end of 1997

Source: Frequent-dining programs. (1997). *Colloquy* (on-line). Web site: http://www.colloquy.com/online/default_matrices.asp

119

Building a database marketing program is expensive, and operations should expect to allow roughly two years to establish a working system. This is also a long-term commitment, because approximately 18 percent of the U.S. population moves each year. Accordingly, continuing effort is required to keep the database current.

In addition to providing a database that may help with marketing efforts, an analysis of guest history information can also help hotels in planning their capacity and revenue management. When the guest history includes the date the reservation is made as well as the date of arrival, analysis of the information can identify reservation lead time for various seasons. This information is useful in assessing the current reservation level. For example, the high season at a resort starts on June 15 and the normal lead time is 60 days. If reservations are weak during the latter half of April, it may be time to offer lower-rate categories and to launch special promotional efforts. Promotions can be aimed at people who have been visitors in the past but have not reserved for this year, as well as people who fit the target market criteria but have never visited the resort.

In conventional mass marketing, the most powerful tools are reducing price and increasing promotion. However, both reduce the profit margin. DBM, on the other hand, builds patronage by offering customers what they want and communicating with them with a certain degree of familiarity. Most fundamentally, DBM is based on the notion that it is not the products or services that provide value to a business, but the customers and their continued patronage.

Summary

With rising marketing expenditures, fact-based decision making, supported by marketing information systems and market research, has become the norm. Marketing information may come from a company's internal sources, such as sales analyses, and external sources, such as marketing intelligence obtained by visiting competitors' facilities. Marketing research relies on published secondary data and syndicated studies, as well as primary research. Common topics for market research include customer identification, product research, promotion evaluation, and tracking studies. The research process starts with problem identification, often based on preliminary and qualitative research techniques. As the research question becomes clear, the design process moves on to consider the type of research to be used, the sample selection, research instrument development, and data collection methods. Once the data are collected, analyses are performed, results are interpreted, and final reports are prepared.

Increasingly, research is being concentrated on getting to know more about a company's current customers by tracking guest transactions, often through frequent-customer programs. Operators seek to establish a relationship with regular guests and to reward guest loyalty.

Key Words and Concepts

Marketing intelligence	Laboratory experiment	Experiment
Environmental scanning	Field experiment	Observation
Marketing information systems	Tracking study	Survey
Marketing research	Research process	Probability sampling
Secondary research	Preliminary research	Nonprobability sampling
Syndicated studies	Literature search	Research instrument
Primary research	Key informant survey	Database marketing (DBM)
Customer base	Qualitative research	Frequency marketing
Product research	Depth interviews	Relationship marketing
Copy testing	Focus groups	

Resources on the Internet

Association of Independent Information Professionals. *http://www.aiip.org/*

Colloquy magazine. *http://www.colloquy.com*

Lodging magazine. *http://www.ei-ahma.org/webs/lodging/index.html*

Market Trends. *http://www.markettrends.com/index.htm*

National Restaurant Association. *http://www.restaurant.org/*

Quirk's Marketing Research Review. *http://www.quirks.com/*

Restaurants & Institutions. http://www.rimag.com

Smith Travel Research. *http://www.str-online.com/*

Statistics Canada. *http://www.statcan.ca/*

Technomic Inc. *http://www.technomic.com/*

U.S. Bureau of the Census. *http://www.census.gov*

Discussion Questions

1. What are the major sources of marketing information? What information do you think is vital at the unit level? At the headquarters level?

2. How is marketing intelligence gathered?

3. What are the principal sources of secondary research? What are the advantages and disadvantages of secondary research?

4. What are some common market research concerns in hospitality? How do you think these concerns could be addressed with market research?

5. What is the purpose of preliminary research? What are some of the techniques used?

6. What are the steps in the research process?

7. How can a study sample be selected?

8. What are the major considerations in questionnaire design?

9. What is database marketing? How is it accomplished?

10. What is relationship marketing?

References

Association of Independent Information Professionals. (2001). *The Association of Independent Information Professionals: An international association of owners of information businesses* (on-line). Web site: http://www.aiip.org/

Barlow, R. G. (1999). Playing catch up. *Colloquy, 7*(1), 2.

Bennett, P. D., ed. (1995). *Dictionary of marketing terms.* 2d ed. Chicago: American Marketing Association.

Churchill, G. A., Jr. (1995). *Marketing research: Methodological foundations.* 6th ed. Fort Worth, TX: Dryden Press.

Colloquy. (1997). Frequent-dining programs. *Colloquy* (on-line). Web site: http://www.colloquy.com/online/default_matrices.asp

Colloquy. (1998). From evolution to revolution: The roots of frequency marketing. *Colloquy, 6*(4), 7–9.

Dunn, W. (1994). Building a database. *Marketing Tools* (July–August), 52–59.

Macdonald, J. (1994). Sheraton building Vegas kingdom. *Hotel & Motel Management, 209*(10), 1, 6.

Mehta, A. (1999). Using self-concept to assess advertising effectiveness. *Journal of Advertising Research, 39*(1), 81–89.

Mortimer, K., and B. P. Mathews. (1998). The advertising of services: Consumer views v. normative guidelines. *Service Industries Journal, 18*(3), 4–19.

Smith Travel Research. (2001). *Smith Travel Research products and services* (on-line). Web site: http://www.str-online.com/

Technomic Inc. (2001). *Technomic information services* (on-line). Web site: http://www.technomic.com/

Marketing Strategy

(Photo courtesy of Four Seasons Hotel Las Vegas. Photographer: Rob Gordon.)

When you have finished reading this chapter, you should be able to:

- Understand the process of corporate strategic planning.
- Differentiate strategic marketing and functional marketing.
- Discuss corporate portfolio analysis.
- Define SWOT analysis and its implications.
- Identify generic strategies.
- Describe four types of growth-oriented grand strategies.
- Explain positioning and its role in marketing.

The hospitality industry in the United States today is experiencing limited expansion opportunities and intense competition among businesses. Operations must take a proactive approach and adapt to this complex and changing environment in order to grow and survive. Historically, the concept of strategy carries a strong military and political connotation. The word *strategy* originated from the Greek *strategos*, which means planning the destruction of one's enemies through effective use of resources. From a business perspective, it is defined as a course of action intended to ensure that a firm will achieve its objectives by matching its internal resources and skills with the environmental opportunities and barriers it faces (Bower et al. 1991). A strategy is a company's "game plan" (Pearce and Robinson 1997), or a large-scale future-oriented plan that looks at the big picture of the company. More specifically,

> *Corporate strategy is the pattern of decisions in a company that (1) determines, shapes, and reveals its objectives, purposes, or goals; (2) produces the principal policies and plans for achieving these goals; and (3) defines the business the company intends to be in, the kind of economic and human organization it intends to be, and the nature of the economic and non-economic contribution it intends to make to its shareholders, employees, customers, and communities.* (Bower et al. 1991, p. 104)

Marketing plays a crucial role in the strategic management process of a firm. Success in marketing can move a company forward in achieving goals established by the strategic plan. Our principal concern is with marketing, but we cannot develop marketing strategies in isolation from other strategic variables. For example, the feasibility of a marketing strategy with the goal of doubling the market share in a particular market will depend on the financial and operational resources required to achieve such goal. Although we focus mostly on marketing here, we have to realize that the strategies of a firm involve issues from many perspectives.

> *Marketing strategy is the analysis of alternative opportunities and risks to the firm, informed by environmental (e.g., competitive, social) and internal (e.g., production abilities) information, which leads management to choose a particular set of market, product, and customer goals . . . the object of marketing strategy is to pose the goals that will direct marketing actions. . . .* (Bonoma 1985, p. 7)

Strategic Marketing

A company can offer value when there is a positive match between customers' needs and the firm's objectives. A better value, based on lower price, better product, or both, will give the company a competitive advantage. When identical or similar value is offered by two or more operations, most consumers cannot differentiate between firms. The result of no competitive advantage could be a price war, which may satisfy customers' needs but not the firms' objectives. Therefore, **marketing strategy** must be defined as an endeavor by a firm to differentiate itself positively from its competitors,

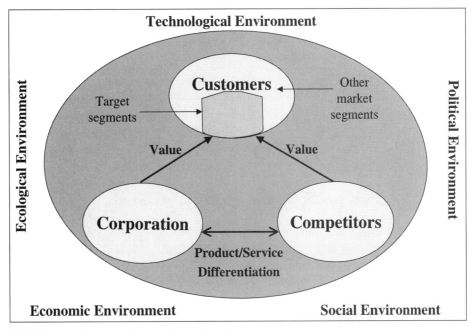

FIGURE 6.1 The marketing strategy triangle.
Source: K. Ohmae, *The Mind of the Strategist* (New York: Penguin Books, 1982), 92.

using its relative strengths to better satisfy customer needs in a given environment (Jain 1997).

Within a given environment, marketing strategies deal essentially with the interplay of three forces, known as the **strategic three Cs:** the customer, the competition, and the corporation (Jain 1997). Marketing strategies focus on identifying ways in which the *corporation* can differentiate itself from its *competitors* and capitalize on its **competitive advantage** to deliver better value to *customers*. Together, the strategic three C's form the **marketing strategy triangle,** as shown in Figure 6.1. To ensure that the marketing strategies developed fit into the overall company aim and direction, a strategic marketing perspective should be taken.

Strategic Versus Functional Marketing

The distinction between strategic and functional marketing is a relative one. In general, **strategic marketing** is concerned with long-term issues that involve basic commitments affecting all or a substantial portion of the organization, and is more concerned with goals and objectives than with actions. Strategic marketing focuses on choosing the right products for the right markets at the right time, or deals with what business to emphasize. Although strategic marketing planning usually draws on research, it is also likely to involve judgments that require the personal experience, talent, and intuition of senior executives. Sometimes short-term performance is sac-

TABLE 6.1 Major Differences Between Strategic Marketing and Functional Marketing		
	Strategic Marketing	Functional Marketing
Time Frame	Long range (3–5 years); decisions have long-term implications	Day-to-day; decisions have relevance in one year
Purpose	Development of strategic perspective to direct future focus	Formulation and implementation of marketing programs
Resources	Broad allocation	Short-term trade-offs
Process	Less formalized and more flexible	More formalized and structured allocations
Environment	Considered ever-changing and dynamic	Considered constant with occasional disturbances
Leadership Style	Proactive	Reactive
Specificity	Tentative, broad-ranging nonroutine issues	Specific, timed actions, expenditures, and controls—often concerning routine issues
Responsibility	Few senior corporate and operating managers	Large number of operating managers

Source: Adapted from S. C. Jain, *Marketing Planning and Strategy* (Cincinnati, OH: International Thomson Publishing, 1977), 32. Copyright 1997 by South-Western College Publishing.

rificed in the interest of long-term results. **Functional marketing,** however, is concerned with the day-to-day actions that implement strategy and respond to minor changes in the marketplace. It deals with running a defined business, as characterized in Table 6.1.

Corporate Hierarchy

The typical decision-making hierarchy of a company is shown in Figure 6.2. At the top is the *corporate level,* composed of the board of directors and chief executives. For a multibusiness firm, the corporate level decides the type of businesses that the firm should operate. For example, in 1997, PepsiCo decided not to be involved in the restaurant business anymore and announced the spinoff of its Pizza Hut, Taco Bell, and KFC operations.

At the *business level,* the managers must translate the statement of intent generated at the corporate level into strategies for the specific **strategic business unit (SBU)** to direct the future focus of the SBU. An SBU may include a single business or several closely related businesses that offer similar products. For example, Cendant Corporation's travel division has hotel franchise, car rental, and Resort Condominiums International as its SBUs. Managers in the hotel franchise SBU must develop long-range marketing strategies to shape the future of this business. Therefore, strategic market-

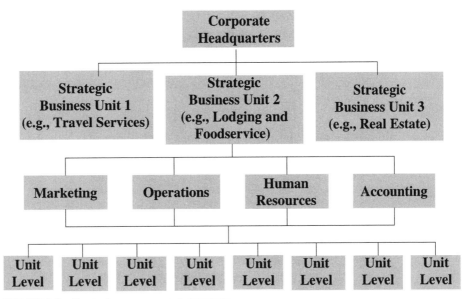

FIGURE 6.2 Strategic management structure.

ing is primarily conducted at the SBU level. For single-business corporations, such as McDonald's, the corporate and business levels are the same.

The next level in the corporate hierarchy is the *functional level,* where short-term functional objectives and annual plans are developed. Traditionally, the success of a business depends on the performance of the marketing, operations, human resources, and accounting *functions. Unit-level* managers are the people who actually implement the activities in those plans. The corporate- and SBU-level managers center their attention on "doing the right thing," whereas managers at the functional and unit levels focus their attention on "doing things right."

Corporation Strategic Planning

Strategic planning begins with the development of a corporate mission, followed by the identification of SBUs, as shown in Figure 6.3. The results of portfolio analysis can help identify viable SBUs and allocate resources among selected SBUs. Each SBU must assess its own internal strengths and weaknesses and external opportunities and threats (SWOT) and develop its own business-level mission and strategies. Based on its mission and strategies, a market position and positioning statement are proposed for each market. Finally, functional strategies and plans are designed to implement the corporate- and business-level strategies. This entire procedure is known as the top-down approach. However, some corporations use the bottom-up method in strategic

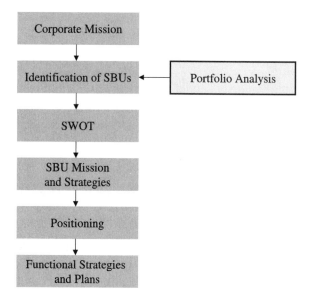

FIGURE 6.3 Corporate strategic planning.

planning. Inputs are generated from the functional and unit levels first and then progress through the SBUs. Eventually, a company mission is derived. Even in the top-down approach, inputs from lower levels of the organization are always important.

Company Mission

An organization's **mission statement** represents what the company seeks to do and to become. It communicates the firm's fundamental and unique purpose. A mission statement sets a company apart from others in the same industry and gives it its own special identity, business emphasis, and path for development. It specifies a company's long-term intentions: Why does the organization exist? What business are we in? What customers do we serve? (Pearce and Robinson 1997). These are the questions that underlie the formation of a business mission statement, such as that of the Hilton Hotels Corporation (1999):

> *Hilton Hotels Corporation is recognized internationally as a preeminent hospitality company. Among our 250 hotels are some of the most well-known properties to be found anywhere, including The Waldorf-Astoria, Hilton Hawaiian Village and Palmer House Hilton. Our hotels offer guests and customers the finest accommodations and amenities for business or leisure. For 80 years, the Hilton brand name has been synonymous with excellence in the hospitality industry.*

A mission statement can be seen as the end, with all other activities as the means to the end. Therefore, a mission statement can be used as a standard to evaluate the company's performance. Mission statements, however, are not eternal. As time goes on and things change, mission statements should be evaluated and revised. The best-worded mission statements are simple and concise.

Portfolio Analysis and Identification of SBUs

Multibusiness companies usually find that their various businesses generate and consume different levels of cash. Some businesses generate more cash than they can use to maintain or expand the business, others consume more than they can generate. Corporate managers have to decide on the best way to generate and use financial resources among the businesses within the company. The **business portfolio** technique attempts to help managers "balance" the flow of cash among businesses. The two best-known business **portfolio analysis** models are the **Boston Consulting Group model** and the **General Electric model.** The role of marketing personnel is to assist strategic decisions by providing information on the viability of various products and markets.

Boston Consulting Group Model. Boston Consulting Group (BCG) is a leading management consulting firm. It developed the *growth-share matrix,* depicted in Figure 6.4, and has made it popular. One of the reasons that this model is so popular is its focus on growth and profitability, which are the primary objectives of most corporations. Managers use the matrix to plot each of the company's

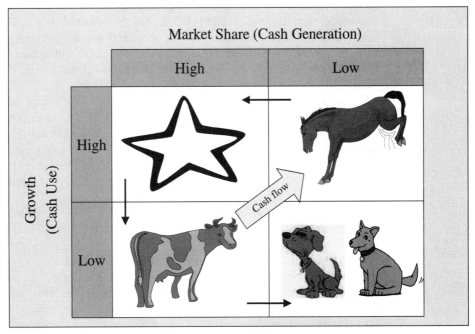

FIGURE 6.4   The Boston Consulting Group growth-share matrix.

SBUs according to its market growth rate and market share. *Broncos* (also called *question marks*) are businesses that operate in a high-growth market but have relatively low market share, as compared with the largest competitor. Most businesses start off as broncos as the company tries to enter a high-growth market. A bronco requires a lot of cash to support the necessary infrastructure to keep up with the growing market. The company has to think about whether to keep pouring money into this business.

If the bronco business is successful, it becomes a *star*. A star is the market leader in a high-growth market. However, this does not necessarily mean that the star produces a positive cash flow. Actually, the company must reinvest most earnings, and sometimes more, to keep up with the high market growth and to fight off competitors. When the market's growth rate falls, if it still has the largest relative market share, the star becomes a *cash cow*. A cash cow generates a significant cash surplus because the market does not need reinvestment as the growth slows down. The company can use the cash generated to support the other types of businesses, broncos in particular and stars to a lesser degree. The cash flow, as indicated in Figure 6.4, represents the desired pattern of investment in growth—a cash cow is "milked" to supply the investment needs of a fast-growing bronco.

A *dog* describes a business that has weak market share in a low-growth market. When a cash cow starts to lose market share and the company would like to maintain its market leadership, a sufficient amount of money has to be put back into the business. Otherwise, the company may become a dog. Sometimes the business becomes a dog through a conscious management decision or because of unforeseen environmental changes. For example, a hotel may be hopelessly outmoded and extensive remodeling is not economically justified. Another example is a roadside motel facing the rerouting of a nearby highway. The growth of motel business has slowed over the years, and now this particular operation's market share will be significantly decreased by the change in traffic pattern. As a result, the motel will become a dog through no fault of the management.

Although a dog is conventionally shown as rather sad-looking, one of the two dogs shown in Figure 6.4 actually looks pretty cheerful. This represents the fact that "harvesting" can still be profitable. For example, cafeteria-style family restaurants were popular in the 1980s, but by the early 1990s the concept had gone out of style. Many cafeterias took away as much cash as possible from their operations without any reinvestment. Other restaurants used the "divestiture" option for a dog (which means to sell or liquidate) and used the cash in other businesses.

The relative position of a business—for instance, as a star or a cash cow—affects its marketing programs. Stars are winners but require continued investment and aggressive marketing to maintain their position in a growing market. Cash cows, on the other hand, require only maintenance marketing because they already dominate the market. They must be alert, however, for others that are out to take the leadership away from them. Broncos need a high level of investment and marketing support if they want to break out of their low market share position. Dogs are most likely to rely on reduced prices or discounting.

General Electric Model. Corporate strategists found the BCG matrix limited in its ability to reflect the complexity of the business situation, because only market share and growth rate were measured. Many companies adopted the General Electric (GE) model, which uses multiple criteria to evaluate *market attractiveness* and *business strength.* Figure 6.5 lists some of the criteria that can be used to assess market attractiveness and business strength; however, each business needs to develop its own relevant criteria for evaluation. The two BCG model criteria, market growth and market share, are usually included in the criteria list.

Each SBU, such as travel services and hospitality operations, as shown in Figure 6.2, should be evaluated and placed in one of the nine cells in the matrix. The matrix is divided into three zones. The three cells at the upper left, or the medium gray zone, indicate strong SBUs. *Build/grow* strategies would be appropriate here. The cells shown diagonally from the upper right to the lower left, or the light gray zone, classify SBUs as medium in overall attractiveness. For these, a company should pursue *hold/milk* strategies. The three cells at the lower right, or the dark gray zone, indicate that SBUs are low in overall attractiveness; the company should consider *harvesting or divesting.*

Marketing plays an important role in portfolio analysis through evaluating market growth potential and estimating market shares. Once the SBUs' positions are identified, management must decide what to do with each business. The idea underlying the business portfolio approach is that not all businesses in the company fall within the

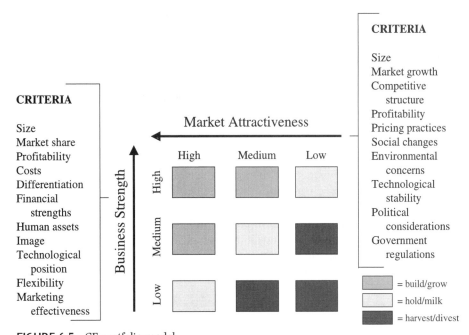

FIGURE 6.5 GE portfolio model.

same BCG model quadrant or GE model zone. A healthy mix of SBUs is critical to a company's long-term success. SBUs in different positions require different marketing strategies. The marketing manager's job is not always to build sales in each SBU. Their job may be to maintain existing demand with fewer marketing dollars or to take cash out of the business and allow demand to fall. Marketing personnel must work with each SBU manager closely and tailor marketing strategies specifically for each SBU.

SWOT Analysis

SWOT is the acronym for the internal *strengths* and *weaknesses* of a firm and the environmental *opportunities* and *threats* facing the firm. **SWOT analysis** is a technique that is easy to use for managers to get a quick overview of a business's strategic position. The analysis is based on the assumption that an effective strategy derives from a good fit between a business's internal capabilities (strengths and weaknesses) and its external environment (opportunities and threats). A good fit maximizes a business's strengths and opportunities and minimizes its weaknesses and threats (Pearce and Robinson 1997).

A strength may be a resource, skill, or other advantage relative to competitors. It gives the firm a competitive advantage in the market. Once strengths are identified, they can be matched with existing or potential opportunities. When opportunities knock, the firm has to be ready to take advantage of them. Knowing its strengths can help the business to identify and capture opportunities. A weakness is a limitation or deficiency in resources, skill, or capability that seriously impedes a firm's effective performance. Weaknesses may be in the area of facilities, in regard to carpet, rooms, or furniture; brand image; marketing skills; or financial resources.

An opportunity is a major favorable situation in the environment. Environmental trends are one source of opportunities. For example, a greater emphasis on healthful diet, an increased number of women travelers, and technological advancement all represent potential opportunities for hospitality operations. A threat is a major unfavorable situation in the environment. Threats pose significant barriers to a firm in maintaining its current position or achieving its desired position. For example, an increase in the minimum wage and lack of skilled workers can be threats to a business's desired growth.

A systematic way to look at the results of SWOT analysis is to categorize the situation according to four types, as shown in Figure 6.6. Cell 1 is the most favorable situation. The operation faces several environmental opportunities and has many strengths that facilitate the pursuit of those opportunities. This situation suggests growth-oriented strategies to take advantage of the situation. Marriott International's growth in various segments of the lodging industry is an example of how a company with a good reputation and many strengths found opportunities in different segments of the market.

In Cell 2, a business with many strengths faces an unfavorable environment. In this situation, the business should use its strengths to explore opportunities in other products or markets. For example, a successful hotel with great marketing expertise

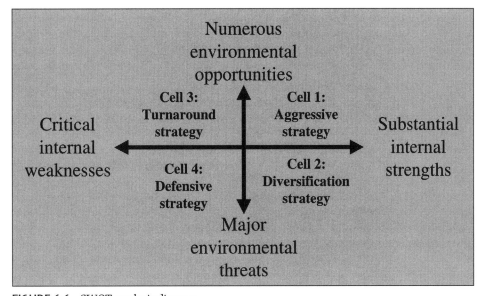

FIGURE 6.6 SWOT analysis diagram.
Source: Adapted from J. A. Pearce II and R. B. Robinson, Jr., *Strategic Management* (New York: Irwin/McGraw-Hill, 1977), 172. Copyright 1997 by The McGraw-Hill Companies, Inc.

might establish a marketing consultant business when the economy is soft and hotel revenues are declining. A firm in Cell 3 faces great opportunities, but has many internal weaknesses. The focus in this instance should be to eliminate major internal problems to effectively pursue the available opportunities. For example, Howard Johnson has turned the company around by improving its products, services, and brand image.

Cell 4 is the least favorable situation, in which a business faces major environmental threats from a weak position. Appropriate strategies include reducing or redirecting resources in the current markets or products. What this business needs is damage control with defensive strategies. Some cafeteria-style restaurants were in this situation when consumer tastes changed, the market became more competitive, and the companies had weak marketing skills and financial resources.

SBU Mission and Strategies

After assessing the internal and external environments, SBU managers should have a clear view of the future direction and achievable goals for their particular businesses. Based on this understanding, an SBU mission statement and strategies are developed. The purpose and format of an SBU mission statement are the same as those of a corporate mission, but with a business unit focus. Consider, for example, the mission statement of Carlson Hotels Worldwide:

Carlson Hotels Worldwide, a division of Carlson Hospitality Worldwide, provides a brand management structure upon which the hotel brands of Carlson Hospitality Worldwide continue to grow as leaders in the luxury, upscale and mid-tier segments of the lodging industry. (Carlson Companies, Inc. 2001)

Generic Strategies. The general philosophy of doing business stated in the mission statement should be incorporated into the strategic planning process. All strategies must be based on a "core idea" about how a firm can best compete in the marketplace. The core idea is called the **generic strategy,** which specifies the fundamental approach to achieve competitive advantage. At the broadest level, three generic strategies can be identified to create a defendable position and outperform competitors in an industry—that is, to create a *sustainable competitive advantage.* These strategies, as illustrated in Figure 6.7, are cost leadership, differentiation, and focus (Porter 1998).

To use a **cost leadership** strategy, an operation has to maximize economy of scale, reduce costs, or use volume to maintain profit. In the hospitality industry, the need to serve customers in many convenient locations limits an operation's ability to obtain economies of scale in production. However, economies of scale are available in advertising and purchasing to such giants as McDonald's. In addition, McDonald's can achieve economies from the accumulation of operating experience in thousands of

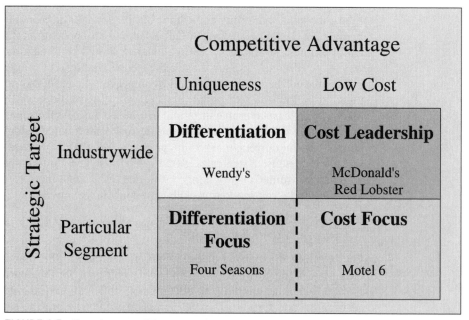

FIGURE 6.7   Generic competitive strategies
Source: M. E. Porter, *Competitive Strategy: Techniques for Analyzing Industries and Competitors* (New York: The Free Press, 1980), 39. Copyright 1980 by the Free Press.

units in many regional, national, and international markets. This accumulation of experience is called the *learning-curve effect.*

When a specialized food product, such as chicken, is the basis of a menu, purchasing economies are likely to occur. For example, a restaurant specializing in fried chicken can maintain a cost advantage over its competitors through volume purchasing and a vertically integrated supply chain. The logic of cost leadership requires a firm to be *the* cost leader, not one of several firms wanting to be cost leader. When there is more than one aspiring cost leader, competition is usually tense and price wars are likely to occur. Eventually, *the* cost leader survives.

A **differentiation** strategy relies on differentiating the product or service offering and creating something that is perceived *industry-wide* as being unique (Porter 1998). The attributes used to differentiate the firm from competitors must be important to customers. Such unique attributes can be used to build customer loyalty, which can translate into higher prices and greater profit margin. The more difficult it is to duplicate a certain attribute, the greater its benefits and the longer the firm can use it as a competitive advantage. In the hospitality industry, unfortunately, innovations are hard to come by and copycats are many. For example, when La Quinta Inns developed the limited-service hotel concept, it was unable to dominate that segment. Because of La Quinta's success, Fairfield Inns, Hampton Inns, and many others followed quickly.

It is true, nevertheless, that an innovator can gain and often maintain a significant advantage by being the first to implement a concept on a broad scale. Although there are many "Courtyard clones," Courtyard by Marriott is still the best-known, most clearly identifiable chain operating in its particular market segment. In fact, one way to succeed is to become the "industry standard." Holiday Inns, in the 1960s and 1970s, had many imitators; however, they were seen as imitators and Holiday Inns and the mix of services that they offered became an industry standard.

Within the quick-service hamburger market, Wendy's successfully differentiated itself from other hamburger chains, in its initial format, based on product, ambience, and slightly upgraded service (no self-busing). These differences supported a higher price and made Wendy's a high-profit, high-growth chain in a market that, at the time, was considered by some to be saturated. Unlike cost leadership, the differentiation strategy can be used simultaneously by more than one company to achieve success, each differentiating according to its own particular attributes.

With a **focus** strategy, a firm attempts to meet the needs of a particular market segment. A firm can achieve a competitive advantage by dedicating itself to that segment exclusively. A focus strategy can be based on cost or on product differentiation. In the luxury market, this strategy works well for Four Seasons, in conjunction with relatively higher prices. It also works in the extremely price-sensitive segment for the North American economy lodging leader, Motel 6. There is often room for several companies using a focus strategy, assuming that they choose different target segments. Case Study 6.1 illustrates one company's success in using a low-cost focus strategy.

CASE STUDY 6.1

Low-Cost Focus Strategy:
Southwest Airlines

Ever since the first Southwest Airlines flight took off in 1971 from Dallas's Love Field airport to Houston, Southwest has been known as a provider of low fares, convenient schedules, and no-frills air transportation. Southwest's mission is to provide customers with an affordable transportation alternative to the automobile. It uses secondary, less congested airports wherever possible and provides a short-haul, point-to-point, high-frequency routing system. Because of its success and continued market development, Southwest Airlines was recognized as a national carrier in 1989. Even with the airline's growth from an intrastate Texas carrier to a major airline serving more than 55 U.S. cities, its "low-cost focus" generic strategy has remained the same.

To offer low-cost flights, Southwest has had to reduce its own operational costs and enhance its operating efficiencies. The no-frills carrier does not serve meals on its flights and does not arrange connections with other airlines, which means that passengers with connecting flights on other airlines have to transport their own baggage and recheck it with the other airlines. To speed the boarding process, it does not offer premium or assigned seating. In addition, it uses only one type of plane (the Boeing

Low-cost focus strategy: Southwest
Airlines

737) to enhance maintenance efficiency. Southwest actually has the quickest on-ground turnarounds in the industry, which means more time in the air.

Southwest's marketing has been creative and reflective of its fun-loving corporate culture. "Price" has been used over the years to support the low-cost focus. As part of Southwest's recognition of its role in the transportation business, it changed its slogan from "THE Low Fare Airline" to "A Symbol of Freedom," which focuses on both low fares and access to nationwide destinations and the philosophy that Southwest is about more than air transportation. It sees itself in the business of giving people freedom to travel for whatever reason they choose. Even before the terms internal and relationship marketing became popular, Southwest practiced marketing to its employees and maintained good relationships with frequent Southwest flyers. Its chief executive officer, Herb Kelleher, cultivated a "loving, family" culture within the organization by knowing employees by name and hosting family barbecues on a regular basis. As discussed in Chapter 2, Southwest involves its most frequent flyers in the employee interviewing process—to show that Southwest treats them as part of the family.

Sources: R. C. Lewis, *Cases in Hospitality Strategy and Policy.* (New York: John Wiley & Sons, 1998); Southwest Airlines Corporation, *Southwest Airlines—A Brief History* (on-line). Web site: http://www.southwest.com/about_swa/airborne.html

Grand Strategies. To achieve long-term business objectives, a firm's efforts must adhere to a set of master strategies so that all activities are focused, coordinated, and effectively implemented. Such a master strategy is called a **grand strategy.** Growth is generally a desired goal of multiunit organizations, and often of independent operators. There are four grand strategies a company can employ to achieve its long-term growth goal, as presented in Figure 6.8.

The objective of **market penetration** is to improve sales of existing products in existing markets. Because companies using this strategy continue to offer the same products and services to the same customers, they usually become more efficient and productive. A company can grow by increasing current customers' rate of use or attracting competitors' customers. The means to achieve this can be as simple as a program to increase sales through suggestive selling of wine, desserts, or better rooms. Promotional activities can also be used to attract more frequent repeat visits or trial visits. This is the lowest-risk growth strategy. However, if a firm is already successful in its operations, this strategy probably offers the lowest rewards.

Product development is a somewhat riskier strategy than market penetration because of the costs involved. A new product can be a modification of an existing product, such as stronger coffee or thicker sauces, or a genuinely new product, such as a pita sandwich in a hamburger restaurant. When successful, such as was McDonald's introduction of breakfast to the quick-service market segment, product development can bring major advantage to the firm. However, the discouraging fact is that the vast majority of new products fail.

Another equally risky strategy is **market development.** It has greater risk than market penetration because the company may lose its market development expendi-

Bed and breakfasts use the focus strategy to differentiate themselves from other commercial lodging operations. (Photo courtesy of Barbeau House Bed and Breakfast, Lenora, Kansas.)

	Existing products/services	New products/services
Existing markets	Market penetration	Product development
New markets	Market development	Diversification

FIGURE 6.8 Growth options.
Source: H. I. Ansoff, "Strategies for Diversification." *Harvard Business Review, 35*(5) (1957): 114. Copyright 1957 by The President and Fellows of Harvard College.

Both established franchise brands and new brands, such as the Wingate Inn, offer market development opportunities. (Photo courtesy of Wingate Inns.)

tures if the effort fails. The most common market development activity is to identify new geographic markets. In hospitality, franchising is the major tool to facilitate a market development strategy. Franchisees supply the necessary investment capital and highly motivated management personnel, which solves the two major problems of market expansion—financial and human resources. A mode of market development currently getting attention from U.S. hospitality firms is expansion into other countries, as discussed in Case Study 6.2.

CASE STUDY 6.2

International Expansion in Foodservice

Most of the major areas in the world—Asia, Eastern and Western Europe, and South America—are experiencing real economic growth. Leading North American companies are moving aggressively into these markets because of domestic market saturation and intense competition. Market development represents the logical next step. More than 160 foodservice companies operate internationally. KFC operates in more than 73 countries. Domino's Pizza makes delivery in 63 international markets. Outside the United States, Dunkin' Donuts has stores in 40 countries, Hardee's is present in 11 countries, and T.G.I. Friday's has 150 restaurants in 51 countries.

McDonald's is the most aggressive foodservice company in international expansion. It already has more than 12,000 units in 119 countries outside the United States. McDonald's added 1,780 restaurants in 1999, with approximately 90 percent outside the United States. Plans for the year 2000 included adding five restaurants per day, also with the majority outside the United States. Most foodservice companies plan to expand faster in international markets than in the domestic market. Subway's projections included a total of 967 locations outside the United States and Canada by the year 2000. Wendy's had 665 international units as of May 2000.

Chain	1999–2000					
	Total	Canada	Europe	Asia Pacific	Latin America	Middle East
McDonald's	12,000+	1,100	4,421	5,055	1,405	314
Subway	2,386	1,419	143	214	249	56
Wendy's	665	300	31*	192	142	
Hardee's	107			48	4	55

*Wendy's has 31 units in Europe and the Middle East combined.

Sources: KFC Corporation. (2000). *International information* (on-line). Web site: http://www.triconglobal. com/triconroot/mainwelcome.htm; Domino's Pizza, Inc. (2000). *About us* (on-line). Web site: http://www. dominos.com/About/Index.cfm; Dunkin' Donuts, Inc. (2000). *About us: History* (on-line). Web site: http:// www.dunkindonuts.com/aboutus/?id=2; Hardee's Food Systems, Inc. (2000). *About us: Hardee's today* (on-line). Web site: http://www.hardeesrestaurants.com/abouts/index.html; T.G.I. Friday's Inc. (2000). *Company Info: T.G.I. Friday's statistics* (on-line). Web site: http://www.tgifridays.com/News/statistics.com; McDonald's Corporation (2000). *McDonald's corporate site: About McDonald's* (on-line). Web site: http:// www.mcdonalds.com/corporate/corp.html; McDonald's Corporation (2000). *About McDonald's: Investor fact sheet* (on-line). Web site: http://www.mcdonalds.com/corporate/investor/about/factsheet/index.html; McDonald's Corporation (2000). *McDonald's 1999 annual report* (on-line). Web site: www.mcdonalds.com/ corporate/inv . . . fo/annualreport/online99/mcd99ar01.htm; Subway (2000). *International Subway locations* (on-line). Web site: http://www.subway.com/web_dics/countrycount.html; Wendy's International Inc. (2000). *Restaurant locations* (On-line). Web site: http://www.wendysintl.com/international/content/loc.htm

Another method of market development is to offer services in nontraditional locations. Quick-service restaurants (QSRs) have demonstrated this approach by opening outlets in schools, college campuses, airports, shopping malls, and supermarkets. Seeking additional market segments in a current market territory can also be used to grow via market development. Usually, this involves the development of a different marketing mix to attract new market segments. For example, to supplement the patronage of weekday business travelers, special pricing can attract families to a hotel on weekends. Companies can achieve similar goals by advertising in specially targeted media.

For instance, a hotel seeking convention business for the first time may begin advertising in *Meetings & Conventions* magazine.

When new products are introduced in new markets, **diversification** occurs. The combination of new products and new markets represents the highest-risk strategy. ARAMARK's expansion, which involved entry into contract cleaning and periodical distribution, was built on existing strengths in the company. However, the diversification was risky because new products and new markets had to be developed and proven successful. The string of unsuccessful acquisitions by Holiday Inns some years ago further illustrate the risk of diversification. Holiday Inns attempted to enter the prefabricated construction, the transportation (with a bus line), and the freestanding restaurant businesses. It eventually divested itself of all of them because of the unsatisfactory returns on investment.

When using a diversification strategy, a company has to create *synergy* among different divisions so that they can complement each other and make the company's overall strength greater than the individual divisions' strengths combined. Perhaps the leading practitioner of this approach in the hospitality industry is Carlson Companies Inc. Carlson Leisure Group manages and franchises travel operations worldwide under a variety of brand names. Carlson Hospitality Worldwide operates or franchises more than 1,000 hotels, including Country Inns & Suites and Radisson Hotels Worldwide. Carlson also operates and franchises more than 560 restaurants, including T.G.I.

Synergy is the goal of Carlson Companies Inc. Country Inns and Suites, Country Kitchen, and Italianni's shown here are located together to complement each other. (Photo courtesy of Carlson Hospitality Worldwide.)

Friday's and Italianni's, which fit in well with many of its hotels. In one of its publications the company says,

> *Propelled by the synergistic relationship between hospitality service, travel agencies, and marketing, Carlson companies brings to the world marketplace a network of companies poised for global leadership in the 21st century.* (Carlson Companies, Inc. 2001)

Positioning

Positioning is the process of establishing and maintaining a distinctive place in a market for an organization and/or its individual product offerings. **Repositioning** involves changing the existing position of a business. The most successful organizations distinguish themselves from "the pack" to achieve a unique position by outperforming their competitors, thus developing a competitive advantage. The marketer's job is to identify the important attributes consumers use to distinguish one operation from another, because consumers usually choose between service offerings on the basis of perceived differences between them.

Positioning plays a crucial role in marketing strategy because it is concerned with how the company will relate to the other two key elements of the strategic triangle, customer and competition. It links market analysis and competitive analysis to internal corporate analysis (Lovelock 1996). Figure 6.9 summarizes these linkages and identifies the basic steps in finding a suitable market position. *External analysis* involves a careful study of customers and competitors, and *internal analysis* focuses on the business's objectives and capabilities.

Customer analysis is used to determine factors such as the overall level and trend of demand and the geographic location of the demand. Based on the size and potential

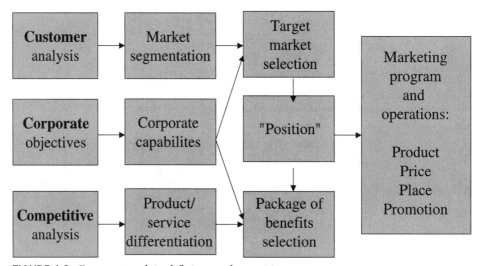

FIGURE 6.9   Forces at work in defining market position.

of different market segments, management chooses a target market or markets. *Corporate analysis* helps identify management goals and objectives, as well as internal strengths and weaknesses in resources and capabilities. Results of the analysis should assist in the selection of target market segments and benefit offerings.

Competitive analysis should include both direct and indirect competitors at the initial stage, and then focus on direct competitors. For example, a fine dining restaurant should be aware of QSRs and family restaurants in its market area because they offer indirect competition. It should, however, pay special attention to other upscale operations. The objective of this analysis is to find a competitive advantage to differentiate the business from its competitors. The outcome of these three types of analysis is the development of a market position, described in a **positioning statement** that specifies the chosen positioning strategy of the organization in the marketplace.

A good positioning statement should be concise, yet create an image for the operation, communicate the benefits offered, and distinguish the operation from its competitors. Positioning statements should be target-market specific. If an operation decides to target two different markets, a positioning statement is required for each market. Consumers in different markets evaluate the operation differently with different criteria. The operation needs different skills and capabilities to serve different markets, and the competition in different markets varies. Therefore, the business has a unique position in each market. The following are two sample positioning statements.

> *The Oak Barrel Brewery and Grills serve a market of middle-aged business and professional people and their families who live in the suburbs of metropolitan areas of 500,000 or more in population. We provide handcrafted beers from our own in-house brewery and the finest Black Angus steaks. Our employee teams provide the most personalized and friendly service in any local market area.*

> *The elegant Capital Square Hotels, located in downtown business districts, provide an "office away from the office" for frequent business travelers. Services from secretarial to client entertainment are some of the features offered to help the guests accomplish more.*

From the positioning statement, the organization can answer the following questions: "What is our product (or service concept), what do we want it to become, and what actions must we take to get there?" (Lovelock 1996). A specific plan of action using the various marketing mix elements can be developed based on the chosen position. Therefore, a company's positioning strategy determines its product, price, place, and promotion strategies. It is important to note that a positioning statement is designed for internal goal clarification, not for external communication. However, a particularly clear and succinct positioning statement may find its way into a company's advertisement.

Functional Strategies and Plans

Based on a company's generic and grand strategies and its chosen position, **functional strategies** are developed. Functional strategies are concerned with how a company will implement its overall strategies formulated at the corporate and business levels. Traditionally, each individual functional unit develops its own departmental plan with the overall company strategies in mind. However, a better approach to successfully carry out the company strategies is a cross-functional, comprehensive approach, with key functional areas working together and providing mutual support. As a result, functional strategies are designed to complement each other. Each functional area and its functional strategies represent a piece of the puzzle. When all pieces are put together, the picture represents the achievement of the overall company strategies.

For example, consider a convention hotel that has decided to use a cost leadership generic strategy and a market penetration grand strategy. Based on the strategic directions set by the corporate management, functional level personnel, including the marketing, operations, human resources, and accounting staff, work as a team to develop their respective functional strategies and plans. Because of the teamwork approach, activities in the marketing plan can help achieve accounting objectives and can be successfully accomplished by operations people. As various functional areas help each other execute their plans, the company's overall strategies are implemented more efficiently.

As characterized in Table 6.1, functional marketing focuses on short-term, specific implementation activities. The process of developing functional marketing strategies and the content of a marketing plan are discussed in the next chapter.

Strategy in Small Firms

The meaning and implementation of strategic planning in small firms, typically single-unit or family-run operations, is different from that of large, multiunit corporations. The existence of sound strategies is equally important, but the approach to them is usually less formal, and rightly so.

Small firms often fail to develop a mission statement because they operate as they "always have," serving their customers "what they like." This works well until something changes, such as the population base (through aging or migration), or new competition appears. When changes occur, businesses without plans are left wondering about what happened as profitability declines. However, an operation may develop a realistic mission statement that says,

> *We provide our guests with a needed opportunity to relax, feel important, be waited on, and experience luxury. We serve hearty steaks and roast beef to the middle-class population in the XYZ area. We are the "favorite restaurant" of our clientele and are committed to maintaining and enhancing that position.*

If business begins to slow, the mission statement provides a basis for investigation before any action is taken. Based on the mission statement, the following logical questions can be asked:

1. Is business poor because our strategy is no longer working?
    a. Is the middle-class population we rely on dwindling?
    b. Has our product mix (steaks and roast beef) lost its appeal?
    c. Has new competition replaced us as the "favorite restaurant" in our market area?
    d. Has the way we communicate with our clientele become ineffective?
    e. Is our market definition incorrect or too narrow?
2. Is business poor because of temporary, local, or broader economic trends?

These are questions of fact that can be researched without an enormous investment of money or time. An action plan can then be designed based on specifically defined problems. Thus, the mission statement guides the daily operation of the business and is the foundation for the rest of its planning.

Many small businesses do have an excellent sense of mission and strategy based on their owners' experience. The mission and strategies may not be written down, but they are carefully thought out and verbalized to employees and guests. One of the reasons for documenting the mission and strategies, however, is that it facilitates communication. A written document can also be examined, or critiqued, when the time comes to question current practices.

The process of strategy formation for small businesses is fundamentally the same as that used by large corporations, as discussed earlier. The implications for positioning strategy are also useful in a local market, but unless a small firm is showing a pattern of rapid growth, the portfolio analysis explained earlier has limited applications. However, the reasoning process employed in portfolio analysis can be used when revenue centers are used as SBUs.

Summary

Strategy can be defined as a course of action aimed at ensuring the achievement of a firm's objectives. The strategic planning process requires input from all decision-making levels: corporate, business, functional, and unit. Marketing perspectives are crucial to all levels of planning.

Strategic marketing, as compared with functional marketing, emphasizes the development of long-term strategic perspectives to direct the future focus of the business. Marketing strategies, based on an analysis of the marketing strategy triangle, are developed by a firm to differentiate itself from competitors by using its competitive advantage.

A corporation's strategic planning begins with the development of a corporate mission statement, followed by the identification of viable strategic business units based on the results of portfolio analysis. The Boston Consulting Group and the General Electric models are popular portfolio analysis techniques. A SWOT analysis is then conducted for each SBU; the results are used to form its mission statement and strategies. The three common generic strategies are cost leadership, differentiation, and focus. The grand strategies include market penetration, product development, market development, and diversification. Each SBU must identify its generic and grand strategies before a market position can be chosen and positioning statement designed.

The market position of a business should be chosen based on an analysis of its customers, competitors, and internal capabilities and resources. The positioning statement delineating the desired position should communicate the benefits offered, differentiate the operation from its competition, and create an image for the business. Based on the positioning statement, functional strategies and plans are developed.

Key Words and Concepts

Marketing strategy	Portfolio analysis	Market penetration
Strategic three Cs	Boston Consulting Group model	Product development
Competitive advantage	General Electric model	Market development
Marketing strategy triangle	SWOT analysis	Diversification
Strategic marketing	Generic strategy	Positioning
Functional marketing	Cost leadership	Repositioning
Strategic business unit (SBU)	Differentiation	Positioning statement
Mission statement	Focus	Functional strategies
Business portfolio	Grand strategy	

Resources on the Internet

The Boston Consulting Group. *http://www.bcg.com/*
Carlson Wagonlit Travel.
   http://www.carlsontravel.com
Cendant Corporation. *http://www.cendant.com*
Country Inns & Suites by Carlson.
   http://www.countryinns.com

The Economic Planning Group.
   http://www.epgcanada.com/index.htm
McDonald's. *http://www.mcdonalds.com/*
T.G.I. Friday's. *http://www.tgifridays.com*

Discussion Questions

1. What are the different levels of decision-making hierarchy in a company?
2. How are strategic and functional marketing different?
3. What is the corporate strategic planning process?
4. What are the roles of different levels of management in strategy formulation?
5. What are the roles of marketing personnel in strategy formulation?
6. How are viable SBUs identified?
7. How can SWOT results be analyzed systematically?
8. What are the generic and grand strategies discussed in this chapter?

9. What is market positioning? How should a desirable position be determined?

10. How does strategic planning differ for small firms, as compared with corporations?

References

Bonoma, T. V. (1985). *The marketing edge: Making strategy work.* New York: The Free Press.

Bower, J. L., C. A. Bartlett, C. R. Christensen, A. E. Pearson, and K. R. Andrews, (1991). *Business policy: Text and cases.* 7th ed. Homewood, IL: Richard D. Irwin.

Carlson Companies, Inc. (2001). *Consumer Solutions* (on-line). Web site: http://www.carlson.com

Hilton Hotels Corporation. (1999). *1998 annual report.* Beverly Hills, CA: Author.

Jain, S. C. (1997). *Marketing planning and strategy.* 5th ed. Cincinnati, OH: South-Western College Publishing.

Lovelock, C. H. (1996). *Services marketing.* 3d ed. Upper Saddle River, NJ: Prentice-Hall.

Pearce, J. A., II and R. B. Robinson, Jr. (1997). *Strategic management: Formulation, implementation, and control.* 6th ed. Boston: Irwin McGraw-Hill.

Porter, M. E. (1998). *Competitive strategy: Techniques for analyzing industries and competitors.* New York: The Free Press.

The Marketing Plan

When you have finished reading this chapter, you should be able to:

- Explain the importance of marketing planning.
- Describe the analysis used for marketing planning.
- Apply the importance–performance analysis.
- Determine a marketing budget using two different approaches
- Discuss the contents of a typical marketing plan.
- Develop marketing plans for hospitality operations.

This chapter discusses the development and content of the functional marketing plan. A **marketing plan** is designed to implement the strategies chosen at the corporate and strategic business unit levels. The development of a marketing plan every year is also important for independent operations, because having good strategies in place is equally crucial to their success. The following section reemphasizes the importance of planning.

Why Plan?

Given the competitive situation in the hospitality industry, the better question is "Why would any organization *not* plan?" It is easy to justify the need to plan, but in a busy operation it is also easy to make the case for a number of other activities. Sufficient staff to do all the work that managers *should* do may be hard to come by. Therefore, busy operators may find it easy to put off marketing planning to "when we have more time."

Even in some large companies in the hospitality industry, marketing planning may get only lip service or may be seen as something the advertising manager does. This low priority for planning activities can result from the dominance of operations people—which is a common occurrence in hospitality organizations. Much of the discomfort with marketing planning sensed by operations people relates to their experience with more concrete operational work requirements.

Marketing planning is sometimes frustrating, inasmuch as such planning usually takes place in an environment with many uncertainties. When a building is constructed, we expect it to look pretty much like the architect's plan. Similarly, operations people know that when they implement a cost-control program, once it is working properly, the operating costs should be close to the budgeted target. With a marketing plan, however, the only thing we can be absolutely certain of is that not all things will go as planned.

Large parts of a marketing plan may operate as projected, but unforeseen and uncontrollable events can happen that may require a change of plan. For example, the economy may go soft; unexpected competition may arise; and bad weather may ruin the sales forecast. In addition, the impact of marketing expenditures is difficult to evaluate. For instance, if there has been an improvement in sales, was it because of promotion, good weather, a rising economy, or other external factors? If the short-term effects of marketing are hard to assess, the long-term impacts of marketing activities are even more difficult, if not impossible, to measure with any certainty. For those who are unaccustomed to marketing planning, the need to measure concrete results may make them feel that marketing planning is impractical and a total waste of time.

Many operators often prefer to follow their instincts and their sense of the market. The problem with this approach is that this leaves the company in a reactive mode and put its competitors, in a very real sense, in control of its marketing planning! For example, hotel X, a competitor, has established a secretaries club. We had better have one as well. Restaurant Y offers free cocktails. Perhaps we should too. Club Z has done a lot of newspaper advertising lately. Should we do the same?

The short-run orientation puts an operation in the position of not knowing where it is going. Yet the need for marketing expenditures, even the reactive ones, does not go away. As a result, an increasing number of marketing dollars are spent just to meet the competition and the opportunity to plan for long-term impact is lost. The fact that the future is always uncertain is especially pertinent in a fragmented business such as the hospitality industry. Having a plan in place gives operators a solid starting point. Plans can always be modified if conditions change unexpectedly.

Although the long-term effects of a marketing program are hard to measure with precision, a look at the power of many trademarks in hospitality offers unquestionable proof that there *are* such things as long-term effects. Ronald McDonald is said to be the second most recognizable name, next to Santa Claus, by children. The face of Colonel Sanders appears in Tiananmen Square in Beijing, as well as in Times Square in New York. Travelers envision universal images when they hear the names Hilton and Holiday Inn. Without effective marketing strategies, these outcomes would not have happened. Therefore, the rationale for marketing planning includes the importance of marketing activities; the increasing level of competition; growing marketing

The worldwide success of American hospitality firms, such as McDonald's and Pizza Hut, is testimony to the impact of marketing and marketing planning.

costs; the need to achieve a competitive advantage; and the need to know where we are going, how we are supposed to get there, and how we will know when we are there.

Content and Development of a Marketing Plan

The order in which a marketing plan is presented varies from company to company. Figure 7.1 shows the table of contents for an annual marketing plan for a hotel property that is discussed in this section. Because a marketing plan generally covers a one-year period, considerable emphasis should be given to activities in the coming year. It is interesting to compare Figures 7.1 and 7.2, which is the table of contents for a marketing plan of a national restaurant chain. Although the latter is more detailed, the general topics covered are basically the same.

This section examines extracts from a hotel's marketing plan, along with descriptions of the appropriate content for each section in a marketing plan. This hotel, Travel Inn, is affiliated with a national franchise chain and is one of the 250 properties owned by a corporation. The property has become somewhat rundown over the years, and the general manager is concerned that it is losing its competitiveness.

Executive Summary

The executive summary is an overview of the entire document and should not be confused with an introduction section. This overview summarizes the analysis, presents key facts, and lists the plan's major recommendations:

> This property's market share has declined from the third highest to the fifth in its marketplace. To maintain volume, a special pricing campaign was introduced. However, the net operating profit decreased from $380,000 two years ago to $190,000 in the past year. A profit of $70,000 is anticipated during the coming year.
>
> The local economic environment is favorable for business-oriented hotels. However, the physical facilities of Travel Inn are in need of improvement. The professionalism of managers and employees should also be enhanced to provide high-quality service.

Executive Summary	Internal Analysis
Mission Statement	Strengths and Weaknesses
External Analysis	Market Segmentation and Positioning
Market Situation	Goals and Objectives
Customer Base	Action Plan
Competition	

FIGURE 7.1 Contents of a property-level marketing plan.

Executive Summary
Introduction
Market Assessment
  Restaurant Market Overview
  Customer Attitudes
  Competitive Environment
  Business Performance
  Mission Statement
Market Objectives and Strategies for the Year Ahead
Positioning Statement
Action Plan
  Advertising
    Role of Advertising
    Advertising Objectives
    Advertising Strategies
    Creative
      Creative Objectives
      Creative Strategies
      Rationale
    Media
      Media Objectives
      Media Strategy
      National Tactics—Timing
  Promotions
    Role of Promotions
    Promotion Objectives
    Promotion Strategies
  National Marketing Calendar
  Local Store Marketing Objectives
  Public Relations Objectives
Pricing
Product Development Priorities
Unit Expansion Program
New Territories Program
Research
  National Consumer Research Commission
  Syndicated Research Participation
  Image Research
  Consumer Perception
  Facilities
  New Product Intelligence
  Media Trends
  Competition: Media Spending and Creative Execution
  Storyboard Testing
Franchise Marketing Support System
  Structure
  Key Marketing Responsibilities
    The Franchisor
    Planning
    Advertising
      Creative
      Media Plans and Buys
      Research
      Promotion
  Franchise Support
    Regional Co-ops
    Local Franchisees
Budget

FIGURE 7.2 Contents of a marketing plan for a national restaurant chain.

Property renovation, professional training, market share development, and loyalty cultivation are the goals of Travel Inn. Specific objectives and implementation strategies are outlined for each market segment in this marketing plan. A short-term, temporary outsourcing option is proposed in the plan to provide sufficient parking and a business center for business travelers.

Mission Statement

A logical starting point of marketing planning is a business's **mission statement.** Reference to the mission statement ties the marketing plan to the overall strategy of the firm. As explained in Chapter 6, the mission statement establishes what business the company is in, what its products are, and in what markets it chooses to compete:

Travel Inn is recognized locally and regionally as a fine hospitality operation, providing guest rooms, meeting facilities, and food and entertainment in a conveniently located facility. We strive to stay competitive in the marketplace and to provide excellent products and services to our guests.

External Analysis

An analysis of its internal strengths and weaknesses and external opportunities and threats (SWOT) is conducted for the operation. Because the customers always come first and constitute an element in the external environment that can be an opportunity or a threat to the business, **external analysis** is conducted first. A discussion of the general environment within which a firm operates helps set the stage for the marketing plan. Both the macro and micro environments should be considered. However, attention will most likely be concentrated on customers and competitors in the micro environment, as well as relevant macro environmental elements in the immediate surrounding geographic area.

Market Situation. A **market analysis** should be conducted to determine the market's size and the growth trends within the market. An individual hotel typically specifies the total market size in number of rooms available, number of rooms sold, and room sales in dollar value for the last year. In addition, an assessment of the local economic outlook should be included. This assessment lists major employers and comments on any prospective new plant openings, major construction projects, or other significant factors in the local market that will increase or decrease employment and travel in the area. Any developments affecting area transportation, such as airport additions or highway improvements, should also be cited.

It is appropriate to present a brief history of the community in this section of the marketing plan and to describe the culture and traditions of the surrounding area, as well as the local political climate. Population statistics and changing demographics should also be summarized. This section may include a discussion of tourism activities, including major attractions, their attendance records, and any pertinent trend data or new developments. This information is needed by senior managers outside the property who review the plan. It is also a helpful review and summary of significant factors for the local management team:

The Travel Inn is located in a suburb of a major southeastern metropolitan area. The suburb is developing quickly with the construction of business complexes and office parks. Most families in the area are upper-middle class with middle-aged household heads. Because of the healthy local economy and growth in business development, the population is expected to increase. The shopping complex, next door to the hotel, is the largest in the region and attracts thousands of shoppers each week within a 200-mile radius. There are 1,415 hotel rooms in this suburb, with an areawide occupancy rate of 72 percent and an average daily rate (ADR) of $89.

Customer Base. An operation should have a clear understanding of its current customers via a **customer base analysis.** The characteristics of customers should be described in the marketing plan. For example, where the customers come from, the kinds of products and services they are looking for, their price expectations, and demographic and lifestyle information about them are all important. The customers' usage occasions also have significant impact on the types of products and services that will be offered. For example, a restaurant should determine whether customers are there for family entertainment, workers' lunch breaks, business dinners, or travelers' quick stops. For operations with multiple revenue centers, such as a full-service hotel, guest profiles for all major operating departments should be analyzed:

Rooms
- A large percentage of our corporate business comes from companies that receive our special local corporate rate.
- There has been a definite improvement in our sports-rate business over the past six months. We believe this segment will become stronger, because many of these guests are young families, which is a growing population.
- The rack rate business, predominantly pleasure travelers, continues to represent a relatively small portion of the business.

Functions/Meetings
- We continue to receive considerable repeat business from local companies for small meetings.
- Arbitration Services uses plenty of meeting facilities but provides little food business.
- Several monthly association dinners with meetings, weekly Rotary luncheons with meetings, and weddings and Christmas parties are held.
- Because of inadequate meeting and recreational facilities, the hotel receives minimum convention business.

Food and Beverage
- During the week, luncheon customers in Maggie's are mostly local business people and those using meeting facilities in the hotel.
- Dinner customers are primarily in-house guests, usually business travelers.
- Weekend business is predominantly local families with young children, taking advantage of the specialty buffets. This is a very value-conscious group.
- The average lounge customer is between the ages of 21 and 30 years, single, and semi-skilled. Many local business executives are also regular customers because of the Dinner Club program.

Competition. In assessing competition, the first thing to do is to identify direct and indirect competitors. **Direct competitors** include those operations that target the same markets and offer products and services similar to ours. **Indirect competitors** are those providing products or services that may be seen as substitutes for those we provide. For example, a casual theme restaurant is a direct competitor of another casual theme restaurant, and a grocery store's hot food counter is an indirect competitor of a casual theme restaurant. For properties with multiple operating departments, all direct and indirect competition should be listed for each department. Direct competitors should be described in detail. The focus should be on their strengths and weaknesses, where they have competitive advantages, and where we have the advantages. The definition of **competitive analysis** summarizes what needs to be assessed:

> *[Competitive analysis is] the analysis of factors designed to answer the question, "how well is a firm doing compared to its competitors?" The analysis goes well beyond sales and profit figures in assessing the firm's ratings on such factors as price, product, technical capabilities, quality, customer service, delivery, and other important factors compared to each of the major competitors.* (Bennett 1995)

For an individual property, considerable information on competitive operations is available from suppliers, employees, and visits to competing properties. We can identify who competitors' customers are by examining their bulletin boards with events listing or the license plates of vehicles in their parking lots. Competitors' business levels, such as occupancy rates and number of meals served, should also be noted. New unit construction by competitors, including additions or remodeling and their progress, should be monitored as well. Figures 7.3 and 7.4 are sample worksheets that can be used to assist in data collection and evaluation.

Other information likely to be reported in this section of the marketing plan includes a rate structure summary to indicate any special rates offered by competitors. All competitor data collected from market research studies should be summarized here as well. For the food and beverage competition, a description of the competitors and a comparison of menu prices should be included. In addition, this section is a good place to analyze **market share.** Table 7.1 shows the calculation of the property's fair market share. From the table, we can conclude that the Travel Inn earned (26.7 percent) slightly more than its fair share (26.5 percent) of the market sales. Properties B and C had higher occupancy rates and earned more than their fair market shares.

It is also useful to compare room sales by market segment with those of the competition. Table 7.2 makes this comparison. The summary of this table reported in the marketing plan looks like this:

> The individual corporate business is our strongest segment. However, we trailed behind competitor A on total rooms sold, and competitors A and C on the proportion of business from this market. We outperformed the local industry average on corporate groups in number of room-nights sold. However, competitor A sold even more rooms in this market and competitor B had a higher proportion of its sales from corporate groups than we did.
>
> We were the local leader in the convention segment, but this was a relatively small part of our business. Our individual pleasure traveler market was a weak spot, and for this segment we were behind the competition. The sports group segment was small but strong for us, with only competitor B selling 30 more room-nights than we did last year.

Internal Analysis

Strengths and Weaknesses. To complete the SWOT analysis, an internal audit is conducted to determine the strengths and weaknesses of the operation. **Internal analysis** is a cross-functional review and assessment of the operation's performance. Even

Name: _____

Location: _____

Number of rooms: _____

Number of employees: _____

Skills and attitudes of employees: _____

Annual occupancy: _____

Business mix:

- Individual business _____%

- Group business _____%

- Individual pleasure _____%

- Group tour _____%

Rate structure: _____
Dining facilities:

- Room service _____ yes _____ no

- Number of restaurants _____

- Number of lounges _____

- Sizes of facilities _____

- Banquet capabilities _____

- Menu types _____

- Menu prices _____

Recreational facilities:

- Swimming pool _____ yes _____ no

- Fitness center _____ yes _____ no

Auxiliary services:

- Car rental _____ yes _____ no

- Gift shop _____ yes _____ no

- Salon _____ yes _____ no

- Valet parking _____ yes _____ no

- Concierge _____ yes _____ no

Meeting facilities:

- Number of rooms _____

- Sizes of rooms _____

- Audiovisual equipment _____

Physical condition: _____

FIGURE 7.3 Competitor information worksheet.

Rate each competitor on each of the following criteria. 5 = excellent and 1 = poor

	Competitor A	Competitor B	Competitor C
Reputation			
Name recognition			
Market share			
Service quality			
Price/value perception			
Promotional effectiveness			
Sales staff			
Employee attitudes and skills			
Employee turnover			
Speed of service			
Cleanliness			
Occupancy			
Room rate			
Financial stability			
Profitability			
Leadership			
Distribution channel			
Customer loyalty			
Location			
Accessibility			
Visibility			
Parking			
Building condition			
Guest room quality			
Meeting facilities			
Food and beverage service			
Banquet facilities			
Organizational culture			
Information technology			

FIGURE 7.4 Competitor evaluation form.

though marketing is the focus, performance and capabilities in other functional areas can affect the implementation of a marketing plan. Therefore, performance in all functional areas should be analyzed.

All performance areas should be assessed and assigned a rating of major strength, minor strength, neutral, minor weakness, or major weakness to more accurately suggest a course of action for management. Figure 7.5 shows a form that can be used to facilitate this evaluation. *Major strengths* are components of an operation's unique ability to gain a competitive edge over competitors. These should be difficult-to-duplicate attributes. *Minor strengths* are areas in which performance is above average but not outstanding. Minor strengths do not help operations to attract new customers,

TABLE 7.1 Market Share Analysis

Property	Number of Rooms (A)	Room-Nights Available (B = A × 365)	Room-Nights Sold (D)	Occupancy % (F = D ÷ B)	Actual Market Share % (G = D ÷ E)	Fair Market Share % (H = B ÷ C)
Travel Inn	220	80,300	57,158	71.2	26.7	26.5
Property A	250	91,250	60,555	66.4	28.3	30.1
Property B	200	73,000	53,114	72.8	24.8	24.1
Property C	160	58,400	43,228	74.0	20.2	19.3
Total	830	302,950(C)	214,055(E)	70.6	100.0	100.0

take customers away from the competition, increase current customers' frequency of visit, or increase their spending. Minor strengths do, however, help to keep current customers and allow the operation to stay competitive.

Minor weaknesses do not present serious threats to an operation, but they prevent the operation from being as competitive as it might be. *Major weaknesses* are serious flaws that require immediate corrective action, especially when they prevent an operation from pursuing an opportunity or avoiding a threat. For purposes of classification, major strengths and major weaknesses are usually quite obvious. However, if there is any doubt about whether a particular factor should be considered as a minor strength, neutral, or minor weakness, the factor should be

TABLE 7.2 Market Segment Analysis

Market Segment	Travel Inn Rooms	%	Competitor A Rooms	%	Competitor B Rooms	%	Competitor C Rooms	%	Total Rooms	%
Individual corporate	26,181	45.8	28,294	46.7	23,857	44.9	20,931	48.4	99,263	46.4
Group corporate	13,682	23.9	14,122	23.3	12,914	24.3	8,858	20.5	49,576	23.2
Conventions	9,114	15.9	8,014	13.2	7,022	13.2	2,910	6.7	27,060	12.6
Individual pleasure travels	7,009	12.3	9,110	15.0	8,119	15.3	10,118	23.4	34,356	16.1
Sports groups	1,172	2.1	1,015	1.7	1,202	2.3	411	1.0	3,800	1.8
Total	57,158		60,555		53,114		43,228		214,055	

(1) Assign each of the following performance areas to a strength/weakness category by using

    5 = Major strength
    4 = Minor strength
    3 = Neutral
    2 = Minor weakness
    1 = Major weakness

(2) Rate the importance of each performance area with 5 = very important and 1 = not important.

	Strength/Weakness	Importance
Reputation	_____	_____
Name recognition	_____	_____
Market share	_____	_____
Service quality	_____	_____
Price/value perception	_____	_____
Promotional effectiveness	_____	_____
Sales staff	_____	_____
Employee attitudes and skills	_____	_____
Employee turnover	_____	_____
Speed of service	_____	_____
Cleanliness	_____	_____
Occupancy	_____	_____
Room rate	_____	_____
Financial stability	_____	_____
Profitability	_____	_____
Leadership	_____	_____
Distribution channel	_____	_____
Customer loyalty	_____	_____
Location	_____	_____
Accessibility	_____	_____
Visibility	_____	_____
Parking	_____	_____
Building condition	_____	_____
Guest room quality	_____	_____
Meeting facilities	_____	_____
Food and beverage service	_____	_____
Banquet facilities	_____	_____
Organizational culture	_____	_____
Information technology	_____	_____

FIGURE 7.5   Assessment of key internal factors.

placed in the less positive category to increase the chances of its being addressed and improved (Reich 1997).

   Once the strengths and weaknesses are identified, they should be prioritized according to their importance to the success of the operation; not all strengths should be equally promoted, and an operation usually cannot afford to correct all weaknesses at once. All functional performance areas can be rated on a five-point scale (5 = very important, 1 = not important). Based on their respective importance, appropriate resource allocations can be made. The **importance–performance analysis** grid in Figure 7.6 uses a graphic display to show where limited resources should be appropriated.

Each quadrant in the importance–performance analysis grid can be summarized into specific directions for operators. Areas that represent major strengths and are important to the success of an operation fall in the "Keep up the good work" quadrant and represent opportunities for operators to promote their competitive advantage. Important areas in which weaknesses are discovered demand immediate attention; therefore, this quadrant is labeled "Concentrate here." Operators should allocate resources to correct actions related to these areas. Issues of lesser importance that are performed well may be given less emphasis; resources can be better spent on "Concentrate here" items. Finally, low performance on relatively unimportant issues may be given a little more attention when resources are available; these are usually "Low priority" areas.

A strengths and weaknesses analysis and importance–performance analysis should be conducted for each individual market segment because the operation may have strength in a particular area for one segment, but not for another. For example, a hotel may have one of the best nightclubs in town; therefore, this is a major strength for the local market. However, the noise from the nightclub may interfere with some business travelers' daily routine. As a result, this is classified as a minor weakness in the business traveler market. In addition, it takes different competitive competence to be successful in different markets. For example, meeting facilities are very important to corporate groups, but leisure travelers could not care less about the size of meeting

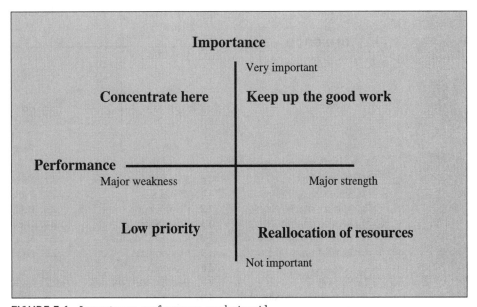

FIGURE 7.6 Importance–performance analysis grid.

rooms in a hotel. Therefore, meeting facilities are rated as unimportant for the leisure market:

> The Travel Inn raised its rates several times during the past few years. The falling occupancy rates and a recent rate reduction caused revenues to decline for two years in a row. Although the food and beverage sales increased last year, combined food and beverage revenues are off this year because of a 5.3 percent decrease in beverage sales, caused mostly by the lower occupancy. This year's monthly operating results show that occupancy has dropped as compared with that of last year in each of the previous nine months, and it is expected to further decrease for the rest of this year.

Results of the internal analysis for the individual corporate market indicate that our top priorities for improvement are service quality, cleanliness, room rate, parking, and guest room quality. Other areas needing enhancement include price/value perception, employee retention, speed of service, occupancy, leadership, visibility, building condition, and information technology.

Travel Inn's importance–performance analysis grid:

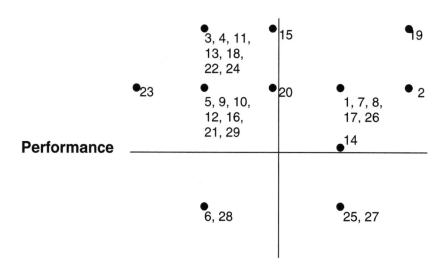

1. Reputation
2. Name recognition
3. Market share
4. Service quality
5. Price/value perception
6. Promotional effectiveness
7. Sales staff
8. Employee attitudes and skills
9. Employee turnover
10. Speed of service
11. Cleanliness
12. Occupancy
13. Room rate
14. Financial stability
15. Profitability
16. Leadership
17. Distribution channel
18. Customer loyalty
19. Location
20. Accessibility
21. Visibility
22. Parking
23. Building condition
24. Guest room quality
25. Meeting facilities
26. Food and beverage service
27. Banquet facilities
28. Organizational culture
29. Information technology

In addition to the importance-performance analysis based on predetermined criteria, a description of the physical facilities and service characteristics can provide further insight into internal strengths and weaknesses. The marketing plan is a document that will be reviewed by the organization's senior management and is therefore a good means of communicating the needs of the unit to headquarters in a constructive way:

Building Exterior: The Travel Inn is located in a low, plain, L-shaped building consisting of two stories. The area in front of the building is mainly a large parking area. The poolside area is beautifully landscaped with plenty of flowers and very attractive. However, the back and east side of the building are rather unattractive and boring. The back of the hotel also faces a poorly maintained vacant field and the rear of a roadside motel.

The main sign faces Fairway Road and can be seen from Highway 8; however, the sign is dated. The two entrance signs from King Street and Fairway Road are very small and hard to see.

Hotel Entrances: The canopy is antiquated, the lobby is small and shows signs of wear, and signage in the lobby is inadequate. There is no coat check area for the banquet hall, no outside entrance to Maggie's, and the entrance to the banquet hall is unattractive.

Main Lobby and Foyer Areas: The dining room and lounge entrances, as well as the entrance to the banquet hall, are all directly off the main lobby. When functions are held at night, it is usually very congested in this area. The noise from the entertainment lounge and from the banquet hall makes it very difficult at times to carry on proper conversations with hotel guests at the front desk. The front desk area is in need of upgrading. The reception and cashier's counter needs to be resurfaced. The key rack also needs to be removed.

Service: We have a loyal base of longtime employees who have good rapport with our guests, especially the regulars. However, their professional manner is often less polished than desired. Although we constantly try to improve their professionalism, we have a very small management staff and none of us is adequately trained to provide a good training program. Our other duties also leave us very little time for such a program.

Market Segmentation and Positioning

Based on the SWOT analysis, feasible market segments can be determined. As discussed in Chapter 4, market segments can be identified using demographic, psychographic, geographic, benefit, or behavioral characteristics. The potential market segments identified can be prioritized according to their size, profit potential, and accessibility. A description of consumers in each market should be included in this section of the marketing plan. Characteristics such as preferences and media viewing patterns can also be noted:

The individual corporate market, defined by occasion, is the most important market segment for the Travel Inn. The potential of this market is tremendous because of the growth in local business and in the economy of the area. Most reservations are made by secretaries/receptionists in local businesses. Individuals traveling for business require prompt and quality service, clean and quality rooms, and convenient parking. An increasing number of business travelers have requested Internet access in their rooms as well as a business center. Local businesses also look for the aforementioned attributes when selecting a hotel for their guests or employees. In addition, competitive room rates are considered very important.

Next, an organization must describe its desired position in each market, based on its SWOT analysis and the results of any marketing research conducted. A comparison of current and desired position can help in developing positioning or repositioning strategies. A positioning statement should be developed to convey the desired position and provide strategic guidelines for each market. The following is the positioning analysis for Travel Inn's individual business traveler market:

> Currently, Travel Inn is a follower in the individual corporate market. We would like to position ourselves as the leader in this market segment based on (1) benefits, such as value for the money and a productive environment for the guests, and (2) product features, such as quality service, clean and comfortable rooms, and accessibility to a business center. The following positioning statement distinguishes Travel Inn from its competitors:

>> Travel Inn is the local leader in serving individual business travelers' needs. Reasonable room rates, convenient parking, quality guest rooms, friendly service, and the availability of a business center are some of the unique benefits our guests receive. In such a productive environment, guests can accomplish more during their stay. Moreover, the personalized attention provided by our employees will make our guests want to come back time after time.

Goals and Objectives

Although marketing plans are usually developed for a one-year period, it is appropriate to include the long-term **goals** of the operation because these plans can be used by unit-level managers as an opportunity to communicate their aspirations for their units to senior management. The first two goals listed here for the Travel Inn require strong corporate- and district-level support. It is interesting that both of these goals involve the *product* element of the marketing mix and require action by operations people, rather than the marketing staff:

> *Goal 1:* Renovate the property so that both front and back exterior will look attractive, guest rooms will be equipped with Internet access and amenities desired by business travelers, and lobby and foyer areas will be able to accommodate crowds.

> *Goal 2:* Improve training capabilities to upgrade service professionalism.

> *Goal 3:* Increase market share in the individual corporate business segment.

Objectives are more specific than goals; they state what the organization would like to accomplish during the next year. Objectives should be result-oriented, stated in numerical terms, and time-specific. When written for a specific time frame and with a numerical target, they can be used as performance evaluation standards at the end of the year. Annual objectives can be further divided into quarterly or monthly objectives to facilitate monitoring and evaluation of accomplishments. For example, suppose that an annual objective is to increase the number of catering events from 50 to 85 a year. Considering the seasonal demand of the market, the quarterly objectives may be an additional 5 events for January through March, 15 for April through June, 5 for July through September, and 10 for October through December. Objectives should be challenging enough to motivate employees, but not so difficult to achieve as to discourage employees.

To accomplish Goal 3 in its marketing plan, Travel Inn has the following objectives:

Objective 1: Increase the number of room-nights sold to individual-corporate market by 2,000 rooms.

Objective 2: Provide a business center in the hotel by the end of June.

Objective 3: Increase the customer satisfaction index on room and service quality by 10 percent.

Action Plan

An **action plan** is a road map leading to the achievement of objectives. It describes the what, when, who, how, and the extent of each **activity.** Activities should be developed for each objective within the individual market segments. Each activity item should also have a **time line** and specify the **personnel** responsible for implementation. If a specific individual(s) is not assigned to each duty, it is likely that the task will not be completed. A deadline for each activity can help the individuals in charge to arrange their work priorities.

The next thing to include in the action plan is a **budget.** There are two ways to determine the budget allocated to marketing and related activities. One is the **top-down** approach, that is, to allocate a percentage of the revenue to marketing. For example, a catering business that had an annual sales of $1 million decided to allocate 5 percent of its revenue to marketing. Of the $50,000 available for marketing, 10 percent ($5,000) was set aside as a **contingency fund.** Contingency funds are used for handling emergencies or unexpected market conditions. An example of putting contingency fund into good use was after the 1993 flood of the Mississippi River. Many convention and visitors bureaus in the Midwestern states used all their contingency funds to convince vacationers that everything was back to normal and that they were ready for visitors. Even a year after the flood, they were still receiving inquiries from potential visitors concerning the safety and sanitation of the tourism offerings! Contingency funds can also be used when unanticipated new competitors come into the market or existing competitors become unexpectedly aggressive.

After deducting overall marketing expenses, such as the salary and benefits for a sales manager and membership dues for professional organizations, the balance of the marketing budget is usually allocated according to the size of various market segments. For example, a catering operation may receive its business from three distinct markets: business meetings, weddings, and family gatherings, which contribute to 50, 30, and 20 percent of the revenue, respectively. The balance of the marketing budget after paying overall marketing expenses is $30,000. Therefore, the business meeting market should receive $15,000, the wedding market $9,000, and the family market $6,000. Within each market segment, the budget is then allocated to the various activities.

If an operator decides to pursue another market or to focus on a particular market based on its revenue-generating potential, the allocation can be adjusted. For example, the owner of the catering business believes that the family gathering market, which includes summer picnics and holiday parties, has potential to generate a lot more business than it currently does. Upward of 20 percent of the available marketing budget can be allocated to this market for future development.

The second approach to budgeting is the **bottom-up** method. A cost is obtained for each activity planned to achieve the objectives. The total costs of all activities become the marketing budget for the coming year. If the operation cannot afford to spend that much on marketing, it means that the marketing objectives are over-ambitious and should be revised to reduce marketing expenses to a reasonable level. The Travel Inn uses this approach to determine its marketing budget for the coming year. The amount required to accomplish the objectives for the individual corporate business is $10,500:

Objective 1: Increase the number of room-nights sold to individual corporate market by 2,000 rooms.

Activity	Personnel	Time Frame	Budget
Design and print corporate rate brochure with room and service features.	Sales manager (C. Carter)	Jan.–Feb.	$2,000
Establish "Office Assistants Club" and host site visits and luncheons.	Sales staff (S. Moser)	Jan.–Feb.	$3,000
Mail brochures to nonreturning guests and local host companies.	Sales staff (S. Moser)	Mar.	$500
Establish "Corporate Partner" program, with reduced room and meeting facility rates as incentives.	Sales director (M. Galen)	Mar.	$1,500
Conduct sales blitzes with help of local college students with hospitality management major.	Sales director (M. Galen) and sales manager (C. Carter)	April–May	$1,500
Follow up on sales blitz leads.	Sales manager (C. Carter)	June–Aug.	$500
Participate in local business fair.	All sales staff	Sept.	$1,500

Summary

Marketing planning is a difficult and frustrating task because of the uncertainty it must face. Major elements of a marketing plan consider both external and internal factors, which are critical to marketing. The organization of a marketing plan varies from operation to operation. However, the overall contents include an executive summary, followed by a mission statement. Next, the external analysis consists of a description of the market situation, customer base, and competition. Internal analysis is a cross-functional assessment of the operation's strengths and weaknesses. Based on SWOT analysis, market segmentation and positioning approaches are identified and goals and objectives are developed. Finally, the action plan is completed, with specific details on activities, time line, personnel, and budget, to implement the marketing objectives.

Key Words and Concepts

Marketing plan	Competitive analysis	Activity
Mission statement	Market share	Time line
External analysis	Internal analysis	Personnel
Market analysis	Importance–performance analysis	Budget
Customer base analysis	Goals	Top-down
Direct competitors	Objectives	Contingency fund
Indirect competitors	Action plan	Bottom-up

Resources on the Internet

Business Advisor, Deloitte and Touche, LLP.
   http://www.dtonline.com/ba/ba.htm
Business Resource Center.
   http://www.morebusiness.com/
Kansas Rural Tourism.
   http://www.oznet.ksu.edu/kansastourweb/

Marketing Plan Pro.
   http://www.palo-alto.com/ps/mp/
U.S. Small Business Administration.
   http://www.sba.gov/

Discussion Questions

1. Why are many people not excited about being involved in marketing planning? Why is such planning important?

2. What elements are considered in an analysis of external factors affecting marketing? In an analysis of internal factors?

3. How should an importance-performance analysis be performed? What do the four quadrants in the importance-performance grid represent?
4. What are the main elements of a marketing plan?

5. How should goals and objectives be written?
6. What should be included in an action plan?
7. How should the marketing budget be determined?

References

Bennett, P. D., ed. (1995). *Dictionary of Marketing Terms.* 2d ed. Chicago: American Marketing Association.

Reich, A. Z. (1997). *Marketing Management for the Hospitality Industry: A Strategic Approach.* New York: John Wiley & Sons.

8

The Hospitality Product

(Mark Ballogg © Steinkamp/Ballogg Chicago. Photo courtesy of Lettuce Entertain You Enterprises, Inc., Brasserie J. in Chicago.)

When you have finished reading this chapter, you should be able to:

- Describe the main elements of the hospitality service offering.
- Explain the role of environment in service transactions.
- Identify elements of a restaurant concept.
- Discuss the role of branding in hospitality marketing.
- Illustrate various types of branding used in the hospitality industry.
- Explain product life cycle and its implications for hospitality marketing.
- Analyze the importance of new products in hospitality marketing.

The Hospitality Marketing Mix

This chapter focuses on the hospitality *product*. The next five chapters discuss these other three elements of the **marketing mix**—place, price, and promotion. Before considering any one element of the mix, it is important to understand why the marketing mix is a necessary concept. A marketing mix, like a football team, calls for a collaborative effort among players, with each member contributing to success in a different yet important way.

Some operators in hospitality see their products as *the* variable to concentrate on. Others think that the key to success is to "get out and sell." These points of view, the product and sales orientations examined in Chapter 1, are not wrong, but only partly right. It *is* necessary to have the right products and services; it *is* essential to make consumers aware of such offerings. But neither of these alone, nor even both of them together, is sufficient for the success of an operation. Price and place of offering must also be considered. The key to understanding the marketing mix concept, and to understanding other marketing concepts, is the consumer. The entire mix is necessary for success, because all elements of the mix are important to guests.

The discussion of marketing mix begins with the product, because the quality of product and service is a central concern. In examining the product element of the marketing mix, it is important to keep in mind the complexity of the hospitality offerings. The term *product* is generally used for the sake of simplicity. However, it is important to remember that product is made up of both goods and services, which are inextricably mixed.

The Service Offering

A hospitality service is a bundle of features and benefits (Grönroos 1990). The **service offering** has three elements: (1) a core benefit, (2) essential facilitating services, and (3) competitive supporting services, as illustrated in Figure 8.1.

The Core Benefit

The **core benefit** is the generic function that a product provides for its guests. For an operation, it is "the reason for being on the market" (Grönroos 1990). For example, a hotel's core benefit is a night's lodging. For a resort, it is both lodging and some combination of recreation and relaxation. A restaurant's core benefit is the provision of nourishment and a pleasant social experience.

Facilitating Services

Facilitating services are absolutely essential to an operation. Without facilitating services, delivery of the core benefit becomes impossible. In a hotel, the absence of a

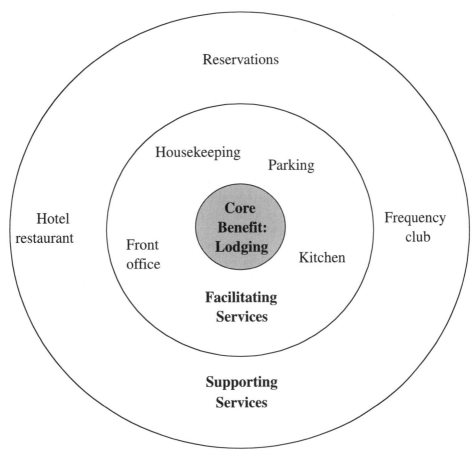

FIGURE 8.1 Three elements of the basic service offering in a hotel.
Source: Adapted from C. Grönroos, *Service Management and Marketing* (Lexington, MA: Lexington Books, 1990), 77. Copyright 1990 Christian Grönroos.

front desk or housekeeping can make the hotel's operation impossible. In a restaurant, a kitchen provides a facilitating service; without it, the operation cannot function. For a resort, recreation facilities are an essential facilitating service. In addition to being essential, facilitating services can be arranged in such a way that they can also be used to differentiate the operation from its competitors. An example is a restaurant that has not just a kitchen but one that provides exceptional cuisine, or perhaps an open kitchen with display cooking.

Facilitating goods are also necessary to the success of an operation. The availability of raw food ingredients is clearly essential. Linen and appropriate furnishings are necessary to a hotel, as is a parking lot for travelers arriving by car. All of these are goods and services that facilitate the delivery of the core benefit.

Supporting Services

Supporting services are not essential to providing the core benefit, but are critical to *marketing* the operation. Supporting services are used to differentiate an operation from its competitors. For example, a restaurant is not a necessary component of a hotel, but the presence of a restaurant can be used to differentiate one property from another. For example, Marriott Hotels offer a variety of foodservices at each hotel property, whereas the company's Courtyard by Marriott properties offer only limited foodservice and Fairfield Inns offer no foodservice. The availability of foodservice is used, then, to differentiate the Marriott hotel products from each other and from other lodging products.

One of the most powerful supporting services in lodging is the reservation system. The convenience, courtesy, and accuracy of a hotel chain's reservation service are important in differentiating one chain from another. The mere availability of a reservation service, however, may no longer be a powerful differentiation factor because reservation services have become so common. Another supporting service offered by most hotel chains and an increasing number of restaurants is membership in a frequent traveler or frequent diner club. This service is intended to bind customers to an operation.

A short transaction time and speed of service are facilitating services of a drive-thru restaurant. (Photo courtesy of Back Yard Burgers Inc.)

Supporting goods are required to maintain an operation's supporting services. For example, membership cards and correspondence are essential for the frequent traveler or diner club service, and reservation confirmations are needed for the reservation system.

To summarize, the basic service offering to guests includes a core benefit, or the generic product, such as lodging or nourishment. The core benefit, however, requires facilitating services, such as front desks and housekeeping, to make delivery of the core benefit possible. Supporting services, such as a frequency club, are critical to the marketing of the product because they differentiate the product offering from those of competitors.

Physical Environment: Managing the Evidence

Because what hospitality operations offer is an experience, the environment in which it takes place is a key part of the product. In a special way, the physical setting is a representation of the experience offered. The perception of a product is "shaped to a large extent by the things that the consumer can comprehend with his five senses— tangible things. But a service itself cannot be tangible, so reliance must be placed on *peripheral* clues" (Shostack 1977). Guests often perceive the apparent luxury or efficiency in an operation as a representation of the reality they experience. A disorderly restaurant or a worn and shabby lobby can also represent the guests' experience. The following sections consider the physical appearance of the exterior first and then the interior, following the usual sequence of guests' experience.

First Impression: The Exterior

A family is driving down a road. Everyone is hungry and ready to stop. A brightly lit shopping area appears, with many signs and stores. Where will the family stop? In just a moment, a decision will be made. Perhaps they will choose the bright red and blue Bob Evans Farms. Maybe the Golden Arches, with its familiar playground, will attract their attention. Or the Long John Silver's nautical theme may catch the eye. Chances are that the visual appearance of the various operations will strongly influence the decision.

If an operation has been properly designed, customers should be able to tell the types of services and products it offers by viewing the exterior. For example, by looking at a Red Lobster restaurant's exterior, a person should conclude that it is a seafood restaurant with a casual atmosphere. The building's exterior design and landscaping must complement the image intended. Clean parking lots imply an efficient operation, perhaps even the cleanliness of the kitchen. Even trash receptacles should be designed to blend with the building design.

Lasting Impression: The Interior

The place in which service is provided is part of the **service delivery system** discussed in Chapter 2. In many ways, the service delivery system is a stage setting (Lovelock 1996). To create the desired impression, or to give the desired cues about the nature of the service to take place there, the design of the interior sets out to achieve certain desired effects, called **atmospherics.** Atmospherics can be defined as the conscious design of a space to create certain effects on buyers. More specifically, atmospherics is the effort to design buying environments to produce specific emotional effects in the buyer to enhance the probability of a purchase (Schmitt and Simonson 1997).

Atmospherics are also defined as the resulting effects of such an effort, and as such have three functions in marketing an environment (Schmitt and Simonson 1997). First, atmospherics are an *attention-creating* mechanism. Color, sound, and motion can be used to make an operation attractive. Second, atmospherics send a *message* about the quality of experience offered. Finally, atmospherics affect the guests' feelings, creating a sense of excitement or serenity, for example. Atmospherics go beyond mere visual appearance. In fact, they involve four of the five senses:

Sight: Designers create a visual effect with color, brightness or dimness, size, and shape.

Sound: The sound of water in a fountain or of soft (or brash or loud) music says a great deal to the guests about where they are and how they are supposed to feel.

Smell: Nonsmoking rooms offer an odor-free environment to the hotel guests. Some restaurants arrange to pipe the odor of baking bread into guest areas; others spread the scent of barbecue near an entrance.

Touch: Luxurious linen napkins and tablecloths are a hallmark of fine dining restaurants. Extra-thick bath towels and deep-pile carpets support the sense of luxury in elegant hotels.

Atmospherics provide a summary statement of the experience offered by an operation. They offer visual, and often auditory and touchable, cues to the guests' experience. Atmospherics also reinforce the food and service (or rest and leisure in a hotel room) experience during a visit. Atmospherics often linger as memories, long after the selected menu items have been forgotten.

Manipulating the Environment

The service interaction setting provides important cues that are, or should be, deliberately introduced by an operation's design. Table 8.1 shows how environmental cues may be manipulated to achieve particular environmental effects.

Experience in hospitality operations clearly indicates the importance of keeping the décor current. Foodservice designs become obsolete in an increasingly shorter period of time as customers constantly look for new and different experiences. In the hotel business, décor packages for franchisees are under constant review and are a major subject

The atmospherics in a restaurant provide guests with important clues as to the kind of experience available. (Mark Ballogg © Steinkamp/Ballogg Chicago. Photo courtesy of Lettuce Entertain You Enterprises, Inc. Mon Ami Gabi in Las Vegas.)

of negotiation at franchise renewal time. In foodservice operations, experience suggests that even though menu and service style are the foundation of a restaurant concept, changes in décor are of major importance in any revitalization program. For example, when menu and service have not been changed but, through remodeling the atmosphere has been altered, the consumers' perception of the dining experience may become quite different. In contrast, when food and service have been changed but no remodeling has taken place, consumers' perception of the operation may stay the same.

Casinos are known to use environmental psychology in designing casino floors. For example, most casino carpets have busy patterns to minimize the idle time visitors may spend staring at the floor. Instead, their attention is attracted by the sight, sound and even smell, of gaming devices—slot machines and tables. Studies have shown that purple slot machines attract more women players, and particular scents given off by slot machines can keep the players betting for longer periods of time (Berko 1996). Many casinos have also replaced bar stools with comfortable chairs to keep players in front of gaming tables longer.

Supporting Cues. In addition to décor, **supporting cues** are used to manipulate the environment. Many restaurants use employee uniforms to support a certain theme.

TABLE 8.1 Achieving Atmospheric Effects	
To Create a Sense of Privacy	**To Encourage Turnover**
◆ Use high-backed booths instead of banquettes to reduce visual distraction	◆ Use banquette or table seating.
◆ Reduce lighting to limit visual contact.	◆ Permit high noise levels by using reflective surfaces.
◆ Use sound-absorbing material for acoustic control.	◆ Use smooth, hard surfaces for seating and tabletops.
◆ Background music can help to diffuse other noise.	◆ Warmer room creates sense of crowding, encourages turnover.
◆ Lower ceiling over perimeter seating.	◆ Brightly lit architectural surfaces tend to move people.
◆ Use varying levels in a large room to define smaller areas.	◆ Bold, primary colors encourage turnover.
◆ Source of illumination (candles) between customers will draw them together.	
◆ Muted, subtle colors create a restful effect.	
To Direct Movement	**To Create Sense of Movement/Excitement**
◆ Use columns, pillars, spindles on tops of booths or other vertical elements to exaggerate movement and encourage specific circulation patterns.	◆ Use vertical elements to break up appearance of large room that may otherwise look like a sea of tables and chairs.
◆ Use different patterned floor covering for aisle areas.	◆ Raise light level.
	◆ Permit higher sound level.

Source: Adapted from R. S. Baraban, "The Psychology of Design," *Proceedings, Chain Operators Exchange* (Chicago: The International Foodservice Manufacturers Association, 1984). Copyright 1984 International Foodservice Manufacturers Association.

Tabletops, including china, glassware, silverware, salt and pepper shakers, and so forth, may be used to support a contemporary theme or reflect baroque luxury. Graphics integrate wall and menu designs, directional signs, the operation's logo, and communication pieces, such as its advertisements and newsletter, to create a unified image.

The Concept as Product

Hospitality operations, such as KFC and Courtyard by Marriott, have been referred to as "concepts." This section explores the meaning of concepts in hospitality in more depth and considers **concepts as products.** A hospitality concept is the total offering provided to guests. From guests' points of view, a concept is an *experience.* From the company's perspective, a concept is an *operating system.* This operating system and its benefits are offered to individual guests for their purchase. The concept is also offered to prospective franchisees as a business opportunity that they may gain the right to operate for their own benefit. For a franchise product to be successful, it must provide a proven business operating format, a substantial marketing program, and the field supervision necessary to succeed. The difference between an idea and a concept can be summarized in that a concept is an idea that can be sold to guests at a profit because its core benefit is of value to them.

Restaurant Concepts

A restaurant concept, as it is offered to guests, includes five elements:

1. *Menu.* The range can be from a single item, such as ice cream or donuts, to a full menu, including appetizers, salads, soups, entrées, and desserts.
2. *Food production strategy.* Some operations rely almost completely on preprepared items, such as ready-to-cook hamburger patties, french fries, and other convenience foods. Other restaurants, such as T.G.I. Friday's, prepare everything from scratch on the premises. There is a wide variety of combinations between these two extremes.

Italianni's restaurant can function as a part of a hotel or as a freestanding operation. (Photo courtesy of Carlson Hospitality Worldwide.)

3. *Service.* A whole range of service options, both formal and informal as well as self-service, are used.

4. *Pricing.* Price ranges from less than a dollar for an ice cream cone to hundreds of dollars for a dinner with wine.

5. *Décor/ambience/environment.* Some operations, such as quick-service restaurants (QSRs), have a clean, functional décor, ambience, and environment. Others are elegant luxury operations. And there are the casual but comfortable varieties in between. Some operations have a noisy, energetic atmosphere that targets younger consumers, whereas others offer a quiet dining environment designed to appeal to more mature patrons.

The range of possibilities in concept is suggested in Table 8.2. Operators can change appropriate elements of the concept to tailor their units to the particular needs of their target audiences. The continuing success of new concepts attests to the guests' eagerness to try new specialty restaurants in their search for diversity. Signature items, foods that are interesting and eye-catching, can be important in setting a concept apart from others. Food bars, such as breakfast bars, salad bars, and dessert bars, have been successfully introduced as signature products that help an operation to develop an image of bounteousness, choice, and value.

Hotel Concepts

Lodging concepts are traditionally divided into two main groups, full service and limited service. Each of these is further divided by price and service levels. The dominant

TABLE 8.2 Concept Variability

Menu	Food Production + Strategy	+ Service	+ Price	Decor/Ambience/ + Environment	= Concept
Basic hamburger	+ Portion and finish fabricated product	+ Self/drive-thru	+ Low	+ Basic	= Wendy's
Upscale hamburger	+ Fabricated on premises (ground beef)	+ Self	+ Mid	+ Casual	= Fuddrucker's
Gourmet pizza	+ On premises	+ Full	+ High	+ Chic	= Spagos
Varied	+ From scratch— all fresh	+ Casual server	+ High	+ Trendy	= T.G.I. Friday's
Individualized; limited choice; changes frequently	+ From scratch on premises	+ Formal	+ Very high	+ Individualized, usually formal or ethnic	= haute cuisine (Côte Basque)

Source: Adapted from R. N. Paul, "Emerging Concepts: Picking the Winners," *Proceedings, Chain Operators Exchange* (Chicago: International Foodservice Manufacturers Association, 1984). Copyright 1984 International Foodservice Manufacturers Association.

concept for many years was the *basic full-service property*. Because of escalating costs, the rates in these hotels, in most locations, often no longer represent a value. Full-service properties positioned above this level include the upscale segment occupied by chains such as Hilton Hotels, Marriott Hotels, and Sheraton Hotels, as well as the luxury segment that includes the Four Seasons and The Ritz-Carlton.

The basic full-service property is gradually being displaced by *limited-service concepts* that offer little or no foodservice and few of the traditional hotel services, such as a bell staff. Fairfield Inns and Hampton Inns are well-known brands in this group. Holiday Inn, which until recently has typified the declining basic full-service hotels, developed its own limited-service concept, Holiday Inn Express. Holiday Inn has also developed more targeted subbrands in the midmarket and a separate identity for its more upscale Crowne Plaza brand. The basic full-service properties, however, remain as cornerstones in many small towns and midsize cities, where they continue to be the premier lodging properties in those communities.

All-suite properties and the extended-stay concept are recent innovations. They were designed mainly to meet the needs of business travelers who desire the extra space of a suite and the convenience and facilities of an extended-stay hotel.

Branding

Branding is seen as a *product* characteristic, because a brand is associated in the consumer's mind with the product it represents. Although advertising has a significant influence on consumers' image of a brand, it is ultimately their experience with the product that determines the brand's success. Even though branding serves basically the same purpose in hospitality as in other kinds of marketing, the role and importance of branding are undergoing significant changes and achieving a new prominence in hospitality. This section discusses some of the recent developments in the use of branding in the hospitality industry, but first considers the major functions of branding.

Branding uses words, symbols, designs, or a combination of these, to establish the *identity* of an operation in the consumer's mind. Brands have played a significant role in the hospitality industry since the beginning of the twentieth century, when hotels like Statler and Ritz began to associate a number of operations in different cities with their brand names. In foodservice, Howard Johnson and Stouffer's are two of the earliest brand names. Since the 1950s branded chains have played a growing role in both lodging and foodservice. Today the use of brand names is in another period of exploding growth.

If an operation achieves superior performance, the identity established by the brand helps to *enhance the image* and raise the profile of the operation. The brand image also *protects the operation from competition*, particularly if it is supported by a strong marketing communications program. Foodservice brands, such as McDonald's, KFC, and Pizza Hut, are among the best-known brand names not only in North America but also around the world. Operations of the same brand can also take advantage of *economies of scale* in name recognition, advertising, purchasing, reservations, and a number of other areas.

Basic full-service properties are being challenged by limited-service operations, such as the Holiday Inn Express. (Photo courtesy of Holiday Inn Express.)

In addition, brands can be used to *segment markets.* The first hotel company to see the value of brand segmentation, in the early 1970s, was the French group Accor (the present owner of Motel 6). A more recent development is Marriott's use of branding. With its Fairfield Inn brand, Marriott targets a price-sensitive segment. Courtyard by Marriott reaches a more upscale segment prepared to pay for limited service beyond a clean, comfortable room. Marriott Hotels serve travelers in downtown areas and other locations, where higher rates are charged and more hotel services are expected. Residence Inn was designed to attract the extended-stay market. Thus, Marriott's brands span most segments of the lodging market.

Brands also help with the *introduction of new products.* When Holiday Inn decided to enter the limited-service lodging market, the name Holiday Inn Express for its "new" product (often older properties converted to the new concept) drew on the reputation built up over the years by the Holiday Inn name. Figure 8.2 summarizes the advantages of branding.

Brand equity is the value that gradually builds up in a brand. Brand equity may be thought of as a reward that accumulates for a company over time for satisfying customers. Superior advertising and other marketing communications can help establish brand equity, but not in the absence of good operating performance. One measure of brand equity, or *goodwill* in accounting terms, is the premium over the book value for its physical assets a brand can bring when it is sold. Another measure is consumers' recognition of the brand. As noted, brand equity was part of Holiday

Identification of operation
Enhancement of image
Protection from competition
Economies of scale
Facilitating market segmentation
Easing introduction of new products

Building brand equity and brand loyalty

FIGURE 8.2 Advantages of branding.

Inn's advantage when it launched Holiday Inn Express. Case Study 8.1 illustrates the value that can be achieved by brand names.

CASE STUDY 8.1

What's in a Name? Brand Equity

Consumer recognition means value for established brands. Cendant Corporation has thoroughly demonstrated the benefits of branding. The *Wall Street Journal* has stated:

> In a celebrity conscious world, brand names, even aging ones, still have cachet and one can do very well exploiting consumers' fondness for the familiar.

Cendant began its rise to the largest hotel franchising group in 1990 when its president, Henry Silverman, acquired the franchising rights to Ramada and Howard Johnson. In 1992, HFS (the predecessor of Cendant) purchased the then-bankrupt Days Inns. In the same year, the company went public, with its stock traded on the New York Stock Exchange. Since then, Cendant has acquired a number of additional hotel brands and has developed one new brand, Wingate Inn. In 1994 the company began acquiring franchising companies in other business lines. It presently owns three real estate franchise companies and Avis, the car rental company. Cendant defines its customers as its franchisees and acts as their brand manager, handling marketing, reservation services, and quality maintenance.

Silverman sees synergy between his mix of brands. As the world's largest hotel franchisor, Cendant can achieve substantial purchasing economies for its franchisees. According to the *Wall Street Journal,* one of the reasons for Silverman's interest in Avis was its reservations network. Cross-marketing arrangements have been made between lodging brands and real estate brands. For example, Century 21 realtors have discount cards for Cendant hotels and Ramada guest folios tout the advantages of using Century 21.

With a stable of "household names," Cendant is reportedly exploring ways to continue its acquisition of franchising companies.

Sources: J. Bigness and K. Blumenthal. (1996). Brand central: Buying Avis would fit unusual business plan of growing HFS Inc. *Wall Street Journal,* 4 June, A1, A8; Cendant Corporation. (1999). *1998 Annual Report.* Author.

Brand loyalty, a goal of branding, can be defined as the degree to which a consumer consistently purchases the same brand within a product class (Bennett 1995). On a basic level, branding achieves *consumer recognition.* Prior to its achieving recognition, consumers do not even know that such an operation exists. Building on recognition with successful operations and continued marketing, a brand can achieve *consumer preference.* Preference suggests that consumers, given a choice, will select the preferred brand over one that is not as familiar. However, guests probably will not go very far out of their way if an acceptable alternative or a less expensive item is available more conveniently. The highest level of brand loyalty is *consumer demand,* whereby consumers insist on a particular brand and make a significant effort to follow that purchase decision and may even pay a premium price (Hesket, Sasser, and Hart 1990).

Types of Branding

As the practice of branding became more common and important in the hospitality industry, variations of branding began to appear. Operations can be branded, of course, but so can individual products or ingredients. Some of the variations of branding are discussed in the following paragraphs.

Umbrella Branding and Subbranding. Although not all food products on a QSR menu are given the distinction of their own brand names, the practice of item subbranding is becoming increasingly common. For example, Burger King is the **umbrella brand** and the Whopper is the **subbrand;** McDonald's is the umbrella brand and the Big Mac is the subbrand. Table service restaurants are also branding house specialties and granting them the treatment of a separate subbrand. An example is Chili's Awesome Blossom.

Ingredient Branding. As competition heats up, companies go beyond their own proprietary brand names to incorporate other companies' branded items on their menus to achieve *category credibility.* **Ingredient branding,** the use of other companies' branded products as ingredients, is becoming increasingly popular and gives us some insight into the power of branding to establish an image of quality and distinctiveness. For example, Hyatt Hotels room service menus include Hillshire Farm and Oscar Meyer products. T.G.I. Friday's serves Jack Daniels' Grill as a featured menu item. United Airlines offers Starbucks coffee. Burger King has introduced Cini-minis, by Pillsbury, for breakfast.

Many local residents call this colocation of KFC, Pizza Hut, and Taco Bell the "Ken-Taco-Hut."

The colocation of Papa John's Pizza and Blockbuster Video makes sense because the traffic they each bring provides desirable exposure for the other store. Consumers at one may "pick up" something from the other store because of the convenience.

Cobranding. This practice, also called **colocation,** involves locating two noncompeting brands in one operation. For example, Wendy's and Tim Hortons (a Canadian donut chain) shared premises, particularly on expressways in Canada, for many years before Wendy's purchased the Tim Hortons chain with the purpose of expanding into more colocations. Some Taco Bell and KFC restaurants are also in one location. In **cobranding,** the two brands are often in quite different fields of retailing. For instance, it is common for a gasoline station and a QSR to share a site. Sometimes a third retail operation, a convenience store, is also located in the same building.

In the lodging industry, operators are increasingly willing to locate national brand-name restaurants on their premises. Some Marriott Hotels have a Pizza Hut outlet at one end of the lobby. Carlson Companies has developed travel brands that are planned to fit well with each other. Case Study 8.2 profiles the Carlson operations. The purpose of cobranding is to derive synergy from the presence of the two or more concepts. Each draws some clientele of its own, and each can serve the needs of the guests patronizing the other operation.

CASE STUDY 8.2

Cobranding Prototype: Lodging and Foodservice

Carlson Hospitality Worldwide has utilized the cobranding concept in many locations. The cobranding usually involves a Country Inns & Suites facility and a T.G.I. Friday's or an Italianni's restaurant. The restaurant offers significant synergies with the hotel.

Country Inns & Suites is a fast-growing midtier chain that has planned a total of 300 locations worldwide by 2000. It has developed a strong U.S. presence and has locations in North America, Europe, Asia, and Central America. Country Inns & Suites operations target both business and leisure travelers and are often located near business parks and local attractions. The brand is attracting an increasing number of first-time guests, particularly among U.S. corporate travelers.

T.G.I. Friday's is the first American casual dining chain, with the highest per-unit sales volume of any casual dining restaurant chain. Distinctive T.G.I. Friday's features include red and white awnings, a blue exterior, and its famous logo. It offers a comfortable, relaxing environment and innovative menu items, including pizzadillas—a Mexican-pizza-like quesadilla. It has also been credited with inventing "potato skins" and has popularized many items, such as frozen and ice cream drinks.

Italianni's, a concept developed on the basis of two years of market research by T.G.I. Friday's, is an Italian-American lunch and dinner house. It features "shared dining"—platters are passed around the table by guests. It also prides itself on an extensive wine list, which includes more than 25 varieties offered by the glass. The dining room has a warm atmosphere, enhanced by the aroma of garlic bread. The menu includes original creations, such as Salmon Oreganato, as well as traditional classics, such as spaghetti and meatballs.

Carlson is not new to cobranding. The company's Radisson Hotels have colocated with T.G.I. Friday's. The Carlson Hospitality Worldwide family also includes Regent International Hotels; AquaKnox, Star Canyon, Friday's Front Row, Friday's American Bar, Timpano Italian Chophouse, the Samba Room, and Taqueria Canonita restaurants; and Radisson Seven Seas Cruises. Other affiliated Carlson companies are the Carlson Leisure Group, Carlson Wagonlit Travel, and Carlson Marketing Group.

Sources: T.G.I. Friday's Inc. (2001). *T.G.I. Friday's Worldwide: Carlson Restaurants Worldwide Inc. files for initial public offering* (on-line). Web site:http://www.tgifridays.com/News/ipo.htm; T.G.I. Friday's Inc. (2001). *T.G.I. Friday's Worldwide: Carlson Restaurants Worldwide Inc.* (on-line). Web site:http://www.tgifridays.com/News/crw_bg.htm

Multiple Branding. In an overbuilt hotel industry, such as in the United States during the late 1980s, operators have found that a larger hotel can achieve higher occupancies in some markets by dividing itself into two brands. For example, a 300-room hotel in Fort Worth, Texas, was converted into a 201-room Clarion Hotel (an upscale Choice Hotel brand) and a 99-room Comfort Inn (a limited-service Choice Hotel brand). In Houston, a portion of a former Holiday Inn was converted into a full-service Days Inn, and its six-story tower became an 89-room Hampton Inn (Bond 1992).

Family Brands and Line Extensions. **Family brands,** in manufactured goods, are brands that are used on several products by one company. For example, Sony sells many electronic products under the Sony brand name. A **line extension** refers to the development of a related product aimed at another segment of the general market for the brand as part of the market development effort. In hospitality, line extensions and family branding usually go hand in hand.

Holiday Inn, for example, operates several related lodging products and most of its products carry the family name, Holiday Inn. Holiday Inn is using these extensions of its product line to reach different market segments. SunSpree Resorts target vacationers by offering activity programs and enhanced swimming pools. The Holiday Inn Select properties target executives and other business travelers with business services and meeting facilities. Holiday Inn Family Suites Resorts are designed for families for business or leisure. Holiday Inn Express is a limited-service product targeting rate-sensitive travelers. These are either horizontal or downward line extensions from the original Holiday Inn brand. The difficulty of moving up the market with a line extension is suggested by Holiday Inn's experience with its Crowne Plaza brand. When the upscale, full-service Crowne Plaza hotels were introduced, the Holiday Inn Crowne Plaza brand was used. Because of consumers' perception of Holiday Inn as a basic, full-service hotel, they were not receptive to this upscale brand that carried the Holiday Inn name. The company finally removed "Holiday Inn" from the Crowne Plaza product name.

Ramada also uses the family brand as its original brand, Ramada Inn, and on its line extensions, Ramada Plaza Hotel and Ramada Limited. As mentioned earlier, Marriott associates its lodging brands by adding the Marriott name to Fairfield Inn, Court-yard, Residence Inn, and TownePlace Suites. The advantage of family branding is that each product can benefit from the promotion mounted by all the others and by the company's overall successful operations.

Individual Brands. One of the most successful companies in foodservice, Tricon Global Restaurants, Inc., chooses to operate its concepts under unique brands: KFC, Pizza Hut, and Taco Bell. KFC and Taco Bell are the leaders in their respec-tive, and quite different, QSR segments, and Pizza Hut is principally a limited-menu table service chain. Cendant Corporation, one of the biggest franchisors in hospitality, has also decided to keep **individual brands** distinctive. Hospitality op-erations under the franchise systems of Cendant Corporation include Ramada, Howard Johnson, Days Inn, Super 8, Travelodge, Villager Lodge, Knights Inn, Wingate Inn, and Avis car rental. Case study 8.3 describes the development of a new brand by the Cendant Corporation.

CASE STUDY 8.3

Birth of a New Brand

The first new-construction-only hotel brand in more than 10 years, Wingate Inn, got its start as a result of the interest expressed by franchisees of HFS, Inc. (the predecessor of Cendant Corporation) in a new-build, midpriced, limited-service product. Rising occupancies and average rates in the hotel business nationally accelerated the devel-opment of this new brand. The first three Wingate Inns opened less than 18 months after the announcement of this new brand.

Market research, consisting of focus groups and individual interviews, was aimed at three target audiences: (1) frequent business travelers who had experience in com-petitive properties, principally Courtyard by Marriott and Hampton Inns, (2) franchisees of other HFS brands, and (3) developers. The result was a hotel designed to please those who would use the hotel and those who would have to finance and build it.

According to research, business travelers spend two to five hours a day working in their hotel rooms. In the initial stage of Wingate Inn development, five room designs were considered, but traveler focus groups rejected some as too officelike and others as not suitable for work. The final plan separates working and leisure areas with an arch. For work, a large, well-lighted desk and an executive swivel chair are provided. Each room has a two-line desk phone with dataport, speaker, conference, and voice mail capabilities, as well as a cordless phone. Each hotel has a board room and two small meeting rooms and provides 24-hour access to a business center. Free local calls and no surcharges on long-distance calls eliminate a complaint of frequent business travelers.

To attract leisure travelers, guest room amenities include a recliner chair, or a chair with an ottoman, and a 25-inch television with remote control, an alarm clock radio, and a coffee maker. Guest rooms are 12 by 28 feet, approximately 17 percent larger than an average hotel room. Each hotel offers a complimentary breakfast (but no other foodservice), an exercise room, and a hot tub. Children stay free with traveling families.

Wingate prides itself on its technology. The hotel offers automated guest check-in without assistance. At either self check-in or at the front desk, the swipe of a credit card retrieves the reservation, verifies credit, assigns the room, and produces an electronic guest room key—all in roughly 15 seconds. The speed of transaction and availability of self-service strike at another common complaint of business travelers, long lines at check-in and check-out.

Developers and potential franchisees are pleased with the simplicity of design, which features a rectangular building of three or four stories, enhancing the efficiency of land use. Straight building lines also help control construction costs.

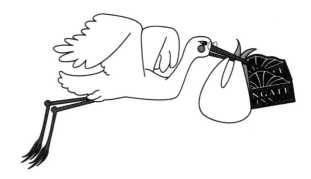

HFS provided a $250,000 development grant and committed to spending another $100,000 on marketing in each new market area. A total of $27 million was committed for marketing in the first five years.

Sources: "The making of a Midmarket Hotel Company," *Lodging Hospitality, 51*(8) (September 1995) 23–25; K. Cassedy, "Inside Wingate," *Lodging, 21*(3) (November 1995), 77–81; B. A. Worcester, "Wingate: A Tech-Based Brand," *Hotel & Motel Management, 211*(3) (February 19, 1996), 17. The assistance provided by Janet Jarosz of Wingate Inn in the development of this case is highly appreciated.

Although many lodging companies have opted for multiple segmented brands, one of the largest and most recognized hotel groups, Best Western, uses its single brand to cover a wide variety of properties and service levels. It achieves an annual renewal rate from its member properties in excess of 99 percent. The rationale of the single-brand strategy is that it makes it easier for consumers who are confused about the numerous brands on the market. Many people in the industry, let alone consumers, cannot tell the difference between one brand and another.

There are, however, many examples of successful segmentation with family brands or individual brands, as well as single brands. Therefore, "Who is right?" is probably a moot question. Rather, we can conclude that a number of different strategies may be successful, depending on the circumstances and how the strategies are executed.

Brand Bundling. The first example of **brand bundling** was food courts in shopping malls. As mentioned earlier, brands, either with or without the same ownership, began to "bundle" in the form of cobranding. In a bundled situation, brand equity from all operations is combined to attract potential customers. In addition, in a food court setting, volume is largely supported by the surrounding environment. As a result, lesser-known brands have a better chance of surviving in these settings than in free-standing locations.

Brands in Institutional Foodservice

Branding is now commonplace in institutional foodservice. Many food courts have replaced the traditional cafeteria lines and scramble system designs. ARAMARK has probably gone further with the development of its **proprietary brands** than any other contract company. A proprietary brand enjoys the major advantage of not having to pay a franchise royalty or advertising fee. Another strategy used by ARAMARK is to invite local operators or new concepts to "try out" at one of the ARAMARK managed locations. In an ARAMARK food court, for example, there may be 4 of its own brands, 4 units operated by a local group, and 4 national brands. Of the 12 units in the food court, only 4 require the payment of franchise fees.

Branding has become so popular on college campuses that the National Association of College and University Food Service (NACUFS) has developed a house brand, Tomassito's Italian Cafe. The concept comes with logos, menus, and promotional materials, as well as information manuals (National Association of Col-

Contract foodservice companies have created their own brands, such as the "Deli Corner" of ARAMARK. (Photo courtesy of ARAMARK.)

lege and University Food Service 2001). Branding is also increasingly popular in high schools. Many school systems operate as a franchise of QSRs, such as Chick-fil-A and Taco Bell.

Health care is certainly no exception to the trend toward branding. The University of Kansas Medical Center is using manufacturers' brands, Weight Watchers and Healthy Choice, as entrées in its vending machines. Other health care foodservices have also served branded entrées in their cafeteria lines. Medical centers across North America offer other franchised products as well. Pizza Hut pizza can be delivered to many hospitals, and local franchisees operate kiosks, such as a Taco Bell point of distribution (POD), in vending areas.

The Power of Branding

Hospitality is a highly fragmented, competitive industry. Although independents are still important, chains with deep pockets for heavy advertising play a major role in almost all sectors of the industry. In such a competitive environment, branding offers a means of establishing a differentiated identity and a basis for attempting to rally consumer loyalty. The exploding uses of branding tactics, summarized in Table 8.3, suggest that hospitality marketers find branding a favored weapon in their struggle for market power.

Brands are a major power in every part of the economy, but perhaps one reason they are especially powerful in hospitality is the *intangible* nature of the hospitality product. The brand, whether McDonald's or the Ritz, helps to identify the operation and provide concrete ideas of the particular product offerings. It helps operators to stand out from their competitors.

TABLE 8.3   Branding Tactics Used in the Hospitality Industry

Tactic	Action
Umbrella branding and subbranding	Brand individual menu items by restaurants.
Ingredient branding	Use ingredient manufacturers' brands on menus.
Cobranding	Operate two noncompetitive brands on the same premises.
Multiple branding	Operate a hotel property under two or more brand names.
Family brands	Put the "family name" on different brands.
Individual brands	Maintain completely unique identities for a company's brands.
Brand bundling	Locate several brands in a freestanding unit or a food court.

Product Life Cycle

Over the life of a product, the consumers' views of that product change. What was once an innovation becomes a common household item and, later, an outdated garage sale item. Things go into and out of fashion. The **product life cycle** concept, in fact, had its origins in the fashion industry. The product life cycle is illustrated in Figure 8.3.

When a new product is introduced, only a few adventurous innovators are likely to try it. Because of high start-up and introduction costs and low sales during the introduction stage, the firm is likely to have a net loss. As the product begins to enter the growth stage, more people become early adopters and try the product. With increased sales, profit increases as well. When the mass market begins to use the product, it enters the maturity stage. The sales level is at its highest. However, the growth rate of sales decreases at this point because most potential buyers have already purchased the product. Profit begins to level off or decline, as many firms have entered the competition. With more firms in the market, competition drives prices down and reduces profit margin. Marketing costs also increase because of market saturation. Once the sales peak is reached, the product and its profit are on their way to the bargain basement and extinction.

The product life cycle can be applied to an industry or to a concept, a brand, or a

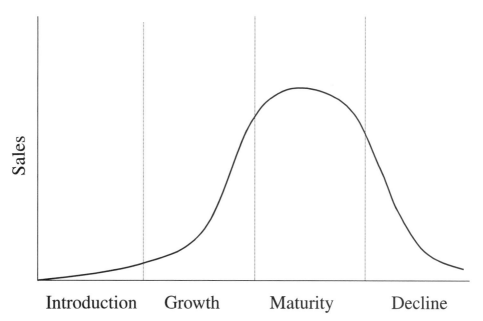

FIGURE 8.3 Product life cycle.

specific product. For example, the family cafeteria concept was initiated, became popular, and was gone in the 1970s and 1980s. Many restaurants in the cafeteria business that did not change with consumers' preferences have also become extinct. Gourmet coffee shops began as a novelty in large cities in the late 1980s. Now, even in small towns, there are two or three coffee shops serving the mass market—an indication that gourmet coffee shops are in the maturity stage. All-suite hotels are experiencing rapid growth and will enter the maturity stage in a few years. On the other hand, roadside motels, introduced in the 1960s, have already reached the decline stage.

When the product life cycle concept is applied to individual brands, it takes a different twist. Whereas restaurants experience cycles in consumer acceptance, the experience of long-lasting brands, such as McDonald's, Burger King, and Pizza Hut, is that brands do not have to die out. They can regenerate themselves, as shown in Figure 8.4. When sales start to fall, companies should review their products and concepts and rejuvenate them with a thorough remodeling, the introduction of a new product, or both. The introduction of a breakfast menu regenerated McDonald's and many other QSRs' lives. Chicken McNuggets have also helped McDonald's to gain sales from snack occasions, as discussed in Chapter 4.

On the level of individual products, blackened redfish is an example of one that has

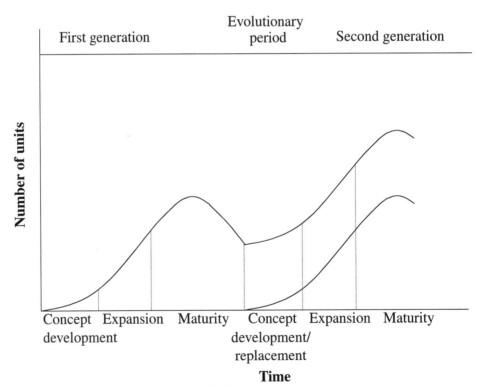

FIGURE 8.4 Product life cycle of an individual brand.
Source: Technomic Consultants.

gone through the product life cycle. The fish is rubbed with spices and then seared very quickly over a hot fire. The result is a product that is cooked on the inside and has a spicy, crisp, blackened crust on the outside. When blackened redfish was introduced to a wider market outside Louisiana's Cajun community by Paul Prudhomme, it was quickly added to the menus of leading upscale restaurants as something new. Over time, the mass-market dinner houses picked up this menu item. As a result, it became too common for most cutting-edge restaurants that seek to distinguish themselves from others. Although still offered at some operations, blackened redfish is no longer as widely popular, nor is it seen as trend setting. It has, in fact, mostly gone out of style.

Even though the product life cycle concept applies to all products, different products have different lengths of life. For example, the Big Mac has been on the market for several decades and still brings in a healthy level of sales. However, McRib sandwiches have a much shorter life—they are taken off the menu before arriving at the late maturity/declining stage so that the product can be introduced again the following year.

Responses to Maturity

One characteristic of a **mature market** is that it is populated by established companies that are excellent operators and marketers with substantial financial resources. The QSR segment is a good example of a mature industry, one in which corporate giants face off against each other in a mass market. To survive and succeed in a mature environment, marketers can develop new products or markets, or revise marketing mix strategies.

Product and Market Development. As sales and profit decline in the maturity stage, operations must either develop new products or new markets to increase revenue and profit. Consider, for example, a restaurant whose appeal is to singles and couples, aged 25 to 34, without children. The size of this market is shrinking because of current demographic trends. The number of individuals in this age category is in decline and will continue to decline for the next 5 to 10 years. This is a time in life when people marry and begin to have children, so the restaurant may lose its appeal to current customers as they mature and have families, because a restaurant targeting young adults may not be perceived as particularly child-friendly.

A market development effort, however, may expand its appeal to include families with children. As a second step, it may appeal to slightly older guests, such as the 35 to 40 age group, as a way of hanging onto its current patrons as they age. The revised operation can thus increase its target population significantly. To accomplish market development, the restaurant will have to change its menu, operating style, services, and perhaps even the décor. For example, children's menus and menu items for older, more weight-conscious adults would have to be added. The offering of a play area, and perhaps a baby-sitting service, would also help broaden its appeal. In addition, servers will have to be trained to take care of families with children.

As the company expands its target market, it takes on new competitors—the operations that are already serving the alternative target market. Therefore, market and product development must be carried out with careful consumer and competitor research and planning. The new offering must include competitive points of difference that will give the operation an advantage, not just a "copycat" pattern that repeats what others are doing in the market. Finally, if the restaurant chooses to continue to serve the declining 25- to 34-year old segment, it will have to sharpen its concept and become more competitive in order to increase its market share of this market and avoid a serious erosion of its profits.

Changing the Marketing Mix. Another approach to maturity involves changing one or more elements in the marketing mix. Facing growing competition, a company might increase promotional discounts or lower some of its prices on a longer-term basis. The most common response to Taco Bell's low-price appeal has been the development of value meals, which bundle products in a way that increases the average check but reduces the total cost to consumers, as compared with purchasing individual items separately. Operations also increase their promotional budgets as a market becomes more crowded. The advertising budgets of QSRs, for example, have increased steadily for years. The most common response to a matured concept, however, is the development of a new product.

New Products

As consumers' needs and preferences change, **new products** must be introduced to maintain customer demand and operating profitability. Even established operations, such as McDonald's, continue to offer successful products and present new combinations of existing products. McDonald's has also introduced genuinely new products—such as McFlurries, adapted from a Dairy Queen favorite—to revitalize its image.

New Product Functions

New products are introduced to build sales by building or holding an operation's customer base, as shown in Figure 8.5. Perhaps the most successful use of new products to expand a market is McDonald's introduction of the breakfast menu. McDonald's is probably the best single supplier of breakfasts away from home to the American public. This success suggests that McDonald's has built a strong customer base with its breakfast menu and has been able to hold onto that customer base in spite of increasingly fierce competition. McDonald's has also been very successful in extending its market into snack occasions, particularly with Chicken McNuggets.

A Schlotzsky's Deli franchisee's idea of adding computers, gourmet coffees, and pastries to units in Miami has boosted its weekly sales to more than three times the chain's average. The company has considered testing the idea in future corporate stores. The Miami Scholotzsky's extended hours, extended concept, and extended menu provide an opportunity to open in the morning and lengthen afternoon and

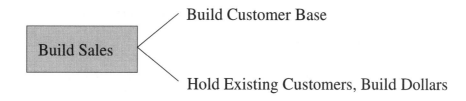

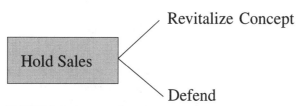

FIGURE 8.5 New product functions.

evening serving hours. The new concept also allows the deli to enter other urban markets (Ruggless 2000).

New products are also used to increase sales to existing customers. Adding daily or weekly specials provides alternatives for regular customers and encourages their more frequent returns. New specialty products, such as a new appetizer or dessert, may also increase existing customers' spending during a visit. Some QSRs have added new items, such as salad and dessert, to offer a full meal. A full-meal offering raises the average check amount and strengthens a QSR's competitive position against family restaurants.

New products have also been used to hold sales by revitalizing an aging concept. Wrapped sandwiches have been used by many operations, such as Wendy's, to perk up existing operations. New products can be used as a defensive strategy as well. When a company finds itself losing market share because it lacks a particular product, it is likely to add that product defensively. For example, KFC added chicken sandwiches to its menu to defend its market share against the burger giants. With an eroded market share due to competition from Papa John's International, Inc. and other upstart pizza restaurants, Pizza Hut developed the Big New Yorker, the 16-inch pizza with sweeter sauce and thinner crust. The product was launched as a special promotion; however, the overwhelming demand prompted Pizza Hut to permanently add the pizza to the national menu (Waters 2000).

Defining New Products

A new product can be defined as any item not currently on an operation's menu, even if the product is available elsewhere. There are many types and definitions of new products; however, most foodservice operations have introduced new products in one of the three categories:

1. *Imitation.* When several operators added chicken nuggets, they were imitating McDonald's successful offering of the product.
2. *Adaptation.* The triple bacon cheeseburger, a modification of an existing product by adding one or more new ingredients, is a good example of adaptation. Another example is pizza by the slice. Godfather's, for instance, originally served only whole pizzas, but introduced pizza by the slice to meet the needs, mainly for speed and single portions, of the lunch crowds.
3. *Innovation.* Wendy's baked potatoes should be classified as an innovation because this offering was unique in its execution—a first for QSRs. The first egg and muffin sandwich, the Egg McMuffin, is another example of true innovation.

Concept Innovation. The most fundamental kind of innovation is **concept innovation.** The power of a total new concept is suggested by competitors' reaction to it. For example, the success of McDonald's and KFC inspired waves of similar restaurants. Holiday Inn's successful development of the motor inn, as opposed to the hotel of the time, set off a surge of imitation that eventually revolutionized the lodging industry. In recent years, the success of Courtyard by Marriott caused many copycat operations to jump into the midprice business hotel market.

Proliferating Service Forms. Some of the most basic concept innovations have been new service forms. The fastest-growing segment of foodservice is off-premise service, such as take-out, drive-thrus, and delivery. Another service form that has added significantly to foodservice sales is late-hour operations via drive-thru or take-out windows. This arrangement avoids the security problems of late-hour operations in some high-crime areas.

New Product Development

New product development often starts with a survey of consumers to identify the "problems" they experience with the hospitality environment. Attending to these problems often helps in developing ideas or solutions to consumer complaints. The researchers narrow their focus as a smaller number of these ideas are identified as feasible projects, and a few of these are then turned into actual products for testing. Only a small number of the products developed will be used in formal market testing, and perhaps one or two of these will be successful. Figure 8.6 summarizes the product development process.

Although many new products are tested, few become successful. For example, the McLean low-fat hamburger was rolled out with much fanfare by McDonald's but subsequently failed completely, except as a public relations exercise. An important consideration in developing new products is that whether they are successful or not, they should add life and novelty to the operation and, as a result, add interest for the customers.

Once a product has been identified as meeting a customer need, several factors

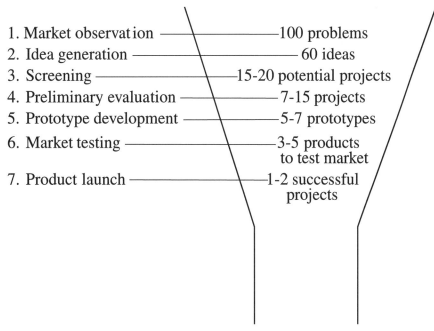

1. Market observation ——————100 problems
2. Idea generation ——————— 60 ideas
3. Screening ——————15-20 potential projects
4. Preliminary evaluation ——— 7-15 projects
5. Prototype development ——— 5-7 prototypes
6. Market testing ——————3-5 products
                                        to test market

7. Product launch ——————1-2 successful
                                        projects

FIGURE 8.6 The new product process: A funnel approach.
Source: R. N. Paul, "New Product Development," *Proceedings, Chain Operators Exchange* (Chicago: International Foodservice Manufacturers Association, 1982). Copyright 1982. International Foodservice Manufacturers Association.

must be considered to determine its fit with the operation. The important factors to evaluate include existing equipment, company image, long-term objectives, volume requirements, profitability contribution, investment required, and existing customers.

During product introduction, the product's attractiveness is assessed in terms of popularity and profitability. The supply of ingredient(s) must be evaluated as well. When Burger King first added bacon to a cheeseburger, the impact on national demand for bacon was so pronounced that pork belly prices rose significantly on the commodity futures market.

A final factor, also important in appraising the attractiveness of a potential new menu item, is its uniqueness. Although a new product may be added defensively in reaction to a competitor's success, it is preferable to have a product that makes a new statement in the marketplace, rather than one that just says "me too."

New Product Hazard: Cannibalization

A potential problem with launching a new product is **cannibalization**—that is, the possibility that the new product will steal sales from existing products rather than add to sales by attracting new customers. Sometimes, in a highly competitive market, new products are added as a defensive measure to keep customers by offering them something new and different, in spite of the danger of cannibalization. However, a desirable outcome for a new product is to attract new customers, not just to spread the existing customers over more choices.

Independent Operations

The introduction of a new product in a chain is a very complex process. This is because the product must be evaluated in several markets, fit with many existing operations' physical plants, and match the image of the chain. In an independent operation the process is much less formalized, because the owner's experience is available to make an informed judgment about the likelihood of the product's success. Although the analysis may be less formal, the same basic factors identified for chain operations should be considered.

Summary

Service is an experience for the guest. For the operation, however, it is a planned event, like a performance. The service product is made up of the core benefit that guests seek, the facilitating services essential to providing the benefit, and the supporting services necessary to the marketing of the service offering.

Because services are intangible, marketers provide cues to help consumers conceptualize a service offering. Among the most important cues are the physical plant and the atmospherics it establishes. The total service offering is referred to as the *concept.* In foodservice, this includes the menu, the kind of food used and the way it is prepared, the service, the price, and the atmosphere. Hotel concepts can be divided into luxury, full service, limited service, and extended stay.

Branding is used to help identify products. Its role in the lodging and foodservice industries is growing. Variations of branding include subbranding, ingredient branding, cobranding, family branding, and brand bundling. Branding also plays an increasing role in institutional foodservice.

The product life cycle is a useful means of summarizing the impact of the aging of a product. Products usually go through the introduction, growth, maturity, and declining stages. The product life cycle concept can be applied to an industry, a brand, or a product. When a brand matures, there are several ways to rejuvenate the concept. The introduction of new products is one way to regenerate a concept or to build or hold sales. The development of a new product is a complicated process. Trials of many ideas are often required to achieve just one successful new product.

Key Words and Concepts

Marketing mix	Branding	Line extension
Service offering	Brand equity	Individual brands
Core benefit	Brand loyalty	Brand bundling
Facilitating services	Umbrella brand	Proprietary brands
Supporting services	Subbrand	Product life cycle
Service delivery system	Ingredient branding	Mature market
Atmospherics	Colocation	New products
Supporting cues	Cobranding	Concept innovation
Concepts as products	Family brands	Cannibalization

Resources on the Internet

Chick-fil-A. *http://www.chick-fil-a.com/*
Chili's Grill & Bar. *http://www.chilis.com/*
Country Inns & Suites by Carlson.
   http://www.countryinns.com
Holiday Inn Hotels and Resorts.
   http://www.basshotels.com/holiday-inn
McDonald's. *http://www.mcdonalds.com*
National Association of College and University Food
   Service. *http://www.nacufs.org/*

Ramada.
   http://www.ramada.com/ctg/cgi-bin/Ramada
Taco Bell. *http://www.tacobell.com/*
T.G.I. Friday's. *http://www.tgifridays.bc.ca/*
Tricon Global Restaurants, Inc.
   http://www.triconglobal.com/
   triconroot/mainwelcome.htm
Wendy's International, Inc.
   http://www.wendys.com/index0.html

Discussion Questions

1. What are the major elements of a service offering? What role does each play?
2. What is meant by "manipulating the environment"? Name some specific examples of manipulations. What are their effects?
3. What are the elements of a restaurant concept?
4. What is branding? What are its advantages?

5. How do umbrella brands and subbrands relate to one another?
6. What is the purpose of ingredient branding?
7. What do you see as the pros and cons of single brands versus family brands?
8. What is product life cycle? How do hospitality operations deal with maturity?
9. What are the functions of new products?

References

Bennett, P. D., ed. (1995). *Dictionary of marketing terms.* 2d ed. Chicago: American Marketing Association.

Berko, A. executive producer. (1996, January). State of the art. In T. Verna, ed. *Dateline NBC.* New York: NBC Broadcasting Company.

Bond, H. (1992). Double-branding seen as sign of the times.

Hotel & Motel Management, 207(19) (November 2), 1, 16.

Grönroos, G. (1990). *Service management and marketing.* Lexington, MA: Lexington Books.

Hesket, J., W. E., Sasser, and C. Hart. (1990). *Service breakthroughs: Changing the name of the game.* New York: The Free Press.

Lovelock, C. H. (1996). *Services marketing.* 3d ed. Upper Saddle River, NJ: Prentice-Hall.

National Association of College and University Food Service. (2001). *National Association of College and University Food Service home page* (on-line). Web site: http://www.nacufs.org

Ruggless, R. (2000). Hot sales at "wired" Schlotzsky's spark plans for broader test. *Nation's Restaurant News, 34*(1) (January 3), 1, 80.

Schmitt, B., and A. Simonson. (1997). *Marketing aesthetics: The strategic management of brands, identity and image.* New York: The Free Press.

Shostack, G. L. (1977). Breaking free from product marketing. *Journal of Marketing, 41*(2), 73–80.

Waters, J. (2000). Better strategies better Pizza Hut. *Restaurants and Institutions, 110*(5) (February 15), 47–48, 50.

Place in Hospitality Marketing: Distribution

When you have finished reading this chapter, you should be able to:

- Define *distribution* in a hospitality context.
- List the major channel members serving hospitality firms.
- Discuss the role of reservation systems in lodging distribution.
- Describe the conflicts in franchise systems.
- List the services provided by franchisors.
- Explain the importance of travel agents.
- Define *intercept marketing* in foodservice.

Place and Places

In hospitality, the marketing mix element "place" covers a number of related topics. In addition to location and site decisions, discussed in Chapter 10, **place** also includes the *distribution* of the product, or making the product conveniently available in many places. **Places** means multiple locations, or chains. Most of this chapter focuses on the distribution problems of chains, but the discussion of *representation* in a market does apply to both chain and independent operations.

The Concept of Distribution

When you are downtown in a large city and are hungry, it does you no good to know that a very nice restaurant is available in the suburbs, unless you have the necessary transportation and lots of time. The same is true for lodging. When your favorite hotel has a room available several hundred miles away, that information is not very helpful.

Being *in place*, or in the many places where consumers are, is critical to hospitality organizations that want to serve guests in regional or national markets. For restaurants, this means having an operation in as many markets as possible. For hotels, having an operation in a major market is advantageous. However, if a hotel does not have a property in a significant market, it is important that it be represented by one or more agencies that can sell rooms in that market. Therefore, *distribution* refers to the strategy of place, of being *present* or *represented* in key markets.

Three broad categories of distribution strategies for manufactured goods can be applied to hospitality services. **Intensive distribution** is appropriate for convenience goods because customers are unlikely to go out of their way to purchase those products. Intensive distribution is required to catch convenience-oriented consumers when they are ready to make a purchase. The distribution strategy of quick-service restaurants (QSRs) belongs in this category. **Selective distribution** achieves fairly wide market representation. Consumers are willing to make a certain amount of effort to purchase the product. Casual dining restaurants usually use this strategy when selecting operation sites. A small town with 50,000 residents and a five-mile radius usually has two or three McDonald's but only one Applebee's. A large shopping area may have five to ten or more competing QSRs, but probably only one or two family restaurants, and perhaps a more upscale casual restaurant. **Exclusive distribution** means only one seller is available in a market. An example is a one-of-a-kind resort, such as the Greenbrier in West Virginia, or a very fine dining restaurant, such as Charlie Trotter's in Chicago.

The Constraint of Market Saturation. The intensity of distribution has a different meaning in the hospitality industry than in manufacturing because there is no inventory in hospitality. A service operation puts in place a capacity. When that capacity is not used at an economically acceptable rate, the operation will have to go out of business. Therefore, there are limits to how many operations a market can support. Where convenience-oriented intensive distribution is the rule, as in QSRs, a big city

A fine dining restaurant, one of a kind in its community, offers an example of exclusive distribution. (Photo courtesy of Resorts Atlantic City.)

can absorb a large number of operations, but not as many locations as are feasible for a manufactured good that can be carried in inventory.

In quite different ways, lodging and foodservice are experiencing increasing intensity of distribution. In lodging, this is achieved through expanding the *representation* of hotels by using a variety of reservation and sales services. In foodservice, such expansion is a result of increasing the number of units. This is often accomplished with a different kind of downsized, specialized unit. More and more restaurants have also used a third-party delivery service, such as the Takeout Taxi, which is a form of representation.

Channels of Distribution

Channels of distribution form the commercial structure of intermediaries between the provider of a good or service and its ultimate consumers. Some channel members in manufactured goods are the more service-intensive *merchant firms,* such as wholesalers and distributors, who take title to the goods, maintain inventories and operate warehouses, and provide delivery services. These firms supply the hospitality industry with most of the goods used in various operations, such as food products, beverages, cleaning supplies, and guest supplies.

Merchant firms of another type are the *retailers* who sell to the ultimate consumers and provide final processing and services. Retailers set final prices and receive compensation in the form of profits generated from markups. In taking title to the goods, retailers assume the risk of resale. The majority of hospitality units are retailers and thus are members of the distribution channels. For example, restaurants are a combination of manufacturing and service organizations. They deal almost exclusively with the ultimate consumers; therefore, they are members of the retail industry.

Agents, another type of channel member, do not take title to the goods and usually do not control the selling price of products they handle. Their compensation is commonly in the form of a commission. Travel agents act as representatives for many hotels, airlines, cruises, and car rental companies. Through reservation systems, travel agents are significant distribution channel members in travel product sales.

Franchise systems are a channel of distribution for hotel and restaurant chains. Franchising companies provide franchisees a number of services, such as marketing and, in lodging, reservations. Franchising has been a major force in both lodging and foodservice for nearly 50 years. If a company with a successful concept does not expand, others will copy its idea and it will lose the advantage of uniqueness. To prevent this from happening, a successful concept must be distributed in all appropriate markets as rapidly as possible. To expand, however, a company must invest substantial capital in its physical plant. In addition, a large organization is needed to manage multiple operations and to guide area and district-level management staff.

Franchising offers a company an opportunity to penetrate many markets quickly, with franchisees providing much of the capital. (Photo courtesy of Taco Bell.)

Franchising offers a company with a successful operating format an opportunity to achieve wide distribution quickly. Franchisees provide most of the capital for expansion; therefore, the job of managing a large and growing organization is made simpler by the motivation of franchised owners.

The basic concept of distribution applies to both hotels and restaurants. However, the way in which they achieve distribution differs in a number of ways. Therefore, lodging and foodservice distribution systems are discussed separately.

Lodging Distribution Systems

Two major forces have shaped the distribution of lodging products. First, franchising has been a potent force since the early 1950s. Although it remains as a powerful force, it has and will continue to change in the direction of being a supplier of specialized services. The second force is the technology-driven revolution in reservation systems. Computerized communications are drastically changing the way hotel rooms are sold and the role of intermediaries in the marketing of hotel products.

In this section, the importance of lodging distribution systems is considered first. Next, we look at the state of reservation systems today and their likely future, as a background for understanding the changing role of lodging franchising and intermediaries. Various channel members are then discussed.

The Need for Distribution in Lodging

There are two ways to view distribution in lodging. The first considers the **physical presence** of properties in various markets; the second, their **representation** in markets. Both are essential to the distribution policy of hotel chains, and representation is helpful to most independent operations as well.

Having a hotel in every major market is a desirable goal because that is what it takes to serve the organization's guests. A hotel has to be *in place* to make it as easy as possible for guests to choose it. Serving guests gains revenue for the hotel, but it also gains *access* to the guests for future sales. Hotels are happy to make reservations for guests' future stays in the same hotel chain, at the same or a different location. An additional advantage of having a property in a certain locale is that the local people become familiar with the brand and are more likely to choose it, as a familiar brand, when they travel.

Representation refers to having some agencies in every market to represent the lodging system. There are several levels of representation. At the minimum level, if you are reading this book in a room with a telephone, there is a "representative" of many hotel chains right there with you in the form of a toll-free telephone reservation service. Or you may prefer to call one of the many travel agencies available to you for advice on where to stay. Travel agents represent all hotels, and generally not any one hotel in particular. Therefore, they are not an especially powerful tool for any *particular* hotel unless efforts are made to *sell* to the travel agents.

Representatives of hotel chains regularly call businesses that generate a lot of travel or are responsible for major conventions. This may be done by the sales office of a chain or franchise group, or by a salesperson from a hotel representative firm. By these means, many hotels are represented in markets where they do not have a property.

Lodging is highly competitive; thus it is important not only to have a known brand name, or a strong local reputation in the case of an independent operation, but also to have some way of being represented in appropriate markets. One way of achieving such representation is through a reservation service.

Reservation Systems in Lodging

Figure 9.1 provides an overview of the **reservation system** serving the lodging industry. To explain the system, this section discusses the role of each player identified in the right-hand column of the figure. Those players made up the traditional reservation system prior to the arrival of the Internet and E-commerce.

Hotel guests, whether for business or leisure, can make hotel reservations in a variety of ways. Travelers may make reservations through *travel agents,* a hotel's **central reservation service (CRS),** or individual *hotel properties.* Travel agents can place reservations for their clients by calling the hotel CRS or individual properties, or by

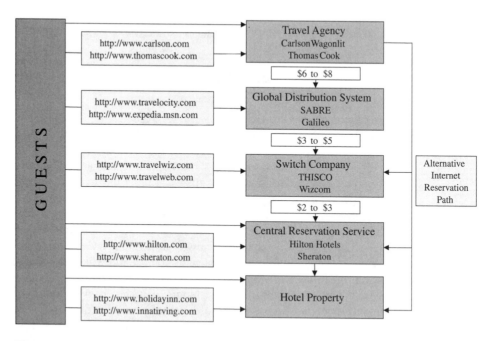

☐ Booking a hotel room through the Internet
▤ Booking a hotel room via traditional reservation structure

FIGURE 9.1 Lodging reservation system.
Source: Adapted from PricewaterhouseCoopers, *Hospitality Directions* "The Internet Transforms the Traditional Hotel Distribution System," pp. 19–29, July 1999.

making reservations through the **global distribution system (GDS),** which consists of the airline CRS. GDS is a popular route for travel agents, because virtually all travel agencies in the United States are on-line to one of the airline CRSs and travel agents can book air tickets, hotel rooms, and car rentals in one session.

For the GDS to communicate with the hotel CRS, a *switch* is required because of the variety of programming languages used. **Switch companies** serve as "interpreters" between the GDS and hotel CRSs. For example, when the GDS receives a request for a hotel reservation, that reservation is dispatched through the GDS and passed on to the hotel CRS through one of the switches, which provides an interface to create a seamless connection between the GDS and the hotel CRS.

The development of the GDS has dramatically increased the distribution channels available to hotels. However, it comes at a price, due to the fees charged by GDS and switch companies for handling reservations. The GDS presents special problems for independent properties because they usually cannot justify the fees charged by GDS to be included in the database. The per reservation cost, including travel agent commission and fees paid to the GDS, the switch company, and the CRS, could add up to $11 to $16 (PricewaterhouseCoopers 1999), which is a particularly difficult problem for midpriced hotels whose room rates are likely to be in the range of $50 to $70. Therefore, there is pressure on independent operations to find other ways of linking to the GDS. This may be a reason for the massive movement of midpriced and economy properties to join a franchise group. Other approaches to becoming part of the GDS include affiliating with a hotel representative firm, contracting with a switch company that provides the GDS connection for a fee, or joining a hotel association that has a CRS linked to the global system. These options are quite expensive as well.

With the arrival of the Internet, guests can make reservations not only through a traditional distribution system but also through the various Web sites. Each member of the distribution channel has its own Web presence, as shown in Figure 9.1. Guests can make hotel reservations on Web sites provided by travel agencies, the GDS, switch companies, hotel CRSs, or individual properties. Internet access is also available to travel agents. Therefore, in addition to making hotel reservations through the GDS, travel agents can book hotel rooms via the Web sites of switch companies, hotel CRSs, or hotel properties. The fewer number of channel members there are involved in a reservation, the lower the cost for the hotel property. Therefore, many hotels offer Internet specials on their own Web sites to encourage travelers and travel agents to make reservations directly through the hotel Web sites.

The Future of Reservations

The adoption of common Internet technology platforms by GDS and hotel CRSs has eliminated the need for traditional switch company services. Many switch companies have developed their own Web sites and compete with the GDS in offering reservation services to consumers and travel agents.

With the continuing geometric growth of individual access to the Internet, the volume of reservations coming directly to hotels from individuals will increase dramatically in the next few years. In fact, on-line bookings are among the fastest-growing forms of distribution. By the year 2002, 12 to 20 percent of all hotel reser-

Consumers can make hotel reservations directly from hotel web sites. Room rates available on the web sites are comparable to, sometimes even lower than, the rates quoted by the hotel CRS, individual properties, or travel agents. (Photo courtesy of Starwood Hotels & Resorts Worldwide, Inc.)

vations will likely be booked on-line. Marriott's on-line booking reached more than $50 million in 1998, an increase of 200 percent over 1997 (Lodging 1999).

Consumers can browse the sites and take a virtual tour, with audio and video features, of specific properties. Small, independent hotels can also develop their own Web sites and be seen by the world at relatively low cost. In light of their lack of name recognition, it is extremely important for such operations to make the proper linkage to major search engines and destination marketing organizations, such as the state tourism office, local convention and visitors bureau, and hotel associations. Because of its availability to *all* hotel properties and the increasing number of users, the Internet has revolutionized the lodging reservation system and will continue to do so in the future.

Lodging Channels of Distribution

The most important channels of distribution in lodging are hotel chains and franchise/ membership systems. Travel agents also play a significant role in lodging distribution. Other channel members include hotel sales representatives and incentive houses. Each is discussed in the following paragraphs.

A franchise system appears to be just one company, but these chains are really an alliance of many independent owners with the franchising company. (Photo courtesy of Holiday Inn Worldwide.)

Lodging Chains. Properties in a hotel chain often *look* very much as though they belong to one company because each of them has the same sign out front and achieves the same standard of services and facilities. However, the ownership of those properties is actually very diverse. Some hotels with the Hilton or Marriott name are owned and operated by the company of that name, but most are owned by an investor group and managed under *management contracts*. Although these chains perform many other services, one of their major roles is to provide advertising and sales representation, as well as a reservation network, for their properties in various markets. Many chains not only manage owned properties and operate for others, but also franchise their names and operating systems.

Franchise Systems in Lodging. The largest group of **franchises** is that of the Cendant Corporation, which operates eight brands covering 6,000 properties and more than 500,000 rooms (Cendant Corporation 1999). Choice Hotels, the second largest group of franchises, operates seven brands with more than 3,600 hotels and 300,000 rooms (Choice Hotels 1999). Best Western, the best-known **membership system** has more than 3,800 hotels and motels (Best Western International 2001). The most critical technical difference between a franchise and a membership system is that in a franchise system properties and their owners are granted a license, whereas in a membership system properties and their owners become members. Their modes of operation are generally similar. However, the membership group is characterized by considerable autonomy for individual properties and tends to have lower charges than a franchise system. One result of the lower charges is a lower advertising budget. Franchise and membership systems usually provide five basic services to their affiliated hotels: a national brand and marketing program, reservation systems, quality assurance, buying cooperatives, and training programs.

A National Brand and Marketing Program. Having a brand that travelers can recognize and trust is advantageous to hotel operators. To support the brand and member properties, franchise companies pool advertising fees to maintain national and regional advertising and promotional campaigns. The system also distributes directories to let travelers know where the system has properties, at what rates, and with what facilities. *Sales representation* in key cities is also an important part of the national marketing program. Specialized sales offices pursue group business, and regional offices call on local generators of travel to sell their brands.

Reservation Systems. The GDS and airline CRSs have an increasing role in lodging reservations. However, the more reservations a lodging group can book directly from guests, the lower its reservation costs will be, because it will not have to pay fees to others. Most large chains operate their own reservation systems, and smaller organizations contract with companies specializing in telemarketing for reservation services. These contracting companies provide reservation services for lodging systems using the hotel names; therefore, guests are not even aware that they are dealing with another organization.

Quality Assurance. With 3,000 to 5,000 individual hotels and motels in a large lodging system, the possibility of problems arising at a few properties is quite real. Given the importance of providing guests with positive experiences to secure repeat business, maintaining quality in the system is essential to all properties. At the time of entry into the system, each property has to meet the minimum physical standards. Inspection programs are established to maintain operating standards. However, it is difficult to punish a property that does not comply. The lodging company may threaten cancellation of the franchise contract, the only effective sanction available, but the legal implications make it almost impossible to carry out. As a result, franchise companies increasingly rely on shorter contracts—five years or less—and simply decline to renew operations that do not live up to standards. Some lodging systems have also begun to rate their own properties and publish superior ratings in their own directories as a way of reinforcing good performance (Club Med 2001).

Buying Cooperatives. Many lodging groups maintain purchasing co-ops for products used in their properties, as well as for local and regional advertising. This is not a distribution-related benefit, but it does have important marketing implications—

operating savings derived from the co-ops can help properties to keep their rates at competitive levels.

Training Programs. Well-operated lodging systems usually provide training programs for property-level managers. Videos and training manuals, to be used by the managers, are also developed for hourly employees. These training programs can help standardize service quality and achieve cost savings in training material development.

The dominance of the market that Holiday Inns once enjoyed is not in sight for any of the current hotels simply because there are so many of them and competition among franchisors is so intense. The most successful franchises in the long run will owe much of their success to wide distribution of their products and effective representation in many markets by various channel members. From the franchisors' perspective, franchising is a powerful form of distribution for their brands.

The number of conversions from chain to independent operations has been falling since a recession-driven peak in 1992, but independent-to-chain conversions have increased since that time. The behavior of franchisees strongly suggests that a very large proportion of them are at least sufficiently satisfied with their affiliations to maintain them, and that many properties without an affiliation are finding it advantageous to join a brand.

Changes in Franchising. In the early days of lodging franchising, the environment strongly favored the franchisors and the franchisees usually agreed to all franchisors' stipulations and requirements. A significant degree of loyalty existed between a franchisee and a franchisor. In the mid-1980s, franchisees gained the right to hold licenses from more than one franchisor's brand. At about the same time "conversion franchising"—a property changing from one franchise to another—began to appear. Between that time and the early 1990s, a period of severe overcapacity and operating losses for most properties, many hotels changed brands and competition emerged among franchisors seeking properties to convert. As a result, franchisors became more like suppliers of services than the quasi-bosses they once were, and franchisees became more like customers than subordinates.

A major factor driving franchisees to consider changing franchises has been cost. Franchise fees typically account for 4 to 6 percent of the total hotel revenue (Ross 1999 a and b). New, lower-cost franchise and membership groups are also entering the market. Price competition appears to be emerging among franchisors as they began to offer discounts as incentives to join the franchise, and it is not uncommon for franchisees to negotiate fees before signing a contract. In fact, competition among franchisors is quite intense in some markets.

Conflict in the Franchise System. **Impact,** in this context, can be defined as the effect on a particular hotel franchisee of the franchisor's converting or developing a property with the same brand affiliation in the same market area. Impact can result in one or more unfavorable effects, such as lost market penetration, a diluted average rate, increased marketing expenditures, lost food and beverage revenues, and a fall in the value of the hotel at resale (Culligan 1995). The owner of one property, for instance, found that the franchisor granted a new license in his market every time the existing hotels achieved a 75 percent occupancy (Turkel 1995). The volume of the franchisor's reservation system gradually spread over more and more properties until, at the end of a three-year period, the original franchisee's room revenue amounted to only 52 percent of the revenues generated by all franchised properties in his market area!

In this very competitive market, the impact problem is not likely to go away for either franchisees or franchisors, but there is every indication that it is on its way to a reasonable resolution. Under pressure from franchisees and state and federal regulations, lodging systems have adopted positive measures to prevent further impact problems. Some lodging systems have developed written impact statements providing for penalty payments where impact can be proved. Some chains have adopted the use of exclusive territories. One chain defines an exclusive territory as the area within a three-mile radius in a downtown metropolitan area or within a radius of 20 miles in a suburban area (Rasinsky 1995). However, the problem of impact is built into the franchise relationship, because the decision to expand favors all parties except the nearby franchisees, whose business is lost to new operations. Continued expansion provides franchisors the desirable name recognition and representation as well as funding for advertising.

The Travel Agent. The advantage for a hotel working with travel agencies is widened representation. Travel agents send hotels business they could not otherwise receive. The cost, of course, is travel agency commissions. Some hotels reason that most travelers make their own hotel reservations and that business comes to a hotel because of its unique features, such as location and service. Therefore, the assistance, and cost, of travel agents is not necessary. However, times have changed. In today's competitive environment, hotels cannot afford to give up any source of business nor the opportunity to work with any distribution channel members.

There are both wholesale and retail channels for hotel rooms. **Travel wholesalers,** such as American Express, buy blocks of hotel rooms and other travel products, such as airline tickets, at discounts and resell them through retail travel agents. The travel wholesalers take ownership of the products and earn profits from the margins on their resale. Retail travel agencies, employing approximately 400,000 agents in the world, sell travel products to end users. Travel agents book more than 95 percent of cruises, 90 percent of airline tickets, 50 percent of car rentals (Schulz 1994), but only 22 percent of hotel rooms (as of 1998) (Dube and Renaghan 2000). The reason is partly that travel agents simply do not ask their clients whether they need a hotel room during the trip.

Travel agents deal with a variety of clientele. They work with individual tourists and business travelers, and some agencies serve as "travel offices" for companies and make all their travel arrangements. The majority of agencies sell individual travel products, such as airline tickets and cruise trips, and some sell packaged tours. Airlines have capped the commissions they pay to travel agents at $50 for each round-trip domestic ticket. This has resulted in travel agencies, in many markets, charging customers a service fee of $10 to $25 per ticket. The limited revenue, along with the growth of the Internet and e-commerce, has put increasing pressure on small travel agencies, which represent the majority of them. The limited airline booking revenue for travel agents, however, represents an opportunity for hotels to present themselves as a potential revenue source for travel agencies.

A problem with selling through travel agencies is that they have no special ties to any particular property. Yet, this situation can be corrected by setting policies that make it attractive for travel agencies to book rooms for a particular property or chain. The experience of successful operators indicates that a hotel chain's commitment to use travel agents must start at the top and must be communicated to hotel staff at all levels. Hilton Hotels maintains a telephone number exclusively for travel agents, staffed by representatives specifically trained to work with travel agents and to answer their questions. Commission payment has been centralized to ensure prompt payment, and Hilton has established a Travel Agent Advisory Board, consisting of travel agents and Hilton executives. Hyatt developed "Travel Agent Golden Rules," a policy that defines how travel agents are to be treated when dealing with Hyatt. As part of the annual Hyatt Exchange Program, 750 Hyatt employees from every U.S. property and 1,000 travel agents nationwide visit each other's facilities to gain a better understanding of their travel partners' functions (Schulz 1994). Marriott has developed a hotel sales training program for travel agents, called Hotel Excellence! and Radisson has the "Look to Book" program. Both are discussed in Case Study 9.1.

CASE STUDY 9.1

Selling Through Channels

Travel agents book about 13 airline reservations for every hotel reservation. A few of the airline tickets do not represent overnight business, but most do. Therefore, the ratio suggests that travel agents are not booking as many hotel rooms as they could. Two hotel companies have developed programs to encourage travel agents to book more hotel rooms.

Marriott believes continuous training will be the key to travel agency success. This organization created the "Hotel Excellence!" hotel sales training program for travel agents, who are a vital bridge between consumers and Marriott. The program was designed to clarify the complex lodging industry, to provide tips on how to qualify, research, and recommend lodging choices, and to enhance understanding of Marriott brands and products. The program consists of a ten-chapter self-study workbook and a computer disk containing test questions. The first five chapters give a broad overview of the hotel industry. Topics include the rating system, types of travelers, hotel types and affiliations, the GDS, hotel sales, and working with groups. The last five chapters focus on Marriott products and services and how the Hotel Excellence! program works.

The disk contains hundreds of questions. Travel agents can take the exam as many times as needed. A random selection of 40 questions is generated every time an agent takes the test. When an agent passes the test at the rate of 80 percent correct, the results can be submitted via electronic or regular mail. Hotel Sales Specialist Certified by Marriott (HSS) and Fam-Tatic certificates are then mailed to certified travel agents. HSS agents will receive a 10 percent commission on rooms booked, whereas non-HSS agents receive an 8 percent commission.* The Fam-Tatic program includes the participation of more than 1,200 properties, across nine brands, each offering a US$49 rate for HSS agents on a space-available basis.

Marriott has also designed a Centralized Travel Agency Commission Service (CTAC). Services include a combined commission for all Marriott brands and a choice of payment frequency. One consolidated commission check is issued to each agent; an agent can choose to be paid weekly, biweekly, or monthly, tailoring the arrangement to the agency's accounting cycle.

Radisson Worldwide has developed the Look to Book program, which rewards travel agents with points that can be redeemed for hotel stays, travel, or gifts, based on the number of reservations they book on-line for Radisson hotels. This "frequent booker" program rewards individual travel agents, rather than agencies. The appeal to agency managers and owners is that the agents now have a personal economic incentive to increase total transactions, which, in turn, benefits the agency as well. The idea is to encourage travel agents to do more than just make airline reservations— especially appealing during a time of airline commission caps.

To support this strategy, Radisson created a seamless interface between its central reservation system and that of the GDS. This allows travel agents to bypass the GDS database and view full English-text room descriptions directly from Radisson's own database. This type of seamless interface has since become an industry standard. A training and support system was also developed to advise travel agents on how to participate in the reward program.

According to Brian Stage, president of Radisson Worldwide, of the approximately 400,000 travel agents worldwide, about 200,000 have participated in the program and about 125,000 are active members, meaning that they have booked multiple reservations in the past year. Look to Book members represent more than 90 countries, including some countries in which Radisson does not even have a property.

Sources: Woodside Travel Trust, *Hotel Excellence! by Marriott: A Hotel Sales Training Program for Travel Agents.* (Bethesda, MD: Author, 1999); L. Dube, C. A. Enz, L. M. Renaghan, and J. A. Siguaw, *American Lodging Excellence: The Key to Best Practices in the U.S. Lodging Industry* (New York: American Express and the American Hotel Foundation, 1999).

*M. Mancini, "The Cruise Phenomenon: Instructional Opportunities" (*International Society of Travel and Tourism Educators Annual Conference*, Vancouver, BC, November 6, 1999).

Hotel chains, franchise organizations, and hotel sales rep firms all have sales staff who specialize in calling on travel agents. The focus of this sales effort is concentrated on geographic markets that generate a great deal of business for a chain or a particular hotel. Selling to travel agents is certainly not limited to the chain hotels. One of the most effective means, especially for resort properties, is the **fam (familiarization) trip,** which provides free or reduced-price accommodations for travel agents who do business with the hotel. Both chain and independent hotels can invite travel agents to experience their products and services and to become familiar with the property, which should facilitate their sales efforts.

Other Specialized Channel Members. **Hotel sales representative companies,** or hotel reps, represent hotels in particular markets. They have their own sales force and often their own reservation centers. Smaller hotel reps operate in only one or a few markets, but larger firms operate on a worldwide basis. One of the largest, Utell International, represents 7,700 hotels, ranging from the Sheraton Kampala Hotel in Uganda to the Sofitel Tokyo Hotel in Japan. Its clients include small independents as well as international chains (HotelBook 2001). Another hotel rep firm, Lexington Services, provides reservation services for more than 3,000 member hotels, including the Historic Hotels of America and Harrah's Hotels and Casinos, in 60 countries, to travel agents through the GDS and consumers via the Internet (Lexington Services 2001).

Incentive houses are firms that arrange travel packages used by companies as special incentives for employees who exceed their performance targets or win sales contests. Incentive trips are usually all-inclusive, meaning that all hotels, transportation, and other travel products are included in the package and paid for by the company.

Distribution in Foodservice

The distribution characteristics of foodservice and those of lodging have both similarities and differences. Franchising plays a key role in both businesses. Distribution in the form of a retail presence in major markets is also important to both lodging and foodservice. The revolutionary development, called **intercept marketing,** in foodservice distribution is the increasing emphasis on multiple **points of distribution (PODs).** A significant difference between foodservice and lodging is that there is nothing in foodservice parallel to the important lodging reservation systems. Another difference between the two is the prevalence of market intermediaries in lodging distribution.

Franchising in Foodservice

Foodservice franchisors provide a range of services to franchisees, just as lodging franchisors do. The services and benefits a franchisor can provide include a national brand and marketing system, quality assurance and field support, new products, purchasing co-ops, and training programs. Field support includes inspection, guest opinion monitoring, and updated operational tools and techniques, such as management information systems. The development of new products is a critical franchise service. The franchisor has a responsibility to develop new ideas into operational concepts, and then into market-tested products. One of the richest resources in the new product development process is the franchisees. The Egg McMuffin, for instance, was first developed by a McDonald's franchisee.

Many franchise organizations work with franchisees to operate a buying co-op. The franchisor has a critical role in providing quality control in approving suppliers of food products. In some cases, the franchisor also sells products to franchisees. For example, at Domino's, 90 percent of the food products used by franchisees are sold to them by a subsidiary of the franchisor. The franchisor's ability to *require* product purchases from its own distribution center is severely limited by antitrust laws. However, in practice there is a gray area that relates to supplies provided for the purpose of maintaining quality. Under the antitrust laws, 11 Domino's franchisees filed a lawsuit in 1995 alleging that they were overcharged for raw dough and that the franchisor, who must approve all suppliers, acted in a manner that discouraged alternative suppliers from entering the market. A similar suit was filed in 1993 by a group of Little Caesar's franchisees (Kramer 1995).

Foodservice franchisees are more closely tied to their franchisors than are lodging companies because of the special-purpose buildings and highly specialized operating skills that may not be transferable to another restaurant concept. Although there has been conversion activity from time to time, much of it has been a result of the purchase of entire chains to secure additional locations for the purchaser. Other occasions for conversion have arisen when a chain was forced to go out of business because of financial difficulties and was acquired by another company. Therefore, the competition among franchisors for other chains' franchisees to change brands has not developed in foodservice as it has in lodging.

Growth Versus Control. Franchising is a tool for rapid expansion, but it also threatens franchisors with losing control of operations as franchisees seek greater freedom and higher profits. Some franchisors expand by issuing a **master franchise,** which grants the right to develop units in a fairly wide territory. The master franchisee usually contracts to develop a certain number of units over a specified time period. The franchisor is likely to choose an individual with a proven record of business success and regards the area developer as a partner. In some cases, the master franchisee has the right to subfranchise to others as a part of the expansion plan. The franchisor gives up a significant degree of control when releasing a large territory to a master franchisee. To recover territorial control and operational profits, many well-established companies limit the number of franchises a franchisee may receive and engage in aggressive buy-back programs.

Encroachment. Encroachment is the term used in foodservice to describe the *impact* problem discussed earlier in relation to lodging. In 1993 a group of KFC franchisees successfully lobbied the Iowa legislature for a bill that would prohibit a franchisor from locating a new franchise within three miles of an existing franchise. The result was that major franchisors slowed or ceased the granting of franchises in Iowa.

Some expansion of franchising is taking place in the form of downsized units. Franchisors argue that even if these locations are near existing franchised operations, they target an entirely different market—shoppers in a mall or supermarket, students on campus, or workers in an office building who are not likely to go outside to eat a quick meal. However, from the franchisees' perspective, the smaller unit downgrades the image of the franchise, and people who have already eaten at a particular hamburger shop are less likely to visit the same brand later that day or in the near future. Some franchisees believe that franchisors are in the business of maximizing corporate revenue, even if it means sacrificing the revenues of some franchisees.

Intensive Distribution: Intercept Marketing

It has always been advantageous for a foodservice chain to have many restaurant locations. More units can reach more customers and achieve a higher level of market share. Over the past few years, QSRs have operated in *nontraditional locations*, such as hospitals, schools, colleges, expressways, and virtually any other viable place, in addition to the typical locations for freestanding restaurants. Learning from this experience, other restaurant companies have begun to think in terms of points of distribution (PODs).

PODs are scaled-down versions of a concept. They often rely on menus that are more limited than those in a traditional unit. Production and service modules are assembled in different ways. They are basically miniaturized, modularized, and, sometimes, mobile units. The presence of a known brand, the careful choice of target market, and a high-traffic site are key points in achieving a successful POD operation (Blumenthal 1995). Several different kinds of PODs are in use. The most common types include the following:

Towers or modular upright merchandisers. These may be self-serve units or visible full-service displays. They usually stand on the floor and are taller than eye level. A merchandiser can be a warmer, a refrigerator, or a display case for shelf-stable products.

Carts or modular cart systems. These are ideal for intercepting customers. Because of their mobility, they can be used as satellite units. Carts are often used as service units rather than "prep" units.

Kiosks. Kiosks are self-contained mini-restaurants. These are "stand-alone" intercept marketing vehicles, with the possible exception of needing outside storage space. A typical kiosk requires approximately 120 square feet.

Two concepts, **hosts** and **venues,** are important to understanding the development of intercept marketing.

Hosts. Hosts are business locations where high traffic is likely to offer potential high-volume sales of food or foodservice products. Examples include discount stores, grocery stores, malls, colleges and universities, airports, manufacturing plants, and theme parks. Hosts seek foodservice PODs to enhance their environment, satisfy consumers, gain revenue, and drive incremental traffic in commercial establishments, such as retail stores (Blumenthal 1995). The main selling point for PODs is that hosts provide foodservice vendors with access to the hosts' traffic.

Venues. The place provided by a host for the operation of a POD is called a venue. In a way, a venue is similar to a location for a freestanding restaurant. A venue not

These scaled-down units in an airport are examples of intercept marketing.

only specifies the place but also defines the customers. A venue on a college campus means that students will provide the bulk of the business, whereas a venue in a mall will have shoppers as the main clientele; in a manufacturing plant, workers can be expected to provide the predominant traffic in the area. Foodservice companies seek venues because good traditional sites are harder to come by and are very expensive. Moreover, as traditional operations face severe competition, venues offer exclusive or almost exclusive access to a significant traffic flow.

Who Operates PODs? Some operators of PODs are QSR companies, such as Taco Bell and Burger King. They often serve products that have been partially prepared in one of their regular units. Other operators of PODs are miniaturized versions of more service-intensive specialty restaurants, such as The Olive Garden, Pizza Hut, and Au Bon Pain. Contract foodservice firms are also major operators of PODs. Some operate under franchised brand names, others use their own brands, and still others may use a combination of franchised brands and their own brands in a food court.

Intermediaries

Restaurants started using third-party delivery services as intermediaries in the late 1980s. There are several hundred such companies in the United States. They usually take orders and deliver foods for 20 or so restaurants, although some provide such services for as many as 100 restaurants in a densely populated area. Some delivery companies charge consumers a $3 to $5 fee; others provide free deliveries to customers. Their profits come from the discounts provided by restaurants using the service. Typically, restaurants sell the food to them at a 25 to 35 percent discount. Many national chains, as well as independent restaurants, have used these services.

The advantages to restaurants include incremental business, name exposure without additional promotional costs, and not having to worry about delivering their own products. Delivery firms usually distribute thousands of copies of updated menus from all signed-up restaurants on a regular basis to local residents and businesses, as well as at hotels and tourist attractions. This service is particularly helpful to restaurants whose volume is not large enough to justify the investment in their own delivery service. Investing in a sophisticated delivery service can cost thousands of dollars for insurance, equipment, additional staff, and advertising. However, using a third-party delivery service means losing control of the food once it leaves the kitchen. Therefore, the selection of a professional third-party delivery firm should be undertaken with caution to ensure that the quality of food and service delivered meet the restaurant's standards and that proper precautions are taken to ensure the sanitation and safety of the food.

Other Intercompany Marketing Agreements: Alliances

Cooperation between companies can take several forms, such as **alliances,** strategic partnerships, or joint ventures. These corporate arrangements sometimes involve franchising. For example, Radisson Hotels formed a strategic partnership in Europe with SAS Hotels. SAS Hotels undertook a joint marketing program with Radisson Hotels and changed its name from SAS Hotels to Radisson SAS Hotels. One of the stipulations of the agreement was that SAS hotel properties would take on the Radisson franchise. Some alliances, however, simply mean cross-marketing. Case Study 9.2 provides several examples.

CASE STUDY 9.2

Corporate Alliances

Corporate alliances are formed to strengthen the partners' brands and to improve their efficiency in marketing and operations. Alliances allow "the partners to retain their independence—and in most cases, their financial control—while they raise revenues or cut costs."* Partnerships improve sales because they help upgrade services while

*D. Ernst and T. D. French, "Corporate Alliances: After the Honeymoon." *Wall Street Journal,* 13 May 1996, p. A20.

each partner reaches new customers. Cost savings come from sharing segments of the business system and from eliminating activities at one or both companies through outsourcing.

Corporate alliances in the hospitality industry involve cross-marketing arrangements between two or more hospitality companies or between a hospitality company and one of its suppliers. In some cases, an alliance is a means of exploring the possibility of a merger, but, in most cases, each firm intends to remain independent.

Pizza Hut has alliances with Hilton Hotels, Marriott International, Choice Hotels, and Cendant Corporation to provide pizza delivery to hotel guests. In their guest rooms, participating hotels display a table tent advertising the service. The alliance provides a service that hotel guests want while helping Pizza Hut to increase its sales. Pizza Hut pays a commission to the individual hotels for each order delivered and a smaller commission to the hotel franchisor. As in any good partnership, everyone benefits.

Carlson Leisure Group developed a cross-marketing arrangement between Carlson Travel and the European firm Wagonlit. Carlson Travel had excellent coverage in North America, and Wagonlit's strength was in Europe. The result of the alliance was that each firm increased its global presence. In this case, the partners merged and became Carlson Wagonlit Travel.

HFS (Cendant Corporation's predecessor) formed an alliance with C.U.C. International, a discount travel firm. When making a reservation, HFS reservationists asked guests whether they were interested in a discount travel club. If a guest was interested, he or she was referred over the phone to C.U.C. HFS brands benefitted because, for example, a Days Inn guest would be enrolled in a "Days Inn Travel Club," which was operated by C.U.C. and designed to build brand loyalty among Days Inn guests. Cendant Corporation acquired C.U.C. in December 1997.

United and eight other airlines from around the world have formed the Star Alliance to better meet the needs of frequent international travelers. The nine airlines work together to make travel less stressful and more rewarding. Gold members of the Star Alliance award program or elite members in any of the nine airlines' frequent flyer clubs, or international travelers flying first or business class on any of the member airlines, have access to Star Alliance Gold lounges and business lounges throughout the network. Travelers can earn qualifying miles when they fly on any member airline. They can also redeem their miles for rewards in the form of travel on any of the airlines. The alliance was designed to provide a seamless experience and convenient global access.

In addition to the Star Alliance, United Airlines has several other worldwide stra-

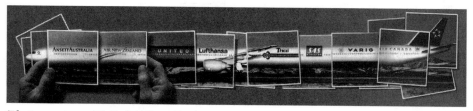

(Photo courtesy of United Airlines, Inc.)

tegic alliances. Together, they serve more than 500 destinations on six continents. Through such alliances, the airline extends the convenience of flying United to destinations beyond United routes. Travelers can enjoy simplified reservations, ticketing, one-stop check-in, reciprocal clubroom access, and coordinated baggage handling. Worldwide alliance members also have "code share" agreements, which means that flights operated within an alliance agreement are code share flights. For example, for a flight to Cancun, Mexico, the flight may be operated by Mexicana Airlines but listed as both Mexicana and United. Such alliances gives United better physical presence and representation around the world.

Sources: United Airlines, Inc. (2000). *United Airlines—Alliances* (on-line). Web site: http://www.ual.com/site/primary/0,10017,1518,00.html. The assistance of Janice Jarosz and Daniel Tarantin at Cendant Corporation, Chris Romoser at Pizza Hut, and Tom Polski at Radisson is greatly appreciated.

Experiences with a wide variety of alliances at McKinsey and Company, an international consulting firm, suggest several points of caution for firms considering alliances (Ernst and French 1996):

1. Customer demographics and usage patterns should ensure a good fit between the partnering firms, and their brand images should be compatible.
2. Expectations and operating guidelines should be agreed upon in advance, and benefits and risks should be balanced between the partners.
3. "Bundling" of products in a joint offer should give guests some real advantage, rather than just offer a package that guests would prefer to put together themselves.
4. Alliances can be costly in terms of executive time and can lead to disagreements, so conflict resolution mechanisms should be built into the agreement.
5. Each party should be assured of its ability to control its service offering and protect its brand image.

Summary

Distribution involves making a product conveniently available to consumers, either by its physical presence in a market or by representation. Convenience products, such as QSRs, use intensive distribution to reach consumers wherever they are. Channels of distribution in lodging include chain and franchise organizations, travel agents, hotel sales representative firms, and incentive houses. The growth of the GDS intensified the role of travel intermediaries, such as travel agents. However, the increased use of the Internet by consumers will revolutionize the GDS and may change the role of travel agents in the near future.

Franchise organizations continue to be important, but have much less power over their franchisees because of growing competition among lodging franchisors for franchisees and the enactment of franchise laws and regulations. Franchise companies form the most significant distribution channel in the foodservice industry. Encroachment, in foodservice, and impact, in lodging, generate the most serious conflicts in hospitality franchising.

The growing use of mobile and downsized points of distribution (PODs) supports the move toward intercept marketing in foodservice. Many foodservices also use a third-party delivery service as an intermediary.

Key Words and Concepts

Place/places
Intensive distribution
Selective distribution
Exclusive distribution
Channels of distribution
Franchise Systems
Physical presence
Representation
Reservation system
Central reservation service (CRS)

Global distribution system (GDS)
Switch companies
Franchises
Membership system
Impact
Travel wholesalers
Fam (familiarization) trip
Hotel sales representative companies
Incentive houses

Intercept marketing
Points of distribution (PODs)
Master franchise
Encroachment
Hosts
Venues
Alliances

Resources on the Internet

American Express.
   http://travel.americanexpress.com/travel/personal/
American Society of Travel Agents.
   http://www.astanet.com
Cendant Corporation.
   http://www.cendant.com/ctg/cgi-bin/Cendant/home
Charlie Trotter's. *http://www.charlietrotters.com/*
Choice Hotels International.
   http://www.hotelchoice.com/

The Greenbrier. *http://www.greenbrier.com/*
Radisson Hotels Worldwide. *http://www.radisson.com/*
Star Alliance. *http://www.star-alliance.com/cgi-bin/*
   sa.storefront/
Travel Weekly. *http://www.twcrossroads.com/*
United Airlines. *http://www.ual.com/*

Discussion Questions

1. What are the differences in lodging and foodservice distribution?
2. What are the degrees of intensity of distribution? Provide an example for each type of intensity.
3. Who are the principal channel members in lodging distribution?
4. What is the traditional lodging reservation system? How do you think the Internet will change the reservation system?

5. Why are travel agents important to lodging operations?

6. What kinds of services are provided by lodging and foodservice franchisors to franchisees?

7. What constitutes the most significant conflict in the franchise system? What is the term used in lodging? In foodservice?

8. What is intercept marketing? How is it changing foodservice marketing?

References

Best Western International. (2001). *Best Western Hotels home page* (on-line). Web site: http//www.bestwestern.com/

Blumenthal, I. (1995). Snapshots of branding. *Proceedings, Chain Operators Exchange.* Chicago: International Foodservice Manufacturers Association.

Cendant Corporation. (1999). *1998 Annual Report.* Author.

Choice Hotels. (1999). *1998 Annual Report.* Author.

ClubMed. (2001). *ClubMed home page.* (on-line). Web site: http//www/clubmed.com/

Culligan, P. E. (1995). Toward a new definition of impact. *Cornell Hotel and Restaurant Administration Quarterly* (August), 38–47.

Dube, L., and L. M. Renaghan, (2000). Marketing your hotel to and through intermediaries. *Cornell Hotel and Restaurant Administration Quarterly* (February), 73–83.

Ernst, D., and T. D. French, (1996). Corporate alliances: After the honeymoon. *Wall Street Journal,* 13 May, p. A20.

HotelBook. (2001). *HotelBook homepage* (on-line). Web site: http://www.hotelbook.com/

Kramer, L. (1995). Franchisees file antitrust suit against Domino's Pizza. *Nation's Restaurant News,* 29(27) (July 29), 7, 115.

Lexington Services. (2001). *Lexington Services home page* (on-line). Web site: http://www.lexres.com/

Lodging. (1999). The reservation revolution. *Lodging,* 24 (June) (10, Supplement).

PricewaterhouseCoopers. (1999). The Internet transforms the traditional hotel distribution system. *Hospitality Directions* (July), 19–29.

Rasinsky, R. (1995). A critical analysis of hotel impact issues. *Cornell Hotel and Restaurant Administration Quarterly* (August), 18–26.

Ross, C. (1999a). Continued growth—A closer look at midscale chains. *Lodging,* 25(2) (October), 55–56, 58–59.

Ross, C. (1999b). A moderate growth in demand—Evaluating the luxury/upscale full-service market. *Lodging,* 25(3) (November), 55–56, 58, 60.

Schulz, C. (1994). Hotels and travel agents: The new partnership. *Cornell Hotel and Restaurant Administration Quarterly* (April), 45–50.

Turkel, S. (1995). The problem with franchising. *Lodging,* 20(8) (April), 41–42.

Place in Hospitality Marketing: Location

When you have finished reading this chapter, you should be able to:

- Describe the major strategic issues related to location.
- Discuss the factors that should be considered in evaluating a restaurant location.
- Conduct a restaurant site evaluation.
- Explain the differences between foodservice and lodging location studies.
- Identify major components of a lodging feasibility study.

One major difference between hospitality marketing and consumer goods marketing is the contrasting ways in which they handle the concept of place. Consumer goods marketing is concerned with "placing products," or getting products from the manufacturers to the retailers and, ultimately, to the consumers. Location, when mentioned in relation to consumer goods, refers to the location of factories and warehouses, rather than the location at which consumers are served. In contrast, this chapter discusses location and site selection as a subject of major importance in hospitality marketing.

Ellsworth Statler, founder of the Statler Hotel chain and one of the pioneers of marketing in our industry, once said, "There are three factors necessary for the success of a hotel. They are location, location, and location." It is the oldest saying in our field; yet it is so true that it is worth repeating because location *is* a crucial issue in hospitality. The following sections consider both the strategic and the tactical issues related to location.

Location Strategies

At the most basic level, companies must decide on the area in which they will locate their units as they expand. In the early days of motel chains, for instance, Quality Courts operated east of the Mississippi and Best Western located to the west of the Mississippi. Holiday Inn began as a regional chain in the southeastern United States and gradually expanded into adjoining states. La Quinta Inns followed a similar strategy of expansion, starting as a regional chain in the southwestern United States. Concentrating in a certain region and expanding the company's territory gradually into neighboring areas allows a company to benefit from the reputation and customer base of established operations. When companies move into a new market, they have to develop themselves as if their products are in the introduction stage of the product life cycle. This was the case, for example, even with a company as well known as Holiday Inn when it first entered the U.S. West Coast market.

Clustering

One strategic approach to location is **clustering,** or locating several units in the same geographic area. Clustering can help establish the necessary critical mass by quickly obtaining the best locations and building consumer awareness and loyalty. Concentrated market development can lead to operating efficiencies in many areas, including management and administration, training, and marketing. It also allows companies to use more expensive advertising media sooner than would be possible with a more scattered expansion strategy. Therefore, clustering offers economies of scale within the cluster. Yet locating a number of new stores in a particular territory involves the risk of **cannibalization**—that is, one of a company's stores stealing business from another of its stores.

Although clustering can cause difficulties, a lack of critical mass can also be problematic. Wendy's expansion into Canada many years ago illustrates some of the problems. Early success in the Toronto market encouraged Wendy's to move into other geographic markets in Canada, some more than 1,000 miles away. In several markets, Wendy's did not have a sufficiently large store base to generate the sales needed to support expensive television advertising or to implement a significant campaign in other media. Operations supervision was also difficult because of the large geographic area covered. As a result, the quality of the operations suffered. Although these problems were subsequently solved by a very energetic turnaround management team, the company experienced several bad years.

Location Type: Freestanding or Part of a Larger Unit

Another issue in location strategy is location type. Some companies seek only freestanding locations, whereas others specialize in locations in malls, office buildings, and other **hosts** for **points of distribution (PODs).** Increasingly, however, companies are choosing to move into malls and other complexes, as discussed in Chapter 9, even though their principal location strategy may favor freestanding units.

The move into host locations results from several factors. The number of available freestanding locations is limited, and many of the best locations are already taken. Limited availability of freestanding sites not only means difficulty in obtaining desirable sites, but also indicates a substantially higher cost for those sites. **Venues** provided by shopping malls and retail stores are expensive; however, they are not overpriced when considering the volume they can deliver.

Market research indicates that the POD visitor market is a particular kind of target market. The principal restaurant patronage motive is convenience. In fact, the host location's traffic provides a customer base and access to a target market that can be reached only by being in that particular location. However, no market is completely captive. Most shopping malls, airports, and office complexes have several kinds of foodservice; therefore, competition is present. Nevertheless, a host location provides privileged access to its users. Although competition *is* present, there is usually only one operation for each concept and this exclusivity is not likely to exist in other locations. In today's mature foodservice market, freestanding units usually compete with several neighboring operations that offer similar concepts.

Host locations present a somewhat different marketing situation than freestanding units. The physical arrangements of PODs are less flexible, and the occupancy cost (i.e., rent) per square foot is usually higher. Accordingly, companies have developed downsized units that can recapture high rents through high sales volume in successful hosts. A key point in a host location is that sales volume is basically a function of the success of the host, such as a busy airport or a crowded mall. A successful foodservice operation in an unsuccessful host is quite unusual. The appearance of a POD is also different from that of a freestanding unit. The unique physical facility and the visibility found in a freestanding unit are not available in a POD because the appearance of the unit is limited to the amount and kinds of signage allowed and the number of feet of counter space available.

A freestanding unit presents a different marketing problem than an in-mall location, where the traffic is provided by mall patrons.

Promotion costs for small chains operating exclusively in host locations are likely to be lower because these operations rely on the traffic provided by the host. Companies that have a significant number of freestanding units, however, probably have to maintain their promotional activities to support their operations. Host locations do offer advantages to new or relatively unknown brands simply because the necessary business is provided by the host's traffic. Yet a strategy of using only host locations will, in time, limit the growth of a brand, because the number of successful host locations is limited.

Large chains that operate several different types and sizes of locations, including PODs, have to realize that not all of their PODs' volume is additional sales. There is a certain amount of cannibalization because, for example, a person eating fried chicken in a mall for lunch is not likely to be a dinner customer for the same fried chicken that evening. This topic is discussed as the concept of *encroachment* in Chapter 9.

Colocation

Colocation, as discussed in Chapter 8, involves putting two or more noncompetitive concepts in one location. McDonald's and Amoco have built many cobranded stations after extensive market testing. McDonald's also has a similar alliance with Chevron's Food Mart, a convenience store. Alliances between foodservice chains and oil com-

When two powerful noncompetitive brands occupy a site together, the result is improved sales, as each brand benefits from the draw on the customer base of the other brand. (Photo courtesy of McDonald's Corporation.)

panies are particularly attractive because service stations often control prime real estate and stations near highways bring travelers who are usually looking for a quick meal.

When a restaurant is colocated with another retailer, it benefits from the traffic the other retailer generates. Likewise, the restaurant enhances the location by providing a service to the retail customers. When a location is shared with another foodservice operation, both partners share the cost of the land and building and gain from exposure to the customers of the other operation. For example, morning donut customers may return for an ice cream treat later, and morning coffee drinkers may pick up a bagel for breakfast or return for a sandwich at lunchtime.

Funnel or Magnet?

Most chain operations and many independent operations seek high-traffic locations. We can equate those locations to a funnel under a waterfall: the water is bound to flow through it. In **funnel locations,** such as those occupied by major quick-service restaurants (QSRs), there are so many prospective customers in the area that stores are almost certain to do a high volume of sales. Funnel locations, however, do have the disadvantage of being located on very expensive real estate, which means higher rent or fixed capital costs.

The Greenbrier Resort serves as a magnet, attracting visitors to this remotely located property nestled on 6,500 acres in the scenic Allegheny Mountains in White Sulphur Springs, West Virginia. (Photo courtesy of The Greenbrier Resort Management Company.)

The analogy of a magnet can be used to describe the very distinctive operations located in rural areas or in small towns, away from major population centers. In **magnet locations,** there is little or no drop-in business; people have to make an effort, or drive a considerable distance, to get there. Rural locations, however, can be used to advantage by creating a unique ambience with scenery, quietness, and open space. In addition, the cost of real estate is likely to be much lower than in high-traffic urban areas. In order for these locations to succeed, the *operation* must function as a magnet by offering a distinctive experience in menu, quality of food, excellent service, recreation, or lodging that draws customers from a significant distance. Many Native American casinos, for instance, located in remote reservations, attract thousands of visitors every day.

In paying for a high-traffic location, operators expect that the location will help *push* volume through their operation. A magnet location, however, requires an operation to *pull* customers to it.

Tactical Issues

Once the broad outline of a location strategy is established, special effort is needed to analyze specific location decisions, which include a **location decision** and a **site decision.** For example, a company may make a location decision to expand into a general part of a city, such as the neighborhood of a new mall or office park, or on a particular side of town. Once a decision is made to locate in an area, a site decision, which involves the selection of a particular piece of land, is required. Usually, several sites are evaluated before a final location is determined.

Restaurant Location Evaluation

A restaurant location is best evaluated in terms of the potential demand it can generate and the access it provides to customers. A trading area can be defined for an existing operation or estimated for a new one. The "quality" of the population is assessed, as is the location's access to that population through the roadway or other transportation system. The likely direction of major traffic flow, as well as competition in the area, must be carefully studied. Each of these factors is reviewed briefly.

Trading Area. A **trading area** is the geographic area containing 70 to 75 percent of the customers of a business. In an existing unit, the trading area is determined from the operation's patronage records. In a new unit, the trading area must be estimated based on the sales volume at other operations in the region, the performance of other units in similar locations, or responses to questionnaires or interviews with prospective customers. When the proposed operation is part of a chain, these data are much easier to come by.

Population Characteristics. When a trading area is identified, its **population characteristics**—density, demographics, and psychographics—are studied in depth. A densely populated area is generally preferred, simply because the more people in an area, the higher the demand for dining out opportunities.

Although population density is key for QSRs and other popularly priced operations, the demographics of that population are also important. For example, the presence of families with children would be a highly favorable factor for some operations but less important for others. For an independent fine-dining operation, population density would be less significant than the income statistics for the area, because the operator is not interested in *everybody* in the trading area but only *selected* market segment(s). A market analysis must consider the current as well as the future market situation. The analysis should project population growth for the area and estimate the size of the total population and market segment(s) for the next five years.

The population's psychographics, or lifestyle, is also of interest. An operation that offers family dining with a country-style barbecue may be interested in one psychographic segment in the area, whereas a Red Lobster may target a somewhat different group. It should be no surprise, however, if these two operations are located side by side, because the trading area they draw from probably has an adequate number of people in both market segments to support both operations.

Relation to Roadway System and Traffic. Paramount to the success of any location is the access it offers to an operation's target populations. Although population in the immediate area is important to many operations, access for people via roadways or other transportation is often even more important. Any changes planned for the roadways should be identified and evaluated to assess the potential impact of such changes. Driving time from the centers of population is a commonly used measure of the convenience of a location. Driving time is affected by the quality of the road system leading to the site, as well as any physical barriers between the site and the population center.

The impact of any physical or social barriers on traffic should also be evaluated. **Physical barriers** include factors such as unbridged rivers or large bodies of water, as well as mountains and freeways that do not have convenient crossings. **Social barriers** include industrial districts, areas with congested traffic, unsafe neighborhoods, rundown communities, and, surprisingly, extremely affluent subdivisions (Thompson 1982).

Distance. As mentioned, distance from population centers is a good *proxy*, or indirect measure, in determining convenience. However, it should be kept in mind that **acceptable distance** is defined differently for different types of operations. For example, most convenience stores serve a trading area within a radius of ¼ mile to 1 mile, whereas a QSR may draw residents from a radius of 1 to 1½ miles. Casual dining concepts usually have a trading area of approximately 3 to 5 miles, and fine dining establishments often pull customers from as far away as 20 miles or more (Reich 1997).

Local Traffic. The volume of traffic in the area is of particular interest to QSRs and other mass-market operations. In downtowns and other highly congested areas, pedestrian, rather than vehicular, traffic can be the significant measure. In general, the more traffic and the greater the traffic flow, the better the location for popularly priced restaurants. For upscale restaurants, however, the right *type* of traffic, including individuals who are willing and able to pay for fine dining on a regular basis, is more important.

Other Sources of Business. In many locations, nonresidential sources of business provide most store traffic. For example, offices and plants, theaters, schools, colleges and universities, and medical facilities have large numbers of employees who are potential customers and also draw a significant volume of visitors. Restaurants near tourist attractions obviously depend on tourists as the major source of business. In central business districts or shopping centers, retail stores' employees and customers are the major source of traffic.

The Gravity of Large Centers and Traffic Flow. The **gravity model** represents perhaps the leading academic theory of location analysis. This model estimates the probability of consumers' patronizing a retail area by considering the size of the shopping area, travel time for consumers to reach the center, and the impact of travel time on patronage at the particular kind of shopping center (e.g., a large regional mall or a small strip mall) (Thompson 1982). Generally, the larger the center, the greater the variety of goods offered, and the shorter the distance from the consumers' homes, the greater the likelihood of patronage. Retail sales volume in the center, therefore, is positively related to the *pull* of the shopping area, reflected in the size and variety of goods, and its proximity to customers. The term "inbound bias" indicates that shoppers gravitate toward centers of retail activities (Thompson 1982). A location between a center of population and a shopping center that serves as a gravity pull has the significant advantage of being along the traffic flow.

Competition. The presence of competition in a neighborhood is often a favorable indicator. "Restaurant rows" are testimony to the fact that a good central location can support several restaurants. Therefore, the presence of several restaurants in an area will increase the draw of foodservice traffic to the area, much like the gravity of large retail shopping centers discussed earlier.

The first step in assessing competition is to plot competitive units on a map of the area and to note each location in terms of street and cross street; size of unit, such as number of seats and square feet; and the type of outlet and its estimated sales. A **competitive analysis** should discriminate between direct and indirect competition. For example, a market study for a quick-service chicken restaurant should analyze competing locations in two direct competition categories—quick-service chicken restaurants and other quick-service restaurants—and one indirect category, including all other restaurants, such as coffee shops and family restaurants.

Although the presence of competition can be a favorable indicator, it is also possible for a location to be oversupplied with restaurants. One way of assessing this possibility is to estimate the sales volume of the competing operations in the area. If the competitors are competent operators but not doing an acceptable level of business, this should signal a warning to the location analyst. A concentration of outdated or inefficiently operated competitors, however, may signal an opportunity. In effect, if they can survive while doing a mediocre job, a well-run operation with a current theme should be able to capitalize on the strong demand in the area. Case Study 10.1 discusses a seven-step location and site selection process used by some restaurants.

CASE STUDY 10.1

Location and Site Analysis with GIS

A geographic information system (GIS) has been used to evaluate retail locations and identify sites that have the greatest profit potential. A seven-step computer-assisted decision strategy has been designed by spatial analysis experts as a guideline in assessing retail locations and developing appropriate geographic expansion strategies.

Step 1: Identify area for store assessment. The company has to answer two questions: (1) Which regions (e.g., states) should we develop in first/next? and (2) Which places (e.g., cities) within the regions should we develop in first/next? The three major patterns of market penetration strategy are contagious, hierarchical, and relocation. Contagious market penetration follows a nearest-neighbor type spatial pattern. An example is a restaurant chain that has clusters of outlets in a region. Hierarchical market penetration follows a pattern of jumping across the landscape to penetrate the "most important" markets first. For example, a hotel company may choose to operate in the 100 largest markets in the world as the first step of expansion.

Relocation market penetration is commonly used after the early stages of a company's development. A company can use a GIS to identify characteristics of successful locations. Those characteristics are then used to explore new locations with potential to succeed. Unsuccessful units are gradually closed or relocated to areas with desirable characteristics. A newly expanding company may follow a hierarchical market penetration strategy, then adopt a contagious strategy by expanding outlets near those "most important" markets. As the company continues to grow, some of the earlier locations may become obsolete and are subsequently closed or relocated.

Step 2: Perform a geographical inventory. Computer mapping programs are available to identify current market saturation by state, metropolitan statistical area (MSA), or other criteria. Legends on the map indicate which markets have had the highest level of competition and which are currently underserved.

Step 3: Assess the relative performance of retail units. The company must establish regional or national benchmarks and compare individual outlet performance to those benchmarks. The comparison will identify geographic markets that have a history of high or low performance and markets that should be targeted for expansion or scaling back.

Step 4: Identify situation targets. The term "situation" refers to the surrounding demographics, businesses, and other environmental factors that may affect the success of an outlet. A GIS can generate a demographic and general situation profile for each outlet's trading area. Information from the entire company can be pooled to identify characteristics that distinguish the most successful units from less successful units within the chain. Locations identified as having similar qualifications can be expected to have similarly good performance.

Step 5: Assess market penetration. Market penetration is the percentage of the total market captured by the company. The total market is the number of people in a particular geographic area whose profiles fit that of the company's target market. The market penetration is calculated by dividing the annual customer count by the total market. A low ratio indicates that the market is less saturated and may support one or more additional outlets. A high ratio identifies markets that may be saturated, with no additional opportunities.

Market penetration ratios of competitors can also be calculated to evaluate the relative competitiveness of each company. Market penetration, therefore, is a measure of market presence, performance, and competitive position.

Step 6: Identify geographic markets for expansion. Geographic areas that have higher than average unit performance (Step 3) and low market penetration (Step 5) can be considered for expansion.

Step 7: Make a judgment. GIS reports for specific locations contain information on population demographics, housing characteristics, locations of competitors, neighboring businesses, traffic generators, traffic volume and patterns, and sales forecasts. Even with all this information in hand, senior managers still need to visit the site and visually assess the area before final decisions are made.

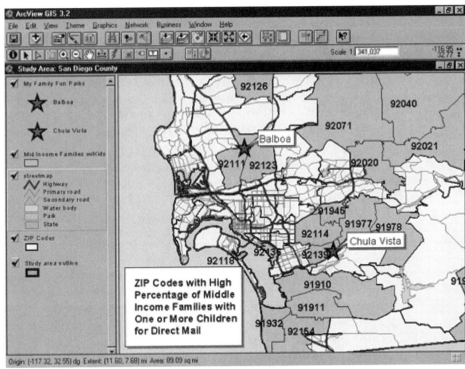

With the Environmental Systems Research Institute's (ESRI) ArcView® Business Analyst™ software, the user can precision-tune target marketing to identify only those zip codes that match a certain criterion. Such information can help in analyzing market potential while conducting site selection. The information can also be used to reduce mailing and printing costs and to increase the success rate of a direct mailing campaign. (Graphic image courtesy of Environmental Systems Research Institute, Inc.)

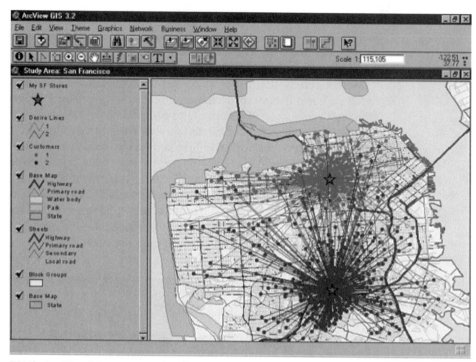

ESRI's Arc View® Business Analyst™ software can illustrate customer draw to allow users to analyze possible cannibalization, identify under- and overserved areas, and visualize where customers come from geographically. (Graphic image courtesy of Environmental Systems Research Institute, Inc.)

Sources: G. I., Thrall, J. C. del Valle, and G. Hinzmann, "Applying the Seven-Step Site Selection Methodology to Red Lobster Restaurants: Steps One and Two," *Geo Info Systems,* 8(2) (1998), 40–43; "Retail Location Analysis, Step Three: Assessing Relative Performance," *Geo Info Systems,* 8(4) (1998), 38–44; "Retail Location Analysis, Step Four: Identify Situation Targets," *Geo Info Systems,* 8(6) (1998), 38–43; "Retail Location Analysis, Step Five: Assess Market Penetration," *Geo Info Systems,* 8(9) (1998), 46–50; "Retail Location Analysis, Step Six: Identify Markets for Expansion," *Geo Info Systems,* 8(11) (1998), 42–45.

Restaurant Site Evaluation

Differentiating between location and site analyses is helpful in understanding the various components of location selection; however, the division is somewhat artificial. Although a general location analysis is usually conducted first, followed by a site analysis, in many cases they are not two separate processes but one multipurpose investigation. If there is no site, then reviewing the location is a waste of time. If there are a number of sites, this immediately raises the question as to whether this is a good location. In practice, landowners and their agents usually approach restaurant chains with proposed sites; therefore, a site proposal could very well initiate the process of location and site evaluation. Location evaluation factors discussed in the previous section are often analyzed more or less simultaneously with site evaluation factors, because they are also fundamental to the analysis of a site. It is true, however, that a detailed review of a site is likely to be the last step before the site is acquired.

As a starting point in site analysis, traffic patterns that are considered in general earlier during location analysis must be reviewed again. This time the traffic patterns should be evaluated based on a specific piece of property. Factors to be considered include traffic volume, ease of traffic flow, and quality of traffic. The type of traffic desired depends on the location of the site and the target market(s). For example, in evaluating a potential bakery site in a retail area near a college campus with limited parking facilities, pedestrian traffic is more important than vehicular traffic. In some cities, public transportation is widely used. If this is the case, a stop near the restaurant site may be viewed as desirable or undesirable, depending on the type of restaurant under consideration.

As shown in Figure 10.1, exposure to traffic is maximized by a corner location, such as Site A. Therefore, Site A has excellent **visibility** as compared with any other sites in Figure 10.1. Within a strip mall building, such as that illustrated in Figure 10.1, Site C is the most preferred site, followed by Site H, from the perspective of visibility. In addition to visibility, *relative visibility* is also a significant factor to consider. Relative visibility refers to the possibility that the site may technically be visible, yet lost in the clutter of other buildings and activities in the area. Under these circumstances, we should explore various ways, such as special treatment of the exterior, to make the property stand out from its neighbors. Billboards and directional signs off

In many downtown locations, foot traffic rather than vehicular traffic is a prime consideration.

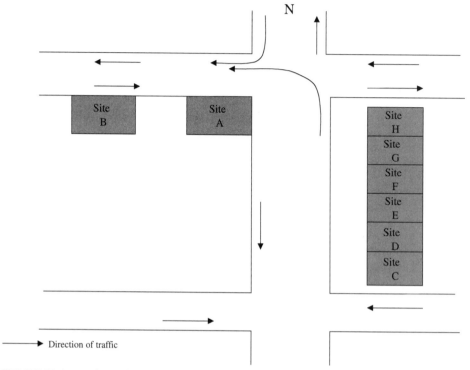

FIGURE 10.1   Analysis of visibility and accessibility.

the property and tall signs on the property can greatly enhance the site's visibility. They may, however, be prohibited by local regulations. Therefore, local zoning codes should be investigated to determine signage possibilities.

Accessibility is another important site evaluation criterion. Access from the roadway to the site is evaluated on the basis of ease of ingress and egress. Left-turn lanes, traffic lights, and stop signs are favorable factors because they facilitate access for left-turning traffic. However, high speed limits and one-way streets can have negative effects on accessibility. Greatly congested traffic at the site and access restricted to right-hand turns can also be seriously unfavorable factors. This may be the case for Site B in Figure 10.1. In evaluating Site A, care should be taken to ensure that traffic from the north, east, and south sides of the site can easily turn into the property. Access to the parking lot from both the north and east sides of the property could greatly enhance accessibility.

Adequate size of the site itself, to provide room for both the building and the necessary parking, is crucial. The lack of parking facilities may be viewed as a barrier and therefore discourage visits to the operation. Many operations in downtowns and near college campus locations face this problem and have limited appeal to people beyond walking distance. The cost of the site is also a significant factor. Demand for prime real estate is strong, and, with many good locations already taken, real estate prices continue to escalate. Building costs for restaurants have risen as well. Therefore, fixed asset requirements, including land and other capital costs, must be reviewed along with the operation's forecasted volume to ensure that the planned restaurant will generate the necessary level of sales and profits to succeed.

Land use in the surrounding area should also be examined. Existing activities in the area can serve as a magnet for traffic, as in the case of a theater, or can be a distinct disadvantage, as in the case of a factory or other activities that pollute the immediate environment with odors, excessive noise, or just an ugly appearance. A final factor is the site terrain and whether it presents problems for the building and required parking.

Given the complexity of location and site analyses, it is not surprising that most restaurant chains have real estate departments that specialize in the analysis and acquisition of land for the company's use.

Hotel Location: The Feasibility Study

Location and site analyses for hotels have many similarities with those required for restaurants. However, there are some fundamental differences. First, a **feasibility study** is conducted to support a hotel construction decision. The decision is more concerned with the overall financial picture of a proposed property than is typically the case with a restaurant. Because a hotel investment decision is very capital intensive, the feasibility study must consider not only the total project cost, but also the financial structure of the project and the tax implications of the project's profit and loss based on the owner's total investment portfolio (Angelo 1985).

Second, a hotel developer looks at a larger service area than does a typical restaurant operation. Most hotel location studies evaluate the entire community as a market. In larger metropolitan areas, specific sections of cities are evaluated, but these sections are generally much larger than a restaurant's trading area. Although the market analysis is restricted to areas near the project site, guests are expected to come from regions far removed from that site. For resort hotels, conference centers, and convention hotels, a study of demand in distant cities may be conducted. However, for most properties, the demand from other cities is inferred from a study of local demand generators and attractions. Demand can also be estimated based on the number of rooms occupied in local hotels and motels (Rushmore 1992).

The content of a hotel feasibility study includes a site evaluation, a **market area analysis,** a **demand analysis,** a **competitive (supply) analysis,** facilities and concept recommendations, a forecast of income and expenses, an estimate of total project cost, and other financial analyses. These factors are discussed next.

Site Evaluation

The size and topography of a site must be assessed to be sure that it is suitable for the proposed project. Surrounding land uses and proximity to major demand generators should also be noted. Similarly, the site's location relative to key highways and interstates should be considered, as should its ease of access for motor vehicle traffic. These characteristics have different levels of importance for different types of lodging operations. For instance, accessibility and visibility are generally more important for operations targeting individual tourists than for properties tailored to business travelers, because individual tourists usually have to find the hotels themselves, whereas business travelers often use public transportation (Andrew and Schmidgall 1993). Proximity to major demand generators, such as a convention center or an airport, is important to lodging operations that depend on business related to these demand generators.

Market Area Analysis

Trends in demographic and economic indicators are employed as a basis to support demand and growth projections. Usually, the history of several indicators is reviewed to identify trends and project visitation. To estimate commercial visitation to the area and meeting and convention volume, the indicators used may include population, income, retail activities, employment, occupied office space, thruway traffic, airport passenger and cargo traffic, and area development. Vacationer visitation estimates can be based on highway traffic, past tourist visit statistics, admissions to nearby attractions, and area tourism development plans.

Demand Analysis

Demand is analyzed by major market segment, such as the commercial, meeting, and vacationer segment. Demand can be estimated by two methods. With the use of the *build-up approach,* demand is estimated through interviews with people connected to travel generators. These interviews determine the amount of demand each market segment provides on a weekly or monthly basis, along with other important visitor information, such as length of stay, number of people in a party, and spending patterns. Another way of estimating demand is by totaling the number of rooms actually occupied in local lodging operations. This information is usually available from local convention and visitors bureaus or by calculating from the room tax figures available from local governments. Demand estimates obtained from the two methods should be compared in order to cross-validate the assessment. Future demand should be forecasted based on current demand and projected growth rates, which can be estimated on the basis of the economic and demographic factors studied in the market area analysis.

Competitive (Supply) Analysis

Competitive analysis identifies existing and planned properties that compete directly and indirectly with the proposed property. Relevant statistics to review include location, number of rooms, room rates, average occupancy rate, target markets, and amenities and facilities. The analysis of the competition should be set in the context of the demand in a particular market. Well-qualified competitors, for example, are not as much of an immediate threat in a market that is severely underbuilt as in a market that has excess capacity. A competitive survey should evaluate the strengths and weaknesses of existing competition. The results may be used to argue for a particular kind of facility to build in a specific locale.

It is also important to assess future known and projected additions to the current supply, and a determination should be made on the probability of their being developed. Many properties that are announced are, for one reason or another, never built. Those that have been granted building permits and have obtained financing, however, are likely to be built. Those that are under construction are almost certain to be completed. Case Study 10.2 reports the lodging supply and demand of various locations.

CASE STUDY 10.2

Lodging Supply and Demand by Location

Smith Travel Research, a leading lodging research and consulting firm, categorizes the lodging industry in various ways. Based on location, the industry is segmented into urban, suburban, airport, highway, and resort categories. The 1999 and 2000 data indicated that the growth of supply and demand of hotel rooms in suburban locations exceeded that of any other locations. Resort hotels, however, had the lowest growth in demand and were one of the slowest-growing categories in supply. Resort hotels also reported the most significant decreases in average rates in both 1999 and 2000.

All locations experienced greater growth in supply than in demand, which shows the continuation of the hotel building boom. Because of the increase in room supply and competition, average room rates decreased in all hotel locations. Nevertheless, hotels in all locations were able to increase their occupancy in both years.

The accompanying table provides detailed information on changes in supply, demand, average rate, and occupancy by location segment. An analysis of statistics such as these should be part of the decision-making process for site selection or expansion.

% Change		Location Type				
		Urban	Suburban	Airport	Highway	Resort
Supply	1999	5.1%	6.3%	4.2%	2.3%	2.1%
	2000	4.4%	5.3%	3.9%	3.1%	3.2%
Demand	1999	3.7%	4.6%	2.5%	1.5%	−0.7%
	2000	3.4%	4.2%	2.6%	2.1%	1.5%
Average Rate	1999	−1.4%	−1.6%	−1.7%	−0.8%	−2.7%
	2000	−0.9%	−1.1%	−1.3%	−1.0%	−1.6%
Occupancy	1999	5.5%	3.9%	4.6%	4.6%	4.7%
	2000	3.6%	2.8%	2.9%	4.3%	5.6%

Note: Percent changes are based on the 12-month periods ending February 1999 and February 2000.
Source: M. V. Lomanno, Smith Travel Research. Personal communication, 30 March, 2000.

Other Study Contents

Based on the analysis of demand and competition, a recommendation on the type and size of feasible facilities is made and the cost of the recommended facilities can be estimated. Revenues are forecasted on the basis of demand projection and competitive analysis. Expenses are calculated on the basis of facilities, services, and occupancy level. Profit is then determined by subtracting expenses from revenues. Typically, the minimum life for a viable hotel is 30 years. Therefore, the entire project involves judgments that go beyond a typical marketing study.

Informed Judgment

It is important to appreciate the degree to which a hotel feasibility study relies on estimates, the judgment of interviewers as to the meaning of various statements, and the judgment of the feasibility study authors on the extent and interpretation of trends. Because of the use of these informed judgments, location decisions in the hotel industry are somewhat less precise than those for foodservice operations. Actually, feasibility studies are commonly used internally to confirm management's prior decision on a proposed location. However, a study's use as a confirmation of decisions that have already been made by senior management is not the intention and proper use of the study and is open to question.

Another and probably more significant use of a feasibility study is to secure debt financing for the proposed property. Because hotel companies spend tens of thousands of dollars on each feasibility study, as it is intended to be used to secure financing, there is often an unspoken pressure on the feasibility analysts to come up with a positive answer.

Site selection sometimes plays a secondary role. Well-known hotel chains are more flexible than no-name operations because of their marketing strength and brand recognition. They are interested in convenience to areas of commercial and recreational activities; however, they can afford to take a location three or four blocks from the very center of such activity because customers are willing to go that far, at least in a central business district location. In addition, good sites, with high traffic and substantial activity, are considerably more important outside the central business district.

Courtyard by Marriott offers an example of the viability of locating at less-than-prime sites because of the strength of the brand. Company officials have indicated that some Courtyard locations are actually hard to get to the first time. However, because of the strong demand for Courtyard properties, guests are willing to make the effort to find the properties. It should be noted that in these locations, the properties are serving guests who have business in the immediate area and therefore want to stay nearby. Such a location strategy would certainly not be appropriate if the property were counting on a significant amount of off-the-road tourist traffic.

Summary

Location strategy involves selecting the general area in which a company will operate and determining whether the company will expand through clustering or a more scattered expansion strategy. Restaurant location strategy also includes a decision on the type(s) of location, such as freestanding or PODs, that the company will use. The tactics of locating a particular operation involve both location and site selections. *Location* refers to a general area within a city, whereas the *site* is a specific piece of property. Restaurant location analysis requires the definition of a trading area and then a study of the area's population, roadway and transportation systems, traffic patterns and volume, and local competition. Site evaluation, which is often conducted simultaneously with location analysis, considers the same factors but with respect to a specific piece of property. In addition, site evaluation considers the site's visibility, accessibility, size, and cost, as well as nearby land use and site terrain.

Hotel location analysis is usually documented in a feasibility study following a rationale similar to that for restaurants. Hotel location decisions, however, emphasize the financing aspects of the proposal, and developers generally look at a larger service area—usually the entire city. The content of a hotel feasibility study includes a site evaluation, a market area analysis, a demand and supply analysis, and other financial analyses. Because most hotels' business comes from other areas, regional and national travel patterns must be considered.

Key Words and Concepts

Clustering

Cannibalization

Hosts

Points of distribution (PODs)

Venues

Colocation

Funnel locations

Magnet locations

Location decision

Site decision

Trading area

Population characteristics

Physical barriers

Social barriers

Acceptable distance

Gravity model

Competitive analysis

Visibility

Accessibility

Feasibility study

Market area analysis

Demand analysis

Competitive (supply) analysis

Resources on the Internet

ESRI GIS and Mapping Software. *http://www.esri.com/*
Geo Info Systems. *http://www.geoinfosystems.com/*
Geographic Information Systems.
    http://info.er.usgs.gov/research/gis/title.html

Strategic Growth Consultants.
    http://stratgrowth.com/

Discussion Questions

1. What are the major strategic issues related to location?
2. What are the advantages and disadvantages of clustering?
3. What are the principal issues in evaluating a restaurant location? How do these issues differ from criteria used in site evaluation? What are the similarities between the two?

4. To what degree is informed judgment a part of a hotel feasibility decision? How does this make a hotel location analysis different from the process for restaurants?
5. How important is "site" in a hotel decision in a downtown market? In a suburban market? How do you explain the differences?

References

Andrew W. P., and R. S. Schmidgall. (1993). *Financial management for the hospitality industry.* East Lansing, MI: Educational Institute of the American Hotel & Motel Association.

Angelo, R. M. (1985). *Understanding feasibility studies: A practical guide.* East Lansing, MI: Educational Institute of the American Hotel & Motel Association.

Reich, A. Z. (1997). *Marketing management for the hospitality industry: A strategic approach.* New York: John Wiley & Sons.

Rushmore, S. (1992). *Hotels and motels: A guide to market analysis, investment analysis, and valuations.* Chicago: Appraisal Institute.

Thompson, J. S. (1982). *Site selection.* New York: Lebhar-Friedman.

11

The Price of Hospitality

(Photo courtesy of Sirloin Stockade International.)

When you have finished reading this chapter, you should be able to:

- Discuss common pricing objectives.
- Explain determinants of price.
- Define common foodservice pricing methods.
- Select final prices for foodservice operations.
- Illustrate hotel pricing practices.
- Understand the yield management concept and strategies.
- List the advantages of package prices.

The basic purpose of price is to present the value of a product to consumers. Price is of interest to sellers because it is their means of recapturing the cost of doing business and making a profit. Consumers, on the other hand, are more interested in what they can get for the price they pay. In other words, they are more concerned about the value they receive. For this reason, some marketers use the term **price/value** rather than simply *price*. In hospitality, value for consumers can be defined as follows:

$$\frac{\text{Product} + \text{service} + \text{location} + \text{ambience} + \text{image}}{\text{price}} = \text{value}$$

The meaning of this equation can be briefly illustrated in terms of enhancements of value with the following examples:

Product improvements, such as guest room amenities or artistic arrangement of the garnish on the plate.

+

Service enhancement, such as employing an unusually well-trained staff or a particularly accommodating central reservations office

+

Extra location appeals, such as a downtown business center location or a location with the social prestige of having the "right address"

+

An attractive ambience—romantic, luxury, or contemporary

+

An image supported by advertising and promotion

Any, or any combination, of these elements should improve consumers' perception of the operation. As these elements are enhanced while the price stays the same, the value of the offering is perceived to be higher.

This chapter examines pricing objectives and the determinants of price and discusses pricing methods in the industry, first in foodservice and then in lodging.

Pricing Objectives

In multiunit organizations, there are usually well-thought-out company policies that support specific **pricing objectives.** In businesses that are smaller and operated more informally, pricing objectives may not be explicitly stated or even consciously thought out; however, closer examination will reveal that unstated goals usually lie behind all pricing decisions. Some pricing objectives emphasize sales, others focus on profits. This is only a matter of emphasis, because profit requires sales and sales usually imply a profit. Therefore, both sales and profit objectives are involved in all pricing decisions.

Sales-Oriented Pricing Objectives

Taco Bell's value pricing strategy began as an experiment by a number of franchisees in a depressed market. Another Taco Bell franchisee explored value pricing to improve Sunday sales. These experiments were so successful in 1986 and 1987 that by 1988, the value concept was adopted and spread across the country. These price *reductions* were intended to drive sales, and they did. Sales from 1987 to 1990 rose 60 percent.

A less dramatic, but more common, pricing practice is to meet the price of competitors. In fact, this is a pattern found not only in hospitality, but also in many other service industries. The **sales-oriented objective** here is to protect market share. The logic of protecting market share is as follows: Prices are set by the competition, and the costs of the operation are set by the going rate for labor, food products, and supplies. Because the operation is, and should be, managed as efficiently as possible to minimize costs, there is a limited range of discretion for pricing. Although a certain premium can be charged for new and unique products, the general rule is that pricing must meet the competition except where there is substantial differentiation. As a result, profit margins are a reflection of an operation's efficiency and its ability to maintain its market share.

What management *can* control, to a significant degree, is sales levels. This can be done by meeting competitive prices and developing more effective strategies based on other elements of the marketing mix, such as service enhancements, new products, and increased advertising and promotion. The upgrading of the ambience of quick-service restaurants (QSRs) by market leaders some years ago, which was quickly followed by other operators, is an example of nonprice competition, as is the growth in promotional spending by hospitality chains. All of these are attempts to differentiate the product and increase sales without engaging in price competition. The rationale is that if you lose your market share, it is difficult to regain your market position.

Profit-Oriented Pricing Objectives

A sales-oriented objective can also be a **profit-oriented objective.** The Taco Bell value pricing initiative increased volume and contributed to the rise in profit by more than 75 percent from 1987 to 1990 (Schlesinger and Hallowell 1994). The significant increase in profit was also a result of restructuring through reducing middle management in the company. In fact, reducing operating costs to become more price competitive is a tactic used by many firms both within and outside the hospitality industry.

Lodging companies usually use a target rate of return on investment (ROI) to evaluate an operation. Price levels are expected to support an operation that generates enough revenue to cover the company's operating format, such as luxury, midpriced, or budget, and meet the company's profit target. Following this reasoning, when a property's occupancy level falls, room rates are raised to maintain target profit levels. This tactic, however, does not work for operators in markets where there is an over-

Taco Bell's value-pricing initiative cut prices but increased profit as sales bounded ahead. (Photo courtesy of Taco Bell.)

supply of rooms, because excess capacity tends to drive down prices regardless of profit levels. When this happens, the building, or at least the land, can be converted to other uses. The fundamental logic is that a hotel is a financial asset that should perform at a certain ROI level. Properties that cannot perform at this level are removed from service.

Restaurant corporations also view restaurant concept and individual operations as financial assets. Foodservice conglomerates acquire smaller firms with the intent of expanding the concept to a larger territory. If a concept does not meet performance expectations, the restaurant will be sold or converted to another concept. For example, after five years of trying to develop a successful Chinese dinner house concept, Darden Restaurants, Inc. closed all of its China Coast restaurants. About half the units were converted to Red Lobster or Olive Garden restaurants, and the rest were sold or otherwise disposed of. Although the Chinese restaurant was a viable concept, the price level it could support was not adequate to generate a sales volume that could meet the ROI target.

It should be noted that although most restaurant companies use profit and ROI in evaluating new locations, they rarely try to maintain revenue in a soft market by raising prices as hotels sometimes do. Higher prices for the same product in restaurants usually mean lower sales, because the dining-out market is more price sensitive, as compared with some segments of the travel market. Business travelers typically have urgent reasons for travel and are usually traveling on expense accounts; therefore, they are generally less price sensitive.

Pricing in Nonprofit Operations

In a certain sense, nonprofit operations have the most rigidly driven profit-based pricing goals. To illustrate this clearly, a special definition of "profit" is needed that includes subsidy as "negative profit." If a school lunch program has a city appropriation of $150,000, then the operation must *lose no more than* that amount. The budgeted loss is best thought of as a negative profit. Therefore, price levels must be set to generate that much "negative profit." A quite different kind of operation, a private club, also subsidizes its food and beverage operations with membership dues.

Some nonprofit organizations, however, set their prices based on consumers' ability to pay. This is true, for example, of congregate meals—government-sponsored meals—for the elderly in the United States. Those who cannot pay anything receive their meals free; others pay what they can afford. The number of meals these congregate meal operations can serve is determined by revenues from sales, per capita subsidies from the federal government, and donations and grants from local governments and charitable organizations.

School lunch prices to the consumer reflect subsidies from several levels of government. (Photo courtesy of ARAMARK.)

The Determinants of Price

The classic **determinants of price** are demand, supply, and competition.

Demand

Demand is a function of people, or the kind of people who make up a population. A young population demands one type of product; older people demand another. Income level and other factors, considered in Chapter 3 as a basis for segmentation, should help us think about changes in demand. For example, as the oldest baby boomers turn 65 in 2010, the aging of the population will probably result in fundamental changes in the nature of demand.

Although price is partly a result of demand, it should be noted that demand is partly determined by price. When hotel rooms cost the same on weekends as they did during the busy weekdays, hotels had very low weekend occupancies. When weekend prices were cut dramatically, occupancy in many urban-center hotels rose just as dramatically—an increase in demand.

Price Sensitivity. The demand for some products is more sensitive to price than the demand for others. Weekend room demand, for example, is **price elastic.** Weekday demand for rooms in a business center, however, is relatively insensitive to price, or **price inelastic,** at least in the short run. People who conduct business away from home *must* have a place to stay and probably require certain amenities and will therefore pay what they have to for accommodation. Yet if guests perceive themselves to have been gouged on price, they may stay away from the business center or stay home and conduct business via alternative means.

Relevant Range. Price sensitivity is not a fixed matter. In the booming late 1990s, people seemed relatively indifferent to fine-dining prices; but during a recession, many fine-dining restaurants may find it necessary to rewrite their menus, introduce lower-priced items, and eliminate costly dishes, as many such restaurants did in the late 1980s and early 1990s. As economic conditions and the climate of opinion change, the relevant range of price sensitivity may change as well. **Relevant range** is the range of prices within which people will accept changes. When the price moves outside that range, chances are that the product will be perceived as over- or underpriced.

Supply

This section considers the **supply** of goods, labor, and capital needed to operate a hospitality establishment. It is possible to estimate, in the short term, the supply of goods, and thus food costs, with reasonable accuracy. *Goods* constitute an essential part of hospitality operations, and, as with any goods, scarcity relative to demand will increase price. For example, a bad freeze in Florida that destroys the orange crop can mean higher orange juice prices for the coming year.

Labor is another basic component of hospitality operations. Because many jobs in our industry do not pay well, they are taken by young people who are working their first jobs or who are still in school. The decline in the youth work force that began in the late 1970s has created a significant shortage of workers in some markets. Although this trend turned around in the early 1990s, there is still a shortage of young workers in many local markets, which adds to the cost of labor. As a result, hospitality operators are forced to pass on the cost to consumers in the form of price increases.

The third element of supply is *capital*. Lodging is particularly capital intensive, and therefore hotel construction is sensitive to interest rates and availability of capital. Foodservice is less sensitive to interest rates, but still requires significant investment in facilities and equipment. Both lodging and foodservice go in and out of favor with lenders and investors. When they are in favor, capital is available with lower interest rates. When out of favor, expansion is more difficult and expensive.

Competition

Competition in virtually all areas of the hospitality industry is intense, which means that it takes a strong competitive advantage to gain any premium in price over the competition. Competitive advantage can be achieved by innovation. However, most successful innovations are quickly copied by competitors.

In addition to competition within the hospitality industry, there is also fierce competition with other industries for consumers' time, attention, and spending. There are many substitutes for hospitality products. For example, communication by phone, fax, E-mail, and teleconferencing may replace some business travel. In foodservice, the toughest competitors are home-cooked meals and the grocery stores that offer a wide variety of convenience foods and prepared meals.

When it comes to discretionary spending, dining out can be sacrificed to purchase a compact disk. A weekend vacation may be skipped to acquire a new computer, camera, or stereo. The prices hospitality operations charge are compared not only with those of other hospitality operations, but also with the costs of other discretionary uses of the consumer's dollar. Therefore, hospitality operations compete with businesses that provide substitutes and alternative products, as well as with other hospitality establishments.

The interaction of demand, supply, and competition creates the broad forces that determine how prices are set. These factors also set the boundaries for pricing practices in foodservice and lodging.

Pricing Methods in Foodservice

This section reviews cost-based and contribution margin foodservice pricing methods. It also discusses demand-based pricing and factors to consider in determining selling prices. Finally, appropriate price range and price change considerations are discussed.

Cost-Based Pricing

Cost-based pricing is the most common practice among most service industry firms, including foodservice. Before calculating the selling price, operators have to establish the desired food cost percentage. Based on the food cost percentage, a multiplier is determined by taking the reciprocal of the percentage (1 ÷ desired food cost percentage). Then the total cost of ingredients is calculated. Finally, ingredients cost is multiplied by the multiplier to establish the tentative selling price. For example: The total ingredients cost for a chicken sandwich with french fries is $2, and the desired food cost percentage is 30 percent. The multiplier is, therefore, 3.33 (1 ÷ 30%). As a result, the tentative selling price is $6.66 ($2 × 3.33).

The tentative selling price is just a starting point, which should be adjusted up or down to stay competitive in the marketplace. If a restaurant cannot produce a product at a competitive price that maintains the desirable food cost percentage, it may want to remove the product from the menu. If the product is a popular menu item that cannot be removed without negative impact on the business, menu placement and other merchandising techniques may be used to move as many customers' choices to other products as possible. Chapter 14 has a more detailed discussion of menu merchandising.

Cost-based pricing is popular because of its simplicity. However, there is a danger associated with this approach—ignoring the consumers' willingness to pay. It assumes that the market or competitive level of prices accurately reflects what people are willing to pay. Actually, it allows the restaurant's suppliers and competitors to tell it what its prices should be.

Contribution Margin Pricing

Contribution margin (CM) refers to the amount left after a menu item's food cost is subtracted from its selling price. The contribution margin "contributes" to pay for the nonfood costs and desired profit. The tentative selling price can be determined by using the following two equations:

Average CM per guest = (Nonfood costs + desired profit)
÷ number of guests expected
Tentative selling price = Average CM per guest + food cost

If an operation expects to serve 7,000 guests per month, with a monthly nonfood cost of $25,000 and a desired profit of $4,000, the average CM per guest would be $4.14 [(25,000 + 4,000) ÷ 7,000]. The tentative selling price of the same chicken sandwich with french fries, at a food cost of $2, would be $6.14 ($2 + $4.14). **Contribution margin pricing** focuses on the *dollar contribution* level, rather than the food cost percentage.

A review of the two menu items listed in Table 11.1 shows the rationale of using the contribution margin pricing method. The pasta has a lower food cost and a lower menu price, and the steak has a higher food cost and a higher price. It is clear from the contribution margin that we would rather sell steaks with the "bad" food cost percentage than the spaghetti, in spite of its "good" food cost percentage, because the pasta does not generate as much dollar contribution. There is much truth to the popular industry saying, "You cannot bank percentages, only dollars."

Another good example of a menu-pricing decision based on contribution reasoning is the cut-rate banquet price discussed in Chapter 1. This was a highly competitive price—a dollar over cost—offered to attract a large volume of business. The contribution margin per meal was modest; however, the total contribution was very large because of the thousands of banquets sold.

Demand-Based Pricing

In some situations in which a product has unique advantages, "what the market will bear" determines the price. Well-located resorts can often follow the practice of **demand-based pricing** during the high season. For example, there are only so many room-nights available in January in five-star resorts in Arizona, and many people want to go to Arizona during that time. Therefore, prices during the high season are usually based on the most that the market will bear. When a product is undifferentiated, however, as with hamburgers and economy rooms, competitive price levels are probably good indications of what the market will tolerate.

When a new hotel comes into a market that is not overbuilt, it can set a price based on the maximum amount that customers are willing to pay and limit discounting practices. This is sometimes called **skimming,** that is, skimming the cream from the market while the property is new. An opposite tactic with a new product is **penetration pricing.** When competition is expected to develop quickly, as it generally does in foodservice, an attractive price may be offered to quickly capture as large a market

TABLE 11.1 Simplified Contribution Pricing Example

Menu Item	Food Cost	Menu Price	Food Cost Percentage	Contribution Margin
Spaghetti	$1.13	$4.50	25%	$3.37
Strip steak	$6.00	$15.00	40%	$9.00

share as possible. The seller's hope is that it can hold on to the customers when competition develops.

Chain foodservice operations can get a clearer picture of what price will maximize revenues through test marketing. Many independent operators, however, assume that they cannot afford to experiment with prices. Therefore, competitive or traditional price levels are often used as indicators of demand. Actually, independent operations, and chains for that matter, that offer table service have a well-qualified source of information for pricing—the service staff (Main 1995). In most operations pricing is done by the chef or food production manager, who tends to be *cost focused.* Servers, on the other hand, are customer focused. They are the ones who are closest to the customers and interact with them constantly. Therefore, it makes sense to ask members of the service staff about what people would be willing to pay for various items. Their input is so important to the final price-setting process that some operators make pricing a collaborative effort by the chef or kitchen manager, front-of-the-house managers, owners or general managers, *and servers.* This process results in a price that represents value to the guests. Servers can also be used as a vital source of intelligence on consumer reaction to prices as part of a continuing effort to reassess menu prices.

Break-Even Analysis and Sales Mix

Break-even analysis, or cost-volume-profit analysis, is a tool used to examine the relationships between costs, revenues, and sales volume, allowing managers to determine the revenue required at any desired profit level (Schmidgall 1997). The **break-even point** (BEP) is the level of sales volume at which total revenues equal total costs. Break-even analysis is helpful in evaluating a decision to add a service or facility and in assessing the price and contribution margins required of a new service or facility. The process of BEP computation, discussed in many managerial accounting textbooks, is beyond the scope of this text; however, the BEP and required contribution margin must be considered in making pricing decisions.

Most menus include multiple items. The price of any one item has a significance of its own but must be evaluated in relation to the prices of other items. The performance of the whole menu is what determines final profit. A high food cost percentage of one item may be balanced by a low food cost percentage of another. Through menu placement, menu language, and other merchandising techniques, low-cost high-contribution items may be featured to push sales. Low-contribution items that must be on the menu because of a need for coherence in product offering or to meet competitive pressure can be "buried" in the menu to minimize their sales.

Because of the many items on the menu that must be considered, any break-even computation must be based on an assumed **sales mix,** as well as on the cost and contribution margin of individual items.

Selecting the Final Price

After tentative selling prices are calculated on the basis of cost or contribution margin, adjustments are made to reflect the operator's best judgment as to the price customers are willing to pay. In the final analysis, it is the entire menu that is being priced. Some items, to meet competition, may be below the target cost percentage, whereas others will make up for that with lower food costs. Next, the final prices must be set.

Price Points. Price points are the final prices selected for individual menu items. Quick-service restaurant prices tend to end in the figure 9 or 5. Some people view adjusting the last digit for psychological reasons as irrational. However, attempts to "prove" that such adjustments do not affect consumers have had mixed results at best. The intuition of operators is that adjusting the last digit in popular-priced restaurants affects the way consumers perceive prices.

The *first digit* is more significant to consumers than other digits. For example, consumers perceive a greater distance between 69 cents and 71 cents than between 69 cents and 67 cents. As a result, operators are more reluctant to move a price from 69 cents to 71 cents than from 62 cents to 67 cents. Consumers are also sensitive about the *length* of the price, or the number of digits in a price. Therefore, the distance between $9.95 and $10.25 is *perceived* as much greater than the distance between $9.65 and $9.95 (Kreul 1982).

In table service restaurants, consumers perceive prices below and above $5 differently. Under $5, pricing should be in increments of 25 cents. If a product can be sold for $3.15, consumers are unlikely to notice the difference if it is sold for $3.25. When the price is over $5, consumers notice increments of 50 cents or more. Therefore, an item offered at $8.75 may be offered at $8.95 without having a significant effect on consumers' perception of value (Main 1995).

Price Range. Most operators have a range of prices they consider as fitting their target market. A family restaurant may eliminate entrées that are priced below $3.50 and above $9.95. Quick-service sandwiches are rarely priced above $2.50 for a single main item or beyond the $4-to-$5 range for a meal deal. One reason for QSRs' limited success in the dinner market may be the consumers' unwillingness to perceive value in those higher-priced dinner items in a QSR setting.

One family restaurant chain found the cost of shrimp, a popular item, escalating in a way that would require an increase in price above its regular **price range.** Management believed that the effect of breaking its upper limit would be to make the whole restaurant appear more expensive to consumers. Therefore, the restaurant chain reluctantly removed one of its best-sellers from the menu and replaced it with another seafood product that fit into the price range.

Lower limits are important, too. For example, the cost of a bottle of wine may justify a price of $12, but that low a price in a fine-dining restaurant could cheapen the appearance of the entire wine list. Therefore, like the item that was too expensive, that particular wine should be eliminated from the wine list if a higher price does not seem reasonable in light of the guests' perception of value.

The distance between the top and bottom of a price range must also be considered. If the spread between individual prices on a menu is too large, customers may be encouraged to choose the lower-priced items. It may also raise concerns about the integrity of pricing in general. Consider the example in Table 11.1. The difference between the two prices may be perceived as large. Customers may doubt the value of the strip steak or be concerned about the quality of the spaghetti. The operator could increase the price of the spaghetti by adding an accompaniment to increase the value of the pasta, thereby reducing the price spread. It is recommended that the most expensive item on the menu should not be priced at more than two and a half times the price of the least expensive item in the same menu category.

Price Changes. From time to time it becomes necessary to increase prices because of rising food and labor costs. The usual practice in the field is to avoid large increments or too-frequent adjustments. Most restaurant chains try to hold the frequency of **price changes** to once a quarter or less. Many operators change their entire menus periodically, adding items that fit in the appropriate price range and deleting items that have become too expensive.

Red Lobster, for example, featured chicken and beef items on its menu in reaction to high seafood costs. It also added shrimp fajitas to the menu, probably because, in combination with tortillas and other ingredients, the fajitas have a lower food cost than a shrimp platter. There are many good reasons for the growing popularity of pasta, one of which is low food cost. When substituting offerings or ingredients with lower-cost items, the contribution margin can be improved without a price increase. Operators must be careful, however, to maintain the quality of the food offered and the image projected.

The decision on whether to automatically match competitors' price reductions should be based on the competitive situation and the customers' price sensitivity. Even in a highly competitive market, there are alternatives to lowering prices. Menu changes, as discussed earlier, certainly are an option. What about using the lost revenue, because of price reduction, on advertising and promotion? Consumers' price sensitivity should also be considered. If price is a major consideration, as it very often is in the quick-service segment, it is hard to hold out against a competitive price reduction. For an upscale operation that has achieved a high degree of differentiation, however, it may be easier to survive competitors' price reductions without reducing its own prices.

Hotel Pricing

The lodging industry is a more capital-intensive business than foodservice and one with a much higher fixed-cost structure. Room rates are typically set in the context of a 30-year or longer property life. Therefore, hotel pricing methods are different from those used in foodservice operations. However, there are some similarities, because the fundamental concerns are the same: recovering costs, assessing consumer demand, and earning a desired profit.

Cost-Based Pricing

For many years, the rule of thumb in estimating hotel room prices has been that the room rate equals $1 for every $1,000 invested in building cost. Like most rules of thumb, this one is more suggestive than precise. The **Hubbart formula,** developed in the 1950s by a committee of the American Hotel & Motel Association chaired by Roy Hubbart, uses **cost-based pricing,** which bases room rates on operating and capital costs to be covered and desired profits to be generated. The revenue required to cover all expenses and provide a fair return is divided by the estimated number of room-nights sold per year to obtain the average room rate. Therefore, the Hubbart formula follows the break-even analysis reasoning.

For a new property, projected rates must be reviewed as part of the feasibility study to see whether they can cover all costs with an adequate margin of safety. Otherwise, under normal circumstances, debt financing is not likely to be approved. When adjusting room rates for existing properties, revenues from other profit centers, such as food and beverage operations, meeting facilities, and retail operations, should be taken into consideration. However, there is no question that room rates are the principal factor, along with occupancy levels, for determining revenue and profitability.

Demand and Supply. When the demand for rooms in a community begins to expand, new hotels are likely to be built and to charge significantly higher room rates. The reason is not only that the investment cost of new construction is higher than the capital cost of existing properties, but also that many guests are willing to pay more for new facilities. As new hotels enter the market, occupancies in older properties are likely to decrease as a result of losing business to the new operations. However, because of the considerably higher rates charged by new hotels, old hotels can often raise their room rates to offset the occupancy decrease.

Lodging supply can be divided into five segments, as shown in Table 11.2. Most guests enter the market with the price range of their favored segment in mind. Competition between properties is most intense within categories, but there is also competition between segments, particularly between adjacent segments, such as between the luxury and upscale, and upscale and midpriced. The designation "all-suite" has a deluxe sound, but, in practice, all-suite properties are available at virtually every price level and the services provided are substantially different.

TABLE 11.2 Lodging Market Price Segments

Segment	Average Room Rates	Typical Brands
Luxury	Top 15%	Four Seasons, Ritz Carlton
Upscale	Next 15%	Hilton, Marriott
Midpriced	Middle 30%	Holiday Inn, Best Western
Limited service	Next 20%	Hampton Inn, Comfort Inn
Budget	Lowest 20%	Motel 6

Note: In rural or nonmetro markets, the top 30 percent of average room rates are classified as upscale and there is no luxury category.

Source: R. A. Smith, "The U.S. Lodging Industry Today," *Cornell Hotel and Restaurant Administration Quarterly* 40(1): 18–25. Copyright 1999 by School of Hotel Administration, Cornell University.

Room Rate Range

Properties in the limited-service and economy segments usually have only one or two room types and charge the same basic rate for each type, with surcharges for each additional person in the room. There are sometimes exceptions to this "one size fits all" approach for suites or larger rooms.'

Luxury, upscale, and to a lesser degree, midpriced properties, generally have several room types that vary in price. The practice of having a minimum of three rates, preferably five, gives front office staff and reservationists an opportunity to "sell up." The objective is to have several levels of rooms and rates, each differentiated from the others by physical features such as size, location, and view. Front office staff and reservationists are trained to sell the higher-priced rooms first, but generally move to a lower category rather than lose guests. If properly executed, the strategy should result in satisfied guests *and* a high average rate.

Discounting. Very few rooms are sold at "rack rate," or the list price traditionally posted on the room rack behind the front desk. A list of 17 special rates, as shown in Table 11.3, was prominently taped to the side of a front office piece of equipment at

Premium prices can be charged for rooms with particular features, such as an attractive view. (Photo courtesy of Renaissance Wailea Beach Resort.)

TABLE 11.3 Some Lodging Discount Categories	
Abbreviation	Full Designation
AAAA	Senior citizen, AAA, any 50 percent discount card, etc.
COMP	Any comp per (manager's name)
CORP	Corporate rate
CRUS	Cruise packages, including food, drinks, room, etc.
EMPL	Employee discount
EXIT	Exit Information Guide coupon
FFAM	Flintstone Family Fun rates
SELL	Discount to sell to keep guests from walking out
SEPT	September Club Member
SPEC	Special company rates
SSSS	Company saver rates
STAY	Any discounted rate due to extended stay or 7+ days
NEGT	Negotiated rates with Drive, Viking Princess, etc.
RACK	Normal rack rate
ROCK	Company rock-bottom prices
GOVT	Government/military rates
SMER	SMERF groups, i.e., athletic, wedding, reunion, etc.

a Florida hotel. The list is an example of all the special rates offered by various hotels. The "SELL" rate, the eighth item on the list, is particularly revealing. Most of these special rates are likely to be offered during periods of slow demand.

Special discount rates are generally a function of demand in a particular geographic market. However, the practice of **discounting** is widespread. The amount of discount and the percentage of discount offered usually increase as rooms price rises. Hotels with higher rates can usually afford to provide a greater discount and still make a profit. When the room rate reaches a certain level, it also takes a greater discount percentage to make a difference in a consumer's mind. For example, when a $59 room is reduced to $49, a 17 percent discount, consumers are likely to take notice of the price decrease. However, when a $260 room is reduced to $216, also a 17 percent discount, few people in the target market are likely to recognize the difference, because, for people who are willing to spend more than $200 on a hotel room, $44 is often not a significant amount of money. It takes more than that to make a difference. If the price is dropped to $199, a 23 percent discount, individuals in the target market are more likely to notice the discount.

Why Discounting? The obvious driving force for widespread discounting in lodging in recent years is overcapacity and heightened competition. More recently, supply and demand have been in better balance. However, discounting activities have not stopped, because, as discussed in Chapter 2, there is no inventory—a hotel's unused capacity has no value the next day. Therefore, there is pressure to sell *now*.

Another factor contributing to the practice of discounting relates to the concept of **incremental cost**—the cost of renting one more room, which includes a few guest supplies, some linen, a half hour of housekeeping time, and a little more use of utilities. The incremental cost is minimal, perhaps between $10 and $20, depending on the services and amenities provided. If the regular room rate is $100 and the incremental cost is $20, the contribution margin could be as high as $80 per room. This leaves considerable room for discounting. Discounting is especially tempting when the high fixed costs of a hotel operation are considered. General operating expenses and other fixed charges, such as administration, marketing, maintenance, utility, franchise and management fees, property taxes, and insurance, can require 30 percent or more of the total revenue (Ross 1999 a and b). These expenses must be paid, regardless of sales volume; therefore, there is a *real need* for any contribution margin that can cover such costs.

In a high-fixed-cost industry, with a product that has a high contribution margin and cannot be inventoried, discounting is a likely practice during any slow period. Providing discounts without a good understanding of their impact on revenue and profitability, however, is very dangerous. Many hotels have adopted the yield management concept to maximize not only occupancy, but also the room rate.

Yield Management

Instead of using a cost-based pricing method, **yield management** is a supply-and-demand driven approach. Yield management has been designed to sell as many rooms as possible while generating the maximum rate possible at any given level of demand. Therefore, yield management is also referred to as *revenue management.* Airlines have used yield management for many years to maximize the number of tickets sold on each flight at rates as high as possible. Travelers seem to have accepted the airline yield management pricing practice.

Adhering to the concept of yield management, when demand is high, operators want to sell rooms at highest rates possible. When demand is low, operators would still like to sell rooms at high rates, but also allow flexibility to build up occupancy. On high-demand days, such as during the vacation season or a major convention, a minimum number of nights stayed may be required. Many ski resorts, for example, have a minimum five- or seven-night requirement during the winter high season. Local promotion is usually limited or eliminated during high-demand days to concentrate on out-of-towners who occupy the guest rooms and use other hotel facilities. Special rates are available only to special categories of guests, such as regular corporate clients. As for groups, in addition to renting rooms at high rates, preference is usually given to those that also book meeting rooms and function space and use food and beverage services. Alternative low-demand days with lower rates may be suggested to rate-sensitive groups.

When demand is low, reservation agents are given maximum discretion with rates. Operators should also go after new markets, especially price-sensitive markets, such as government and education groups as well as leisure travelers. The offering of special weekend rates by many business-oriented hotels is an example of the various efforts to fill rooms during low-demand weekend days. The focus is on maximizing revenue *every day*.

Critical Areas of Yield Management

Forecasting. To effectively use yield management, a hotel must have the ability to forecast long-term demand with a high degree of accuracy. Convention planners, tour operators, and similar rate-sensitive groups usually book their rooms far in advance. It is not uncommon for conventions planners to negotiate rates and block rooms two or three years prior to the convention dates. Business travelers and other rate-insensitive guests, however, usually plan their travel only a few days before departure. Therefore, an accurate long-term forecast is extremely important to accommodate the rate-sensitive low-paying groups that plan ahead to secure occupancy *and* the rate-insensitive high-paying guests who do not plan ahead so as to increase average rates.

Historical data on daily occupancy, number of individual reservations, average number of no-shows, number of inquiries, and number of people being turned away by the hotel are all important information to consider. Demands from groups and individuals must be monitored regularly to project demand on a day-by-day basis. Because of the large amount of data and the need to constantly evaluate supply and demand levels, most hotels implementing yield management techniques rely on computers to keep track of everything and suggest up-to-the-minute room rate categories.

Training. To ensure successful implementation of the yield management technique, all employees involved in selling rooms, such as front office staff, reservation agents, and sales staff, should be properly trained to sell rooms under different conditions of supply and demand. Employees must be competent in dealing with complicated yield management issues, and they must also be tactful when interacting with guests. Achieving such competencies is no small task, because rate structures have become extremely complex. Regrettably, it sometimes happens that an experienced traveler understands the rate structure better than the reservationist and must either explain it to the employee or, worse, argue with the employee. This leads to loss of respect for the hotel or chain and cynicism in regard to hotel rates.

When special rates are advertised during an off-period, once reservations reach a certain level, the reduced prices will no longer be available. If the reservationist is properly trained, he or she will tactfully tell a caller, "I'm sorry, all of those rooms are sold," and try to book the guest at a higher rate or offer alternative dates or accommodations elsewhere within the system. A reservationist who is not properly trained, may say,

"Sorry, the lower rate category is closed and the rooms are now more expensive." Improperly trained employees, as well as disgruntled or indifferent employees, have enormous potential for harming the system's reputation in a situation like this.

Evaluation. A hotel sales staff's performance evaluation and compensation should also support the yield management concept. For example, performance should be evaluated on the basis of a staff member's contribution to the "yield" or revenue of the hotel, not just on the number of rooms sold or the average rate of the rooms sold. A sales manager who can sell rooms at good rates during the low season is more valuable to the hotel than one who brings in groups only during high-demand periods.

When implemented properly, yield management creates a win-win situation for the hotel and the guests. A hotel's revenue is maximized when proper strategies are used during both high- and low-demand periods. Guests' needs are better met by being able to accommodate price-insensitive guests who must have a room on high-demand days. Price-sensitive guests are also better served with lower rates in low-demand periods. The keys to success are accurate early forecasting, a proper employee training and reward system, and pricing flexibility. Case Study 11.1 discusses the revenue management program of one hotel company.

CASE STUDY 11.1

Marriott International's Revenue Management System

Marriott International has a long history of collecting and using consumer behavior data to make sound product development and marketing decisions. The company began to invest in yield management in 1985. Data collected through the computerized yield management system help track room demands from various market segments and make appropriate pricing decisions. For example, Marriott found that weekend leisure travelers usually make their reservations two to three weeks in advance, whereas business travelers tend to book their rooms five to ten days before departure. The timing of demand should be taken into consideration when decisions to open and close different rates are made.

Marriott's current yield management system ensures that all distribution outlets receive the same inventory and rate structure so that customers are quoted the same rate regardless of the inquiry method. For example, a potential guest will find the same rate on the Marriott homepage, on any other commercial travel Web sites, and given by the toll-free reservation center and all travel agencies. The yield management system also recommends the number of rooms to overbook, property by property, based on cancellation, early departure, and stay-over statistics.

Because of the complexity of the yield management system, the reservations manager position has been upgraded to the equivalent level of a director of sales and requires this staff member to report to the sales and marketing director. According to

Marriott, strong leadership from top management and extensive communication and training are required to implement the yield management system successfully.

In addition to a revenue increase in the "hundreds of millions of dollars," yield management provides the properties with a better profile of their guests and identifies weak occupancy periods for additional promotional efforts. Through effective inventory control and pricing, customers are more likely to have a room when they need it. Price-sensitive customers can be accommodated at discounted rates on days when available inventory is high.

Source: L. Dube, C. A. Enz, L. M. Renaghan, and J. A. Siguaw, *American Lodging Excellence: The Key to Best Practices in the U.S. Lodging Industry.* (New York: American Express and the American Hotel Foundation, 1999.)

Package Prices

Selling a package of goods and services, instead of individual items, can be advantageous to both lodging and foodservice operators. **Packages** can be designed with specific target markets in mind and, therefore, can appeal to particular target markets. Properly designed packages can also enhance customer satisfaction by serving their special needs.

Packages may include some products or services, such as a wine seminar and a back-of-the-house tour, that are not normally available. A special offer may stimulate more frequent repeat visits, increase per-capita spending, and extend the guests' length of stay. Packages can also include a few weaker or unknown products or services, such as a new entrée or a special spa treatment, that customers would not have purchased if not for the package. This offering may also enhance exposure and sales of new or unpopular items.

Hotels and resorts usually offer packages during the off-season to increase demand. Foodservice operations often provide packages during slow days of the week (e.g., Tuesday night is family night) or a slow time of the day (e.g., early bird specials). When the purchase of packages must be reserved in advance, operations can enjoy easier forecasting and improved efficiency in staffing and operation. Unique packages may also gain favorable publicity from the media (Kasavana 1998).

Many consumers like to purchase packages for greater convenience and economy. For example, instead of their having to make individual arrangements for transportation, lodging, sightseeing, and dining, a package tour takes care of everything. Packages usually sell for less than the total price of the items if purchased separately and therefore represent greater value. Packages also enable guests to know the total cost of an outing or vacation. In all-inclusive resorts, package prices usually cover all the costs of a vacation, including transportation, ground transfers, food, lodging, entertainment, and the use of recreational facilities. Alcoholic beverages are also included at some resorts.

Package tours usually include transportation, lodging, sightseeing, and some dining. Consumers do not have to worry about individual arrangements. Once a package is purchased, they can sit back, relax, and enjoy the trip.

Although packages reduce the profit margin percentage somewhat, the incremental sales they generate can actually improve total profits. For example, most quick-service restaurants offer value meals consisting of a sandwich, fries, and a soft drink. These items are discounted in the package to provide value to the customers. However, the incremental sales volume is more than enough to offset the increase in food cost percentage. Value meals have also increased the average check for most QSRs.

Summary

Price represents value to customers and is a means to recapture costs and generate a profit for operators. Sales-oriented pricing objectives seek to maintain or increase market share. The most common pricing practice is to meet the price level in the market. Increasing market share not only helps to maintain profit but also enhances it when the increase in volume is large enough. Profit-oriented pricing objectives treat the operation as a financial asset and seek to support a planned return on investment.

Demand, supply, and competition practically determine the prices that operations can charge. As price increases, demand generally declines, but this relationship depends on the price sensitivity of the customers. Price sensitivity is relative to economic conditions. As economic conditions change, the relevant range of price sensitivity may change as well. Price is also affected by supply. When the supply is plentiful, the price is usually lower. Competition within hospitality is intense, and hospitality operations also compete with other industries for discretionary consumer expenditures.

Foodservice operations can use cost-based pricing, contribution margin pricing, or the demand-based pricing method to establish tentative selling prices. Break-even analysis and sales mix evaluation are helpful in making pricing decisions. In setting the final prices, consumer perceptions are critical to determining the exact price points, range, and changes.

Hotel pricing has traditionally been cost-based to recover capital and operating expenses. However, it has also responded to demand and competition levels by providing various types of discounts. The minimum incremental cost, high fixed cost, and the inability to inventory have also contributed to the discounting practice in the hotel industry. Yield management is a supply-and-demand-driven pricing technique used to maximize revenue. To successfully implement a yield management system, the operation must have the ability to forecast accurately, have proper employee training and reward systems, and be flexible in pricing.

Package prices have been offered by both foodservice and hotel operations to increase low-period demand and appeal to special target markets. Package prices usually reflect a discount from the list price; however, the increased sales volume generally offsets the increase in operating costs and results in greater profit.

Key words and Concepts

Price/value	Competition	Price points
Pricing objectives	Cost-based pricing	Price range
Sales-oriented objective	Contribution margin	Price changes
Profit-oriented objective	Contribution margin pricing	Hubbart formula
Determinants of price	Demand-based pricing	Discounting
Demand	Skimming	Incremental cost
Price elastic	Penetration pricing	Yield management
Price inelastic	Break-even analysis	Packages
Relevant range	Break-even point	
Supply	Sales mix	

Resources on the Internet

Foodservice Central.com.
  http://www.foodservicecentral.com/content/homepage/
Hotel and Motel Management.
  http://www.hmmonline.com/

International Yield Management Research Site.
  http://mugca.cc.monash.edu.au/~kfarrell/iymrs/
Lodging Online. *http://www.lodgingnews.com/*
Smith Travel Research. *http://www.wwstar.com/*

Discussion Questions

1. What is the significance of the term "price/value"?
2. Did Taco Bell's use of value pricing pursue sales-oriented or profit-oriented objectives? Why?
3. What are the advantages and disadvantages of cost-based pricing and contribution margin pricing?
4. What is demand-based pricing? How can a foodservice operator find out what the market will bear?
5. What factors must be considered in setting the final prices of menu items?
6. What are the common cost-based hotel pricing methods?
7. Why do hotels discount?
8. What is yield management? What are the appropriate strategies for high- and low-demand periods?
9. What are the critical areas of yield management success?
10. Why are packages popular?

References

Kasavana, M. L. (1998). *Managing front office operations.* 5th ed. East Lansing, MI: Educational Institute of the American Hotel & Motel Association.

Kreul, L. M. (1982). Magic numbers: Psychological aspects of menu pricing. *Cornell Hotel and Restaurant Administration Quarterly*, 23(2), 70–75.

Main, B. *Menu Marketing.* (1995). Alexandria, VA: Wells Walker and Company, Inc.

Ross, C. (1999a). Continued growth—A closer look at midscale chains. *Lodging*, 25(2) (October), 55–56, 58.

Ross, C. (1999b). Evaluating the luxury/upscale full-service market. *Lodging*, 25(3) (November), 55–56, 58, 60.

Schlesinger, L. A., and R. Hallowell, (1994). Taco Bell Corp. (Case No. 692058). Boston: Harvard Business School.

Schmidgall, R. S. (1997). *Hospitality industry managerial accounting.* 4th ed. East Lansing, MI: Educational Institute of the American Hotel & Motel Association.

12

Marketing Communication: Advertising

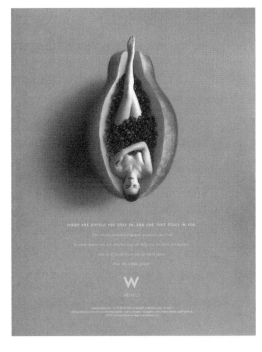

(Photo courtesy of W Hotels.)

When you have finished reading this chapter, you should be able to:

- Describe the major components of marketing communication.
- Identify the appropriate types of communication strategy under different circumstances.
- Explain the objectives of promotion.
- Discuss the five key considerations in advertising planning.
- Identify four advertising audience segments.
- Understand advertising media characteristics.
- List the major media used in advertising.

The terms "promotion" and "communication" are sometimes used interchangeably in marketing. Because marketing communication, or *promotion,* includes activities such as advertising and selling, it is the element of the marketing mix many people think of first when marketing comes to mind. Indeed, some people confuse promotional activities with marketing. They think that selling or advertising *is* marketing. We saved our consideration of communication to end the discussion of the marketing mix to emphasize that the success of marketing communication depends on the *products and services* offered, the *place* in which they are offered, and the *price* at which the offer is made. However, this is not to say that promotion is not as important as the other three elements of the marketing mix. Actually, promotion is so important that we devote two chapters to it. In this chapter we consider advertising, and in the next we examine sales promotion, public relations and publicity, and personal selling. Before we discuss advertising, however, it is appropriate to introduce the major forms of marketing communication.

Communication Mix

The **communication mix** includes advertising, sales promotion, public relations and publicity, and personal selling. All but personal selling are methods used to address mass audiences. We begin with a brief definition of each.

Advertising employs various paid, impersonal mass media to communicate with potential buyers. Mass media advertisements include not only newspaper advertising and radio and television commercials, but also signs and billboards and other media, such as direct mail, that can be used to address large numbers of people without any personal contact.

Sales promotion is used to stimulate immediate first-time or repeat purchases. Financial incentives are usually provided to increase consumer demand. In foodservice, the most common forms of sales promotion are "deals," such as coupons, premium merchandise, and games. Hotels use family packages, seasonal promotions, special events, and frequency programs to encourage patronage. Sales promotion strives to enhance value and is generally aimed at achieving a specific sales goal.

Personal selling generally refers to sales calls made by a company representative to prospective or existing customers. These calls can be conducted face-to-face, but hospitality operations have increasingly used telephones to initiate personal selling. Personal selling also includes "selling up" by servers and front office agents to persuade guests to increase their level of spending.

Public relations (PR) is a form of communication used to influence the feelings, opinions, or beliefs about a company, its products, or services, or about the value of its products, services, or activities, by buyers, prospects, or other stakeholders (Bennett 1995). **Publicity** is directed specifically at the media to generate unpaid media coverage of a company's products, services, and activities.

Objectives of Marketing Communication

You are planning to open your own restaurant and realize that you have to let people know about your business. Your first job is to *inform* potential customers that your restaurant will be open soon and will offer certain benefits. Next, you must *persuade* potential guests that your offer is a good one. After you have been open for a while, you will have to *remind* guests of your restaurant and its offerings in order to compete with similar operations' communication programs. In other words, you need to *promote* your restaurant.

Product Life Cycle

As indicated in the preceding example and in Figure 12.1, operations or products in different stages of the product life cycle can emphasize different types of communication. There are many strategies associated with the various stages of the product life cycle, the most common of which are discussed in the following paragraphs.

The major goal during the introduction phase is to build volume by reaching those individuals who are most likely to patronize new operations or try new products. Informative communication is usually the best way to introduce new prod-

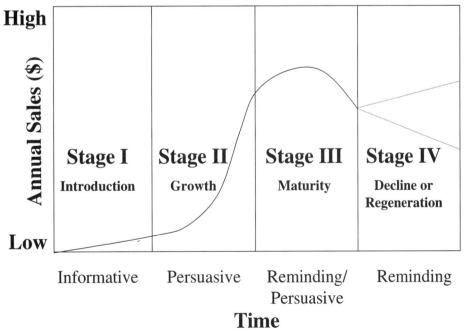

FIGURE 12.1 Principal communication strategies for various product life cycle stages.

ucts or operations. This approach is especially important for independently owned operations because, unlike national chains, they are little known by the public. Every effort should be made to reach potential customers and encourage their first-time patronage.

During the growth stage, the emphases are image building and sales volume increase. Therefore, persuasive communication is generally employed to convey positive aspects of the operations or products, retain current guests, and entice new customers. Comparative messages are sometimes used to stress the special advantages offered by an operation or its products and thereby differentiate it from competitors.

Note, however, that only successful operations reach the maturity stage. Operations that do achieve this level are usually well established and have the advantage of a recognized name. Customers know their products and services well. Therefore, the primary communication function is to remind the public that the operation still provides the products and services that customers have always enjoyed. The occasional use of persuasive communication to reinforce the benefits offered is appropriate. However, reminding communication is generally sufficient on a regular basis.

For operations in the declining stage, persuasive communication is often too expensive to support because of the decreasing sales volume. An occasional reminder to current customers is usually the only financially viable option. A possible variation during the maturity and declining stages is the situation that occurs when a business contemplates the idea of repositioning the operation or a particular product. When a new product or concept emerges, and the product or operation moves into the regeneration stage, the operation will have to introduce the new product or concept to the market—and eventually go through another product life cycle, using the various communication strategies appropriate for each stage.

Decision-Making Process

The stages in the customers' decision-making process should also be taken into consideration in selecting appropriate communication strategies. Many operators have been successful in making consumers aware of a certain need, or "want" may be a more accurate description. For example, consumers are told that they have worked hard all year and they *need* a vacation. When consumers have recognized the need and are ready to search for information, relevant operation and product information should be readily available to those potential customers. The communication should be informative, so as to increase consumers' awareness and introduce the operations' benefits and features.

At the evaluation and purchase stages, communication should be persuasive so that consumers will perceive the products as being better than those of the competitors and make a purchase. During postpurchase evaluation, reminding communication is effective in positive reinforcement and refreshing customers' memory about the services. Figure 12.2 matches the types of communication with the stages of the decision-making process.

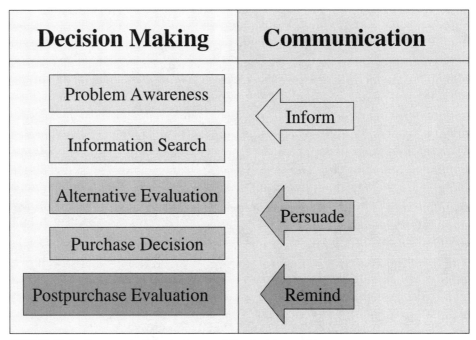

FIGURE 12.2   Communication strategy and the decision-making process.

Stimulating Demand

A primary objective of marketing communication is persuading consumers to purchase, that is, stimulating demand. We should distinguish, however, between stimulating primary and selective demands. **Primary demand** refers to a generic demand for the product itself, such as the demand for food and shelter. Much of the primary demand for hospitality products exists naturally. However, some organizations, such as state travel promotion agencies, see stimulating primary demand as one of their objectives.

Individual firms may need to promote primary demand when they have a new product. An example is the hospitality condominium companies' sale of timeshares—the ownership of the right to use a condo for a specified period of time—when they first came on the market. The companies had to explain the timeshare concept to consumers and how swapping networks, or arrangements to trade a timeshare in one place for use of a facility in another place, gave them a flexible vacation medium.

Market leaders who hold the lion's share of a market sometimes advertise to stimulate primary demand because, in the event that the overall market size increases, their total sales are also likely to increase. McDonald's lifestyle advertising, for example, depicts quick-service restaurant (QSR) dining occasions (e.g., father and son, mother and daughter) as socially approved ways for families to get together.

Selective demand is the demand for a specific brand marketed by a particular

Make it yours.

Another canoe will be along any minute.

Call for your Free Vacation Planner   1-800-661-8888   www.travelalberta.com

State/provincial tourism boards and other travel promotion agencies have charge of stimulating primary demand for travel, as well as selective demand for their particular state or region. (Photo courtesy of Tourism Alliance.)

firm (Bennett 1995). This usually happens in an established market where the battle is for the consumer market share. The emphasis of communication is on product differentiation to generate selected demand for "our" brand rather than "theirs."

Hierarchy of Objectives

Table 12.1 shows the various levels of consumer involvement with a company's offering. All marketing, of course, is ultimately aimed at securing purchases and a loyal customer base. The primary goal of a new operation, or of the first unit of a chain in a new territory, is to gain consumer *awareness* of the business. Intensive preopening promotional activities and grand opening events should capture the community's *interest* about the operation's offerings and help move consumers on to the next level, *desire*. A desire to purchase should, then, lead to *action*, or trial. The acronym **AIDA** should help you remember these key stages.

Although promotion continues to be important in keeping the company name and offering before its target markets, once a trial occurs, the quality of the operation will

TABLE 12.1	Hierarchy of Marketing Communication Objectives: The AIDA Model	
	Stage	Consumer Reaction
A	Awareness	I see there's a new . . .
I	Interest	I wonder if . . .
D	Desire	I'll give them a try on . . .
A	Action	Well, here I am.

be crucial to the guests' decision to return. "Reminder" advertising is appropriate and essential in most markets. However, advertising cannot fill dining room seats or hotel rooms very long unless the operations deliver what the customers want.

Figure 12.3 shows that promotion plays a key role in fulfilling all marketing objectives up to the point where a trial is secured (the dotted line in the figure). As promotional efforts increase, consumers' awareness, interest, and desire can also be heightened over time. Once a trial is achieved, however, the quality of the product becomes crucial. Promotion has taken on a secondary role, that of a reminder. Operations now play the primary role in pleasing the guests and moving them on to becoming repeat customers—adoption and repeat patronage—a true goal for all hospitality operations.

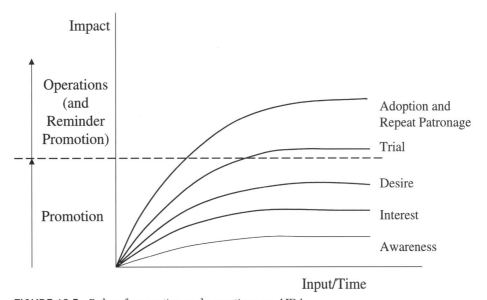

FIGURE 12.3   Roles of promotion and operations on AIDA.

Note that all elements of the marketing mix have a place in the AIDA process. A convenient and viable location helps in gaining awareness. A pleasing ambience can be an important factor in acquiring repeat patronage. Once customers are aware of an operation, a competitive price can also be a supporting factor in developing interest, evaluating the offer, and making a trial purchase. Actually, special price offers can even be used to gain awareness.

Advertising Goals and Objectives

Believe it or not, advertising in the hospitality industry was once perceived to be unimportant. In the earlier days of product-oriented management, most restaurants limited advertising to a promotional push when a new unit opened. Hotels generally limited advertising to informational purposes, such as billboards along highways and announcements in the hotel trade press to obtain referrals from fellow professionals in other cities. Those days are gone, probably forever. With the increased importance of advertising and the growth of advertising budgets, the clear formulation of the goals and objectives of a company's advertising program becomes essential.

Image Versus Promotional Advertising

Two basic and somewhat different goals of advertising are building or sustaining an image and creating immediate sales. The latter goal often supports other promotional activities, such as a coupon campaign or other special offers. Advertisers that have limited budgets often make a difficult choice between the two extremes of image and immediate sales. Some operators believe that using advertising to secure sales damages the image of a business, proposing that advertisements should be a long-term investment that helps to create a personality for the brand. Using advertisements to push sales, they say, contradicts the image-building effort. Yet, some operators argue that building image is wonderful, but one has to survive to enjoy the image and, therefore, advertisements should be designed to move sales.

There is no clear-cut answer as to whether advertising to support image or to encourage sales is the better choice. In practice, operators do both, and sales promotions can be designed to support image. For companies with generous advertising budgets and strong competitive positions, there will probably be more image advertising. McDonald's, for instance, is a leading image developer in the hospitality industry. However, the need for short-run sales results drives some chains to a much higher proportion of sales promotion ads. McDonald's is also one of the most efficient practitioners of sales promotion. Its Monopoly game is a good example of a promotion that drives traffic and yet builds image. McDonald's projects a "fun" image with its McDonaldland characters, including the Hamburglar, Grimace, Mayor McCheese, the Fry Kids, Officer Big Mac, Birdie the Early Bird, and the McNugget Buddies (McDonald's Corporation 2001). The Monopoly game is a logical extension of the fun theme, of-

Ronald McDonald and other familiar McDonaldland characters build a "fun" image for Mc-Donald's. (Photo courtesy of McDonald's Corporation.)

fering a chance to play America's most popular board game for instant wins with 100 million prizes and an opportunity to win the top million-dollar prize.

Measurable Objectives

For an advertising campaign to "get the most bang for its buck," it must have objectives that are specific, measurable, and attainable. The following are examples of appropriate objectives:

1. Increase consumer awareness level by 10 percent during a two-month campaign period.
2. Improve consumer perception of the company from "average" to "good."
3. Increase sales by 5 percent during lunch hours.
4. Support the summer vacation promotional program to reach an average occupancy of 80 percent during July and August.

The growth in both marketing sophistication and the typical advertising budget is a response to the increasing level of competition across all segments of the industry. In a mature market, operators fight for market share and try to develop new products or new concepts to gain a competitive advantage. All of these activities require expensive advertising and promotional support. The restaurant industry actually spent more than $3 billion on advertising in 1998. Because advertising expenditures are escalating rapidly, consumers are bombarded with commercial messages to a point that many prospective customers have become indifferent to promotional efforts. Therefore, advertising has a special and growing need to "cut through the clutter" of the saturated media with advertising that can gain and hold the audience's attention. The situation has made advertising planning even more important.

Advertising Planning

The five key considerations in **advertising planning** are target audience, message, media, timing, and budget. Table 12.2 summarizes these considerations and lists the major concepts related to each factor. They are discussed in the following sections.

Target

Like any marketing activity, advertising planning begins with research on customers. Specific considerations include customers' product/service preferences and their media viewing, listening, and reading habits. A necessary precondition for advertising planning is a good comprehension of the operation's consumer profile. Demographics are important, but an understanding of *lifestyle* is perhaps more revealing. A household made up of two 35-year-olds with a combined income of $100,000 may, after all, include two lawyers or two plumbers.

Audience Segments. Four key **audience segments** must be considered in designing advertising. Each requires a somewhat different approach (Stewart 1994). The first

TABLE 12.2 Advertising Planning	
Considerations	Key Concepts
Target	Emergents, loyals, switchers Multiple decision makers Diverse population
Message	Unique selling proposition (USP) Cut through the clutter
Media	CPM, GRP, waste, reach, frequency, impact Electronic, print, outdoor, direct mail, due bill
Timing	Continuity, flighting
Budget	Objective oriented

group are *nonusers* who are aware of the products but have rejected them. For example, some consumers refuse to patronize QSRs because of health concerns. Nonusers of this type are relatively unimportant because the products do not have a good fit with their preferences. There is, however, another group of nonusers who *are* important, the *emergents*—people who are new to the market, such as young people and recently arrived immigrants or international students. These newcomers are a growth segment of the market because they have not yet formed their buying habits. Advertising aimed at them should follow the principles of introducing new products to create awareness and build brand image.

The two established audience groups are the *loyals* and *switchers.* The goal with loyals is to reinforce brand loyalty and discourage switching. Advertising should help them justify their behavior and reassure them that they are making the right choice so that they will remain loyal. Loyal customers are important because the majority of an average operation's business comes from current satisfied customers.

Loyal users of competitive brands, however, present a more difficult picture. It is hard even to get their attention and harder still to get them to try an alternate product. Because of their loyalty, they are willing to pay a premium for their brands of choice. Therefore, it takes a significant discount to coax the loyals to change brands.

Switchers are inconsistent in their patronage behavior. Price promotions can attract their business, but they are likely to switch to something else when the discount is no longer available. Being a familiar brand with a good image is helpful to an operation when top-of-mind awareness is a major factor in a purchase decision, such as selecting a QSR. Even so, the effect of advertising on switchers is only temporary. The four audience segments are presented in summary form in Table 12.3.

Multiple Decision Makers. Not all advertising is directed at the ultimate consumers. For example, meeting planners purchase travel services for the end users, including corporate travelers, social groups, and professional associations; and school boards purchase foodservice contracts for students, who are the consumers. Although advertising is often used, these organizational segments are the most common targets for personal selling.

TABLE 12.3 Four Target Audiences

Audience	Possible Appeals	Comment
Nonusers		Not really potential customers
Emergents	Similar to selling a new product; creation of awareness and image	Have not yet formed their buying habits
Loyals	Confirmation of loyalty as the "right choice"	Majority of business comes from repeat users
Switchers	Name awareness, price, deals	Hard to retain as customers

Diverse Population. The marketplace in North America consists of a diverse population, including many ethnic minority groups. For example, the African American, Hispanic, and Asian American populations made up 22.3 percent of the U.S. population in 1990. By the year 2005, these minority groups will represent 29.6 percent of the total population in the United States (Population Projections Program 2000). Advertising to ethnic market segments often requires a different approach than is appropriate for the general market. Burger King's ad agencies designed different ways to communicate with diverse audiences. The Pointer Sisters' song "Baby Come and Get It" was used to target African Americans, and a rock-and-roll version of the song "My Way" was used to entice Hispanic consumers (O'Connor 1999).

Many advertising agencies and marketing consulting firms specialize in various ethnic markets. They provide ethnic-specific market research, customer profile analysis, and advertising planning.

Message: Unique Selling Proposition

A **unique selling proposition (USP)** states the theme for a campaign and often becomes its slogan. It needs to demonstrate that the offer is of *value* to the consumers. It should speak to the consumers' needs, wants, problems, or concerns. In addition, a USP's *uniqueness* must be clear to achieve differentiation; it cannot be a "me too" offer. A USP should only make a promise that is *believable* and that can be fulfilled. An effective USP also summarizes the *benefits,* or reasons, to buy. Benefits can be supported by product features, or characteristics and attributes of products; however, we should always sell benefits, rather than features, because benefits have the strongest appeal to buyers.

Motel 6 has used the same spokesperson, Tom Bodett, for about 15 years to sell the benefits of Motel 6—clean comfortable rooms without high prices. It has used the USP, "We'll leave the light on for you," to communicate the motel's reliability and accessibility. No matter where or why you travel, it tells consumers, there will be a Motel 6 leaving the light on for you at a convenient location where you can always get the best price of any national chain (Motel 6 2001).

When McDonald's says, "You deserve a break today," the underlying message is that a McDonald's meal or snack will be a pleasant experience, or a deserved reward in the midst of a harried life. In addition, the USP implies the notion of solving time-pressure problems. A "break," as compared with a meal, saves time. Visually, a McDonald's ad also suggests a particular experience that goes well beyond food to include social acceptability, family togetherness, and fun times.

Just as slogans in a television commercial sum up the message in words, the visual content, such as smiling faces, happy people, and good times, is often used as a summarizing device. Pictures play a similar role in print ads, particularly for hotels. Photographs or images can be used to provide concrete ideas of the intangible benefits promised by the hotel.

Cut Through the Clutter. As noted earlier, consumers are bombarded with commercial messages. The term **clutter** is used to describe the extent to which multiple

Memories are simply moments that refuse to be ordinary.

How does one capture a moment that lasts a lifetime? Here, it is often a daily occurrence. For reservations, please call a travel professional or The Ritz-Carlton at 1-800-241-3333.

THE RITZ-CARLTON®

www.ritzcarlton.com

The picture in this Ritz Carlton print ad provides tangible clues of the "extraordinary memories" customers will have after visiting the hotel. (Photo courtesy of The Ritz-Carlton Hotel Company, L.L.C.)

messages in one medium, such as television, or one place compete for consumers' limited attention (Bennett 1995). Advertisements must have the ability to "cut through the clutter" to gain and keep the audience's attention—a key goal of designing an ad that gets the operation's message across.

One way to get people's attention is to use a *headline* in print ads. A headline provides a hook to attract the reader's attention. Some are simple, such as "50 Percent Off!" and others strive to be catchy. For example, Sheraton Hotels & Resorts has used the headline, "In Latin America, vacations that start out in ruins end up beautifully at Sheraton."

Humor can attract consumers' attention; however, it is difficult to be amusing to everyone. Little Caesars is known for its humorous television commercials. The Little Caesars' logo is a toga-clad character wearing sandals and the traditional laurel wreath of a Roman statesman, carrying a pizza on a spear. Since Little Caesars first advertised on national network television in 1988, the animated Little Caesars' humorous persona is recognizable worldwide. In fact, Little Caesars' commercials have been voted several times as being the most memorable ads among all TV commercials (Little Caesars 2001).

Another technique to get consumers' attention is the highly aggressive *comparative advertising* campaigns that have become a centerpiece of marketing for runners-up among the hamburger chains: the much discussed burger wars. The Wendy's 1984 commercial, "Where's the beef?" challenged other burger chains in regard to the size of their hamburger patties. It registered the highest consumer awareness levels in the history of the advertising industry (Wendy's International, Inc. 2001). This technique is certainly not limited to burger chains. Papa John's pizza has challenged Pizza Hut in several advertisements. In one ad, a Pizza Hut cofounder who was introduced at a corporate meeting appeared in a Papa John's polo shirt. That cofounder of Pizza Hut simply said he had found a better pizza! Dominos and Pizza Hut have also been rivals over the years with comparative advertising.

Humor helps attract consumers' attention and cut through the media clutter. (Photo courtesy of Chick-fil-A.)

Spokespersons are often used to cut through the clutter by personifying the company and its appeal. Big Boy, a mythical figure atop Bob's Big Boy restaurant signs, has become a landmark in many cities. Probably the most successful spokesperson is Ronald McDonald, who has been suggested as the second most recognized figure in America, next to Santa Claus (McDonald's Corporation 2001). The visual image associated with the company and its message, through constant repetition, makes for effective communication. Most people in North America can instantly associate the clown with McDonald's restaurants. The Chihuahua has also done wonders for Taco Bell. A survey of kids 6 to 17 years old indicated that the Chihuahua commercials motivated 83 percent of them to want to buy Taco Bell products (O'Connor 1999).

Real people are also often used as spokespersons with great success. Dave Thomas, founder of Wendy's, has been very appealing as an easygoing, humorous spokesperson for his company. Bill Marriott has also served as an effective representative for the Marriott Hotels. Tom Bodett, as indicated earlier, is the spokesperson for Motel 6. His voice is recognized by millions of radio listeners and has become synonymous with Motel 6. Even spokespersons, however, can wear out. KFC's long-time symbol, the Colonel, was shelved and replaced with campaigns that portrayed families. In 1988, however, the Colonel was brought back as a result of the demand by many franchisees and his popularity among consumers.

One danger in clever and ambitious copywriting is overpromising. Consumer expectations established by advertising will haunt the operators who cannot fulfill them. Therefore, advertising agencies must work with an operation's people to make sure that the messages communicated are real and achievable.

Advertising Media Characteristics and Alternatives

The principal **advertising media** used in the hospitality industry are electronic, such as television and radio, and print, such as newspapers and magazines. Outdoor advertising, direct mail, and due bills are also important media. The telephone and telemarketing are increasing in significance, especially for hotels and resorts.

Media Characteristics. There are two common benchmarks used in assessing advertising media, **cost per thousand** (**CPM,** in which M stands for thousand) and **gross rating points (GRPs).** To compute CPM, the cost of the ad is divided by the number of audience members in thousands. For example, for an ad that costs $10,000 and reaches 500,000 people, the CPM would be $20 ($10,000 ÷ 500). CPM should be viewed as a rough benchmark because it ignores the issue of *waste* circulation—people who are exposed to the medium but do not really pay attention to the ad, and people who pay attention to the ad but are not potential customers. Yet, CPM also undercounts the number of exposures of print media because it figures only *primary* circulation and ignores *secondary* circulation, whereby a newspaper or magazine is read by more than one person. Finally, the CPM measure overlooks the *impact* or effectiveness of the particular medium on the target audience.

In addition to cost, media have three key characteristics: reach, frequency, and impact. **Reach** refers to the number of *households* exposed to a particular ad during a particular time period. **Frequency** means the number of times within that time period a *household* is exposed to the message. Based on estimates of the number of people viewing or reading a medium in an average household, reach and frequency can also be expressed as the number of *persons* reached and the number of times each *person* is exposed to the message.

Reach and frequency can be specified numerically and used to compute gross rating points (GRPs). Reach is usually presented as a percentage of the total population in a target market (Bennett 1995). GRPs are computed by multiplying reach by frequency. For example, if an ad reaches 70 percent of the homes in a market with an average four-time frequency, that advertising schedule or plan has a GRP of 280. The term "gross" is used in GRP because there is likely to be duplication in coverage. A very high GRP does not mean that *everyone* in the audience has been reached. Many people may have missed the ad, whereas others may have seen it several times.

GRPs are a measure of the weight of advertising delivered by a particular schedule. If a schedule delivers 350 GRPs, it would have more weight than the 280 calculated earlier. However, the GRP figure does not reveal the combination of reach and frequency used. The media planner, therefore, faces the decisions on reach and frequency as separate considerations. The choice is whether to emphasize high reach with extensive coverage of a large audience, or high frequency with intensive coverage of a more limited target. Exposures that are too frequent can result in boredom; overemphasizing reach at the expense of frequency may mean that an ad makes no impression at all because it is seen so infrequently. In general, some repetition is helpful; however, too much repetition results in consumers' tuning out.

Impact involves a more subjective judgment on the quality of the exposure. An ad attempting to reach women executives is likely to be more effective in the magazine *Working Women* than in tabloids, because the credibility of the magazine tends to be higher and the reader's respect for it is likely to be greater as well.

Media Alternatives. A summary of the available media alternatives and their advantages and disadvantages is provided in Table 12.4.

Electronic Media. *Television* advertising often results in the lowest CPM reached, even though it has a very high *total* cost. For this reason, large chains that have large enough advertising budgets to afford the efficiency of the **electronic media** are the major users of television advertising. Television is so significant to restaurant chains that its **areas of dominant influence (ADI)** boundaries are an important consideration in restaurant expansion planning. In fact, an advertising threshold can be calculated to indicate the number of operations required in a market to justify TV advertising. If TV advertising is necessary to the success of a concept, **market entry threshold** calculations, as shown in Table 12.5, can indicate whether it is feasible to enter a particular market.

The power of television comes from its ability to combine sight, motion, and sound. In addition to informing the audience about the products offered, more and more TV commercials tell a heartwarming story or provide some entertainment value to catch people's attention and increase their likelihood to recall the message.

TABLE 12.4 Types of Media and Advantages and Disadvantages of Each

	Advantages	Disadvantages
Electronic media		
Television	Excellent reach Combination of sight, motion, and sound Ability to catch people's attention Ability to target with cable and satellite stations	High total cost Clutter High waste Audience's ability to switch channels
Radio	Ability to target Less costly than television Good reach of travelers	Sound only Less attention getting than TV Clutter
Internet	Relatively low cost Amount of information Ability to provide sight, motion, and sound Interactivity Flexibility Buyer seeking seller	Constant update required
Other electronic media	Excellent visual and audio quality of CD-ROM Ability to target Amount of information Flexibility	Expensive to design
Print media		
Newspapers	Timeliness Broad-based readership Local audience	Poor production quality Clutter Inability to target
Newspaper inserts	Good campaign distribution vehicle Higher coupon redemption rate	More expensive than newspapers
Magazines	Ability to target Prestige High-quality reproduction High secondary circulation	Long lead time More expensive than newspapers
Collateral materials		
Brochures	Informative Ability to target High production quality	Outdated easily
Specialty items	Relatively inexpensive High recall rate by consumers	
Outdoor media	Good reach Good frequency Relatively uncluttered	Brief message High waste
Direct mail	Ability to target Personalized mailing pieces Good coupon distribution vehicle Low minimum cost	High CPM Junk mail image
Due bill	Low cost Positive public relations	Displacing paying guests if poorly planned

TABLE 12.5   Calculation of Market Entry Threshold

Assumptions:

Typical unit sales volume	$1,000,000
Percentage of sales to local advertising	4%
Local advertising budget available per unit per year	$ 40,000

Experience in this company is that 250 GRPs every other week are required to get its message across.

Cost in this market for a 250 GRP schedule is $10,000 per week.

An every-other-week 250 GRP schedule will cost $260,000 per year.

$$\$260,000 \div \$40,000 = 6.5 \text{ restaurant units}$$

On the basis of these calculations, the company should not enter this market unless it thinks the market can support seven restaurants or that some alternative advertising schedule can be made to work.

Yet despite its strengths, TV advertising receives frequent criticism. The escalating cost, particularly of network television, means that previous budgets may no longer support sufficient frequency. Because of the expensiveness of airtime, there is a growing use of shorter commercials, which has led to the problem of increasing clutter as the number of commercial messages rises. Also because of the high cost of network TV, cable and satellite TV stations have effectively challenged the networks' early dominance of the medium. An advantage of cable and satellite stations is that they are a highly targeted medium because individual channels have a distinctive group of viewers. The production costs of TV ads can also be prohibitive for small operations. A professionally produced TV ad that can attract an audience's attention can easily cost $8,000 to $10,000.

Although TV offers the greatest reach, a logical by-product of extensive reach is poor selectivity. Chances are also very good that television has a high waste factor, or reaches many people who are not in the target market. The ability of the audience to mute commercials and channel surf during commercials has also had an impact on TV's effectiveness. Despite all the reservations we may have about television, however, it is clearly the most powerful medium for mass marketers who can afford it.

Radio is less expensive in terms of absolute costs, and can therefore be used by a wider range of operations. Radio is also more selective, because most stations are target market specific, offering news/talk, easy listening, classical, hard rock, and country/western, with a highly differentiated listenership. Radio is often used in conjunction with television to provide *frequency* in an overall campaign. For example, the desirable frequency for an operation to reach the homes in a market is five times during an advertising campaign period. Because of budget constraints, three exposures are provided via television and the other two via radio.

Radio can also be used to reach people in their cars and thus is a good medium for reaching travelers and people commuting to work during the daily "drive times"—roughly, 6:00 to 10:00 A.M. and 3:00 to 7:00 P.M. A disadvantage of radio is the limited attention of the listeners, because most of them are doing something else, such as housework, driving, or studying, while listening.

The *Internet* has been used as an advertising medium by many hospitality operations. A Web page on the Internet is a must for those operations targeting business travelers, the educated, and the young. Those individuals are more likely to be technologically savvy and to use the Internet as a source of information and a way to make travel and dining reservations, as well as to find special deals. Most hotel Web sites provide information on facilities and amenities, directions to the hotel, and information on local attractions. Some Web sites also provide a virtual tour of the property with video clips. Guests can make room reservations directly from the homepage, and some hotels offer special rates for their Internet customers.

Restaurants have also taken advantage of Internet technology by providing menus, nutrition information, and franchise and employment opportunities on their Web sites. Some restaurants' Web sites provide a restaurant locator and allow visitors to order delivery on-line. In addition, several corporations provide archives of their past TV and print advertisements for viewing. The major advantage of the Internet as a medium is the relatively low cost. Even small, independent operations can afford to have a Web presence; and their Web sites can be just as effective as those of the major corporations. A challenge for operations with a Web site is to continuously update the information.

Other ways of using the Internet include purchasing of banner ads, the commercial messages visitors see when they first log onto a site, and being a sponsor of a Web site. The costs of banner ads are also reasonable, as compared with TV or print ads. The actual cost of banner ads and sponsorships depends on the nature of the Web site and the popularity of the site.

Other electronic media, such as videocassette tapes and CD-ROMs, have also been used by various hospitality operations. Some corporations send a videocassette to their stockholders, along with their annual reports, to illustrate the highlights of their accomplishments in a livelier manner. Usually, a few commercials are included as part of the highlights. CD-ROMs are mostly designed for organizational buyers and potential franchisees. Because of the ample storage capacity of CD-ROMs, detailed information can be provided along with video clips and full-color pictures. The audio and visual quality of CD-ROMs is extremely high; therefore, the products shown may have enhanced appeal.

Print Media. *Newspapers,* the most popular **print media** among restaurants, are generally published once a day. Therefore, they can provide great flexibility, because the message can easily be adjusted daily, if needed. Newspapers provide a broad-based readership that helps to build awareness of an establishment among key audiences. Moreover, the different sections of a newspaper, such as Sports, Travel, and Finance, offer opportunities to target particular groups of readers. Newspapers are also often used to distribute coupons to a wide audience, either as part of a newspaper itself or as special inserts.

Newspaper inserts can be in either co-op or solo format. Co-op inserts are supplements shared by several advertisers. The inserts are usually printed in color and offer greater flexibility and lower costs than newspaper advertising. Coupons distributed by inserts tend to have higher redemption rates than those in newspaper ads. Co-op inserts usually contain advertising from only noncompetitive products and services. Solo inserts are generally of one or two pages and cost three to five times as much as co-op inserts. Therefore, the use of solo inserts is usually limited to chains and large operations. They do make an effective medium, however, for special events, such as grand openings.

Magazines offer demographic selectivity, and many national magazines publish regional editions that offer geographic targeting. Special-interest magazines, such as those focusing on sports, hobbies, and fashion, offer psychographic targeting opportunities as well. Local and regional magazines are also available, and these are appropriate for independent operations whose target markets are local or regional in scope. Many magazines have an excellent reputation and high-quality production, both of which improve the impact of the messages. Superior reproduction of photos is especially important in destination and resort advertising. Because magazines are often read by more than one person, they have a strong secondary-circulation advantage built into their distribution numbers.

Moving billboards offer a good way to communicate with the public, especially in a tourist area.

Outdoor Media. **Outdoor media** include signs and billboards. The major difference between an operation's signs and billboards is that the *signs* are on the operation's grounds, whereas *billboards* are placed away from the operation. Some signs have a reader board, or an area for temporary messages. A reader board is a good place to announce specials, new facilities and services, or local activities, which help build public relations with the community.

In selecting billboards, circulation figures and visibility should be considered. *Circulation* statistics are based on the number of vehicles that pass a display each hour. *Visibility* depends on the number of other billboards in the area and the surrounding environment. The audience for billboards and signs is usually in moving vehicles, therefore the message should be brief and the design easy to follow. Case Study 12.1 shows one property's creative use of billboards.

CASE STUDY 12.1

City Buses as Moving Billboards

The Inn at Essex, an AAA four-diamond hotel, is an independent quintessential Vermont country hotel that offers "Country Inn Charm . . . Luxury Hotel Service." The Inn has 120 colonial-style rooms, each with its unique decorations, on 18 acres of land. The Inn's location has less than desirable visibility and was recently facing a

(Photo by Linda Seville.)

poor economic climate. Standard billboards are not allowed in Vermont; therefore, the Inn's creativity was challenged.

The "moving billboard" idea was developed by the hotel marketing staff and accepted by the local transportation authority. A city bus was covered with a huge vinyl wrap featuring pictures of the hotel's exterior, meeting and convention spaces, and fine dining facilities on both sides of the bus. The pictures have an excellent reproduction quality, better than paintings on the sides of the bus—a second display option. They show the hotel in a much livelier manner and illustrate vividly the experiences guests can expect at the Inn.

The bus drives through various downtown areas and has stops right outside the competitors' hotel properties. This solution has provided the much needed exposure to area residents and tourists. The innovative use of a city bus as a moving billboard has also received free press coverage. When a second bus was added, the Inn passed out cider and cookies to passengers and distributed hotel brochures and coupons for dining in its restaurant. The buses traveled hundreds of miles a week, and the Inn enjoyed greater exposure than it could have received with any other form of advertising. According to the Inn, the volume of meetings and conferences, as well as restaurant business, has increased.

Sources: L. Dube, C. A. Enz, L. M. Renaghan, and J. A. Siguaw, *American Lodging Excellence: The Key to Best Practices in the U.S. Lodging Industry* (New York: American Express and the American Hotel Foundation, 1999); The Inn at Essex. (2000). *The Inn at Essex: Home* (on-line). Web site: http://www.innatessex.com/

Collateral Materials. **Collateral materials** include brochures and specialty items such as coffee mugs, mouse pads, and key chains. *Brochures* are probably the most important collateral items, especially for hotels and resorts. Other forms of advertising may get consumers' attention, but brochures deliver the information that help sell a product. It is necessary to develop target-market-specific brochures, rather than a one-size-fits-all brochure, to address the different needs of the various markets. For example, a hotel brochure targeting leisure travelers might emphasize recreational facilities, while the brochure designed for convention planners might focus on meeting facilities and banquet services. *Specialty items* are economical sales tools that can be remarkably effective. If consumers use the items on a regular basis, they can easily recall the sponsoring organization's name. When they use the items in public, they also become walking advertisements. Specialty items can be used as a promotion themselves or in conjunction with other promotional activities.

Direct Mail. **Direct mail** offers opportunities to target specific groups of individuals and personalize the mailing pieces. Specialized mailing lists are available from list suppliers. Operators can request a list containing individuals of the particular demographic and psychographic profiles that characterize their target markets. House lists, composed of names and addresses of current customers, are also useful in encouraging repeat visits. It is important to realize that a direct mail campaign is only as good as

Providing mini-brochures containing restaurant menus is a creative way of using collateral materials. This type of display can be found in tourist information centers and hotel lobbies.

the mailing list used. Operators can request the post office to return undeliverable mail to help "clean up" the database. Direct mail represents an option for operators who cannot afford the large-circulation media, such as television, radio, and newspapers, in spite of their favorable CPM because of the high total cost.

Some operations mail newsletters that feature items about staff and guests, as well as information about special events, such as holiday meals, wine tastings, and other promotions. In a "feathered" mailing, only a certain percentage of the list is used each week so as to avoid the crush of sending out thousands of pieces all at once. To overcome the image of junk mail, direct mail pieces can be personalized or convey an "insider" feel in a newsletter. Including a coupon or a certificate can also entice the receivers to review the material.

Due Bills. **Due bills,** or trade-outs, are a means of trading merchandise or services for advertising. They are attractive because of the low incremental costs to hotels. Even with foodservice, food and labor are the primary costs in a trade-out. However, operators should limit trading to slow periods so that they do not have to turn away paying guests. Trade-outs can often be arranged with local media by unit managers. In addition to the monetary benefits of trades, these arrangements can have a positive public relations impact when handled properly because of the personal contacts made with local media personnel. Brokers are also available to make such arrangements on a national or regional basis. Case Study 12.2 is an example of a hotel owner using direct mailings and due bills to generate its much-needed business.

CASE STUDY 12.2

Using Direct Mailings and Due Bills to Generate Business

Arun Bivek owns the Knights Inn, Econo Lodge, and Travelodge in a small, sleepy town in South Carolina. Other than fishing and golfing, there is no local industry or tourist attraction. The town does not even have a quick-service restaurant or a gas station that is open past 9:00 P.M. Knowing that many golfers come from other states, Bivek hired a retired golfer to compile a list of players using the local golf courses. He merged this mailing list with the hotels' guest history databases and mailed out 10,000 advertising pieces to golfers in 11 Southeastern states. The promotion was so successful that he was able to negotiate better rates and preferred tee times with the local courses.

Bivek has also worked with the local Chamber of Commerce, and his is the host hotel for various fishing tournaments. For one of his hotels to become the exclusive hotel, he gave 10 complimentary rooms to the Chamber of Commerce. He has also worked with other organizations in similar trade-out agreements. From the local fishing guides, he learned that people who are serious about fishing like to leave early in the morning, therefore he started opening his restaurant at 5:00 A.M. The new hours not only serve his hotel guests better, but because no other restaurants in town serve breakfast that early, have also attracted customers who do not stay at the hotel.

Bivek had a net loss of $20,000 during his first year because of the initial investment in advertising. However, he generated $180,000 in new revenue in the second year and was also profitable in the third year of the direct mailing campaign.

Source: L. Dube, C. A. Enz, L. M. Renaghan, and J. A. Siguaw, *American Lodging Excellence: The Key to Best Practices in the U.S. Lodging Industry* (New York: American Express and the American Hotel Foundation, 1999).

Timing

The **timing** of an advertising campaign often relates to the timing of customers' purchases. A direct mail program aimed at selling office Christmas parties would be inappropriate in July and probably just as untimely in December. If decisions are usually made in November, a late October or early November mailing would fit well with the timing of the information search. Radio ads promoting a Mother's Day special should start approximately one month before the event.

There are two possibilities in advertising schedules, continuity and flighting. Some advertisers adopt **continuity** by scheduling ads evenly throughout a campaign. The alternative scheduling pattern is **flighting.** A "flight" refers to the repeated use of advertising in a certain medium during a campaign—an "on-period." The flight is then followed by a period of silence in that medium—an "off-period." Flighting is used in some cases because of budget limitations. For the case presented in Table 12.5, if the advertising budget is only $7,500 a week, less than the $10,000 required, the operator may consider having three on-periods followed by one off-period, and then repeat the pattern as shown in the following chart. When flighting is used with television advertising, continuity is often maintained in another less expensive medium, such as radio.

Schedule	Week															
	1	2	3	4	5	6	7	8	9	10	11	12	13	14	15	16
Continuity	on		on		on		on		on		on		on		on	
Flighting	on		on		on				on		on		on			

Budget

A common way to set the **advertising budget** is as a **percentage of sales** that is judged affordable or comparable to competitors' spending. The advantage of this method is simplicity. Some may even argue that the method is oversimplified. For example, in a poor performance year, the advertising budgeting is decreased, but this is a time when more advertising is needed. Moreover, spending the industry average percentage on advertising, in effect, lets the competition set the advertising budget for you.

A preferred method, called **zero-based budgeting,** is to set advertising objectives first and then spell out the steps necessary to accomplish the objectives. For example, a company may seek to increase consumer awareness for an operation in selected markets, secure a heightened level of name recognition, or increase the level of trial purchases. The steps necessary to achieve any or all of these goals can then be designed and costs estimated for each activity. If the total cost of attaining these goals exceeds the budget, more realistic objectives can be set, perhaps moving toward the desired goals over a longer period of time. The advantage of this approach is that the results of the advertising program can be measured against the objectives.

Advertising Agencies

Advertising agencies come in all sizes, ranging from one-person shops to international agencies with revenues in the billions of dollars. Full-service agencies provide *creative, media-buying,* and *market research* services. These agencies also offer *campaign planning.* In many cases, they are involved not only in the advertising but also in the design of sales promotion programs and in all elements of a company's marketing program.

There are also a wide variety of specialized agencies, such as creative boutiques, independent media-buying services, and market research firms. The disadvantage of using a group of specialized agencies is that the client, the hospitality company, has to coordinate the work of a group of highly specialized experts, and hospitality managers often lack the expertise to undertake such coordination. The result can be expensive and frustrating.

Although large companies generally use major agencies, a town of almost any size usually has a small independent agency that is interested in assisting the independent hospitality operators or providing local advertising services to franchised operations. Small agencies may not have the depth of larger firms, but they do have people experienced in the creative work of developing ad campaigns, including layout and artwork. They generally have experience in media-buying processes in the local community. Besides, small accounts usually get the attention of the top personnel in small agencies.

Some firms develop their own in-house ad agencies to maintain tighter control over advertising and to save the commission or fees that an outside agency would charge. A problem with this approach is that these companies lack an outside independent perspective on the company's marketing program, which is one of the vital advantages a strong agency can offer its clients.

Summary

Advertising is one of the major forms of marketing communication. Others include sales promotion, personal selling, and public relations and publicity. Marketing communication can be informative, persuasive, or reminding. The appropriate type of communication to be used depends on the stages in the product life cycle and the consumer decision-making process. The objective of advertising is usually to generate selective demand for a particular company, but market leaders and firms introducing unknown products may seek to stimulate primary demand.

Advertising aims first to move consumers to awareness and then to interest and desire and, ultimately, to action (AIDA). Advertising has a primary role up to the point of consumer trial. From that point on, pleasing the guests through good operations becomes the key, while advertising retains an important reminder role. Some advertising is designed to build an image, and other advertising is intended to encourage immediate purchase.

Five considerations underlie advertising planning: target, message, media, timing, and budget:

Target. The audience for advertising can be divided into segments of nonusers, emergents, loyals, and switchers.

Message. The unique selling proposition (USP) is often summarized in a tag line. A USP should offer value to consumers, be unique and believable, and communicate benefits. A message must be designed to cut through the clutter of other advertisements. Headlines, humor, comparative advertising, and spokespersons are usually utilized to make an ad stand out from the crowd.

Media. Two common benchmarks in assessing advertising media are cost per thousand (CPM) and gross rating points (GRPs). Other key media characteristics are reach, frequency, and impact. Advertising media options include electronic (television, radio, computers, and other electronics), print (newspapers, newspaper inserts, and magazines), outdoor media (signs and billboards), collateral materials (brochures and specialty items), direct mail, and due bills.

Timing. Advertising must be timed to reach customers at the point at which they are most likely to be influenced to purchase. Continuity and flighting are alternative advertising schedules.

Budget. The advertising budget may be set as a percentage of sales or determined by using the zero-based, objective-oriented, budgeting method—a preferred approach.

Advertising agencies may be divided into full-service and specialized firms. A key advantage of a strong agency is that it brings an expert outside independent judgment to a hospitality firm's marketing decisions.

Key Words and Concepts

Communication mix	Unique selling proposition (USP)	Print media
Advertising	Clutter	Outdoor media
Sales promotion	Advertising media	Collateral materials
Personal selling	Cost per thousand (CPM)	Direct mail
Public relations	Gross rating points (GRPs)	Due bills
Publicity	Reach	Timing
Primary demand	Frequency	Continuity
Selective demand	Impact	Flighting
AIDA	Electronic media	Advertising budget
Advertising planning	Areas of dominant influence (ADI)	Percentage of sales
Audience segments	Market entry threshold	Zero-based budgeting

Resources on the Internet

Abbott Wool's Market Segment Resource Locator. *http://www.awool.com/awool/*
The Ad Council. *http://www.adcouncil.org/*
AdWeek Online. *http://www.adweek.com/*
Advertising Research Foundation. *http://www.arfsite.org*
American Advertising Federation. *http://www.aaf.org*

American Association of Advertising Agencies. *http://www.aaaa.org/*
Idle Minds: Advertising, Internet Consulting, Web Site Design & Hosting. *http://www.idleminds.com/*
International Advertising Association. *http://www.iaaglobal.org/*
Internet Advertising Bureau. *http://www.iab.net/*

Discussion Questions

1. What are the elements of a communication mix?
2. What types of communication are appropriate for the different stages of the product life cycle and consumer decision-making process?
3. What is AIDA? How does it relate to marketing communication? How does it relate to operations?
4. What are the pros and cons of image and promotional advertising? What determining factors influence the decision on which to use?

5. What are the main considerations in advertising planning? What are the key points related to each?
6. How can an effective USP cut through the clutter? Give examples of campaigns you believe to be effective in achieving this goal.
7. What are the benchmarks used to evaluate media? What do *reach, frequency,* and *impact* mean in media evaluation?
8. What are the commonly used advertising media?
9. How should an advertising budget be set?

References

Bennett, P. D., ed. (1995). *Dictionary of marketing terms.* 2d ed. Chicago: American Marketing Association.

Little Caesars Enterprises. (2001). *Little Caesars homepage* (on-line). Web site: http://www.littlecaesars.com

McDonald's Corporation. (2001). *McDonald's Corporation homepage* (on-line). Web site: http://www.mcdonalds.com

Motel 6. (2001). *Motel 6 homepage* (on-line). Web site: http://www.motel6.com

O'Connor, P. (1999). Getting the message. *Restaurants and Institutions, 109*(14), 105, 108, 110, 112, 118, 121.

Population Projections Program. (2000, January 13). Washington, DC: U.S. Census Bureau, Population Division. No. 20233.

Stewart, D. W. (1994). Advertising in a slow growth economy. *American Demographics, 16*(9) (September) 40–46.

Wendy's International, Inc. (2001). *Wendy's International, Inc. homepage* (on-line). Web site: http://www.wendys.com

13

Marketing Communication: Sales Promotion, Public Relations/Publicity, and Personal Selling

When you have finished reading this chapter, you should be able to:

- Identify the major types of sales promotion.
- Describe the primary purpose of various sales promotion techniques.
- Provide examples of public relations and publicity.
- Explain the steps in effective crisis management.
- Discuss the sales process.
- Illustrate how to build credibility and confidence during a sales presentation.
- Understand the importance and techniques of closing a sale.

This chapter continues the discussion of the important topic of marketing communication. Sales promotion and public relations/publicity are impersonal activities that target a large number of consumers. They are often used in conjunction with advertising. Personal selling, however, is directed at individual decision makers.

Sales Promotion

Sales promotion is a media and nonmedia marketing effort applied for a limited period of time to encourage trial or more frequent repeat purchases, introduce a new product, encourage consumers to trade up, or neutralize competitors' marketing activities (Bennett 1995). Unlike advertising that is used to influence consumer attitudes over a period of time, a sales promotion usually includes the provision of a financial incentive to build immediate sales. A good sales promotion, ideally, should also support the company's image. Figure 13.1 lists the probable reasons for using sales promotions.

The most common form of sales promotion in foodservice is a deal that offers coupons, discounts, or premium merchandise. In upscale operations, instead of decreasing prices, special events are used to enhance perceived value for the customers. Most sales promotion activities are also keyed to the prevailing economic conditions. For example, coupons and value pricing are especially popular during a recession, when consumers either have less money in their pockets or are afraid that they will soon have less money to spend. In more prosperous times, the emphasis usually shifts to activities that focus on value enhancement.

Like any other element of the marketing mix, promotions should be designed to target a specific audience, such as families, teens, or business travelers. Sales promotions are not spur-of-the-moment activities, and, especially in multiunit companies, they require considerable advance planning. A means of evaluation should also be built into the promotion plan. Customary practice in the industry for measuring the impact of a promotion is to compare the operating results in the period immediately preceding the promotion with the period during the promotion and the period immediately following it. Sometimes the results of the corresponding period of the preceding year is used. These comparisons must be adjusted if unusual events, such as a major concert or a football game, occur during any of these periods.

A number of concerns about promotions have been expressed. Many operators use

- Encourage trial purchase
- Stimulate repeat business
- Build customer loyalty through rewards
- Increase sales during specific time periods
- Increase customer spending or length of visit
- Introduce new products or services
- Compete with other operations for spotlight
- Capitalize on special trends or events
- Add excitement
- Motivate employees

FIGURE 13.1 Reasons to use sale promotions.

promotions as a quick fix for declining sales without identifying the real reasons for the business's deterioration. Moreover, deal-seeking customers attracted by promotions tend to lack loyalty. When the sales promotion ends, their patronage may end as well. The quality of a product or service may also be, or may be perceived to be, inferior to the quality provided during nonpromotion periods. In addition, discounts provided to current customers do not really increase sales volume, because these customers would have made the purchases anyway. Finally, if they are used improperly, promotions can cheapen the image a company has created over the years.

Types of Sales Promotion

The most common forms of promotion are coupons; discounts; premiums; games, sweepstakes, and contests; merchandising; packaging; and sampling.

Coupons. Coupons basically reduce prices for consumers. Because coupons usually have an expiration date, they encourage consumers to buy *now*. Coupons are most often distributed by newspapers or direct mail and are used most frequently during economic downtimes and off-seasons. Coupons are most commonly used by quick-service restaurants (QSRs), but hotels sometimes use them as well. Hotel coupons are usually distributed by mail or in magazine ads to promote weekend or off-season business, to encourage repeat visits, or to expand the customer base.

The larger the discount offered, generally, the higher the redemption rate that can be obtained. A **BOGO** (buy one, get one free) is the most popular offer with consumers when dining out or ordering take-out food, as shown in Table 13.1. However, a BOGO drastically reduces the profit margin of an operation. For example, if an operation has a food cost of 30 percent at full price, it will have a 60 percent food cost for a meal when a BOGO coupon is redeemed. But because the beverage cost for soft drinks is usually below 10 percent and most customers order a soft drink with their meals at full price, the combined food and beverage cost percentage may be in the 50 percent range, which leaves another 50 percent to cover other expenses. A successful coupon promotion should increase customer traffic in an otherwise slow period. The extra profit margin, even though smaller than that of the nonpromotion period, makes a welcome contribution to the bottom line and provides the cash flow operators need to meet ongoing costs.

Bounce-back coupons are given to customers at the time of purchase to encourage their repeat visits. For example, many pizza restaurants tape coupons on pizza boxes as part of the take-out or delivery orders. Bounce-back coupons have a significantly lower cost because they involve no distribution fee, a particularly important consideration for small operations. Because of the targeted audience, bounce-back coupons usually have a higher redemption rate than coupons distributed through newspapers. Bounce-back coupons can also be designed to bring customers back for designated periods, such as Monday nights, or to get them to try particular products.

Discounts. Discounts, or sales, are another common form of sales promotion. Discounts can be supported by other advertising or simply by in-store signage, such as a

Many operations distribute coupons on their Internet homepages, with no additional distribution cost to the company. This gives consumers another reason to visit the Web site and find out what's new with the company. (Photo courtesy of Long John Silver's. Reprinted with permission.)

"special" clip on the menu. Like coupons, discounts work on the price side of the price/value equation. They are most often used during off-peak business periods. "Early-bird specials" invite people to eat the evening meal early when the dining room is not crowded. The offer of a special price for a second entrée is occasionally given for slow days. For example, "Tuesday night is family night" when kids can eat free or for a minimum charge. Another use of discounting is to introduce new products. The introductory rate offers are usually for a "limited-time only." Sometimes another item, such as a soft drink, is offered free or at a reduced price when the new item is ordered.

The danger of discounting is that it can cheapen the product's or the operation's

TABLE 13.1 Likelihood of Using Meal Deals			
Incentive or Promotion	All Adults	Men	Women
Two-for-one specials	51%	49%	53%
Coupons	44	38	49
Complete-meal specials	44	43	45
All-you-can-eat specials	42	46	38
Price reductions for dining during off-peak hours	33	36	30
Senior citizen discounts	30	30	30
Early-bird specials	24	26	22
Games and sweepstakes	14	14	13

Source: National Restaurant Association, *Tableservice Restaurant Trends—1999*. Copyright 1999 by National Restaurant Association (Publication CS509).

reputation for quality and service. If discounts are provided too often, customers can become accustomed to their availability and may not purchase the items without discounts. For example, if a restaurant offers a discount on its fish sandwich every Thursday, it is likely that most of the sales from the fish sandwich will be generated on Thursdays. When customers dine in the restaurant on any other day of the week, they tend to order something else from the menu because they can *always* get the fish on Thursdays at a lower price. When used properly, however, discounts can stimulate incremental business during slow periods.

Premiums. **Premiums** are merchandise usually sold at cost with a purchase of a food or beverage item. Toys and special drinking glasses are common premiums. They are often offered in sets of three to six items, the goal being to get customers to collect the entire set. With a different item becoming available each week, customers are encouraged to return once a week for the rest of the promotion period. The "bargain" provided by such merchandise is an extra incentive to visit the store because it is seen as adding or enhancing the value of the purchase. Premiums are sometimes referred to as **self-liquidating promotions** because the cost of the merchandise is usually covered by the amount paid by the customers.

Games, Sweepstakes, and Contests. **Games** involve the use of game pieces, such as scratch-and-win, match-and-win, and peel-and-win tickets. This form of promotion requires frequent visits by customers to increase the probability of winning and therefore promotes repeat business. Small prizes, such as free soft drinks or other food items, are given frequently to make the game interesting, particularly for younger customers. The top prizes offer an incentive to continue playing and the satisfaction of a fantasy about a trip to the Caribbean or a new car.

Pull big prizes out of little boxes.

Head into Harrah's® Prairie Band Casino and you could be heading out in a new Lincoln LS6. Or with extra cash in your pocket up to $2,500!

January 17 – March 27

- 1 free entry per day
- Earn additional entries based on play
- Weekly drawings Mondays at 7 p.m. beginning January 24
- 5 winners weekly
- Amounts range from $250 to $2,500

PRAIRIE BAND CASINO

Cash & Car Craze

January 17 – March 27
Final Drawing Monday, March 27, at 7 p.m.

How To Play
All cardholders will receive one free entry per day Sunday through Thursday just by presenting their card at the Total Gold® Center. Then, for every hour of tracked play, Total Gold members will receive one entry form. Upon presenting their Total Platinum Card, members will receive two entry forms for every hour of tracked play, and Total Diamond Card members will receive three entries.

Before you leave, stop by the Total Gold Center to pick up your Cash and Car Craze entries. Good Luck!

Weekly Drawings
Five guests will win per drawing. In order of name called, each will pick one of 10 keys. Each key opens one of 10 boxes. They'll try the key in each box until the key works. Each box has cash in it, and every winner wins cash. Amounts will range from $250 to $2,500.

5 winners per week — Every Monday at 7 p.m. beginning January 24.

Final Drawing
On Monday, March 27, at 7 p.m., Harrah's® Prairie Band Casino will give away ten grand prizes. You must bring your entry forms back on the day of the drawing. Entry forms will be placed in a drum which will close 2 minutes prior to drawing time. Entry forms will stop being distributed 10 minutes prior to drawing time. Ten winners will be selected and if you are a winner, you'll have 2 minutes to report to the stage or alert Harrah's staff. Each of the ten winners will be given $1,000 and a key. One key will start the engine to a new Lincoln LS6.

PRAIRIE BAND CASINO

A sweepstakes program can be used to increase traffic on slow days. (Photo courtesy of Harrah's Prairie Band Casino.)

Sweepstakes require participants to submit their names and addresses, and winners are drawn randomly. These are great opportunities to gather updated customer information to build an in-house mailing list. For a sweepstakes to have a significant impact, top prizes must be large enough to compete for consumers' attention among other activities. **Contests,** such as a coloring contest for kids and a name-the-product contest for customers of all ages, are competitions based on certain characteristics or skills of the participants. Contests can generate excitement among consumers because of the activities involved. Therefore, the top prizes usually are not as large as those that can be won in games and sweepstakes.

Merchandising. **Merchandising** is an on-premises promotion that targets in-house guests. The purpose is to increase customer spending during the current visit or to encourage repeat visits. Merchandising usually involves displays of products or promotional materials. Both restaurants and hotels use this technique extensively. Promotional materials include table tents, wine lists, room service menus, and elevator posters. Products can be displayed via dessert trays, tableside cooking, in-room minibars, and lobby exhibits. Menus are the best merchandising devices a restaurant can use to promote specific items. A detailed discussion of various merchandising techniques is included in Chapter 14.

Packaging. **Packaging,** discussed as a pricing method in Chapter 11, can also be used as a means of sales promotion. Many independent and chain restaurants have found that suppliers are happy to work with them on promotions. For the suppliers, a successful promotion means increased sales of their products and a closer relationship with their customers—the operators. A wine-tasting dinner offers a good opportunity to use packaging as a promotional tool. Wine suppliers are usually willing to provide restaurants with wines for tasting, free or at reduced prices, as well as promotional materials such as booklets, regional wine maps, and posters. Sometimes the purveyors even provide a representative to discuss wines at the tasting. Restaurants may offer their regular customers an interesting "free" event, or perhaps charge a fee that still makes the tasting a bargain for the guests. The result is likely to be a full house for dinner. A wine tasting can also provide an excellent kickoff for a new wine list and a campaign promoting the sale of wine with dinner.

Hotel restaurants can use all the promotions that freestanding restaurants use, plus a package of room and meals. Hotels can also offer special weekend packages that include tours of local attractions or packages built around sporting or cultural events, with tickets included. The results are usually favorable publicity and increased room and food sales on otherwise slow weekends.

Sampling. **Sampling** means giving away free samples of products or services to encourage sales. For example, an operation may provide sample foods or hotel room amenities at a local business fair to increase awareness and encourage patronage. Hotel rooms are not likely to be given away to the general public, but familiarization tours may be given for travel agents, which is another example of sampling. Free upgrades in room assignment are also used to allow guests to experience a different type of room and thus encourage future paid upgrades.

Public Relations and Publicity

As defined in Chapter 12, **public relations (PR)** is a form of communication used to influence consumers' feelings, opinions, or beliefs about a company, its products, or services, or to convey the value of its products, services, or activities to buyers, prospects, or other stakeholders (Bennett 1995). **Publicity** is directed specifically at the media to generate unpaid media coverage of a company's products, services, and activities. PR and publicity are activities with different purposes. However, a well-planned public relations activity should create complimentary publicity, and the gain of publicity should generate positive public relations.

Public Relations

Public relations activities are performed to maintain a firm's relationship with its *special publics*, as well as the *general public*. Special publics are those that have direct relationships with the firm: consumers, employees, suppliers, intermediaries, and stockholders. Each of these has a somewhat different perspective and interest in the company. Other special publics include people working in the firm's political and regulatory environment, as well as community opinion leaders such as clergy, teachers, or key people in civic and business organizations. The general public comprises everyone in a community or, in the case of a chain operation, in the region or nation.

Public relations activities include positioning the firm as a responsible business citizen and communicating that position to the appropriate publics. A key starting point in PR is simply to have the public's interest in mind in developing operating policies and procedures. That is, a firm must intend to be a good citizen and to behave responsibly and honestly. To be good, however, is not enough. The company must make sure that its publics are aware of its admirable actions.

Publicity

One of the major advantages of publicity as a medium of communication is its credibility. The news is written by a neutral third party. An ad or commercial obviously presents the advertiser's point of view. But a news article, even if it is an edited version of a firm's press release, is seen by its readers as objective and factual. In addition, with the escalating cost of advertising, it is in an operation's best interest to present information in a news format and encourage press coverage.

To gain the media's attention to an operation's story, however, is not easy. Many hospitality managers do not understand the concerns and interests of the media and present stories that are of relevance to the operators, but of very little value to the

Programs such as the Ronald McDonald House build goodwill in the community and help involve franchisees in a company-wide program, which enhances franchisee loyalty.

media. They simply do not know what is *newsworthy*. Operators should look at each story from the perspective of the media's targeted audience. An expensive new banquet room may be news to an operator, but a release about its features and costs probably looks like a solicitation of free advertising to the media. However, if the room is named after a prominent local leader and the dedication ceremonies are held with appropriate dignitaries in attendance, its opening may be viewed as legitimate news to the media.

Hazards of Publicity. The very strength of publicity—that the message comes from an impartial third party—contains a real hazard. With advertising, the advertisers control the content. Publicity, however, is controlled by the editorial staffs of the media. In some cases, the message as presented is vague and incomprehensible, which may confuse the audience and create problems for the hospitality operation. An even worse situation arises when an editorial staff chooses to make fun of the operation or to give the story a negative spin in some other way.

Tools of Public Relations and Publicity

Events and happenings, such as speeches, public service activities, news conferences, and festivals, are sometimes staged for PR purposes. Grand openings and dedications of new or renovated facilities often have a news angle, or a news angle can be created to bring attention to the event. The planning of any such event should include the development of a *press kit,* including **press releases,** fact sheets, and photos. The inclusion of photos can result in a substantial increase in the amount of space allocated to the story, if the photos are used. Photos can also enhance the potential impact on readers. When culinary-related events are held, recipes or a biography of the chef can be included, as appropriate, to generate interest.

Favorable publicity can be built around the owner/operator or employees of an organization. Special achievements, recognition, and even hobbies can be used to generate interest. Celebrity visits are often interesting, and the cost of having a photographer on hand is a worthwhile investment considering the potential press coverage. If the celebrity is of sufficient interest and the media are notified in time, television stations may send camera crews. Whatever coverage is provided, however, must be acceptable to the celebrity guest.

Corporate charities are often developed, and fairly so, with a view to doing well by doing good. That is, they accomplish charitable goals while also gaining favorable publicity. It often happens that a company assumes permanent sponsorship of an activity to increase its PR impact and establish a link between itself and the charitable event in people's minds. Ronald McDonald House, which provides residences for families with seriously ill children, is probably the best-known charitable activity in our industry, but smaller organizations can also make a significant impact in their communities. Many hospitality operations in college towns sponsor fraternity or sorority events or other student organizations' activities. Operations can also be involved in local festivals and sporting events, community affairs, and charitable fund-raising activities.

Chains and large operations may have a PR person on staff. Smaller operations usually rely on a talented manager, part-time PR consultant, or assistance from their advertising agencies. Case Study 13.1 includes some examples of corporate charities.

CASE STUDY 13.1

Corporations Care!

Many hospitality corporations, besides being responsible members of society, are involved in charitable organizations and sponsor community events. Some of them include generous donations as part of their regular activities; others have special giving programs during the holiday seasons. This case study represents only a small fraction of all the contributions made by hospitality operations.

The Burger King Corporation is involved in several community programs. Burger King is a founding member of the Welfare to Work Partnership. As of July 1999, Burger King has hired more than 12,800 welfare recipients in company-owned restaurants since October 1996. Three hundred franchisees have signed on as partners, employing another 2,700 former welfare recipients.

Burger King has also worked with Communities in Schools, Inc., the nation's largest stay-in-school organization, in forming a national network of 24 academies. These are designed for students who have dropped out of school or are functioning below their potential in a traditional school setting, including those who have encountered problems with the juvenile justice system. These youngsters are given a second chance within the personalized environment of the academy.

Burger King's BK Cares is a formal employee-volunteer program run by a committee of approximately 50 employees, representing all levels of management. BK Cares allows corporate employees up to two hours per week during their work schedules to perform volunteer work within the community.

Pizza Hut has sponsored the Book It! National Reading Incentive Program for 15 years, as of 2000. The program is part of the curriculum in more than 895,000 classrooms in nearly 53,000 elementary schools in all 50 states. Teachers set monthly reading goals for each student in the class. The goals vary from student to student and from month to month. When a child meets a monthly reading goal, the teacher gives him or her a Pizza Award Certificate. When the child brings the certificate to a participating Pizza Hut restaurant, he or she is rewarded with a free one-topping Personal Pan Pizza, a program button, a sticker for the button, and praise from the manager. On each subsequent award visit, the student receives another pizza, another sticker, and more praise.

If a child meets the reading goals in all six months, he or she qualifies for the Reader's Honor Roll, a record of achievement signed by the principal and the teacher, and receives a Book It! Program All-Star Reader Medallion at Pizza Hut.

Inter-Continental Hotels and Resorts was the first hotel chain to issue an Environmental Operating Manual to all properties. In 1991, Inter-Continental shared its in-house manual with competitors around the world. In conjunction with the Prince of Wales Business Leaders Forum, Inter-Continental recommended setting up an independent forum in which environmental practices could be shared. Eleven hotels became the founding members of the International Hotels Environment Initiative, whose charter agreed to develop practical environmental guidelines for hotels. Inter-Continental also launched its Internal Environment Awards to recognize the efforts of its corporate staff and hotels in protecting their local environments.

Inter-Continental has also been involved in fund-raising activities for the United Nation Children's Fund (UNICEF). Activities included an Internet charity auction that allowed participants to raise money for UNICEF while they bid on one-night weekend stays at more than 200 Inter-Continental hotels throughout the world. All proceeds went directly to UNICEF.

Sources: Burger King Corporation. (2001). *Welfare reform* (on-line). Web site: *http://www.burgerking.com/community/welfare.htm;* Burger King Corporation. (2001). *Welfare academies* (on-line). Web site: *http://www.burgerking.com/community/bkacademies.htm;* Pizza Hut, Inc. (2001). *Book It! Information* (on-line). Web site: *http://www.bookitprogram.com/whatbook.html;* Bass Hotels & Resorts, Inc. (2001). *Inter-Continental Hotels and Resorts: Press office—Social responsibility* (on-line). Web site: http://www.interconti.com/news.html

Crisis Management

Unfortunately, bad news about a hospitality operation is reported from time to time. Accidents, fires, food poisoning incidents, crimes, and other disturbing events do happen. Most operators prefer to keep these events hush-hush, but if the news does get out, experience suggests that getting the facts straight and telling the truth is the best policy. It is also wise to develop procedures in advance to deal with emergencies. Unfavorable publicity can often be avoided by careful planning and proper handling of a situation.

The first steps in **crisis management** must be taken *before* a crisis occurs. A company's policies and procedures should be constructed with care and must be in the public interest. This is not only the conscientious thing to do, it also minimizes the possibility that any crisis will be traced to the company's negligence. Another step to take before any crisis happens is to have a **contingency plan** in place. Such plans should identify the company's potential crisis points and anticipate how these situations may be handled if any of them do arise. However, because of the uncontrollable nature of any crisis and the demand for information it may create, contingency plans should be flexible.

In most cases, there should be a designated spokesperson for the organization. This person should be a decision maker who has access to the facts. If some facts are in doubt, the spokesperson should offer to get the information and make it available. Within the company, the communication process should be structured so that it is easy to follow in emergencies, when people are likely to be confused. The two greatest dangers in a crisis are *panic* and a *sense of urgency*. Panic often leads to extreme reactions, and a sense of urgency causes people to rush and become unreasonable. Knowing who the spokesperson is releases employees from unnecessary pressure and keeps communication in the hands of one person who has the essential information and training to handle the press.

There should also be clear channels of communication within the company to disseminate information about a crisis to its employees. This is important not only for the morale of the employees, but also because employees, both on and off the job, are in contact with the public and should know the facts. Employees should never answer guests' queries with "No comment."

The Cost-Effectiveness of PR and Publicity

With the escalating costs of paid media advertising, PR and publicity efforts have become increasingly desirable. Yet PR and publicity are not free. There are costs in preparing press releases, photos, and media events. These costs are usually minor, however, as compared with the cost of purchasing similar space or time for advertisements. Even though specific selling messages cannot be incorporated into PR and publicity activities, the impact of PR and publicity is often greater than that of a comparable amount of space or time obtained from advertising, because news coverage has higher credibility than an ad.

Personal Selling and the Sales Process

Selling is something we all have to do. We have to sell our abilities and personality in order to be employed and sell our ideas to have a successful career. Selling to customers, or having direct contact with customers, is often part of the jobs of entry-level hospitality employees and managers. As people work their way up in an organization, they reach a stage at which they must represent their organization to the public—another form of selling. Therefore, directly or indirectly, selling is something we all do at one time or another.

Although the main concern of this discussion is the work of a sales staff, the total sales effort is contributed by the entire crew, especially those guest-contact employees, or "marketing ambassadors," such as front office agents and food and beverage servers. A 180-room hotel, with a 75 percent occupancy and 1.2 persons per occupied room, caters to approximately 60,000 guests a year. There is no way for the sales staff to deal with that many people, yet all guests are targets of selling while in the hotel. Therefore, front office agents should try to upsell rooms to increase the average room rate, and servers should make an effort to raise the check average by selling drinks and desserts as well as meals. Moreover, the quality of guests' interactions with service staff is what sells repeat visits.

All employees are part of the sales team.

Personal selling is a very expensive medium for getting an operation's message across. Costs include the overhead required to support a sales staff, their training, travel, entertainment, and office space and supplies. The actual "selling" time, when a salesperson has face-to-face contacts with potential customers, is relatively brief. Most of a salesperson's time is spent in preparation and follow-up, which makes the actual "contact time" even more expensive.

Personal selling should be used only when the size of the sale justifies the expense. For example, hotels hire sales managers to sell rooms to groups, solicit referrals of guests from companies that have a significant visitor volume, and promote meetings, banquets, and other group functions. Selling to travel agents and other distribution channel members is also important to hotel chains. Personal selling is the major medium used by contract foodservice companies to obtain new accounts, as well. However, this discussion of the sales process focuses on hotels to provide examples.

Selling begins well before a sales call takes place and is a never-ending process—retaining current customers is an important part of any sales rep's responsibility. The major activities of selling include prospecting, planning the sales call, making the presentation, closing the sale, and following up with the sale and the customer.

Prospecting

Prospecting involves developing sales leads and identifying prospects from the leads. Prospects are people who need to use the property and can afford the rate structure. Therefore, the heart of prospecting involves reviewing sales leads and identifying prospects among them.

Sales Leads. **Sales leads** can be generated by a drive around town or a visit to the local Chamber of Commerce. New construction can indicate new business activities, and the Chamber usually has a list of businesses due to open and information on the nature and size of those businesses. A scan of the classified directory in the Yellow Pages can identify businesses that may require guest rooms or meeting spaces, that are not already being served by the hotel. There are also directories of trade associations and membership lists for local organizations that can suggest particular people within the organizations to contact. A review of the daily listing of meetings posted in competitive hotels is both customary and quite productive. Friends in the community and current customers are also good sources of leads. At the lead-gathering stage, we may say, "The more the merrier." However, at the next stage the emphasis is on quality, as we move from leads to prospects.

Qualifying Prospects. A **qualified prospect** is a person who has a need for, or an interest in, using the property and who can generate enough business to justify the expense of a sales call. Qualified leads include people who book a significant number of guest rooms or meeting spaces and the people who make decisions about these bookings. Therefore, qualified prospects can include secretaries, office assistants, office travel managers, sales or training managers, and other management people. Hotel sales reps should spend most of their time talking to people who are responsible for placing or referring business. Secretaries are often key *gatekeepers* in an organization, that is, people who control access to decision makers. They are also often decision makers themselves, choosing which hotel to use for visitors. Therefore, many hotels have developed secretarys' clubs and host regular luncheons for these decision makers.

Not all sales calls, however, are made on qualified prospects. One way of generating leads and qualifying them is to make **cold calls** on new prospects—people the salesperson knows little about. Sometimes these calls are made because the salesperson is in a certain area for other business and has some time to spare. To use this time productively, the salesperson visits a few businesses in the area.

Cold calls may also be made as part of a coordinated effort called a **sales blitz.** A sales blitz is an organized and concentrated series of sales calls, usually cold calls, within a particular market or markets by a number of people. In many cases the target may be a geographic area, such as "the business complexes on the west end of town." The target may also be a particular type of organization, such as all colleges and universities in the city. Sales blitzes are sometimes conducted with the assistance of hospitality management students. More commonly, however, sales blitzes are performed by the sales staff of several of a chain's properties in the area. Occasionally, operations staff also join the blitz.

Cold calls are basically information-seeking activities. They may occasionally result in actual sales, but the realistic goal is to generate leads and qualified prospects.

Planning the Sales Call

A successful sales call requires careful planning. A planned sales call, in contrast to a cold call, is made on a particular prospect. The more a salesperson knows about a prospect, the better he or she will be able to develop a strategy for selling. Two general types of information are helpful, company information and personal background on the individual prospect. Company information includes the size and nature of the business, the history of its using the hotel and meeting facilities, and its preferences in products and services. Personal information may comprise hobbies, interests, club or civic affiliations, and social position. Personal information can offer opportunities for smalltalk to break the ice. However, a sales call is a business meeting, not a social visit. Considerable care should be taken not to intrude on the privacy of the prospect. A good deal of company and personal information may be obtained from the prospect just by listening carefully.

Getting in the door is not always easy. To avoid wasting time and creating an unprofessional impression, an appointment should always be arranged. This is usually done by phone. However, if the prospect is difficult to reach by phone, a letter or E-mail stating the purpose of the visit and requesting an appointment may be a better choice. This communication can be followed with a phone call to set an appointment. Once an appointment is confirmed, further planning and preparation are needed.

The key to planning a sales call is to have particular objectives in mind. We should know what we want to sell and what approach we intend to use to generate the strongest response from the prospect. We should also know what information we still need, what points we propose to make, and in what logical order. For hotel sales, a canned pitch—a standardized and memorized sales presentation—is not likely to be effective. A prospect's specific needs should be identified and clarified before preparing the presentation. Based on the needs, the presentation must show that the lodging organization presents the solution to the prospect's problems. The sales presentation should be logically thought out and organized to include the necessary information and appropriate appeals. The people we call on are usually busy and accustomed to giving and receiving information in an organized manner.

The Approach. The first few moments with a prospect are crucial—first impressions are lasting. Therefore, it is worthwhile to develop an **approach** that will gain the prospect's attention and interest and provide a smooth transition into the sales presentation. The most common way to address the prospect is the *introduction approach:* "Hello, I'm J. D. Smith from the ABC Hotel." It is important to be polite; it is even more important to know what to say after the initial introduction to gain interest and attention.

The *consumer benefit approach* is effective in telling prospects about what can *they* get from the purchase. When seeking referrals of individual visitors from a secretary, the presentation may begin by giving information about the hotel's secretarys' club or other ways in which the hotel recognizes people who refer guests. It is important, however, to avoid sounding as though we intend to bribe this person. A friendly invitation to the secretarys' club, with an explanation of the club benefits and functions, should be sufficient.

In addressing the person who is responsible for booking meetings and seminars, the consumer benefit approach may come as a question: "How would you like to have a meeting where *all* the coffee breaks and meals are served *on time?*" Whatever distinctive difference the property offers can be used as the basis for an opener. If the property is ready to offer price concessions, the appeal may involve a flat statement: "With our excellent food and service, we still can save you *X* percent on your next meeting."

Probably the best setting for a sales call is the property itself. When the level of business warrants the time and cost of a property visit, an invitation to a meal can be offered. An invitation to a dinner may be justified; however, breakfast and lunch are the more common business meals.

When the prospect is a guest in the hotel, a tour of the property is in order. The prospect should be shown those areas that concern the sale, such as the guest rooms and banquet facilities. People are also interested in the back of the house, and passing through this area may provide a chance to cater to that interest and show "how things really work." The prospect can also be introduced to some of the key players at the property, such as the chef and the executive housekeeper. These people can be influential in making the sale. Furthermore, letting operations people know that they are helping to land a sale can strengthen the alliance between them and the sales office.

It is essential to give operations departments advance notice of a tour so that people can reserve some time to meet with the guests. Those responsible for the respective units can also see to the cleanliness and order of their areas prior to the visit. An unannounced tour into a dirty-looking kitchen may very likely cost a sale.

The Presentation

Depending on the preferences of the prospect, the **presentation** can be quite formal, with computer-generated slide shows as visual aids and operations portfolios with fact sheets and photographs as handouts. The sales presentation can also be a small group meeting between the sales rep and the major players in the buying organization. Informal conversations and exchanges are the primary elements of the presentation. Regardless of the format, good sales reps establish the *credibility* of the property, the organization, and themselves and aim to gain action, or sales, *now*.

Building Credibility and Confidence. There is no perfect script that can secure a sale every time. However, there are some general guidelines and time-tested techniques:

Make Conservative Claims. We should never claim more than we can produce. If we are conservative early in the conversation, we are more likely to be believed later.

Be Positive. We should never criticize our own organization, the boss, the competition, or other sales associates. Positive statements should always be used. When negative comments have to be made, we should still accentuate the positive side of things.

Describe the Property and Experience. We should not assume that everyone knows how good the property's service is. We may hesitate to brag about our products and services, but it is really important for prospects to have a good understanding of the quality we can provide, especially those who have never been to the property. A "story" often catches the listener's interest, so we should not hesitate to briefly talk about successful functions at the property or how it won the repeat patronage of a particular loyal guest.

Use Testimonials. Testimonials from customers may help convince a prospect of the organization's excellence. One method is to use the implied testimonial—invite the prospect to call one of the regular guests, after obtaining permission from those guests to do so. Not many people actually make such phone calls; however, they are impressed with the sales rep's confidence in the property's ability to perform. Some sales reps also like to carry copies of letters thanking the hotel for particularly successful events.

Engage in Friendly Interchange and Listen. Although a sales rep should not act as the prospect's old pal, the sales call is supposed to be a friendly visit. In addition to presenting the information prepared, sales reps should be willing to listen during the conversation. If we, as sales reps, do all the talking, not only do we appear to be pressuring the prospects but we also cannot hear what they have to say. Active listening involves making eye contact and observing body language. We should also use our own facial expressions and body language to show our interest and engagement.

Ask Questions. When the prospect does not have much to say, we may want to ask questions to find out where we stand. The tone, as well as the content, of the prospect's reply may signal belief or doubt, thereby giving a strong clue as to how we are doing. Some salespeople actually feel that they are best able to control the direction of the conversation by asking questions. Questions give the prospect a chance to talk, the sales rep gets some feedback, and the questions can be used to steer the conversation from topic to topic.

Do Not Argue. If we win an argument and lose a sale, we are *not* ahead. When disagreement seems unavoidable, it is probably best to indicate interest in hearing another point of view on the subject, and then listen.

Handling Competition. We cannot ignore our competitors, but it is wise to heed one of the oldest sayings in selling: "Don't knock the competition." Criticizing the competition makes us sound petty and our motives questionable. Possibly the best approach is to say, "It's a fine organization, but we can probably fit your needs better because . . ."

It is generally best not to raise the subject of competition, but chances are that the prospect will. For this reason, we should know our competition—its strengths and weaknesses relative to those of our organization. We should be able to anticipate the points a prospect will raise and, by preparing for the sales presentation, we should have the answers ready. We acknowledge the strengths of the competitors, but we must be confident that we will come out ahead in an overall comparison.

Handling Complaints and Objections. It is only natural that people have heard both good and bad things about an operation. When confronted with a complaint or question, sales reps should never challenge or dispute the complaint or justify mistakes; they should never argue with guests and they can never win an argument. Instead, an apology should be offered for any mistakes, and the sales reps should be appreciative of the information. This information is not only helpful to operations people in correcting mistakes, but also useful to sales reps in identifying areas needing additional attention.

Closing the Sale

No salesperson can make every sale he or she tries for. Yet most are aware that **closing** is the moment when the success or failure of the sales effort is revealed—this is the moment they have been working toward. However, many salespeople shy away from asking for an order. Perhaps the reason is fear of failure, or perhaps some people believe

If a sale is the objective of a call, the salesperson must ask for the order. (Photo © Leif Skoog-fors—Woodfin Camp and Associates.)

that it is impolite to ask directly for something. Some salespeople may think that their presentation has been so effective that all prospects are ready to buy and there is no need to ask for an order. Regardless of the rationale for such hesitation, if a sale is the objective of the visit, it is necessary to *ask for the order.*

Assumptive Close. One way to close is simply to assume that we have made the sale and act on that conclusion. Questions such as these can be asked to confirm the close: "How soon do you think we can have your rooming list?" "Do you want to write up the menu now or would you like some time to consult with other people in your organization?" Another way to test the assumption is to ask to use the phone "so that I can block the space for you."

Standing Room Only. When we are not certain whether the sale is secured but feel that now is the time to close, we may indicate that the proposed time of year is a fairly busy one and suggest that the prospect reserve the rooms now. This may give the prospect a sense of urgency and move him or her closer to a decision. It is important, however, not to use this tactic in such a way that we make untruthful exaggerations about demand. Eventually, the truth will come out, and overstatements used to close the deal will diminish the client's trust and the operation's reputation for honesty.

The Trial Order. If the prospect is not ready to buy, we may consider asking for the order as a trial, saying, "We'd like a chance to prove ourselves to you." Or a commitment of another, smaller event might be suggested as a trial order.

If we cannot get a firm order, we should try to get a tentative commitment and indicate that we will call back for confirmation at a time agreeable to the prospect. The point is to obtain, if at all possible, some form of positive resolution at the visit. Even if a deal is not made this time, the movement from lead to prospect is a positive development that can result in sales in the future.

Follow-up

Even when a prospect does not give an order, a thank-you note and additional appropriate information should be sent as a **follow-up** of the presentation. Information about the prospect and reasons for not getting the sale should be recorded and kept in an active file for future reference. Additional follow-up calls can be made to identify future lodging and meeting needs. Repeated sales calls are usually necessary to land an account.

When a sale is closed, it is important to follow through on service. Prior to the event, the sales rep must update the guests on the progress of preparations for the function. During the event, the sale rep who booked the business should be at the property to check with the guests and make sure that everything is performed as agreed. When there is a problem, the sales rep is in a better position than the guests to pass on the concern to the *right person* in the organization, because the guests do not know the operating staff as well as the sales rep does. The danger, however, is the perception that the sales rep is trying to tell operations people what to do, which may create friction between the two departments.

After the event is over, additional follow-up is needed for several reasons. First, a few days after the function, the person arranging the event may have received reactions from others in his or her organization. If the comments are unfavorable, it is important for the sales rep to make whatever amends seem appropriate. If the feedback is favorable, it provides an ideal lead-in to sell the next piece of business.

Another reason for follow-up is to fend off the competition. As mentioned earlier, leads can be obtained by reading the function listings in the lobbies of competing hotels. The competitors may have picked up a lead from our hotel's information board and called on that prospect. Therefore, aggressive follow-up calls should be made to protect the business.

Sometimes a call-back on an account simply serves the purpose of keeping the lines of communication open, maintaining contact, and staying current on what is happening in that organization. Calls of this kind are usually brief and can be fitted between scheduled calls on other accounts in the same area.

Sales efforts can sometimes be discouraging. Turndowns happen quite often; and many calls have no tangible results. Baseball batting averages can be used as an analogy: Nobody bats 1.000, and people who bat .300 are real heroes.

Summary

Sales promotions offer an incentive to immediate purchase. The most common forms of sales promotion include coupons, discounts, premiums, games/sweepstakes/contests, merchandising, packaging, and sampling. Bounce-back coupons are a good option for small operations with limited marketing budget. Premiums are also called self-liquidating promotions. Deals enhance consumers' price-value perception by offering a bargain or adding to the excitement of the operation. In upscale operations, special events play a similar role.

Public relations (PR) and publicity are activities with different purposes, yet often complement each other. PR and publicity can be built around events, personnel, and charity or community involvement. Information about an operation is usually communicated through press releases. With rising media costs, PR and publicity are becoming increasingly cost-effective. However, a crisis management program should be developed to minimize negative publicity. To prepare for any crisis that may occur, policies that are in the public interest should be developed. Contingency plans should also be in place, and a spokesperson designated.

Everyone in hospitality operations is involved in some kind of personal selling. Professional sales staff usually go after accounts that can generate high business volumes, because personal selling is a very costly promotional medium. The major steps in selling include prospecting, planning the sales call, making the presentation, closing the sale, and following up.

Prospecting includes developing sales leads and qualifying prospects from the leads. Sales blitzes are sometimes conducted to generate leads. A prospect's needs should be identified prior to planning the sales presentation so that it is tailored to the prospect's specific preferences. During a sales presentation, complaints, objections, and questions about the competition should be handled professionally. Sales reps should also recognize the need to close the sale—the objective of any sales call. Finally, follow-ups are important regardless of the presentation results, sale or no sale.

Key Words and Concepts

Sales promotion
Coupons
BOGO
Bounce-back coupons
Discounts
Premiums
Self-liquidating promotions
Games/sweepstakes/contests
Merchandising

Packaging
Sampling
Public relations (PR)
Publicity
Press releases
Crisis management
Contingency plan
Personal selling
Prospecting

Sales leads
Qualified prospect
Cold calls
Sale blitz
Approach
Presentation
Closing
Follow-up

Resources on the Internet

Hospitality Sales and Marketing Association International. *http://www.hsmai.org*

PlanSoft Network: The meeting professional's destination. *http://www.plansoft.com/*

Public Relations Online Resources and Organizations. *http://www.webcom.com/impulse/resource.html*

Public Relations Society of America. *http://www.prsa.org/*

Sales and Marketing Executives Marketing Library. *http://www.MarketingLibrary.com/sme-fr1.htm*

Sales and Marketing Management. *http://www.salesandmarketing.com/smmnew/*

The Sales and Performance Group. *http://www.redhotsales.com/*

Discussion Questions

1. What are the major purposes of sales promotion?
2. What are the major forms of sales promotion used by foodservice and lodging operations?
3. What are bounce-back coupons?
4. What are the advantages and disadvantages of publicity?
5. In what ways can public relations and publicity be created?
6. What are the major steps in crisis management? Have you ever been involved in a crisis in an operation where you work(ed)? If so, how do you assess the way it was handled?
7. Under what circumstances is personal selling appropriate?
8. What are the main steps in the sales process?
9. How should complaints, objections, and comments about the competition be handled during a sales presentation?
10. Describe the various ways to close a sale.

Reference

Bennett, P. D., ed. (1995). *Dictionary of marketing terms.* 2d ed. Chicago: American Marketing Association.

14

Marketing at the Unit Level

When you have finished reading this chapter, you should be able to:

- Explain the basis for local marketing.
- Discuss why local marketing is growing.
- Describe concerns of chains in regard to local marketing.
- Explain the necessary steps in establishing a local marketing program.
- Illustrate appropriate merchandising techniques for foodservice.
- Describe the role of community relations in local marketing.
- Discuss the elements of property-level marketing communications.

Marketing at any level of a company draws on the same basic body of knowledge, but the *perspective* at the unit level is different. Not surprisingly, marketing at the unit level is characterized by a "hands-on" approach and is more specifically targeted. It brings managers closer to consumers and offers opportunities for personal touches that are just not possible in regional or national programs. Local marketing is also an area in which individual managers can make a real difference. They can contribute significantly to an operation's success and, as a result, to their own success.

The content of this chapter should be of particular interest to hospitality management students because it is likely that most new graduates will work at the unit level for several years. Whereas marketing at the corporate level is the responsibility of marketing specialists, unit-level marketing is likely to be done by unit managers. Although medium- and large-sized hotels typically have sales managers, many smaller properties do not have a specialized sales staff, nor do many restaurants have sales representatives. Therefore, unit-level marketing and sales fall on the shoulders of managers and other operations people. An understanding of the broad perspective of a company-wide marketing program is vital for hospitality management students, but competence in local marketing may prove to be a practical skill that will be useful to them in the near future.

Marketing in a multiunit company is usually a top-down process. The company's image and market position are determined at the headquarters level, and units operate under the umbrella of the chain's concept. The goal of corporate-level marketing is to establish and enhance the identity of the company in the marketplace on a very broad scale. The marketing challenge at the local level, however, is very different. At the local level, the concern is to develop a local identity as an integral part of a community. A community can be defined as a town, part of a town, a shopping mall, or a few city blocks. In fact, unit-level marketing is sometimes referred to as **neighborhood marketing** (Feltenstein 2001), particularly for foodservice operations. By becoming an important local institution with a network of contacts and activities, an operator can make an international brand, such as McDonald's or Holiday Inn, the hometown's very own McDonald's or "our" Holiday Inn to the local people.

Local marketing is no substitute for a national or regional strategy in a multiunit company. In fact, the more the local attempt can support the national effort, the better. The goal of coordinating local with company-wide marketing is to achieve the best of both worlds—a strong national image *and* a solid local identity. In this chapter, the examples used are units of regional and national chains that needed to establish their local identity to complement their national image. This does not mean, however, that independent operations do not have to be concerned with local marketing. Actually, for the independent, *all* marketing is unit-level marketing, and successful independents are usually the best local marketers in any area. Virtually everything in this chapter applies to independent operators as well as to units of larger organizations.

Basis for Local Marketing

Like any marketing task, local market analysis begins with the *customers* and must include the *competition*. The nature of the *operations* also has a major impact on localized marketing. These are the components of the **marketing strategy triangle** discussed in Chapter 6. *Database marketing* is another important element of local marketing because it enhances an organization's ability to target customers. These four topics, which affect all hospitality organizations' unit-level marketing, are examined briefly in this section.

Customers

The analysis of customers involves a study of local consumers' characteristics, such as the demographics of the market area, and of the unit's current customer base. Figure 14.1 shows a portion of a population analysis for one market area. Data for such a profile can be drawn from local census reports or purchased from marketing consulting firms.

Local marketers have to understand the customers' behavior—for example, what brings guests into the area and what they are doing while they are here. Also included in this analysis is a review of the major traffic generators, such as shopping centers, schools and colleges, amusement parks, theaters, and sports centers. Another important part of the analysis is to identify major centers of economic activities, such as factories, office buildings, and retail centers.

Although this information is useful to provide a market overview for a hotel, the hotel is more interested in those particular segments that generate a significant volume of out-of-town business. Customer segments that can be of interest to hotels include corporate business travelers, potential conference and meeting customers, tour groups, athletic teams, and members of local governments. For hotels with a restaurant, local foodservice customers are also of interest, not only for the sales they generate, but also as a source of referral for lodging business.

As mentioned earlier, major economic activity centers should be identified because different local economic environments require different marketing strategies. For example, two similar restaurants, one in a booming suburban market and the other in a depressed town or region, would face quite different marketing challenges. The suburban unit may be successful with value-added offers, such as service enhancements, premium merchandise promotion, or new products. The unit facing an adverse economic climate may find that special pricing, such as provided by coupons and value meals, is the approach likely to succeed.

The kind of economic activity that characterizes the local market is also important. A hotel operating in a manufacturing center, such as Pittsburgh or Dayton, for instance, would present a different marketing outlook than a hotel at a major recreation destination, such as Orlando or Las Vegas. Personal selling to key local accounts can play an important role in a manufacturing center, whereas selling to travel agents, offering a national reservation system, and engaging in consumer advertising may be more important for a recreational destination market.

	A.S.A.P.	Abbreviated Store Area Profile	
	Total U.S.	Kansas City A.D.I.	2104 Broadway, Kansas City, MO Neighborhood (3-Mile Radius)
POPULATION (#)	248,709,873	1,566,280	14,502
Projected Growth 1990–98 (%)	8%	10%	6%
Historical Growth 1980–90 (%)	10%	9%	4%
Historical Growth 1970–80 (%)	11%	4%	5%
HOUSEHOLDS (# HH's)	91,947,410	608,347	6,252
Average HH size (1990 People/HH)	2.63 people	2.55 people	2.63 people
Historical Growth 1980–90 (%)	14%	46%	10%
Historical Growth 1970–80 (%)	26%	15%	12%
Historical Growth 1960–70 (%)	20%	22%	10%
URBAN/RURAL MIX (%) HOUSING	75%/25%	89%/11%	100%/0%
1990 Median Home Value (Owner-Occupied)	$79,100	$66,500	$69,050
% Owners/% Renters	68%/32%	65%/35%	60%/40%
% Built 1980–90	21%	20%	15%
% Built pre-1980	79%	63%	70%
% Built pre-1970	57%	43%	52%
% Built pre-1960	41%	41%	45%
AVERAGE HH INCOME ($)	$35,894	$31,613	$32,837
RACIAL MIX			
% Black	12%	13%	5%
% White	80%	84%	88%
% Other	8%	3%	7%
AVERAGE AGE	35	33	34
GENDER (Male/Female)	49%/51%	48%/52%	48%/52%
MARITAL STATUS (Persons aged 15+)			
% Married	55%	60%	55%
% Single	27%	24%	35%
% Other	18%	16%	10%
% HH'S WITH CHILDREN (age 0–18)	49%	44%	40%

FIGURE 14.1 Population report for a restaurant market.

Source: Population Estimates Program, Population Division, U.S. Census Bureau, Washington, DC.

Competition

A listing of *all* competitive operations in the market area and their locations should be compiled as background information for developing a unit's marketing program, but detailed analysis can generally be limited to direct competitors. A hospitality unit's direct competitors are those operations targeting the same market segments, with facilities, services, and prices similar to those of the unit in question. If there is any doubt as to whether an operation is a direct competitor, that operation should be included in the analysis. Any known, or even rumored, plans for expansion by competitors should also be noted.

For hotels, a competitive analysis should include size, location, rate categories, and facilities of all competing operations. Competitors' quality of service should also be assessed as part of the analysis. For restaurants, the investigation should include size, operating hours, menu offerings, pricing, physical plant and ambience, parking, and quality of food and service. Estimated sales volume by meal period for each day of the week is also vital information. Figures 14.2 and 14.3 show two forms that can be used to facilitate competitive analysis. Figures 7.3 and 7.4 also display worksheets available for evaluating competitors.

	Our Operation	Competitor 1	Competitor 2	Competitor 3
Date opened/renovated				
Location				
Number of seats				
Type of food				
Top-selling items/prices				
Breakfast price range				
Lunch price range				
Dinner price range				
Quality of food				
Customer count				
Seasonal variation				
Training/uniforms				
Service consistency				
Theme				
Physical condition				
Reason for patronage				
Customers:				
Mix of male/female				
Mix of singles/ couples/families				
Age range/average				
Occupations				
Income range				
Advertising media used				
Promotion				
Community events sponsored				

FIGURE 14.2 Restaurant competitor analysis.

	Our Hotel	Competitor 1	Competitor 2	Competitor 3
Type of hotel				
Mobile/AAA rating				
Location				
Date opened/renovated				
Number of rooms				
Occupancy				
ADR				
Business mix %				
Rate structure:				
Single/double				
Commercial				
Group				
Miles to downtown/airport				
Miles to major attractions				
Hotel courtesy van				
Room amenities				
Room service hours				
Restaurant name/type				
Lounge name/type				
Type of entertainment				
Concierge desk				
Car rental/travel agency				
Gift shops and other services				
Number of parking spaces				
Fitness facilities				
Swimming pool				
Meeting facilities:				
Total square footage				
Number of meeting rooms				
Largest room—square feet				
Audiovisual equipment				

FIGURE 14.3   Hotel competitor analysis.

For both restaurants and hotels, a vital piece of information is who the competitors' customers are. A profile of customers should be prepared on the basis of observation and conversations with suppliers and competitors' management. Another valuable source of information is the unit's employees, who are often acquainted with employees at competitive operations.

The purpose of competitor analysis is not simply to accumulate information. Rather, it is intended to provide the unit with a foundation for evaluating competitors' strengths and weaknesses as compared with its own. From this comparison, a differentiation strategy covering all elements of the marketing mix should emerge for the *local* market.

Operations

The brand identity of a chain or franchise system usually dictates the target markets and the operation's format, including the quality and price levels of the product offering and even the ambience, size, and other physical characteristics of the operation. There is, however, considerable opportunity within these parameters to individualize a product to the local market. For example, a hotel must decide whether to seek local business for weekends, as well as *which* group rates to offer and *when*. A high-occupancy hotel may decide to maintain full rates and to limit the availability of rooms at low rates for such markets as government employees and college athletic teams, even though other properties with the same brand may go after those businesses in other markets.

A local franchised restaurant also has an opportunity to decide whether to seek tour bus business. The sales volume provided by tour buses is attractive, but it can also disrupt service to regular patrons unless special arrangements, such as a party room, are made to take care of the tour groups. Moreover, if a restaurant is located in a downtown commercial district with high luncheon traffic but low evening business, it may seek out special evening targets, such as senior citizens living in downtown apartments and special-event groups. This practice may be different from any other units within the same chain.

If a competitor has a particular advantage in the market or the local consumers favor a particular product, the unit managers should develop products or services to compete in that local market and serve the local customers. Many restaurants offer local menus, and hotels provide entertainment based on the taste of the local patrons. These examples define "who we are." Although a brand's umbrella identity can define the "personality" of all units to a certain extent, individual operations can customize their own characteristics significantly to meet local market conditions.

Operations and Marketing. In a **hospitality marketing cycle,** as shown in Figure 2.4, conventional marketing communications are used to attract customers, but the performance of service employees determines an operation's success in converting interested prospects into customers and first-time customers into regular guests. Therefore, good working relationships between operations and marketing people at the unit level is extremely important in providing satisfactory experiences for the guests.

Database Marketing

The term **database marketing,** as discussed in Chapter 5, refers to the use of information about an operation's existing customers to improve its efforts in target marketing to those customers and people like them. Database marketing is not new to the hotel business. Upscale hotels, for instance, have maintained guest histories for years. Restaurants have recently begun to collect similar information, using data from registrations for promotional programs—such as frequent-guest programs and "Birthday

A newsletter for Friends of The Cornhusker—

Nebraska's Grand Hotel

The Connoisseur

As winter once again comes to a close, we can reflect and breathe a sigh of relief knowing that spring is just around the corner. This is one of the most splendid times of the year as the flowers are just waiting to bud and the birds are anxious to begin their chirping routine. The Cornhusker is excited to bring you an update on all we have planned this spring.

Jumping right into the season, there will be a special wine tasting event for Friends of The Cornhusker in Terrace Grille on **Thursday, April 17**. Read inside about the select Fetzer wines to be featured along with some tantalizing food. Also, mark your calendar for a special Meritage Dinner to be held in The Renaissance on **Thursday, May 1st**. We'll reveal how to create the perfect blend between a delightful dinner and the featured Fetzer Select Barrel wines at the tasting. Look inside for the menu.

A veritable clue that spring has sprung is the celebration of Easter. Within you'll find a personal invitation to spend this Easter morning with us to enjoy a fabulous brunch in The Cornhusker's Grand Ballroom. Of course, Mother Goose and the Easter Bunny will be there to greet the children and bring smiles to the faces of all. Additionally, don't forget mom on her special day. Our Mother's Day Brunch buffet is sure to impress even the most discriminate of tastes.

With the season comes a flurry of wedding invitations and engagement announcements. If you have such an event to plan, you will enjoy the feature on how The Cornhusker can orchestrate and personify your distinguished affair.

You may notice a few changes in this issue, beginning with the name. We have chosen **The Connoisseur** to better describe our purpose and to give Friends of The Cornhusker expert opinions and information regarding our special events. You'll also find convenient pull-out recipe cards inside. Start collecting Executive Chef, Reese Hummel's recipes prepared exclusively at The Cornhusker. Enjoy this issue of The Connoisseur. You'll surely find something just right inside.

Sincerely,

Lisa McMeen
Food & Beverage Director

A newsletter is a targeted communication medium used by many hotels in establishing relationships with current guests and local residents. (Photo courtesy of The Cornhusker, Nebraska's Grand Hotel.)

Clubs," which offer a free or reduced-price meal to guests, usually children, on their birthdays.

Building a customer database is an expensive and time-consuming process, but it offers several advantages. It allows an operation to segment its customers, communicate with them on a personal basis, and offer products and services tailored to their preferences. A customer database usually contains information such as customer name, address, occupation, preferred payment method, usage frequency, average spending, product and service preference, and response to promotions. For hotels, the database often includes sources of and lead time for reservations.

Database marketing is also referred to as **loyalty marketing**, because the information in the database is used to reinforce the loyalty of current customers in three ways: with rewards, with recognition, and by making it costly for them to switch. First of all, customers are *rewarded* for repeat patronage with bonuses such as free meals, complimentary or upgraded rooms, or other special privileges. The airline frequent-flyer clubs are probably the best known and most widely established means of rewarding customers, and many hotel chains have copied the technique. Most casinos offer "comps" based on players' betting statistics, including average bet, largest bet, frequency of visit, and length of visit.

Recognition, sometimes called a **soft benefit,** is one of the strongest motivators of repeat visits. Most hotels and full-service restaurants strive to address customers by name to create a sense of recognition. Guest history files can provide details about guests' preferences, such as favorite food and beverage, guest room and dining seat location, and newspaper. The recognition of an individual addresses the ego needs of that individual at a basic level.

The accumulated rewards in a loyalty program, such as a frequent-diner club, make it *costly to switch* to another operation. If a guest stops patronizing an operation and switches to a competitor, he or she loses the accumulated points and therefore incurs an actual cost of lost benefits. No one would count on this potential loss as the major motivation to continued patronage. However, it can be counted on to provide a guest with a reason to give an operation another chance when the unfortunate—a less-than-satisfactory experience—happens.

There are significant details in local marketing practices that differ between the restaurant and hotel businesses. Accordingly, the needs and practices of each segment of the industry are examined separately.

Local Marketing in Foodservice

The definition of a local area varies from one restaurant company to another. Some firms use a 1½ mile radius, whereas others talk of a 10-minute drive time. For companies operating expressway restaurants, "local" target markets include such segments as trucking companies, tour line operators, and commuters. The customers in these cases do not live near the restaurants. What makes these guests "local" is their transportation patterns, which lead them to travel through the unit's market area on a regular basis. Settling on an appropriate definition of *local* for a particular operation is important; however, the focus of the following section is on *what to do* about the local markets.

Why Is Local Marketing in Foodservice Growing?

Perhaps the most important reason for the growing emphasis on local marketing is that the local market is where the customers are. As mentioned in Chapter 10, a quick-service restaurant (QSR) may draw customers from a radius of 1 to 1½ miles. Casual dining concepts usually have a trading area of approximately 3 to 5 miles, and fine dining establishments often draw patrons from a radius of 20 miles or more (Reich 1997).

Competition is another reason for foodservices' growing interest in local marketing. The competitive conditions in the foodservice market have changed both qualitatively and quantitatively. Foodservice organizations used to face independent operations, with unsophisticated marketing programs, as typical competitors. Today, well-established regional and national restaurant firms, with deep pockets and large advertising budgets, dot the landscape. The number of restaurant units in most markets has also increased dramatically in the past 25 years. Therefore, the North American foodservice market is saturated, experiencing intense competition.

The way the restaurant industry looks to consumers has also changed after a half century of growth by chain restaurants and limited-service concepts. In the 1960s, standardized chain restaurants were *welcomed* as they pushed aside many less-than-desirable operations with varying standards of cleanliness, service, and quality. Standardization was new, and consumers were glad to see it as a safe haven, especially when traveling. Today, standardization is the rule and the trick is, increasingly, to deliver standardized quality, with national or regional brand recognition, *and* a local flavor.

Local marketing is needed to deal with local competition because economic and social conditions vary widely from city to city and even between the various neighborhoods in a city. Different strategies are needed in an upscale suburb, a declining neighborhood, and an expressway location. In each of these and many other location types, customer needs and wants are different. The competitive environment in each of these locations is likely to be different as well. Moreover, various locations have different time-of-day and day-of-week peaks and valleys, therefore lending themselves to different marketing techniques.

A final reason for using local-area marketing relates to firm size and the degree of market penetration a firm has achieved. Independents and small chains cannot compete in the conventional advertising media against larger and better-financed national chains. Even large chains may sometimes have too few operations located in a market to afford traditional media advertising; there are simply not enough units to absorb the cost of using the media, particularly television. In these circumstances, local marketing is a viable opportunity.

Many corporations, such as the IHOP, have realized the importance of local marketing. (Photo courtesy of IHOP Corp.)

Local Marketing Issues for Chain Restaurants

Although local marketing is gaining increasing use, not all multiunit organizations emphasize local marketing, because local store marketing presents challenges that some chains may not want to deal with. Their reasoning is summarized in the following paragraphs.

Budget Priorities. At the headquarters level, the view is often that setting aside a portion of the marketing budget for local marketing is inefficient, because national brand marketing benefits *every* unit, whereas local spending helps only one or a few units.

Organizational Issues. At a headquarters marketing department, extensive market research can be conducted to help design the marketing program, with various scenarios simulated and tested. This effort increases the likelihood of having successful marketing programs to enhance corporate profitability. The budget available for local marketing is generally not large enough to justify extensive study or to hire marketing specialists to develop and implement marketing activities. Therefore, local marketing decisions are usually made by operations people who lack the necessary training, background, and skills for formal market research. In addition, they are pressed for time and thus unlikely to favor time-consuming, formalized market studies. Many companies also have a concern that any time spent on local marketing is time away from unit operations, inasmuch as marketing is done by unit managers.

Another organization issue involves supervision of local marketing programs by headquarters marketing staff. Because each local marketing environment is different, unit-level marketing efforts place a tremendous demand on the time of corporate staff. As a result, central-office marketing people tend to avoid involvement in local marketing decisions. One way of addressing the problem of time pressures on headquarters marketing staff is to establish an intermediate supervisory marketing position. The person in this position, whose primary responsibility is to assist unit managers in the district in conducting marketing programs, reports to the corporate director of marketing but has an office in the field at the area or district level.

Organizing Field Marketing. Essential elements in a successful local marketing program include resources, standardization of decisions to increase control and reduce corporate executive time commitments, and provision of expert marketing support to operations people who are making decisions outside their main area of expertise. Resources needed for local marketing include not only a local marketing budget, but also local marketing manuals and a planner's guide, including camera-ready copy for ads and other suggested campaign material.

A further important resource is a standardized financial planning formula, which indicates to the operators the break-even point for any promotion. Knowing the level of **incremental sales** required to pay for the costs of a promotion, operators can make a reasonable estimate of whether the proposed local promotion will be profitable or not. For example, at one company, the rule of thumb is an increase in sales by X, where X = cost of promotion ÷ 35%. Therefore, if the program costs $100, the *incremental sales* required to carry it are $286 ($100 ÷ 35%). Headquarters can also develop standardized deals that are proven in test markets. All that is required, then, for a store manger to implement one of these "approved deals" is an estimate of the incremental volume and approval by the area manager.

Some companies provide local marketing specialists in the headquarters marketing department to act as expert advisors to area and store managers. They also respond to specific problems encountered by various store managers. Whereas some companies have full-time staff to work on local marketing, others hire a marketing firm to assist in developing chainwide local marketing policies and work with store managers and area supervisors in implementing the programs.

Establishing a Local Marketing Program

From a unit manager's perspective, the first step in developing a local marketing program is to define its objectives. The manager, then, should identify the unit's customers and competitors to assess the local market. Finally, the operation's en-

This ad is prepared at the corporate level to achieve the high-quality visual presentation that food advertising requires. Blanks are provided for each unit to imprint its store location and the exact offer based on local market conditions. (Photo courtesy of Pizza Hut.)

tire marketing mix needs to be evaluated in the context of local market conditions.

Objectives. Local marketing programs should have concrete goals—for instance, to increase traffic or check averages. Objectives should be stated in specific terms, such as "To increase morning snack sales by 10 percent next month" or "To increase early dinner sales by 50 customers per week over the previous month."

Customers. The restaurant's trading area can be specified either in miles or in travel time. A useful technique to visualize the trading area is to drive, in prime mealtime traffic, 20 minutes in each direction from the restaurant and mark the end of each trip on a local map. When the points are connected, the probable limits of the unit's local market have been defined. Figure 14.4 illustrates this technique.

Once the boundaries have been determined, the manager needs to know who the people are who live and work in the area. Census data give a great deal of information on the demographics of the census tracts that make up the trading area. Scouting the area by driving through it during the day helps in estimating the size and characteristics of the working population. Driving through the area also helps in locating concentrations of customers, such as people who live in apartments or senior citizen housing centers and people who work in offices or industrial complexes. These and other *destinations*, such as schools and colleges, recreation centers, shopping malls, and churches, should also be marked on the market map. Estimates of the relative size of these centers can be verified by a visit or a few phone calls. Conversations with

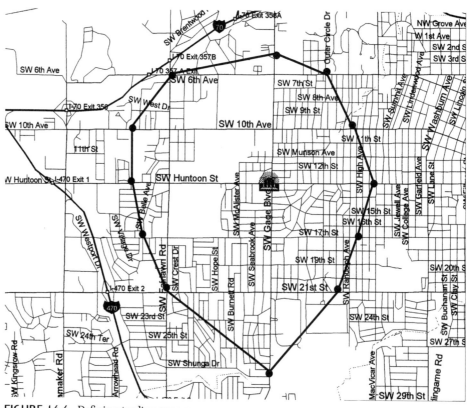

FIGURE 14.4 Defining trading area on a map.

employees, customers who live in the area, and suppliers can complement the gathering of marketing intelligence.

Competition. Just as in any other competitive analysis, direct and indirect competition should be identified and marked on the map. Classifying competitors as direct or indirect involves a judgment of the marketplace. For example, all QSRs are usually viewed as direct competitors of each other. Their indirect competitors are family and casual restaurants. However, in a particular market, some operations in another category may be viewed as direct competitors because of a special condition, such as location. For instance, a family restaurant and a QSR located next door to each other may see each other as being directly competitive.

Once direct competitors are identified, their strengths and weaknesses should be assessed in the local context. It is also important to keep tabs on what competitors are doing on a continuing basis. One way to gain valuable information while boosting staff morale is to offer to pay the cost of a "shopping visit" to competitive operations by staff members, with the visit to be followed by a report to management. This technique has the added advantage of making the unit's staff more aware of the competitive pressures.

Marketing Mix. Modifying products to meet local demand creates both potential risks and rewards. Adding a local item to a chain operation's menu may add local appeal, but may also run the risk of confusing the public. Still, when an item is identified as a "local favorite," even a company with a tightly focused concept can benefit from efforts to accommodate local preferences. An interesting approach to this dilemma of whether to localize product is demonstrated by the buffet offered in many KFC units. Although only 30 products are offered at any one time, operators may choose from more than 300 items approved for the buffet. Therefore, locally popular items may be included in what is still a standard product, the buffet.

The general price level for a menu is usually established on a chainwide basis; however, "specials" and "limited-time offers" may be promoted locally to meet the immediate competition or special local conditions. Early-bird specials are widely used, offering reduced prices to increase sales in the slow mid- to late-afternoon period. Early-bird programs are usually successful in markets with a significant number of seniors or others attracted to the special time or reduced prices. Another popular price promotion is to establish a "coffee club" to build volume in an off-peak period. Club members, by purchasing a personal mug, can use it between mealtimes to receive coffee at a discount without other purchases or at no cost when food is purchased.

Local Marketing Communication Methods

Although product and pricing are important local marketing variables, the most prominent element in local marketing is communication, accomplished through merchandising, advertising, sales promotion, personal selling, and community relations.

Focal point of a single-sheet menu   Focal point of a folded menu opening from the right

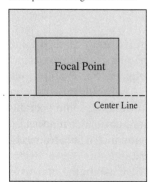
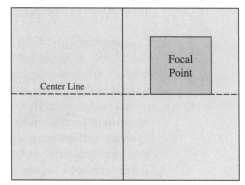

Focal point of a folded menu opening from the center

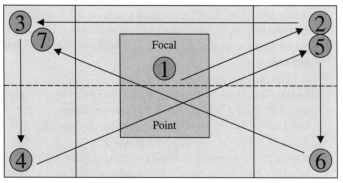

The numbers indicate the order of eye movements, given that no special graphics are used.

FIGURE 14.5 Menu focal points and reader's eye movements.
Source: Adapted from J. D. Ninemeier, *Planning and Control for Food and Beverage Operations,* 4th ed. (Lansing, MI: Educational Institute of the American Hotel & Motel Association, 1998). Copyright 1998 Educational Institute of the American Hotel & Motel Association.

Merchandising. The classic examples of **merchandising** in foodservice are wine display and dessert carts, but merchandising extends beyond these obvious representations. Actually, in a restaurant, **menu merchandising** is the most potent promotion tool. It is an advertising medium presented to *all* guests dining in the operation. However, guests usually do not "read" the menu; instead, they scan it quickly without paying attention to most content areas. Thus, *page positioning* can be important. Figure 14.5 displays the focal points of various menu formats and guests' usual eye movements. Signature menu items or items with the highest profit margin should be placed in a focal point area to draw diners' attention. The second most profitable menu item group should be placed in the spot to which the guests' eyes move next. The same logic applies to the areas labeled 3, 4, 5, and so forth. Other menu merchandising ideas are discussed in Case Study 14.1.

CASE STUDY 14.1

Menu Merchandising

A menu is a restaurant's best merchandising material, even though the average diner spends less than three minutes reviewing a menu. To help hurried guests choose items with a high profit margin, menu planners must use techniques that highlight the more profitable items. *Page positioning,* discussed in the text, is one way to draw people's attention. More profitable items should be placed at the focal points of a menu. *Special effects,* such as boxing and shading, can generally increase the sales of featured items by 15 to 20 percent. Asymmetrical descriptors, such as "Special" and "New," printed to the side of certain menu items, can also draw attention. Placement of a signature icon, or the restaurant logo, is another way to alert diners of a particular option.

The *placement* of an item in a group can also affect its visibility. For example, customers tend to order the first item in any categorical listing most often, followed by the last item in the category. Therefore, the most profitable item in a category

---

Soups & Salads

Each day we offer a SPECIAL SOUP. Your server will know all about it.

My Mom's Minestrone
One incredible bowl of soup
with sourdough bread & butter
$4.95

ALL YOU CAN EAT
Bottomless bowl of Minestrone
PLUS a Pete's garden salad
$5.50

SPINACH SALAD
Leaf spinach mixed
with balsamic vinaigrette topped
with bacon, mushrooms,
sliced egg, tomato wedges,
pine nuts & grated parmesan
$5.50

CLASSIC COBB
Avocado, chicken, bacon,
crumbled bleu cheese,
diced tomatoes & sliced egg,
on a bed of crisp romaine
& iceberg lettuce
$5.95

should be listed as the first item in that group on the menu, and the second most profitable item should be listed as the last item in the group. Items that have to be on the menu because of customer demand, but carry a low profit margin, should be "buried" in the middle of the menu listing.

Menu *description* is another area that deserves thought. Words and phrases that stimulate the senses should be incorporated into menu descriptions to help sell items with emotional appeal. Special food preparation methods, ingredient selection procedures, food origins, or special growing conditions may also be depicted to build the character of the items.

> A medley of . . .
>
>   Toss lightly with . . . .
>   Tender pieces of . . .
> Freshly baked . . .
>   Generous serving of . . . .
> Mouth-watering . . . .
>   Lively blend of . . .
>   . . . grilled to perfection
> . . . mounded with fresh . . .
>   Fresh Florida redfish . . .
>   . . . . melt in your mouth . . .
>   . . . organically home-grown . . .
>   Pan seared to a golden brown . . .

In addition to merchandising through the menu, there are many great opportunities for merchandising within the restaurant. Efforts to "upsell" and to direct attention to high-profit-margin selections contribute to improved sales volume and profit. Figure 14.6 shows the restaurant as a promotional medium. It summarizes some of the major **merchandising zones** for selling to in-house guests.

Besides guests, employees should also be targets for merchandising as part of the internal marketing effort. A brief preshift meeting of employees who are in contact with guests can be a powerful merchandising technique, ensuring that they are familiar with the day's menu and specials, and reminded of proper service procedures. Such meetings also are great opportunities to restate the goals and methods of suggestive selling programs. Other **internal merchandising** tools include an employee suggestion box, incentives, and communication media such as a newsletter and a bulletin board in the employee break room.

Many national chains, including contract foodservice companies, develop **turnkey merchandising programs** that have all the details worked out for the unit managers. For instance, special events can be used in this type of promotion. Special event kits are developed and distributed, which include recipes, promotional ideas, templates for printing flyers, other printed media, training manuals, and supporting merchandise. Examples of special events are Mardi Gras, St. Patrick's Day, and parties with a "Seventies" motif.

Merchandising at this fine dining restaurant includes a point-of-purchase display of wine in the dining room.

Advertising. Local advertising can be used to support local promotion, publicize local sponsorship, and reach key local target audiences such as college students, senior citizens, and tourists. Direct mail, usually including coupons, is a common local medium and especially helpful in response to a new competitor's opening or an established competitor's aggressive sales drive. Local image advertising, emphasizing the unit's local identity, may also be useful. Low-cost media for such promotion include bulletin boards in community centers and supermarkets, bus benches, buses and subways, and local cable television. Much of a chain restaurant's local advertising may be accomplished through an advertising co-op made up of all operators in the area. This type of advertising is usually an areawide effort that receives considerable assistance from the district or headquarters office.

Sales Promotion. Local sales promotion can help an operation respond to local competitive conditions. When all competitors in a market issue coupons, a unit in that market should probably use coupons as well, whatever the chain's national strategy

All Restaurants		Table-Service Restaurants	Quick-Service Restaurants
Lobby Zone	*Bathroom Zone*[a]	*Dining Room Zone*	*Front Counter Zone*
Welcome mat	Audio	Menu	Menu board
Clothes hangers	Posters	Specials board	Register toppers
Displays	Special event calen-	Matches	Counter cards
Host preselling	dar	Posters	Wall posters
Brochures	Cleaning schedule	Displays	Premiums
Sampling		Wine cart	Condiment stand
Wall posters	*Office Zone*	Dessert tray	Bag stuffers
	On-hold message	Sampling	Bounce-back coupons
Pay Phone Zone	Answering machine	Gift certificates	
Signs and posters		Bounce-back coupons	*Drive-Thru Zone*
Memo pads	*Delivery and Carry-*		Menu boards
	Out Zone	*Bar Zone*	
Tabletop Zone	Car signage	Point-of-purchase	
Table tents	Bulk order pads	displays	
Place mats	Take-out menus	Drama drinks	
Menu clip-ons	Magnets	Bar menu	
Wine list	Bounce-back coupons	Drinks coasters	
Napkins		Specials board	
Comment cards	*Parking Lot Zone*	Upselling	
	Cleanliness	Entertainment	
Property Line Zone	Landscaping		
Restaurant marquee	Directional signs	*Car Valet Zone*	
Sign on the building	Ease of access	First greeting	
Awnings		Vacuum car	
Banners		Wash windshield	
Posters		Thank-you card	
Outdoor menu			
Outdoor dining area			
Children's playground			

[a]Forty percent of customers go to the bathroom before ordering dessert.

FIGURE 14.6 Merchandising zones and merchandising media in restaurants.
Source: T. Feltenstein, "The Newest Wave in Neighborhood Marketing," Presentation at the Marketing War College, Palm Beach, Florida 1995.

is. Promotion also offers unique opportunities to polish a local image by partnering with successful local enterprises—a technique called **joint promotions** or **cross-promotion.** This tactic pairs two complementary businesses. For example, a movie theater and a dinner house restaurant may promote each other by distributing each other's coupons. In return for their effort, each establishment gains access to a somewhat different stream of customers. When a locally well-known partner is chosen, there is the added advantage of being associated with that firm, a kind of indirect endorsement. Careful advance planning is important to ensure that each party has potential to gain a significant advantage from the partnership, both groups are fully

This four-story, glass-and-stainless-steel wine tower houses 10,000 bottles of wine. Located in the center of a restaurant, it takes merchandising to new heights. (Photo courtesy of Aureole.)

committed to the project, and costs and other efforts are shared equitably. Examples of such alliances at the corporate level are discussed in Case Study 9.2.

Personal Selling. Restaurants cannot afford the cost of personal selling to reach individual guests, but calling on organizations with large numbers of members makes good sense. For example, large plants or office complexes may be willing to distribute coupons with paychecks, offering an additional fringe benefit to their staff at no cost to themselves. Nearby churches may also have organizations, such as a seniors' club, that may be willing to accept and distribute coupons to their members. To make the necessary contact to launch such a program, a personal call by the operation's manager is essential.

The manager should first identify major institutions that have large numbers of potential customers. The initial contact could be made by phone or a letter introducing the organization. The company's interest and involvement in its neighborhood activities should be emphasized to create a positive impression. Then a meeting should be set up to conduct a formal sales call. As indicated in Chapter 13, preparation for a sales presentation is of crucial importance.

Community Relations. One way to build a local identity is for unit personnel, especially the unit manager, to be involved in local activities in order to establish good **community relations.** The manager's membership in a service club, local Chamber of Commerce, or convention and visitors bureau, as well as involvement in local charities, gives the unit desirable visibility. These types of involvement also provide the manager with opportunities for networking, which can be a significant source of business. Although such activities have little or no dollar cost, a manager's time away from the unit *is* a significant cost because of the competitive pressure for excellence in operations. The value of being a local notable is difficult to measure, but being a good local citizen is not without real benefits for the business.

Some activities enhance an organization's image and, at the same time, increase its sales volume. Among the most popular and effective activities are team sponsorships. In some cases, the restaurant provides team uniforms bearing the restaurant's name. The understanding is that the team's meals and other functions will occur in the restaurant. A typical arrangement is for the restaurant to give a discount for all team meals and to credit the same amount to the uniform fund. A related approach involves community clubs, churches, and other organizations. To support a fund-raising project, the restaurant contributes a set percentage of the sales of any group function to the charitable group's treasury, or pays a set percentage on receipts turned in by an organization's members. Efforts of this kind tie the contribution to the sales volume generated by the organization.

A highly effective local promotion is a joint effort with a local radio station, called a **remote.** The station broadcasts from the restaurant, often in conjunction with a drive for a local charity. Both the radio station and the restaurant gain from supporting a local initiative. The broadcast often brings significant traffic to the restaurant, resulting not only in increased sales but also in new customers. In most cases, however,

Team sponsorship builds local identity. Team meals can also be a source of revenue. (Photo courtesy of Pizza Hut.)

the restaurant is required to purchase a certain amount of advertising from the radio station.

Property-Level Marketing in Lodging

Property-level marketing activities have long been a tradition in lodging, but until recently they have been largely limited to personal selling. Today, three elements of the mix—product, price, and promotion—are vital components in a hotel's local marketing program. Although place, in the sense of location, is unchangeable once a property has been built, it does determine who the target markets are.

The techniques discussed in the previous section on foodservice local marketing can also be applied to hotel restaurants. In fact, hotels with restaurants have an ideal opportunity for gaining local referrals for lodging business. Successful, well-promoted restaurants and bars are perhaps the only means to attract local people into hotels on a regular basis. The discussion in this section, however, deals primarily with the marketing of rooms and group functions.

Product

In most hotels, the physical facilities already exist, but the product for sale—predominately the guests' experience—can be designed and redesigned by the joint efforts of marketing and operations personnel. For example, packaging the property with nearby attractions, such as theme parks, shopping centers, theaters, and other cultural institutions, defines the experience offered to leisure travelers. Partnering with these attractions makes sense, too, because joint marketing ventures make marketing dollars go further.

The way a property is positioned, or which customers it should target and which competitors it should compete with, shapes the product as well. For example, many chain hotels have two or three properties in one city, with similar numbers of rooms and facilities. One is usually located near the airport and positioned at a convenient location. The other properties may be positioned as part of a downtown business center or an urban resort. Although there is some competition among them, only one property would target airline crews, one would go after the sports business, and one would position itself as a business conference hotel.

Price

Rate-setting is almost entirely a property-level decision. Rack rates, or the list prices, are generally set by the property's management team and used as a base in setting other rates, such as corporate, weekend, and tour group rates. In some chains, however, rate setting is done with the advice and approval of headquarters. Special rates are sometimes negotiated at the chain level with very large buyers, such as airlines and travel wholesalers; however, most discount rates vary from property to property and the degree of discount is set by the unit managers. Property-level managers generally make the decisions on which rates are offered to which groups.

Yield management decisions, as discussed in Chapter 11, on when to open and close special rate categories are also made at the property level, based on frequent assessments of probable demand for specific periods. Some headquarters monitor the practices of individual properties in real time, based on on-line supply-and-demand information. Such monitoring, however, is basically done for advisory purposes.

Promotion: Marketing Communication

For a property to succeed, it is crucial to offer the right product to the right customers and to price the product competitively and profitably. Once the product and price are determined, the offer must be communicated to the customers. Product offering and pricing are usually the concern of the general manager and the operations management team. The sales function is often an important, but additional, duty of the managers in smaller properties. In larger hotels, a staff of one or more salespeople carries out this work.

Advertising. Database marketing is increasingly used to transform advertising into "narrowcasting" rather than broadcasting. That is, advertising is used to communicate with a hotel's regular guests as well as with people like them. Database marketing can be especially powerful in crafting individualized advertising, such as direct mail and telemarketing. Advertising an individual property in the mass media is more common among resort hotels and upscale properties. It is also usually limited to media in major feeder markets and in the local market to support special promotional events. Internet homepages are likely to be designed at the headquarters level. However, individual properties can "localize" their Web sites with local information on attractions, special services, and a welcome message from the unit manager.

Personal Selling. As indicated in Chapter 13, personal selling is an expensive medium and must generate significant revenue to offset its cost. Therefore, sales calls target sources of multiple room-nights or meeting and banquet business, rather than individual reservations. The target of a sales call is often not the guests but the individuals making the buying decisions, such as secretaries, office travel managers, and travel agents. Local sources of multiple room bookings include local social clubs; fraternal, religious, and ethnic organizations; government agencies; tour operators and motorcoach companies; convention and meeting planners; airlines; educational institutions; and sports teams. Therefore, sales managers' involvement in community and professional activities can help generate potential leads and prospects.

Sales Promotion. Advertising often has long-term goals, such as making a property better known and enhancing its image. Sales promotions may strengthen the property's image through partnering with a successful company or an entertainment or cultural institution, but their major purpose is to stimulate immediate sales during a specific time period. Weekend packages are a common promotion aimed at raising a hotel's sales during a soft part of the week. In addition to possibly establishing a prestigious association, partnering, in which cost sharing is part of the arrangement, can also stretch the property's marketing budget further. Lodging properties also present great opportunities for merchandising: in-room minibars; table tents, restaurant menus, and room service menus in guest rooms; displays in lobbies and elevators; and gift shops selling hotel merchandise.

Public Relations and Publicity. Although the general public in the local market is an important target, there are *many* publics to which a property can direct its PR efforts. Travel agents, local corporate accounts, customers in distant cities, and trade and professional association executives are all *publics* to a property. A hotel's own employees also constitute a critical public. General media publicity about the property as well as targeted media, such as an in-house employee newsletter, are all important PR and publicity tools for an internal marketing program.

A basic tool in publicity is the press kit. A press kit may be prepared for special occasions, such as a hotel's grand opening or a special promotional event, because specialized promotions may be of interest to the news media. It is also helpful to have a general kit describing the property and its features so that a request from the media can be met immediately and comprehensively. A press kit should include a general description of the hotel; a "fact sheet" giving critical data, such as size, capacity, and history; pictures of the main features; and copies of recent press releases.

An important aspect of PR is community involvement. Executives and other employees are encouraged to be active in local organizations to heighten the visibility of the hotel among local residents and other publics. These activities may be the focus of new releases, when appropriate. Similarly, employee achievements, awards, and sometimes even hobbies, offer potential for news stories. Case Study 14.2 tells a success story of an independent country inn.

CASE STUDY 14.2

Marketing via Books of Historical Fiction

Farmington Inn, a quintessential New England inn, is nestled in the heart of one of Connecticut's oldest towns, Farmington. This beautiful and charming country inn is decorated with fresh flowers, antiques, and original local artwork. The Inn is situated among the Farmington River Valley region's many recreational activities and shopping opportunities. The uniqueness of this country inn, however, lies in the way the director of sales and marketing, Richard Bremkamp, promotes the property.

Bremkamp first wrote *The Farmington Lady*, a work of fiction based on historical facts and lore, to introduce guests to the Inn and to the community. The story incorporates sights in the city and at the Inn, as a little girl repeatedly encounters a ghost at various historical locations in the area. A copy of the book, which takes about 30 to 40 minutes to read, is placed on the pillow in each guest room so that the guests can read about the local attractions and their history. The guests can take the book with them when they leave. As a result, *The Farmington Lady* has been reprinted several times for a total run of 10,000 copies. It has become a wonderful marketing tool. In fact, the Inn has received requests for copies of the book from all over the world.

Because of the popularity of this book, *The Spirit of Simsbury* was written for a sister property and *Julia's Journey* was also written for the Farmington Inn. *Julia's Journey* was intended to complement *The Farmington Lady* and to encourage repeat business among those who enjoyed the first book. All of these books are part fiction, part fact, and part history. They have generated tremendous publicity for the Inn. This is a perfect example of connecting a hospitality operation with its host community. The public relations and publicity created have not only helped the Inn to project its image as a good community member, but have also enhanced its business and profitability.

Sources: L. Dube, C. A. Enz, L. M. Renaghan, and J. A. Siguaw, *American Lodging Excellence: The Key to Best Practices in the U.S. Lodging Industry.* (New York: American Express and the American Hotel Foundation, 1999); The Farmington Inn. (2001). *Farmington Inn home page* (on-line). Web site: http://www.farmingtoninn.com

Summary

Local area marketing is action oriented with a hands-on approach. More often than not, local marketing is done by unit managers. The design of any local marketing effort should be based on the characteristics of the customers, the competition, and the operation itself. Database marketing can improve local targeting efforts; loyalty marketing provides regular customers with rewards and recognition for repeat patronage and tries to make it costly for them to switch to other operations.

Local area marketing in foodservice is growing in importance for many reasons. First, many patrons come from nearby areas, and competition has become more intense because there is less growth in the market. Changing consumer tastes also encourage national brands to focus on a local identity. Moreover, different local markets have widely varied conditions. Finally, many restaurants cannot afford to compete in the major media, such as television, but can afford a local marketing program.

Some chain restaurants question the value of local marketing because it takes resources away from national brand advertising and because local efforts are usually not backed by extensive market research. The role of a company's headquarters in local marketing is to provide financial resources and expertise and to develop standardized programs and procedures.

Products can be adapted to the local market in foodservice through the development of local specialties. Lodging companies use local partnerships and positioning to adapt their products to local conditions. Prices in foodservice largely follow the pattern of the chain, but specials and limited-time offers can be used to meet local competition. In lodging, pricing is a property-level function that includes setting rack rates and making yield management decisions.

Local restaurant advertising often involves advertising co-ops, but some advertising is also done by individual units. For both restaurants and hotels, sales promotions at the local level can involve partners. Menu merchandising is a powerful tool for restaurants, and many other merchandising zones and media are available. Personal selling, usually done by unit managers, can be used by restaurants to reach concentrations of customers. Lodging firms use personal selling to reach accounts that book multiple room-nights. Public relations and community involvement, although not free, are cost-effective ways of establishing local identity for both restaurants and hotels.

Key Words and Concepts

Neighborhood marketing

Marketing strategy triangle

Hospitality marketing cycle

Database marketing

Loyalty marketing

Soft benefit

Incremental sales

Merchandising

Menu merchandising

Merchandising zones

Internal merchandising

Turnkey merchandising programs

Joint-promotions/cross-promotion

Community relations

Remote

Resources on the Internet

AdPlex. *http://www.adplex.com/*
RUF Strategic Solutions. *http://www.ruf.com/core.htm*
Tom Feltenstein's Neighborhood Marketing Institute.
  http://info@feltenstein.com/html/asktom.htm#

You Are Where You Live! *http://www.dellvader.claritas.com/YAWYL/Default.wjsp*

Discussion Questions

1. What forces are driving the increasing interest in local marketing in foodservice?
2. What problems does local marketing present for some chain organizations?
3. What resources are vital to the success of a local marketing program?
4. What are the local marketing communication methods commonly used in foodservice?
5. What are the possible merchandising zones for a restaurant?
6. What are a hotel property's key responsibilities with regard to pricing?
7. What are the sources of leads for a hotel property?

References

Feltenstein, T. (2001). *Tom Feltenstein's Neighborhood Marketing Institute* (on-line). Web site: http://info@feltenstein.com/html/asktom.htm#

Reich, A. Z. (1997). *Marketing management for the hospitality industry: A strategic approach.* New York: John Wiley & Sons.

Note: The authors acknowledge their indebtedness to Tom Feltenstein and the Neighborhood Marketing Institute whose frame of analysis is reflected throughout this chapter.

Index